MAKING CINELANDIA

MAKING

CINELANDIA

AMERICAN FILMS
AND MEXICAN FILM
CULTURE BEFORE
THE GOLDEN AGE

LAURA ISABEL SERNA

DUKE UNIVERSITY PRESS   DURHAM AND LONDON   2014

© 2014 Duke University Press
All rights reserved
Printed in the United States of America
on acid-free paper ∞
Designed by Heather Hensley
Typeset in Minion Pro by
Tseng Information Systems, Inc.

Library of Congress Cataloging-in-Publication Data
Serna, Laura Isabel
Making cinelandia : American films and
Mexican film culture before the Golden Age /
Laura Isabel Serna.
pages cm
Includes bibliographical references and index.
ISBN 978-0-8223-5641-7 (cloth : alk. paper)
ISBN 978-0-8223-5653-0 (pbk. : alk. paper)
1. Motion pictures, Mexican—History—20th
century. 2. National characteristics, Mexican, in
motion pictures. 3. Motion pictures—Mexico—
History—20th century. 4. Motion pictures,
American—Mexico—History—20th century.
I. Title.
PN1993.5.M6S47 2014
791.430972—dc23   2013042800

Frontispiece: People in front of the Cine Progreso
Mundial, Mexico City, circa 1920. © (88896),
CONACULTA.INAH.SINAFO.FN.MÉXICO.

In memory of my paternal grandparents,
JOSEFA L. SERNA (1911–2007) and
TEODORO "LOLO" SERNA (1908–1981),
and for ESMÉ SIMONA, with love

Asistimos al cine
cómo quién no sabe el papel
y va a verlo ensayar por profesores

El director sabe siempre
cómo acabarán las cosas
y nosotros deberíamos ya saberlo.

—SALVADOR NOVO, "CINE," 1925

Un beso
is not just
a kiss—

—FRANCISCO X. ALARCÓN,
"UN BESO IS NOT A KISS," 2002

CONTENTS

A NOTE ON TRANSLATIONS AND FILM TITLES

All translations from the Spanish are my own unless otherwise indicated. I have identified films in the text by their Mexican release title or titles if I encountered them in my Spanish language sources. When a film title appears solely in English it is because the source I drew on was in English. I contend that these films were transformed by their travels into distinct cultural objects.

At the end of the book I list all of the films referred to in the text. For the convenience of the English-dominant reader, I have organized them by English-language title. The production information there has been drawn from the American Film Institute's Catalog. For serials, I have primarily relied on the index compiled at the website Silent Era (http://www.silentera.com/PSFL/indexes/serials.html); for films produced in Mexico and other parts of the world, I have consulted online databases, published filmographies, and indices, and I give as complete information as I am able.

PRÓLOGO (PROLOGUE)

In the (very) short story "Frente a la pantalla" (Before the screen), published in the Mexico City weekly *El Universal Gráfico* in 1926, María—a common name for women in Mexico and thus perhaps an everywoman—goes to the movie theater alone to enjoy a "cinedrama" announced as "*the* cinematic super production."[1] Surrounded by couples and "carloads of entire families," she waits with her fellow spectators for the evening's program to begin. The cinema's jazz band attempts to smooth over the projectionist's delay, while various advertisements projected on the screen urge the public to patronize a provider of unadulterated milk, a restaurant, "Los Antojitos Michoacanas," and other local establishments.

Finally, the show begins. Tonight's feature is the last installment of a serial, *Abnegation*, whose plot concerns the frustrated romance of a heroine, "alone, weak, and unprotected," and her "completely noble" hero. During the course of the emotional final reel in which the pair are finally reunited, María's neighbor slides first a foot, then both hands, and ultimately both feet and both hands over María's exposed calves. Realizing that these attentions were not "part of the program," María slaps her molester, who is subsequently escorted out of the theater by the police, accompanied by the shouts of the audience—who "having seen the nobility of a celluloid man became indignant in the face of such a rogue."[2]

This short sketch of moviegoing in urban Mexico in the mid 1920s presents a constellation of characteristics that defined Mexican film culture from the end of the revolution to the mid-1930s. It features a foreign film, advertised in the hyperbolic register common to studio marketing departments, that offers a perhaps unrealizable vision of romantic love as the source of all suffering and all happiness. The film's presentation involves popular American music and advertisements, which encourage the public to participate in local manifestations of the consumer culture that was spreading across the globe. Inside the cinema the anonymity of new public amusements provide a cover for sexual activity (whether invited or not), strangers from a range of walks of life form a community of viewers who filter their everyday experiences through the stories and images they have seen on the screen, and the state exercises its power over citizens' behavior.

This story's appearance in a popular, illustrated publication hints at the circulation of U.S. films and film culture across Mexico. It is a fitting figure for the film culture, constructed out of transnational and local elements that took shape in Mexico in the period between the end of the revolution and the emergence of Mexican national cinema as a significant cultural and economic force. If, as Dolores Tierney suggests, some analyses of classical Mexican cinema privilege audiences at the expense of texts,[3] the reverse has been true of English-language scholarship on the silent period, which tends to privilege the few films that survive at the expense of the popular experience of Mexican audiences. This book seeks to redress this imbalance by focusing not on Mexican silent films, but on Mexican silent film culture in both Mexico and Mexican migrant communities in the United States, audiences that were bound by affective ties to the nation. Focusing on exhibition, distribution, and reception rather than production, I unpack the meanings made out of Mexican encounters with U.S. films to reveal the way that the cross-border circulation of cultural objects (films), cultural formations (fan culture, for example), and individuals (migrants) created a film culture that was at once transnational and national.

ACKNOWLEDGMENTS

The debts I have incurred in finishing this project are legion. I would like to begin by thanking the archives that graciously gave me access to their collections and the archivists who offered their expertise: Barbara Hall at the Academy of Motion Picture Arts and Sciences, Margaret Herrick Library; the staff of the Performing Arts Division of the New York Public Library, especially the pages; the Center for American History at the University of Texas at Austin; the staff of Special Collections at the University of Texas at El Paso; the Bancroft Library at the University of California, Berkeley; my colleagues at the Filmoteca de la UNAM, especially Ángel Martinez; the staffs of the Cineteca Nacional, the Biblioteca, and Hemeroteca Nacional and the archivists, especially Maestro Beristein, at the Archivo General de la Nación; El Archivo Regional de Monterrey and the municipal archives of Guanajuato, Ciudad Juarez, El Paso, and Los Angeles.

Generous fellowship and research grants made the completion of this project possible. Summer research grants from the David Rockefeller Center for Latin American Studies and the History of American Civilization Program at Harvard University facilitated early phases of the research. A Fulbright–García Robles research fellowship, a Sheldon Traveling Fellowship, and a Finishing Fellowship from Harvard University supported the research and writing in Mexico City, as did a Beca para Estudiantes Extranjeros from the Instituto Nacional de Estudios Históricos de las Revoluciones Mexicanas. An Andrew W. Mellon Postdoctoral Fellowship provided time for me to think through the revision of an early version of this project, and a First Year Professor Grant from Florida State University allowed me to conduct follow-up research.

For their intellectual support and mentorship I thank Shelley Stamp, Chon Noriega, and Kathleen Newman. I am also indebted to many colleagues: Sally Hadden, Jennifer Koslow, Ralph Berry, and Robin Truth Goodman at Florida State University; the attendees of the Tepoztlán Institute for Transnational History in 2004 and 2007; Claudia Brittenham, Sergio de la Mora, Halbert Jones, Seth Fein, Katie Flom Kline, Alexis McCrossen, Enrique Plasencia Parra, Stephany Slaughter, Tamara Falicov, Jeffrey Middents R.; members of the Houston Area Writing Group, especially Raul Ramos; George Sanchez, Vicki Ruiz, Patricia Torres San Martin, Mark G. Cooper, Jennifer Bean, Patrice Petro, Dan Streible; members of the Society for Cinema and Media Studies Latino/Latin American Caucus; and many others, including Dr. Cynthia Verba, the Society for Cinema and Media Studies dissertation award committee, and the American Studies Association's Ralph Henry Gabriel Prize committee.

The members of my dissertation committee, who read a very early version of this project, deserve a huge thanks. Lizabeth Cohen and Werner Sollors stuck with me even when they weren't sure where all this was headed, and Ruth Feldstein modeled the best practices of cultural history and graduate student mentoring—for which I will be eternally grateful. Eric Zolov gave my dissertation a careful and valuable reading; I appreciate his comments and suggestions.

Areli Ramírez helped me gather images from Mexico City archives and libraries, while Jorge Cuellar and Alex Cohen have helped from Los Angeles—*gracias*. Elizabeth Palchik Allen has been both a friend and a careful reader of this work in various forms, for which I am very grateful. Finally, my colleagues in the Bryan Singer Division of Critical Studies at the University of Southern California's School of Cinematic Arts made finishing the manuscript a happy task. Thanks also to my editor, Ken Wissoker, for his interest in this project and to the press's two anonymous readers, who offered extraordinarily helpful comments and suggestions.

I also want to thank my friends Faith Adiele, Ellen Hanspach, Sarah Kareem, Mashariki Kudumu, Rachel Levine, Amy Lin, Darinka Mangino, Gina Mistretta Small, Monica Guerra Robinson, and Simona Schaefer for putting up with my single-mindedness, and Françoise Carré for modeling what it means to be a researcher, a feminist, and a friend. Most importantly, I'd like to thank my family for their support and love. My father provided material and emotional support at various stages of this project, and my extended family cheered me on over the years. My family in Mexico—*tíos* Conrado Gomez and Margarita Sandoval de Gomez and my cousins, especially Miriam and Esmeralda—provided me with a home away from home, and Mexico City welcomed me, *pocha* that I am, with open arms. Finally, this book was completed during the first three years of life of my daughter, Esmé Simona. I can't wait to go to the movies with her.

INTRODUCTION

In 1920 revolutionary warlord Saturnino Cedillo catalogued the changes he hoped to see in his home state of San Luis Potosí. He told an American journalist: "I want land and I want plows, and I want schools for my children and I want teachers, and I want books and pencils and blackboards and roads." "And," he added, "I want moving pictures for my people, too."[1] Cedillo seemed convinced that motion pictures, like property ownership, education, and improved transportation systems, would contribute to San Luis Potosí's "material progress and social advancement."[2] Convinced, despite the fact that seeing a moving picture in Mexico in 1920 generally meant seeing an American film. One might expect a revolutionary like Cedillo to rail against the motion pictures readily available to Mexican audiences as a form of cultural imperialism that worked against one of the revolution's primary goals: wresting Mexico from the shackles of foreign influence.[3] Some in Mexico certainly held this view, but Cedillo and many others saw motion pictures and moviegoing as evidence not of American cultural imperialism, but of Mexico's modernity.

From the late 1910s to the early 1930s American films dominated Mexico's movie screens. During this period Mexican imports of U.S. films increased dramatically, part of the success of American studios' efforts to edge out European filmmakers in the global market.[4] Fast-paced westerns, crime films, domestic dramas, and serials produced in the United States pushed European comedies, historical films, and melodramas off Mexican screens. Films sponsored by American corporations that showcased technological advances impressed Mexican audiences at movie theaters, schools, and other venues.[5] What is more, through the concentrated publicity efforts of the producer-distributors that came to dominate the U.S. film industry in the late 1910s, American films and film culture permeated Mexican visual and popular culture. Images of American screen idols like Douglas Fairbanks and Clara Bow dominated the illustrated sections of popular magazines, decorated Mexican homes—however humble those homes might have been—and dotted the walls of urban centers and smaller towns alike. Film reviews, advertisements, motion picture fiction, and gossip about stars and studios—some written by Mexican journalists, some translated and reprinted from U.S. sources—could be found in abundance in Mexican periodicals on both sides of the border. The U.S. Department of Commerce estimated that the dollar value of American movies sent to Mexico increased more than twentyfold in this period, from $6,614 in 1914 to $143,921 in 1922.[6] Over 78 percent of the films screened in Mexico between 1920 and 1929 came from U.S. film studios; on average, five hundred American titles were screened each year.[7]

In contrast, between 1916 and 1929 Mexican filmmakers produced a scant ninety feature-length films, an average of just six per year.[8] The Mexican silent film industry had occasional commercial successes, notably the extraordinarily positive reception of the twelve-part crime serial *El automóvil gris* (Rosas, 1919), which was based on the story of a criminal gang that plagued Mexico City in 1915; a series of well-received feature films produced by the actress Mimí Derba in the early 1920s; and a handful of popular *noticieros* (newsreels), which presented local and national current events to Mexican audiences.[9] Critics applauded the efforts of filmmakers to make national films and even reviewed many of them in glowing terms, but with few exceptions these productions disappeared quickly from the country's motion picture theaters. Though some Mexican film companies were able to produce multiple films, domestic production remained artisanal in nature, as companies emerged to produce one or two films before dissolving. Some would-be filmmakers turned to the relatively more lucrative activities of film distribution and exhibition.[10]

As World War I brought European film exports to a trickle, American films met exhibitors' need to have something to offer Mexico's growing motion picture audiences. Despite the fact that Mexico had been engaged in a civil war for almost a decade, motion picture theaters and other exhibition spaces had proliferated. The armed conflict had brought migrants, refugees, and soldiers to larger towns and cities, increasing the cinema's reach. Evidence documenting attendance figures is elusive, but venues that sat thousands at a time were constructed not only in the capital but also in large industrial centers in northern states. What is more, many small towns had one or even two movie theaters that operated several days a week, and film exhibitions were offered either sporadically or regularly in *rancherias* (farming settlements) and company towns. In a predominantly rural country, the cinema had become popular enough that virtually every state boasted at least a dozen theaters, and several states—Yucatán, Veracruz, Coahuila, Puebla, Nuevo León, and Jalisco—had numerous theaters relative to their respective populations.[11] During this same period, Mexican immigrants to the United States saw the same films their compatriots in Mexico did (sometimes much sooner), most often in barrio theaters that catered specifically to Mexican audiences.

At the time many Mexican film critics and journalists referred to this shift in Mexican film culture as "the *Yanqui* invasion."[12] As Kristin Thompson notes, the invasion metaphor "would become almost universal in discussions of expanding the American film trade abroad."[13] For Mexicans, however, the threat of an American invasion seemed more than a figure of speech or rhetorical gambit. The country's historically fraught relationship with the United States, defined by a grossly unequal distribution of economic and political power, loomed large in the public imagination. Most Mexicans remembered quite vividly the U.S. invasion of the capital during the war between the two countries in 1847–48 and the U.S. seizure of nearly half of Mexico's territory as a result of the Treaty of Guadalupe Hidalgo at the end of that war. More recently, the United States had made numerous attempts to meddle in Mexican domestic politics during the revolution that had just ended, sending marines to the Port of Veracruz in 1914 and a contingent of soldiers into Mexican territory in search of the revolutionary general Pancho Villa, after his attack on Columbus, New Mexico, in March 1916. Anti-Mexican sentiment and discrimination directed at Mexican immigrants in the United States aggravated Mexicans' resentment over the U.S. government's continued lobbying for favorable terms regarding investments and property ownership after the signing of the 1917 Mexican constitution, which restricted foreign ownership of land and subsoil rights.[14]

Resistance to just such imperial machinations—"Mexico for the Mexicans"—was one central impetus of the revolution and, rhetorically at least, shaped Mexico's intense quest for a national identity in its wake. The governments that came to power after 1917 focused on the consolidation and centralization of power in the name of the revolutionary state and the production of modern citizens.[15] One key way in which they went about shifting the allegiance of Mexicans from the church, their regional or local communities, and "tradition" was to elaborate national myths and identify distinctly Mexican characteristics around which a national identity could be created and sustained. Postrevolutionary nationalism—a collection of rituals, practices, and symbols—was mobilized to legitimize political power by weaving together a discourse on the revolution and its legacy with myths and symbols from Mexico's indigenous past.[16] At the same time the government and cultural elite turned their attention to modernizing Mexico's infrastructure, economy, and educational institutions, while urging citizens to modernize their private lives.[17] Most relevant to my concerns, participation in commodified leisure activities—like going to the cinema—became highly politicized, as Katherine Bliss has argued.[18]

At the very moment when Mexico's revolutionary government was developing public works projects, instituting literacy programs aimed at the country's vast indigenous population, and nurturing a national arts movement that was both distinctive and readily exported abroad, an intense cultural exchange between the United States and Mexico was taking place at the popular level in motion picture venues across Mexico.[19] Though the output of Mexico's film producers and directors, activities of actors, and even the rise of film criticism as a profession during this period have received scholarly attention, this seeming contradiction between nationalist rhetoric and the everyday experiences of popular audiences remains relatively unexplored, especially in English-language scholarship.[20] Instead, this period has been treated as something of an embarrassing imperialist interregnum. The film historian Aurelio de los Reyes marks the late 1910s as a missed opportunity for national filmmakers: "Despite the country's isolation because of the Revolution and the fact that the First World War had offered Mexico the opportunity to develop its own industry . . . cinematographically speaking, Mexico would be for the Americans."[21] In turn, Charles Ramírez Berg proposes that Mexican displeasure with the stereotypes of Mexico and Mexicans in American silent films "helped foster the desire to create a national cinema."[22]

In this way, scholarly accounts of the silent era tend to privilege national cinema production even in absentia, focusing on, to borrow Andrew Higson's pithy phrase, "what ought to be the national cinema" rather than the experiences of audiences.[23] Indeed, in most histories of Mexican film, mass audiences take shape only with the emergence of a strong national film industry in the 1940s, which the cultural critic Carlos Monsiváis argues offered viewers "links between real situations, collective fantasies and the faithful reproduction of popular behavior."[24] It is true that the audience for cinema increased in the mid-twentieth century as Mexico's wartime economy grew and cities attracted yet another wave of migration, but to assume that cinemagoing was not popular in the 1920s, particularly in urban or urbanizing areas, or was the pastime of only a privileged few distorts our understanding of the cinema's spread during the silent period.

Quite to the contrary, filmgoing appears with regularity in accounts of Mexican life penned by both social scientists and everyday people during the

1920s. For example, in his 1931 portrait of what was in his view a persistently traditional Mexico, the American economist Stuart Chase describes a traditional fiesta in a town where, he writes, "the inroads of the machine to date are not great."[25] In the same breath, he notes of fiesta attendees: "Many of course will attend the town movie, where Hollywood dumps its more dismal failures, titled in both English and Spanish."[26] In turn, Mexican written recollections or *memorias* that include accounts of moviegoing in urban areas in the 1910s and 1920s frequently begin not with accounts of national films, but with the experience of seeing foreign films. To offer just one example, in his memoir—written in the 1950s—Alfonso de Icaza begins his reminisces about the cinema by recalling a long list of motion picture theaters that dotted Mexico City, remarking on the popularity of foreign stars, first European and then American, and remembering the activity of going to see motion pictures. Only as his narrative moves into the 1930s do national productions take center stage.[27] Both Chase's casual dismissal of popular film culture, motivated in large part by his desire to cast Mexico as a primitive Eden in contrast to the United States, and the structure of Icaza's personal history of cinema support Higson's recommendation that "the parameters of national cinema should be drawn at the site of consumption as much as at the site of production."[28]

Taking up this call for a more expansive definition of national cinema, this book focuses not on national production but on exhibition practices, moviegoing, and fan culture. The protagonists of this story, which takes place in distributors' offices, neighborhood theaters, and the pages of the popular press, are not famous directors or stars but anonymous fans, exhibitors, municipal inspectors, reformers, and journalists. I have mined newspapers, magazines, the records of U.S. distributors, diplomatic correspondence, the minutes of city council meetings, and published and unpublished studies of the exhibition industry in Mexico and about Mexican immigrants to the United States to explore the texture of Mexican encounters with American cinema. Rather than engaging in close readings of individual film texts or even audience reactions to specific films, I analyze the discursive practices that comprised the social and cultural space of cinema as an institution and an idea.[29]

Focusing on the agency of Mexican audiences, distributors, cinema owners, and journalists in this exchange of culture calls into question the power relations presupposed in accounts of the circulation of American mass culture as exclusively or even primarily a tool of cultural imperialism.[30] Instead the encounter between Mexican audiences and American cinema can be seen as a "contact zone," which Mary Louise Pratt defines as "social spaces where disparate cultures meet, clash, and grapple with each other, often in highly asymmetrical relations of domination and subordination," rich with productive possibilities.[31] I use the phrase "making cinelandia" to describe this social space where Mexican audiences' productive engagement with U.S. films and film culture generated meanings beyond those imagined by either American filmmakers or film companies. *Cinelandia* was both the title of a Spanish-language fan magazine published in Hollywood by a group of American investors, and a term employed by many Mexican journalists in the 1920s to describe American film culture, specifically Hollywood, as seen through Mexican eyes. This dual meaning seems to aptly capture the geopolitical dimensions of this transnational cultural exchange.[32]

Mexican viewers shared a set of referents — most insistently national identity — through which they read American films and film culture and identified with the American films and the situations, characters, and stories they presented as a means of crafting modern identities as individuals. This process of "negotiated reading" facilitated the production of modernity marked as distinctly Mexican.[33] In this way, I contend, exhibition and moviegoing practices, discussions about what cinema should be and do in Mexican society, and the fan culture that emerged around the cross-border circulation of American cinema were as important for the production of a distinctly national film culture — perhaps more so — as any film produced in Mexico during this period.

How could the widespread consumption of American films contribute to, as Saturnino Cedillo phrased it, Mexico's "material progress and social advancement" rather than make Mexico a cultural vassal of the United States?[34] What did Mexican audiences make of the foreign films and film culture that came across the U.S.–Mexico border and circulated in urban centers, along transportation networks that linked those centers to smaller towns, and in Mexican enclaves on the U.S. side of the border? How did Mexicans square their love of American films and desire to be part of a global film audience with the American film industry's typically racist representations of Mexico and Mexicans? Key to answering these questions is an understanding of the relationship between Mexicans' perception of cinema as a global expression of modernity and instrument of modernization, as Miriam Hansen's formulation of cinema as a form of "vernacular modernism" suggests, and the nationalist discourses that conditioned that perception in Mexico.[35]

Postrevolutionary Mexico's preoccupation with becoming modern represented a point of continuity with the autocratic regime of Porfirio Díaz (1876–1910) that the revolution had overthrown.[36] In the wake of the signing of the 1917 constitution, cities wasted by war were rebuilt, public health cam-

—¡Y para esto compra uno zapatos!...

FIGURE INTRO.1 The uneasy coexistence of tradition and modernity in Mexico City: "For this one buys shoes?" Note the posters advertising the "Cine." Ernesto García Cabral, "El avaro" (The miser), editorial cartoon, *Excélsior*, September 7, 1923.

paigns were mounted to eradicate disease and improve sanitation, and educational programs that aspired to bring Mexico's peasants into the modern world were initiated. This elite discourse on development and modernization was paralleled by a popular perception that everyday life was changing rapidly and radically. Journalists animatedly discussed what they called the "vertigo" of modern life, while editorial cartoons and news accounts enumerated the dangers of modern city life. New forms of work—wage labor and increased industrial production—as well as new ways of traversing cities and borders and of thinking about citizenship, community, and family coexisted, sometimes uneasily, with traditional practices, social relationships, and beliefs.[37]

Néstor García Canclini characterizes this coexistence as a "multi-temporal heterogeneity" in which "traditions have not yet disappeared and modernity has not yet completely arrived."[38] Although García Canclini conceives of modernity as a state one can leave and reenter and that coexists with other temporalities, I have approached the question of modernity in spatial terms. Provincial cities, small towns, and even rural areas had unique encounters with U.S. film during this period, but I focus on Mexico City and the U.S. cities of El Paso and Los Angeles, which were major nodes along a migration corridor from Mexico to the United States and the areas of Greater Mexico most saturated by U.S. mass culture and at the vanguard of Mexico's modernization.

Whereas dependency theory might have categorized early twentieth-century Mexico as undeveloped, I propose that this diffusion of urban spaces, even across national borders, characterized Mexican modernity: uneven, dispersed, but connected by a web of transportation networks and intimately tied to a powerful neighboring country. In contrast to the economic and social developments in the United States and Europe, which have dominated definitions of modernity, modernity brought Mexico persistent social inequality; migration on a massive scale; a contested relationship with tradition; the coexistence of traditional forms of labor, entertainment, and social life with modern capitalism and its attendant cultural forms; and, above all, a deep desire to "become modern."[39] That is, rather than being unmodern or even possessing multiple temporalities, as García Canclini's formulation suggests, postrevolutionary Mexico's self-consciousness about what was and was not modern can be understood as a symptom of an alternative modernity that emerged out of a unique relationship among technology, political power, and the exigencies of nation building.

While in the United States and Europe cinema became a symbol of the radical potential and dangers of modern life and an inspiration for avant-garde experimentation, in Mexico writers, artists, and intellectuals seemed simultaneously fascinated by and indifferent to cinema. As literary critics Jason Borge and J. Patrick Duffey discuss, some writers in the Mexican literary avant-garde took up cinema—including Hollywood—as well as other new technologies such as the typewriter, radio, and airplane as a source of formal inspiration and themes.[40] Members of avant-garde literary groups— most visibly *los contemporaneos*, who aligned themselves with European modernism, and *los estridentistas*, a loosely affiliated group of modernist poets, writers, and artists with strong nationalist tendencies—who disagreed vehemently about what should constitute modern Mexican literature— agreed that Charlie Chaplin represented the epitome of modernity. Los estridentistas sang Chaplin's praises in the group's 1923 manifesto.[41] The "angular, representative, and democratic" star could propel Mexico, they wrote, beyond "stale, meaningless patriotism." At the same time, los estridentistas member Manuel Maples Arce was critical of American popular films like the westerns that featured William Duncan, which he designated the "interventionist 'film' of empire."[42] In another register, the prolific writer and public intellectual Salvador Novo—who was a member of los contemporaneos—would recall afternoon visits to the Cine Vicente Guerrero, where watching American films he came to terms with his desire to be on the receiving end of "the kiss of a cinema hero."[43] For Novo, popular cinema became a major force in his self-fashioning as a gay man, artist, and intellectual. However, the leftist artists and intellectuals most commonly associated with revolutionary Mexican culture during this period, such as Diego Rivera and José Vasconcelos, had little use for cinema—especially American cinema, which some of them considered vulgar.

It is in the pages of the popular press that we see most clearly how cinema became a lens for understanding life in contemporary urban Mexico. Journalists used cinematic metaphors to describe the social upheaval—broken families, crime, suicide, cross-class conflict, and economic uncertainty—that characterized postrevolutionary Mexico. For example, during the highly publicized 1922 murder trial of a young woman named Magdalena Jurado, one newspaper reported that "scenes and characters paraded by as in a film reel."[44] The murder of an Englishwoman, Rosalie Evans, in the town of Texmelucan, Puebla, was composed of "real life scenes" worthy of "being copied by cinema studios."[45] Another newspaper story described the murderer of a cuckolded husband fleeing down a highway with a pistol in hand, the authorities in "cinematic pursuit."[46] And a sixteen-year-old girl who stabbed herself to prove her fidelity was accused of acting out "cinematic scenes."[47] In this way, everyday events took on a new cast, as American films about crime, family drama, and personal tragedy permeated Mexican popular culture. At least for some Mexicans, cinema became an important means of understanding the changes that characterized Mexico's postrevolutionary period. Although films produced by Mexicans performed some of this work, the broad-based film culture that arose out of the exhibition and reception of imported films also "enabl[ed] viewers to participate and promote whatever forms of [that] modernity were available locally."[48]

But Mexican audiences' responses to American cinema were far from univocal. For some Mexicans, the widespread popularity of American films was simply an expression of U.S. imperialist designs and an unwelcome catalyst for the Americanization of Mexican society. Others, including cultural nationalists of all political stripes, used American cinema as a foil against which mexicanidad could be defined, without taking a definitive stance against it.

Still others, like Saturnino Cedillo, saw motion pictures—even imported ones—not as a form of cultural imperialism, but as evidence of Mexico's modernity. Indeed, many Mexicans, primarily but not exclusively young people, embraced U.S. cinema and the new forms of sexuality, social relationships, and practices of consumption it presented as a means of asserting their independence from what were being framed as traditional Mexican cultural norms and expectations.

The spread of these new modes of self-presentation, behavior, and values became the subject of heated debates about the effects of American mass culture on Mexican society. For example, women's fascination with film culture, which has been studied in the North American context by Kathy Peiss, Lauren Rabinovitz, Shelley Stamp, and others, raised urgent questions in Mexico.[49] As in the United States, some of those questions revolved around new types of sexual behavior and women's place in the public sphere, but they also took up the issue of how or if American culture should be integrated into Mexican society. Just as film exhibitors in the United States sought the patronage of middle-class women as a means of conferring respectability on films and filmgoing, Mexican exhibitors and municipal inspectors sought to make theaters welcoming places for honorable families—ostensibly from any class, but particularly those who essentially conformed to a middle-class model and represented the fundamental building block of the nation. At the same time, officials discouraged behavior that resembled the distracted viewing habits that Hansen argues were common to early cinema audiences, and that Stamp has shown were associated with female audiences during the 1910s.[50] In this way, theaters were made part of the process of educating Mexico's heterogeneous moviegoers—workers, women, young people, and others—into the middle-class norms whose adoption many believed necessary for Mexico's progress.

The effects of American mass culture on migrants, many of whom returned to Mexico after a sojourn in the United States, constituted another key point in the Mexican debate about American cinema in the 1920s. Though scholars, most notably Hansen, have unsettled the paradigm of early cinema as a uniformly acculturating force for European immigrant groups, the idea that American cinema Americanized Mexican immigrants or became a catalyst of generational conflict persists in the literature on Chicano/a audiences.[51] Countering this tendency, José Limón, Rosa Linda Fregoso, and Curtis Marez have suggested the productive possibilities of interpreting exhibition practices and moviegoing as sites of Chicana/o agency.[52] Departing from the Chicana/o studies framework that guides much of this work and focuses on the development of a distinct ethnic identity and community, I argue that in the 1920s the racism that kept Mexican patrons out of mainstream or Anglo theaters fostered the formation of a transnational Mexican audience that stretched across the U.S.-Mexico border.

Without conflating the experiences of migrants to the United States with those of residents of Mexico City, I propose that moviegoing and film culture nurtured a sense of what it might mean to be Mexican on both sides of the border. Turning our attention south, away from Eastern or Midwestern cities, and examining the commonalities between the parallel film culture that emerged to serve Mexican audiences in the United States and the exhibition practices and film culture in Mexico allows us to see how moviegoing could strengthen rather than weaken attachments to home countries. Indeed, the rhetoric of *Mexico de afuera*, thinking of migrants as part of the nation that happened to reside outside its borders, which had particular force in the 1920s, when many migrants expressed intentions to return home and often did so if they could, brought migrant communities into the sphere of Mexico's nation-building projects.[53] What is more, migrants' understandings and responses to U.S. films and film culture were as conditioned by their exposure to discourse on progress, modernity, and nationhood in Mexico as they were by the experience of migration and cultural shock, as historians Vicki Ruiz and Douglas Monroy have argued.[54]

That Mexican audiences, on either side of the border, loved American serials, dramas, and comedies; adored American actors and actresses; and even dreamed of stardom does not mean that they viewed American films or film culture uncritically. Indeed, Mexicans were keenly aware that Mexican characters occupied a particular place in the racial hierarchy of American silent cinema. Like black characters, they were often confined to humorous bit parts or doomed to perpetual villainy. These representational strategies worked to popularize racist images of Mexico, participating in the construction of Mexicans as unfit for inclusion in the American melting pot. These stereotypes have been well documented and analyzed by Arthur Pettit, Charles Ramírez Berg, and many others, but we know far less about how the traffic in what Mexicans referred to as "denigrating images" affected Mexican film culture before the emergence of the Chicano movement.[55] However, I treat Mexican responses to these images—in the main, resistance—on either side of the border as a central but not exclusive shaper of Mexican film culture in the 1920s.

Making Cinelandia is divided into two parts. The first, "The *Yanqui* Invasion," tracks American cinema as it made its way into Mexico. In chapter 1 I examine how U.S. film companies gained control of the lion's share of the Mexican market beginning in the late 1910s.[56] American film companies wanted to increase their profits and staunch the film piracy that was rampant in Latin America, and the U.S. State Department was enthusiastic about using film as a diplomatic tool. However, local distribution and exhibition practices and audience preferences forced U.S. film companies to adapt to local conditions. What is more, U.S. film company representatives brought racist perceptions about Mexico and Mexicans with them that were met indignantly by cinema patrons and workers alike, who asserted their right to be treated with dignity and respect as consumers and laborers.

Chapter 2 examines the place of movie theaters, motion picture exhibition, and the social practice of moviegoing in Mexico's postrevolutionary nation-building project. The cinema—not filmic texts per se, but the exhibition practices that surrounded them—was imbued with nationalist import. Although foreign companies dominated the distribution business and even, to some extent, the exhibition business in the capital, most motion picture theaters were owned by Mexican nationals and were considered a potentially important part of Mexico's modern economy by the federal government. Purpose-built theaters, which emerged in the 1920s, became icons of Mexico's modernity regardless of the country of origin of the films they showcased. The performative aspects of film exhibition, whether home-grown jazz bands, marimba bands, or other live performers from the local entertainment scene, likewise served to localize foreign texts. And when exhibitors wove the cinema into patriotic celebrations or government entities included film exhibitions—whether at a theater or another site—in educational programs, the distance between American films and rituals of Mexican citizenship grew smaller. At the same time, cinemas and audiences became the target of reform, as municipal inspectors sought to curtail the often rowdy behavior of working-class audiences and clandestine sexual activity by members of all social classes. In the process, they invoked the honorable family, an avatar of the revolutionary family, as the ideal spectator for whom the cinema would prove educational and uplifting.

Municipal inspectors had a vision of the types of behavior and values they hoped audiences would adopt. The discourse on cinema in the popular press offered another vision of Mexican audiences. Chapter 3 focuses on the ways in which the press served as an efficient disseminator of American film and fan culture, which addressed Mexican audiences, primarily conceived of as female by these publications, as part of a global audience of consumers.[57] At the same time, Spanish-language newspapers, periodicals, and even the Mexico-specific sections of internationally circulated fan magazines offered Mexican audiences a space in which they could engage with American films and film culture as an audience marked by language, sentimental attachments to the nation, and the history of U.S.-Mexico relations. Mexican journalists and critics became important interlocutors between the U.S. film industry and Mexican audiences, at once providing instruction in the practices of fandom and offering a window onto Hollywood and the film industry from a Mexican perspective. In this way, they transformed American cinema, adapting and appropriating it in order to produce audiences who identified with the nation.

The second part of the book, "Border Crossings," tracks the ways in which the diffusion and popularization of American cinema in Mexico prompted movements across figurative and literal borders. Though the evidence suggests that both men and women went to the movies, Mexican women's engagement with U.S. film culture became the source of much anxiety; it is the main focus of chapter 4. Critics held American mass culture responsible for the appearance of the *pelona*, a flapper-like figure who defied traditional gender and class norms and took part in new forms of sexual behavior and practices of consumption. Coded as a particularly pernicious effect of American mass culture, women's longing for glamour, the public visibility of stardom, sexual freedom, and social mobility motivated Mexico's cultural elite— Catholic women's groups, newspapers, and even government officials—to look for ways to strategically mobilize those desires for the good of the nation. Through beauty contests and fashion shows, they cast engagement with the American film industry as a service to the nation, while the new practices of consumption encouraged by American films and film culture were channeled toward the respectable sites of home, family, and citizenship.

While the pelona and her peers embraced U.S. films and film culture as a model for self-fashioning, the Mexican state decried the negative depictions of Mexico and Mexicans in American films. Mexican diplomats recognized that Hollywood's racist representational practices, which portrayed Mexico as a land of bandits, buffoonish revolutionaries, or uncivilized savages, tarnished Mexico's public image abroad. Chapter 5 takes up Mexico's struggle to censor these images. Unlike countries such as the United States and the United Kingdom, where moral concerns were paramount, representations of the nation and its citizens became the primary concern of Mexican censorship regulations.[58] That preoccupation came to the fore in 1922, when the Mexican government issued an embargo against American films that portrayed Mexico in a denigrating manner. The story of Mexico's attempts to influence American production practices, first via the embargo and later by assigning diplomatic corps members the role of preproduction consultants, ends predictably with Mexico's having little more influence over how Hollywood represented Mexico or Mexican-like characters. The debate over these efforts illustrates how Mexico's censorship regime produced the nation and national identity, even when those ideas were interpreted in different ways, as a central element of Mexican film culture.

Stereotypical representations of Mexico affected the country's reputation abroad, but they also shaped Mexican migrants' day-to-day experiences in the United States. Chapter 6 examines how racism shaped Mexican migrants' experience of moviegoing in the United States. Mexican observers acknowledged the way that Hollywood's racist representational and labor practices could alienate Mexican migrants from their host country and encourage their identification with Mexico. In turn, Anglo-American social scientists' and reformers' perception of the effects of moviegoing on Mexican immigrants sprang from their beliefs about Mexicans' racial characteristics. Though some reformers and social scientists believed that moviegoing could serve an educational function, many believed that unbounded and unguided viewing habits could encourage criminality or inappropriate sexual behavior in populations considered prone to vice. In many parts of the United States, anti-Mexican racism also determined the conditions under which Mexican audiences could view films. Segregation and discrimination at movie theaters prompted the development of a parallel film culture, as it did for the African American audiences studied by Jacqueline Stewart, Mary Carbine, and Gregory Waller.[59] Theaters operated by ethnic Mexican entrepreneurs or serving Mexican audiences became sites for the fostering of community solidarity and the affirmation of national identity.[60] In El Paso, this parallel film culture constituted part of a transborder, regional film culture that contributed to northern Mexico's development and progress. In Los Angeles, where many Mexican immigrants not only indulged in the pleasures of moviegoing but hoped to find work in the film industry, if only as extras, the city's Spanish-language daily, *La Opinión*, criticized Hollywood's racism. In both cities, performative elements of exhibition practices, promotional strategies, and critical discourse nurtured Mexican nationalist sentiment.

Neither purely entertainment nor exclusively empire, Mexico's encounter with U.S. films and film culture in the 1920s facilitated the construction of Mexican national identity as much as it spread American values and political ideology. Although Mexican audiences were encouraged to immerse themselves in a cosmopolitan film culture that connected them with other audiences around the world, they were also encouraged to invest in U.S. film culture as Mexicans. Between the revolution and the introduction of sound films, purpose-built cinemas were offered as evidence of Mexico's economic and social development, regardless of the national origin of the films they showed; young women's longing for Hollywood stardom could, likewise, be framed as serving nationalist ends; and when Mexican migrants in the United States encountered American racism in the form of on-screen representations, studio labor policies, or restrictions on where they could see motion pictures, such encounters could become the catalyst for deeper identification with Mexico. In this way, Mexico's engagement with American cinema in the 1920s became part of the revolutionary state's broader nation-building project and set the stage for the national cinema culture to come with the advent of sound. Looking at the variety of ways in which the nation filled the space around the screen—in cinemas, the popular press, censorship regimes, and government correspondence about the cinema industry—throws into high relief how Mexican audiences, marked by national identity, language, and an often fraught relationship with the United States, used their encounters with American cinema to negotiate their own entrance into modernity, a modernity in which the nation mattered.

PART I

THE *YANQUI* INVASION

Stands selling sweets and street food in front of the Cine San Rafael, Mexico City, circa 1925. © (161861), CONACULTA.INAH.SINAFO.FN.MÉXICO.

1 | U.S. MOTION PICTURE COMPANIES GO SOUTH OF THE BORDER

The Yankee invasion; slow heartless, corrupting; today one zone, tomorrow another, and another, and finally, everywhere! . . . [N]obody, I mean nobody—this is the sad part—dares to resist it.
—FEDERICO GAMBOA, *RECONQUISTA*

Film men and exhibitors [from the Southwest] have turned to the land of the Aztecs as an almost virgin field for unlimited business.
—"SCREEN 'COMING BACK' IN MEXICO," *MOVING PICTURE WORLD*, JULY 27, 1918

In 1917 the Mexican film critic Rafael Pérez Taylor penned a scathing review of the serial *La hija del circo* (*The Adventures of Peg o' the Ring*; Universal, 1916). "Trains, cowboys, attacks, shootouts, beasts, struggles, jumps, and brutally painted eyebrows form the entire story," he complained.[1] "After the protagonists have sweated an inconceivable amount, Lind [*sic*; Lund, the male lead, played by Francis Ford] marries Arabela [Peg, the female lead, played by Grace Cunard], and everyone is happy, satisfied, and nothing has happened." And with that, Pérez Taylor dismissed all "North American film" as a "synonym for vulgar film."[2] The banality, at least according to his assessment, of *La hija del circo* convinced him that this film—and, by extension, all others created north of the Río Grande—was a form of entertainment best appreciated by children.

Despite such pronouncements, views like Pérez Taylor's were becoming marginalized in Mexico by the late 1910s, much to the dismay of Pérez Taylor and other arbiters of culture. The commentary of critics throughout the late 1910s and early 1920s attests to the growing dominance of U.S. cinema in Mexico, not merely in terms of the

FIGURE 1.1 Still from *The Adventures of Peg o' the Ring* (*La hija del circo*, 1916), displaying some of the melodramatic excess that Rafael Pérez Taylor deplored. From the Robert S. Birchard Collection.

number of films screened but also in terms of American cinema's hold on the Mexican cultural imagination. In 1920 an unnamed writer acknowledged in the popular magazine *Revista de Revistas* that "North American talent has dethroned the old queens. . . . [A] picaresque smile from Mary Pickford is more interesting than the most languid gesture of Bertini; to all the funny feats of the dandy Max Linder, contemporary spectators prefer the amusing comedy of Chaplin."[3] Three years later, another reviewer nostalgically recalled the "reign of European cinema" before confirming that U.S. films had pushed Italian and French films to the margins of Mexican screen culture.[4] By the mid-1920s, the *yanqui* film had clearly arrived.

Taking advantage of the opportunity created by World War I, U.S. producers expanded their operations in Mexico. This expansion, as Kristin Thompson has documented, was part of a broader strategy to solidify the U.S. film industry's hold on global markets, but film producers also had very specific aims in looking south of the border.[5] Mexico was not the most lucrative market in Latin America, but American film companies perceived it as the principal gateway to even larger and more lucrative audiences in other parts of Latin America. Beyond gaining access to markets further south, film companies sought to curtail the rampant piracy that flourished along the porous border between the two countries. As it did in other parts of the world, the U.S. government supported the interests of American producers and distributors in Mexico as a means of cultivating new markets for U.S. consumer goods and spreading American political ideologies, a particularly important goal during this period, given the civil unrest that had recently rocked Mexico, jeopardized American business interests south of the border, and threatened to spill over into the United States.[6]

The history of the distributor United Artists in Mexico, which I focus on in this chapter, documents on a smaller scale the processes that Thompson sketches more broadly. As the United Artists case study shows, the "*yanqui* invasion" was not the result of U.S. film companies' unilaterally exercising their superior cultural and economic power, but rather the result of interactions between U.S. film companies and their representatives, who often brought with them racist ideas about Mexico and Mexican nationals involved in the motion picture business. While U.S. producers offered what they considered to be a superior product — and many Mexican audiences agreed with them — they were nevertheless forced to negotiate local contexts of distribution and reception, including the radicalization of Mexico's film exhibition workforce.

AMERICAN FILMS TAKE OVER

From 1896, when motion pictures were first introduced in Mexico City, to 1907, Mexican film culture had the decidedly cosmopolitan flavor that marked the diffusion of the new medium across the globe. Flexible modes of exhibition and distribution quickly made cinema, which had initially been the province of foreign entrepreneurs, an exciting new field of activity for domestic entrepreneurs, many of whom already dealt in photographic and phonographic equipment. Mexican filmmakers, who were very often distributors as well, followed the example of Lumière and Edison representatives in filming scenes of local life — national dignitaries, disasters, social life, and "typical" Mexican scenes, such as bullfights — and crafting exhibition programs that combined those films with titles they ordered or procured from abroad. By 1899 motion pictures had become part of everyday life in Mexico City, in highbrow as well as more popular settings, and had spread to the provinces thanks to the itinerant exhibitors who traveled the extensive railroad system completed under the Díaz regime.[7]

Between 1907 and 1917 the exhibition and distribution sides of the industry became more firmly established. Programming consisted first of a mix of European shorts and later feature-length French historical dramas and Italian comedies and melodramas featuring the histrionics of actresses such as

FIGURE 1.2 This *calavera*—a poem written on the Day of the Dead, November 1, that criticizes the living, here illustrated by printmaker José Guadalupe Posada—shows both the mania for cinemagoing in the capital and the fear of the infectious diseases that plagued the city's cinemas. At the bottom the artist offers portraits of typical audience members: an old *lagartijo* (dandy), a stupefied visitor from the provinces, and a light-hearted seamstress. "La brava calavera del cinematografo," 1906. FG0012, Fernando Gamboa Collection, Center for Southwest Research, University Libraries, University of New Mexico.

Pina Menichelli.[8] The revolution, which erupted in 1910, demonstrated the power of motion pictures as a shaper of public opinion and created the conditions for a truly indigenous cinematic tradition, as various revolutionary factions and figures used cinema to influence public opinion.[9] Those films played to enthusiastic audiences across Mexico and the American Southwest, which were hungry for news about the conflict.[10]

Despite or perhaps because of the armed conflict, moviegoing became increasingly entrenched as a part of daily life. Soldiers quartered in provincial cities and the capital became reliable audience members, and refugees and residents found cinemagoing almost a necessary diversion from the fighting.[11] In fact, audiences were so faithful—most cinemas in Mexico City opened even on the day that Francisco I. Madero, the first leader of the revolution, was toppled in a coup—that ticket prices remained the same despite the economic crisis the revolution engendered.[12] By the time the 1917 constitution was signed, signaling the end of the military phase of the revolution, live-theater owners and performers in Mexico City had initiated a campaign against cinemas, which they argued were driving them to ruin.[13]

On the cusp of peace, Mexico's cinema exhibition infrastructure consisted of larger theaters (often repurposed existing buildings) both in Mexico City and provincial capitals, which advertised in daily newspapers, along with smaller theaters that served provincial towns, *cines de barrio* (neighborhood cinemas) that often did not advertise at all, and itinerant exhibitors who served Mexico's extensive rural areas. Distributors were primarily Mexican nationals, some of whom were also film producers. Coverage of motion picture releases—still primarily, though not exclusively, informative—shared space with news and reviews of live theater performances.

During the revolution, most movie theaters typically featured some combination of Italian and French films, with the occasional American film added to the program when available. This dominance of European film stemmed from the fact that most distributors imported films directly from Europe, using the long-established commercial ties between Mexico City and France and reaching the rest of Europe through France.[14] For example, in an ad in the capital's most widely circulated weekly, *El Universal*, in October 1916, the distributor Gonzalo Varela announced that his company had received a shipment of Italian films. Those films included *Romanticismo* (Ambrosio, 1915), *Triste deber* (*Triste impegno*; Caesar Film, 1915), and *Gespay o el jockey caballero* (*Gespay, fantino e gentiluomo*; Caesar Film, 1915).[15] During the same month another distribution company, Cinema México, offered exhibitors a different selection of Italian films: *Sierpe contra sierpe* (*Serpe contra serpe*; Bonnard Films 1915); *Maciste* (Itala Film, 1915); two Aquila Films productions, *Medusa* (*Medusa: L'ammaliatrice*, 1915) and *El herrero de Luozon* (*Il fabro di Lauzan*, 1915); and *Los misterios de Nueva York*, the retitled popular American serial *Exploits of Elaine* (Pathé, 1914) starring Pearl White.[16]

The dominance of European films was, however, on the wane. As early as 1916 one reporter for a trade publication wrote that the mere mention of American actors could guarantee a film's success.[17] As the revolution drew

FIGURE 1.3 An advertisement touting film dealer Gonzalo Varela's most recent shipment of European films. *El Universal*, October 9, 1916. From the collections of the Hemeroteca Nacional de México.

to a close, industry watchers began to assert the "absolute predominance of North American films over European films" in Mexico City, while other reports indicate that U.S. films had become popular well beyond the capital.[18] Industry watchers observed that North American films had been "received very favorably" in Guadalajara, and that the "artistic tastes, tendencies, and aspirations" of the population of Morelia, in Michoacán, were "completely satisfied by American films."[19] By 1918 many cinemas, like the Salon Paris in Morelia, reported that they showed *only* films produced in the United States.[20]

Serials in particular had become popular with Mexican audiences in the late 1910s, as they had in the United States, changing the popular perception of American cinema. Valente Cervantes, who, with his brother, owned the Cines Imperio, Blanco Popular, Pathé, and Parisien in Puebla, the capital of the state of the same name, remembered that initially "the *pueblo* [the people] found American films repugnant, they didn't make any headway, [and] they [Mexican audiences] only saw American 'churros' (low-quality movies)," but "Americans were astute enough to make the first serial films and thus gained acceptance."[21] Indeed, in 1917 *Cine-Mundial*'s Mexico correspondent wrote excitedly: "The films that have awakened the most interest in the last few months have been *Las aventuras de Elena* [an alternate Spanish-language title for *The Exploits of Elaine*] starring Pearl White."[22] Serials, the correspondent continued, consistently provided "fabulous profits" to cinema owners. By way of proof, he cited the "extraordinary success" of the exhibition of two older serials, *La llave maestro* (*The Master Key*; Universal, 1915) and *La caja negra* (*The Black Box*; Universal, 1915).[23] In the summer of 1918, when shaky distribution channels placed re-released European films on almost every program, the public in Mexico City flocked to theaters screening American serials. And, of course, the film that had grated on the aesthetic sensibilities of Rafael Pérez Taylor, *The Adventures of Peg o' the Ring*, was a fifteen-part serial with a circus theme.

That serials made up the vanguard of the *yanqui* invasion is clear from both the ongoing reporting on the Mexican film scene that can be found in *Cine-Mundial* and retrospective accounts of early Mexican film culture. Nothing indicates that the audience for serials was not exclusively or even primarily women, as was the case in the United States, nor were there attempts at re-creating prose tie-ins. Indeed, at least some exhibitors saw serials as something of a liability. For example, Jacobo Granat, a film distributor in Mexico City, claimed in a 1917 interview with *Cine-Mundial*'s Mexican correspondent that patrons who missed the first episode or happened to come to the theater when episodes from the middle of the series were being shown might turn to another theater, in which a full feature or even a number of episodes were being shown successively at one screening.[24] Granat's comments suggest the existence of a heterogeneous set of exhibition practices. Evidence indicates that some theater owners received and screened multiple episodes at one time. For example, in Matehuala, San Luis Potosí, one of two local theaters programmed three episodes of *La caja negra* on one evening in October 1919. Other theaters programmed serials with long lags between episodes, showing them as they became available.

Clearly, something about the personalities and narratives that animated American serials resonated with Mexican audiences. Scholars have framed the appeal of stars such as Pearl White to audiences in the United States in terms of their portrayal of modern womanhood on the screen and off, their

U.S. industry. And both French and Italian exhibitors had to import films to satisfy domestic audiences. The *yanqui* film stood poised to triumph in markets "deprived of national production . . . whose external commerce hasn't been paralyzed by the war," as in Mexico.[35] That triumph required a concerted effort on the part of American film manufacturers, in cooperation with the U.S. government, to take advantage of the opportunities created by the war.[36]

POLITICS AND PIRACY

Film producers in the United States had paid little attention to Latin America before 1916. In part, this stemmed from their perception that Latin America in general, and Mexico in particular, was a difficult place to do business. Prior to the revolution, Americans had invested heavily in agriculture, mining, and industry in Mexico, leaving the market there for imported goods largely to European companies. Yet as the revolution wound down, American firms of all stripes began to see Mexico as ripe with economic possibility. After the revolution, the relative buying power of many poorer Mexicans grew, and the middle class began to expand. In 1920 an American Protestant missionary to Mexico observed that the country's peasants, who constituted the majority of the population, were "economically . . . better off than before": "They are now better able to sustain their churches and their schools. Labor unions, political leaders, current papers appeal to their opinions and seek their support. A strong and growing middle class is emerging from them."[37] *Americas*, a publication of the New York Commercial Bank, summed up the businessman's perspective on Mexico when it declared excitedly "opportunities for trade with Mexico are increasingly rapidly" and encouraged entrepreneurs to look southward for new markets.[38]

As part of this broader trend, motion picture companies in New York began to express interest in Latin American markets. In January 1916 *Moving Picture World*, which had become the leading publication for film exhibitors in the United States, began publishing a Spanish-language version called *Cine-Mundial* (literally world-cinema), which declared itself "dedicated to the promotion of cinematographic interests in the United States and Latin American countries." More accurately, the magazine was dedicated to the promotion of the interests of the U.S. film industry in Latin America.[39] Throughout the first two years of the publication's existence, editorials and feature articles focused on the potential of the Latin American market, including Mexico, and on chronicling the industry's efforts to tap that potential. The staff of *Cine-Mundial* observed that not only was the Latin American market full of potential, but U.S. companies that were astute enough to recognize this fact were guaranteed to reap handsome profits because of the lack of domestic competition. According to one unsigned article in the first issue, "the companies of this country [the United States], recognizing the bottomless resources and future of Latin America, now propose initiating an intense advertising campaign in all those republics."[40] Each issue featured country-specific reports on the state of the cinema business that offered encouragement to distributors and exporters alike.

The magazine's monthly "Crónica de México" column documented the expansion of cinema in Mexico. For example, in 1917 the magazine reported encouragingly: "The activity of the rental houses has multiplied to the extent that it's not difficult to find impresarios that dedicate themselves to the importation of films even in the most remote settlement."[41] Declarations like these about the vibrancy of the Mexican market supported information found in the English-language trade publications, like the announcement in *Moving Picture World* in 1917 that gold and silver currency had displaced the paper money that had been issued during the revolution; producers and distributors could now safely and profitably do business in Mexico.[42]

Pragmatic industry concerns about doing business were often overlain by a discourse on cinema as a medium for spreading democratic cultural values and fostering pan-American cooperation. An editorial in *Cine-Mundial*'s first issue urged hemispheric solidarity, asserting that World War I had demonstrated the need for the Americas to "live with total economic independence from the influences of the old continent."[43] Feature articles suggested that Latin American countries, including Mexico, shared fundamental political values with the United States—values that permeated films produced by U.S. studios. American motion pictures, wrote the publication's editor, Francisco G. Ortega, "emanate[d] equality," while European films perpetuated class differences.[44] In contrast to Mexican cultural nationalists who decried the *yanqui* invasion as a species of cultural and economic imperialism, the editors of *Cine-Mundial* promoted the idea of hemispheric unity through modern capitalism and its accompanying political, social, and cultural formations.

Cine-Mundial's pan-American rhetoric fit well with the general views of the U.S. State Department during this period. As the historian Emily Rosenberg observes, during the 1910s and 1920s the State Department began to see culture as a tool that could be used to achieve diplomatic objectives, including the spreading of American social values and the nurturing of American commercial interests abroad. This perceived power of culture guided government policy, in which film played a central role, during World War I.[45]

After the United States entered the war in April 1917, films destined for export to neutral countries such as Mexico were subject to "strict censorship" that tried to ensure that any films shown would generate sympathy for the United States and its allies.[46] Mexico was of special concern because of the lingering, if not very realistic, possibility that Mexico might ally itself with Germany. (The German government had offered military and financial aid in exchange for Mexico's support.)[47] President Woodrow Wilson's propaganda office, the Committee on Public Information, sent films deemed appropriate to Mexico City, where they were made available to local distributors. Though the archival record is unclear, it seems that these films were a combination of productions of the Committee on Public Information and commercial films that the State Department approved of, such as Charlie Chaplin's *Shoulder Arms* (Charles Chaplin Productions, 1918).[48]

State Department documents reveal that U.S. government officials believed film would be a particularly effective means of countering the pro-German sentiment that they believed had spread to Mexico's illiterate and semiliterate populations.[49] One diplomat wrote: "All Mexicans, especially that large percentage which can neither read nor write, attend the film shows, and this is the best means we have to hand to get before them pro-American Peace Propaganda."[50] Other diplomats urged the State Department to facilitate the exportation of pro-Allies films to Mexico, especially along the increasingly militarized U.S.-Mexico border. In November 1917, for example, George Woodward, the U.S. consul in Matamoros, Tamaulipas—just across the border from Brownsville, Texas—beseeched Secretary of State Robert Lansing to send more films with Spanish-language intertitles to Mexico. According to Woodward, motion pictures were the only effective way to convince the "pro-German element" among Mexico's "lower classes" of the United States' military capacity.[51]

In September 1918, Woodward appealed to the First National Exhibitors Circuit office and the Pathé Exchange in Dallas, Texas, to secure the film *Pershing's Crusaders* (Committee on Public Information, 1918) and the weekly newsreel *The Official Weekly War Review* (Committee on Public Information, 1918) for exhibition in the town's movie theater, without having to pay the usual high duties levied on films that came across the border or wait for them to make their way to Matamoros—which was, as Woodward noted to the State Department, "off a regular film circuit in Mexico."[52] Because he was unable to negotiate the necessary licenses and permissions, *The Official Weekly War Review* never screened in Matamoros, probably to the relief of the theater manager, an American citizen, who felt that such blatant propaganda might "interfere with other business interests" that he had in the region.[53]

Pershing's Crusaders, however, did show in Matamoros in September 1918. The reportedly small audience seemed underwhelmed by the "first official American war picture" from the front lines of Europe. Woodward reported that "there was absolutely [a] lack of applause and . . . the American shield was slightly hissed." This reaction seems somewhat reserved, given that for many Mexicans along the border Pershing was an extremely controversial figure: he had led the punitive expedition that crossed U.S.-Mexico border in search of Pancho Villa after his attack on Columbus, New Mexico, in March 1916. Nevertheless, the consul believed, perhaps naively, that the film "changed the view of many that the military preparations of the United States were not limited to the Mexican borders [sic]."[54] While the film's reception in Matamoros might be best characterized as tepid, the film caused a small scandal a month later when it was shown in Mexico City. An article in the newspaper *El Demócrata* declared that the "charitable gesture of Pershing's troops" had been the "seed of hundreds of orphans and widow's [sic] weeds"—definitely not the impression the consul had hoped to make.[55]

After World War I ended, the U.S. government turned its attention to using motion pictures to encourage trade and helping the film industry "develop in increasing proportions" in Mexico and the rest of Latin America.[56] Propaganda took a back seat to films that would not "arouse antagonism between Americans and Mexicans" and would "secure Mexican friendship and trade."[57] In a 1919 publication, *Selling in Foreign Markets*, an official in the U.S. Department of Commerce noted of Mexico: "In practically every community the display of motion pictures is as common as in this country [the United States]. It is being used for advertising purposes and arrangements can be made with many dealers for the display of slides advertising American products."[58] The consul at Ciudad Juárez, Edward Dow, asked that more instructional motion pictures be sent to that region, noting not only that films and slide lectures helped educate the "illiterate classes" about the "greatness of our country," but that films about agricultural technology and techniques were "productive of sales of inexpensive farming implements" and "facilitated the sale of other products."[59]

In addition to promoting commercial and industrial products, motion pictures could presumably generate profits of their own. However, rampant film piracy, much of which originated in Mexico, made the business of exporting films to Latin America a tenuous endeavor at best.[60] Prints of American films frequently surfaced in Havana that had been obtained illegally in Mexico. From Cuba, they were made available to distributors and exhibitors throughout Central and South America. In *Cine-Mundial*'s April 1918 issue, the general manager of the New York–based Central American

Film Company declared in an interview: "There is nothing more laughable than making big orders to get 'exclusives' in New York while others obtain material in bulk in South America or Mexico."[61] When *Cine-Mundial* announced the imminent arrival of Abraham Carlos, a representative of Fox Film Corporation, in Mexico with over one hundred eight-reel programs, including the D. W. Griffith film *Hearts of the World* (1918), the publication noted that his mission in Mexico was not only to broker distribution deals but also to confront piracy. Lax regulations had allowed twelve counterfeit copies of the Universal serial *The Broken Coin* (1915) to circulate in Mexico and turned *Intolerance* (Triangle Film, 1916) into *La doncella de Orleans* and the serial *Who Is Number One?* (Paramount Pictures, 1917) into *La subasta de virtud*, title changes that allowed the illegally duplicated—duped in industry parlance—films to be exhibited undetected.[62]

The proximity of the two countries and the relatively porous border region made trafficking in films, like other illicit goods, quite easy.[63] Trade papers estimated that over 60 percent of all films, particularly American films, shown in Mexico in the late 1910s were the product of illicit trade.[64] In 1919 L. H. Allen, the Vitagraph distributor for Latin America, wrote a lengthy letter that was published in *Cine-Mundial*, detailing how illicit copies of Vitagraph material had reached Mexican theaters. He reported, for example, that three titles had been "rented" by the company's representative in Dallas for an "imaginary" theater in San Antonio, Texas.[65] But the films never arrived in San Antonio. Instead, a man identified only as "Silva" picked up five boxes of films in the border town of Laredo, Texas. A series of transfers followed, involving the complicity of a train conductor on the Mexican side of the border, and before long the films wound up in the possession of Roque Castillo and his Mexico City–based company, Imperial Cinematográfica. Presumably, once in Mexico City, a new negative would be made and multiple prints struck. In other cases, Mexican film entrepreneurs in the border region simply ignored the international line and circulated films without paying the appropriate international rental fees or customs duties, as when the El Paso Film Exchange offered the serial *Por venganza y por mujer* (*Vengeance and the Woman*, 1917) to exhibitors in the northern Mexican states of Sinaloa and Sonora at deeply discounted rental fees.[66]

Film companies asked for the U.S. government's help in fighting piracy. In the spring of 1918, a new set of customs regulations called for the meticulous inspection of films and their accompanying paperwork as they left the country. Producers and exporters also sent customs officials a list of falsified or stolen films in hopes that film smugglers would be caught and prosecuted.[67] The impact of regulation remains unclear, but the continued furor suggests that they failed to quell the illicit trade.

Through *Cine-Mundial*, studios and distributors appealed directly to Mexicans in the film industry. These entrepreneurs, many of whom were anxious to legitimize the film business in Mexico by establishing the industry as respectable and important, appear to have supported U.S. companies' attempts to stamp out piracy. Allen, the Vitagraph distributor, claimed that after the publication of an announcement in *Cine-Mundial*, he received letters from Mexican exhibitors informing him about illegal prints circulating in their region or city.[68] In 1920 three distribution companies in Mexico City—Universal Film Manufacturing (associated with the U.S. studio), International Pictures, and Mundial Cinematográfica—formed a "union" that they hoped would both help them compete with the much larger and more powerful distribution company owned by the Austrian immigrant Jacobo Granat and protect them from losses related to piracy.[69] They agreed to withhold prints from those cinemas that had obtained pirated films for which any of the three companies held exclusive distribution rights.

This type of self-regulation differed markedly from that practiced in the United States. There, the industry's creation of institutions such as the National Association of the Motion Picture Industry, which was founded in 1916, and its successor, the Motion Picture Producers and Distributors of America (MPPDA), served primarily to "buttress its [the industry's] fight against censorship and efforts to reposition its cultural status," as Lee Grieveson puts it in his account of the industry's negotiation of the censorship issue during the early part of the twentieth century.[70] In Mexico self-regulation was not about censorship—most of these firms did not aspire to produce films themselves—but about establishing film distribution and exhibition as a viable industry. To do so, Mexican distributors needed to develop "mutually beneficial" relationships with the U.S. companies that were their primary suppliers and to demonstrate that Mexico was a profitable place for them to do business.

The complaints that continued to surface throughout the early 1920s indicate that the efforts of Mexican exhibitors and distributors at self-regulation achieved only partial results. In 1919 the manager of Goldwyn's Export Division, George E. Kann, sent a four-page letter to the U.S. secretary of state detailing the illegal procurement and exhibition of an unnamed Goldwyn film in Mexico. Two Mexican distributing companies (Germán Camus & Company, which Kann called an "old hand at pirating films" despite its being the official Goldwyn distributor in Mexico, and N. Gonzalez & Company) had managed to secure a court order allowing the film to be shown until the suit was decided.[71] The company appealed to the State Department for help in communicating to the Mexican government that this was "purely a case of theft and should not be tolerated." Kann emphasized: "American distributors of motion pictures are annually losing hundreds of thousand [sic] of dollars."[72] Yet—in contrast to its support of the claims of American landowners and industrialists for damages and losses suffered during the revolution—the Department of State refused to take action on behalf of U.S. film distributors. The companies' losses, the U.S. government opined, resulted from "the action of a private concern in Mexico and not from the action of the Mexican authorities."[73] Thus, the U.S. government held to a firm line: it was willing to help promote general U.S. commercial interests in Mexico, but it often left American film companies to negotiate their own day-to-day relationships with the Mexican government.

With regard to film piracy, the Mexican government was similarly of little help. Mexico's copyright laws, like those of the rest of Latin America, did not offer explicit protection for motion pictures. At the Fourth International Conference of American States in 1910, members of the Pan-American Union signed a new convention regarding artistic and literary property that recognized those copyrights that had been registered in one signatory country. The conference also adopted the language of the recent revisions to the Berne Convention, which included motion pictures as literary and artistic property.[74] Mexico's civil code ostensibly provided protection that could be obtained by submitting a synopsis of the film and the appropriate fee to the Archivo General de la Nación's (Mexico's National Archive) copyright section, Propiedad Artistica y Literaria (Literary and Artistic Property), which holds the synopses for many—though certainly not all—of the U.S. films exhibited in Mexico in the late 1910s and the 1920s.[75] Though some companies may simply not have bothered to register their properties, it is clear that by the mid-1920s fewer films were being registered, perhaps because piracy was no longer such a pressing concern. American film companies had devised their own strategies for ensuring that profits from the exhibition of their films in Mexico accrued to them.

U.S. FILM COMPANIES IN MEXICO

The time was ripe for American film companies to solidify their presence in Mexico. A David P. Howells Inc. report from 1920 that was featured in *Motion Picture News* noted that the effects of social and economic stability in Mexico could be seen in the boom in theater construction and remodeling projects, which included cinemas that could seat four to five thousand spectators (the subject of the next chapter). The efforts of Mexican distributors during the previous decade to establish the legitimacy of their business and prove that Mexico was a profitable market seemed to be reaching fruition; the film industry in Mexico increasingly operated on what the Howells auditor called a "more substantial and more responsible basis."[76] The exhibitor E. H. Roth of San Francisco took an exploratory trip to Mexico in 1921 and asserted that, in spite of President Álvaro Obregón's commitment to making Mexico safe for U.S. capital, "moving picture development is seven or eight years behind the United States."[77] Roth saw this as an opportunity rather than a deficit. He reported confidently that "the masses are an amusement-loving type and moving pictures will appeal strongly to them when our best offerings are available."[78] *Cine-Mundial*'s Mexican correspondent, José Navarro, had predicted as much in 1916 when he attributed the paucity of American films to the "scarce propaganda [advertising] of American producers."[79] In an interview two years later, a studio representative concurred: "The [Mexican] public that has seen the top brands from here [the United States] won't settle for the common European program."[80]

By the late 1910s and early 1920s, studios increasingly strove to put their names in front of Mexican audiences. They did so by establishing more formal relationships with the Mexican distribution and exhibition industries (often one and the same), which were centralized in Mexico City. Coverage of the exhibition and distribution arms of the Mexican film industry in *Cine-Mundial*'s monthly "Crónicas" column shows this shift clearly. Correspondents' emphasis in the mid-1910s on individual film titles and the theaters that showed them gave way in the late 1910s to a focus on *los alquiladores* (exchanges). By the mid-1920s the focus had shifted again to the company branch offices and the cinema circuits they supplied.

Indeed, in the mid-1910s Mexican distributors typically sent agents to New York to obtain slates of films or worked through export companies that packaged films for the international trade—*Cine-Mundial* noted in its inaugural issue that "direct exportations [to Latin America] have been very rare."[81] By the late 1910s Mexican distributors began working directly with specific "brands," functioning effectively as authorized exchanges. Paramount Pictures executives stated the benefits of establishing relationships with authorized distributors for their industry peers: "The establishment of an authorized exchange in Mexico is expected to curtail considerably the operation of film thieves and will assure the distribution of Paramount Artcraft Productions outside of Mexico City itself . . . the Mexican people will be able to see in their theaters the same stars and feature products that appear in theaters in the United States."[82] As Paramount's strategy suggests, companies also hoped to create more diffuse distribution networks, essentially bringing their products closer to cinemas across Mexico. Above all, direct sales would eliminate intermediaries who, according to *Cine-Mundial*, "only hamper and restrict operations . . . create prejudices, hide the true origins of trademarks, and . . . work in the long run to the detriment of all interested parties."[83]

Authorized exchanges proliferated. Pathé began to supply complete programs via authorized Mexican distributors in 1918, a strategy that the company hoped would give Mexican exhibitors access to a constant flow of new material associated with its trademark.[84] *Motion Picture News* reported in 1919 that the establishment of Paramount-Artcraft's exchange in Mexico, Continental Film, had generated a "great increase in the public interest" in the studio's productions, furthering the company's goal of "standardizing the Paramount-Artcraft trademark throughout the world."[85] The International Pictures Company, which had offices in El Paso, Mexico City, and New York, became the exclusive distributor of Vitagraph productions not only in Mexico but also in Central America.[86]

Other companies began to establish branch offices in Mexico.[87] Fox Film led the way in March 1919, when it sent two representatives to Mexico "for the purpose of extending the Fox distributing organization throughout Mexico."[88] Fox's foray into Mexico represented part of a hemispheric strategy that included Venezuela, Cuba, Argentina, and Brazil. *Cine-Mundial* praised the company's approach—"complete organization; aggressive publicity campaigns; comprehension of the needs, tastes, and manners of the publics they are trying to cultivate"—as ideally suited to entering new markets like Mexico.[89] By June 1923 *Cine-Mundial* reported that most of the major companies—Fox, Paramount, Universal, and United Artists—and some independents had offices in Mexico City and branch offices or authorized representatives in major provincial cities and port towns.[90] In the mid-1920s Hollywood studios even began to sporadically acquire exhibition spaces in Mexico City. In 1924 Universal Pictures' representative in Mexico City leased the Cine Regis and promised to offer "high-class movie programs" composed entirely of Universal material.[91] The following year the Cine Olimpia—whose parent company, the Circuito Olimpia, had featured films from studios such as Fox, First National, and, most important, Paramount—reopened as the Fox-Olimpia.[92] These changes reflected broader shifts in distribution in the United States, as major studios either incorporated or marginalized smaller, independent competitors and exerted increasing control over production, distribution, and exhibition.[93]

American studios' more systematic approach to the Mexican mar-

FIGURE 1.4 An advertisement for the Granat Bros. Film Distribution Company featuring material from Goldwyn and Fox, serials, and (off to the side) European productions, and promising "success" to exhibitors. *Excélsior*, April 11, 1920. From the collections of the Hemeroteca Nacional de México.

ket promised to bring benefits to audiences, exhibitors, and studios alike. Studios emphasized that the new mode of distribution would be "mutually lucrative" and ultimately benefit the Mexican public, which they claimed, somewhat disingenuously, had suffered from neglect.[94] Mexican audiences were excited by the prospect of being able to see the latest releases. Previously some had felt that Mexico had been closed off from the advances being made in the film industry "by a sort of Great Wall of China," as *Cine-Mundial*'s correspondent in Mexico phrased it.[95] As late as 1921 the editor of *Excélsior's* cinema page lamented the fact that many theaters in Mexico exhibited films that were two or more years old. This lag meant that it was difficult for Mexican spectators to develop loyalty to the films of any given studio since "artists had changed their contracts" but were "still being announced as

FIGURE 1.5 Paramount makes its presence in Mexico known with a New Year's greeting printed in the newspaper *El Universal*, January 1, 1923. From the collections of the Hemeroteca Nacional de México.

stars of the company that made the film."[96] *Cine-Mundial* likewise acknowledged that Mexican audiences deserved better than "films . . . scratched and incomplete; new films . . . with photography inappropriate to the brand names they carry; film divided arbitrarily into innumerable parts with no other objective than to squeeze out rentals until the last drop."[97] Studios' sustained attention to the Mexican market promised to modernize Mexico's film culture and place it "at the same level that Argentina, Brazil, the United States, and a great part of Europe had reached."[98] But even as film companies and their representatives perceived themselves and were perceived as agents of modernization, they were forced to adjust their formula for box office success—a formula rife with ideological and cultural assumptions—to local tastes, politics, and business practices.

ARTISTAS UNIDOS: A CASE STUDY

The history of United Artists in Mexico illustrates the challenges faced by U.S. film companies once they moved from establishing authorized distribution exchanges to actually opening distribution offices in Mexico. United Artists was founded by Mary Pickford, Douglas Fairbanks, Charlie Chaplin, and D. W. Griffith as a distribution outlet for its principals' independent productions; its history has been well documented, as have its activities throughout Latin America.[99] Though United Artists was somewhat anomalous in terms of its business model, it is the established company for which the most extensive records of activity in Mexico exist.[100] These sources provide an invaluable window onto the company's foreign operations, its on-going analysis of the preferences of Mexican audiences, and its interactions with the country's radicalized cinema workers.

According to historian Gaizka Usabel, methodical expansion into foreign markets, including Mexico, was essential to the business strategy of United Artists.[101] In 1922 the company opened an office in Mexico City. Artistas Unidos S.A. was legally incorporated as a separate entity and placed under the administration of Harvey Sheahan, a U.S. citizen with a reasonable grasp of Spanish. As a separate company rather than a branch office, Artistas Unidos purchased a three-year license to "exploit, market, and distribute" United Artists' titles in Mexico—among them, *His Majesty the American* (1919), *Robin Hood* (1922), *Pollyanna* (1920), *Orphans of the Storm* (1921), *A Tailor Made Man* (1922), and *A Small Town Idol* (1921).[102]

Establishing its Mexican office as a separate company gave United Artists protection from any potential economic instability in Mexico. Perhaps more important, it served as a strategy to maximize foreign box office profits. The contract entered into between United Artists Corporation and Artistas Unidos S.A. provided for a 75–25 percent split of gross receipts and a 70–30 percent split of marketing expenses. This arrangement allowed the Mexican company to operate with a permanent deficit and thus avoid paying taxes in Mexico. Occasional infusions of cash from the home office covered extraordinary expenses and capitalized expansion.[103] The branch carried heavy deficits until 1927—two years after the company had altered its agreement with the branch to create a 60–40 profit split—when it began to operate with just a slight deficit.[104] Incorporating the office in Mexico also put the company in a better position to pressure the Mexican government to intervene, as Sheahan put it, "more directly in cinema related issues, which are tarnishing the good name of all the country's [Mexico's] businesses."[105] Finally, having a branch office in Mexico facilitated business transactions in Central and South America. Prints could be sent to Mexico, either by train across the border or by steamer to Tampico, and then via rail to Central America. Just as Argentina was typically the point of entry for film in South America, Mexico served as the entrepôt for United Artists' films destined for Nicaragua, El Salvador, Honduras, and Guatemala.[106]

Reports from employees on the ground in foreign countries helped Artistas Unidos stay abreast of political developments that might affect its profits. Sheahan, for one, believed that the Mexican market was unique in its sensitivity to political events. In one of his weekly reports from December 1926, Sheahan discussed the effect that the Cristero Rebellion, a three-year civil conflict that pitted conservative Catholics against the government of President Plutarco Elías Calles (1926–29), was having on United Artists' business. "The moving picture industry here [in Mexico] is more sensitive to political unrest than any other," he wrote. "Politics here are usually accompanied by parades, and there is often some disorder and shooting. These manifestations take place always on Sundays in the morning, and when anything occurs the people stay in their houses all day, which, of course, hurts the 'cines' very much, as this is their one revenue-producing day."[107] Sheahan enumerated the effects of the civil unrest—delays in paying government salaries, looting, the suspension of all credit operations, and the high price of food—all of which "seriously" affected people "who normally patronized the 'cines.'"[108] Indeed, even before the Cristero Rebellion erupted into an armed conflict, conservative Catholic activists—known as the Liga Nacional de la Defensa de la Libertad Religiosa, who would unite under the motto "Viva Cristo Rey" (Long live Christ the king)—had called for a boycott of all cinemas, resulting in significant losses in parts of the country where the group was most active.[109] Sheahan reported to the New York office in August 1926: "The Catholic party is at the present making the boycott stick. There have been committees organized throughout the Republic to pick on all the moving picture houses."[110] In September Vice Consul George Waters appended statements from U.S. film distributors indicating that movie attendance had fallen 75–80 percent to his alarmed report that "the boycott in Mexico City is very serious."[111]

Although the Liga Nacional would discard the boycott in favor of militant action, U.S. film companies found that in general periods of intense religious activity were bad for the film business in Mexico. For example, in January 1924 Sheahan reported that "the reason for holding back *A Woman of Paris* is that the Lenten season in this country is a poor one for business."[112] In 1928 S. C. de la Garza, who succeeded Sheahan as manager for Artistas Unidos S.A, reported that the 1928 death of the archbishop of Mexico in San Antonio, Texas, where he had gone into exile during the Cristero conflict, had become the "cause of mourning in Catholic centers" and "reduced the attendance at all amusements," including the cinema.[113]

In addition to tracking the idiosyncratic rhythms of the film exhibition business in Mexico, having offices in Mexico provided United Artists with direct information about the preferences of the Mexican public. Sheahan regularly advised United Artists' home office in New York on which new releases should be sent to Mexico, based on his firsthand observations. For example, although the 1924 re-release of *A Woman of Paris* (Charles Chaplin Productions, 1923)—the tragic story of a country girl corrupted by the big city, directed by Charlie Chaplin—"went over very big in Mexico City,"

Loving Lies (Associated Authors, 1924), a melodrama, which the home office considered a surefire success, "did not make much of a hit with the Mexican Public [*sic*]. It was taken as an ordinary program picture."[114] The plot of *Loving Lies* revolved around marital deceit, childlessness, and adoption and took place in a harbor town. *Woman of Paris*, in contrast, told a story that many audience members might have recognized as a version of the popular novel *Santa*—published in 1903 by the Mexican author Federico Gamboa and brought to the screen in 1918 by the director Luis Peredo—in which a small-town girl is corrupted by the city. Perhaps even more relevant, *Loving Lies* did not have an association with Chaplin, so beloved in Mexico that in 1920 one commentator noted that figures of the actor "modeled out of cardboard and filled with firecrackers" had been burned in place of the traditional effigies of Satan that marked popular celebrations of Holy Saturday, the day before Easter Sunday.[115] Chaplin's appearance as part of a popular celebration of mischief indicates the degree to which the Mexican public had integrated American film culture into everyday life.

Some cultural character types, United Artists found, simply did not translate. Although Mexican audiences seemed to enjoy Gloria Swanson's performance in the film *Sadie Thompson* (Gloria Swanson Productions, 1928), in which Swanson played a former prostitute who becomes the object of a missionary's affections when they find themselves thrown together on a South Sea island, the film's Protestant missionary character apparently made little impression on Mexican audiences. "As they do not have reformers in this country," de la Garza wrote, "the plot was not generally understood."[116] In truth, Mexican audiences may well have known what a missionary was and still been unimpressed by the character. After all, the presence of Protestant missionaries was a highly contentious issue in Mexico at the time. Whatever the case, this lack of cultural resonance led, predictably, to a drop in box office receipts. In contrast, the success of films such as Cecil B. DeMille's 1927 *The King of Kings*, marketed in Mexico as *Creo en dios*, was attributed to its relevance to the ongoing armed conflict over the state's anticlerical policies. "Because of the ensuing difficulties existing between the government and the church," de la Garza wrote, "the Catholics supported the picture tremendously." De la Garza had spent over 6,000 pesos (approximately $2,880 in 1928) marketing the film; he was sure "no other picture [could] gross as much for this market."[117] According to documentation from DeMille's holding company, the Cinema Corporation of America, which handled the film's international distribution and had arranged for Artistas Unidas to distribute the film in Mexico City and perhaps elsewhere in Mexico, generated over $27,000 in contract revenue from Mexico alone.[118] The critic Cube Bonifant, writing as Luz Alba in *Revista de Revistas*, praised *Creo en dios*, saying "everything [in it] is delicacy, refinement, spirituality," and spoke approvingly of DeMille's "believing heart." She complained, however, that the film was only being shown at one upscale cinema, at prices beyond the "reach of the majority of people."[119]

Political instability, the liturgical calendar, and even the weather (Mexican theaters were typically not heated or cooled; in the winter they could be incredibly cold) could affect business conditions; in addition, U.S. film companies in Mexico had to contend with a markedly different business culture. When Henry Muller, United Artists' traveling auditor, came to Mexico City to investigate accounting irregularities that would result in Sheahan's suspension, he noted: "Exhibitors rarely come alone . . . some one had to get up and offer them a seat, otherwise they would never stay long enough to do any real business."[120] "No work whatsoever," he expressed with frustration, could be accomplished during the two-hour lunch period that was customary in Mexico. Muller reported not even being able to start his audit until he had rented two more rooms and had the appropriate furniture made. He complained about having to write out his notes by hand because the office's one Corona typewriter was being used by a traveling agent of the company, and the "public stenographer [was] drunk again and of no use." Muller's frustration may have emerged from his inability to speak Spanish and his unfamiliarity with the rhythms of Mexican urban life, but his observations reinforced his and others' preconceptions that Mexico was an undeveloped and uncivilized country.

The activities of the business-centered American expatriate culture, which U.S. film company representatives inhabited, often had little to do with fostering the "hemispheric understanding" promoted by publications such as *Cine-Mundial*.[121] Sheahan's sojourn in Mexico, while personally profitable—despite being accused of embezzlement, he managed over the course of two years to make lucrative investments in a garage in Mexico City and oil wells in Tampico—did little to change his racist perceptions of the country and its inhabitants.[122] At the height of the Cristero conflict, he wrote to his superiors bemoaning the political situation in Mexico and hoping that President Calvin Coolidge would deal firmly with Mexico and the rest of Latin America. "All of this trouble," he declared, should "convince our State Department that she cannot treat these people like white folks."[123] Sheahan's perception of Mexicans as a less civilized race suggests that despite assertions about the democratizing nature of consumption, being part of the market for American motion pictures did not necessarily mean that one would be thought of as a citizen, global or otherwise.

Such racist attitudes infused everyday business interactions between the staff of U.S. film companies and their Mexican clients and employees, and even the public with whom they did business. Although the presence of U.S. film companies in Mexico, like the presence of other U.S. businesses, generated employment for Mexicans, U.S. expatriates typically occupied the best-paid and most powerful positions. Artistas Unidos employed seven people, not including the staff in its office in Torreón in the state of Coahuila. Sheahan earned $100 per week, while the Mexican staff—two film reviewers, a bookkeeper, a stenographer, a shipper, and a janitor (Pedro Canales, who received $3 per week)—earned significantly less.

These types of skewed inequalities in pay and power, coupled with racist rhetoric, could easily lead to tensions. For example, both the employees and patrons of the Cine San Hipólito, which was owned by Universal Films, complained about the attitude of American manager, Charles Rich. In one report a Mexican cinema inspector noted that Rich "possesses absolutely no grasp of the national language" and treated both employees and patrons "despotically, insultingly, and in a denigrating manner."[124] The inspector continued: "He constantly offends the public . . . as much for his personal conduct as for his poor administration of the theater." Similarly, in 1928 C. P. Margot, the manager of the Paramount office in Mexico City, was denounced by Mexican distributors for his "despotic" treatment of cinema owners and managers and was blamed for the deterioration of the Circuito Olimpia (with which Paramount had negotiated an exclusive contract, displacing Fox Films).[125] His behavior irritated Mexicans in the industry so much that they asked Paramount to transfer him. It is unclear what happened to Margot. Reports of other clashes between *yanqui* cinema representatives and the Mexican public surface periodically in municipal records, indicating that although Mexican audiences appreciated the quality of U.S. films, expatriate managers often failed to treat Mexican nationals with the respect and professionalism that audiences felt they were entitled to as patrons.

Formal labor relations proved to be another source of tension between Mexican employees and American-held or -managed companies. Cinema workers—projectionists, the inspectors who checked films for damage, ticket sellers, doormen, and janitors—used labor strikes to demand that cinema owners conform to Mexican labor standards and pay living wages.[126] In 1922, for example, Circuito Olimpia, which by that time was not only the largest cinema chain in the capital but also completely under American control, cut its Mexican staff in response to the decline in business caused by the Mexican government's embargo on U.S. films (the topic of chapter 5). The chain's workers had organized themselves as the Unión de Empleados Confederados de Cinematógrafos (Confederated Union of Cinema Workers) the year before, and they went on strike. After two weeks the union settled with the company, which agreed only to reinstate the workers who had been let go, leaving the union's other grievances unaddressed. In 1924 the union became an affiliate of the Confederación Regional Obrera Mexicana (Regional Confederation of Mexican Workers), which was one of the most influential political organizations in the country, and at the time under the leadership of the powerful Luis Morones.

American film companies quickly came to resent the amount of power wielded by cinema workers' unions, which despite initial setbacks exerted increasing pressure on American-based producers and distributors. Sheahan reported that the unions had begun using the practice of "embargos"—asking distributors not to send films to exhibitors who refused union demands for salary increases, vacation time, or the power to place their members in vacant positions. At the beginning of 1925 three "embargos" took place. Two of the affected urban centers, Tampico and "Monterey" (sic) were, as Sheahan reminded his superiors in New York, "big revenue producing cities."[127] And in 1926 the employees of the Circuito Maximo, which had taken the Circuito Olimpia's place as the largest cinema chain in Mexico City, went on a sympathy strike in support of the musicians' union.[128] The federal government's Departamento del Trabajo's (Board of Labor) board of conciliation ultimately ruled against the unions, but the strike closed the chain for two months. Disturbed, Sheahan wrote to New York that the strike "came on just as we are about to put *Son of the Sheik* [a popular Valentino film] in the circuit." As a result, he argued, our business "has been very seriously affected."[129] Labor activism on the part of cinema workers, Sheahan reported, was contributing to "very ugly" conditions in the Mexican film industry.

American film companies reacted to Mexico's unfavorable labor climate by forming their own national "union" of producers and distributors in May 1925.[130] The union, later designated the "Film Board of Trade," was formed explicitly to resist the demands of labor, maintain "friendly" relations with theater owners, and protect the studios' mutual business interests. Because of the centralized nature of the Mexican film industry, the board, located in Mexico City, wielded a tremendous amount of influence. At the time, Sheahan noted, the U.S. embassy in Mexico City was "filled with complaints from both British and American concerns against the unreasonable demands of labor."[131] Sheahan recognized that the employer-employee relations that characterized the movie industry were part of a larger conflict between the two countries and counseled his fellow film company representatives to speak to Morones before forming the Film Board of Trade.

Despite his politically savvy advice, the board appears to have continued to attempt to arbitrate labor disputes on behalf of U.S. studios, convinced that its members knew the best course of development for the Mexican cinema industry.[132] Ironically—in contrast to the situation in countries such as Britain, where similar bodies represented domestic film production companies that were fighting Hollywood's influence—the Film Board of Trade in Mexico was composed of representatives of American companies.[133] In the 1930s, as Mexican film production increased under the auspices of the country's government, one of its key characteristics would be a highly organized labor force, a direct legacy of the activities of cinema workers in the 1920s.[134]

CONCLUSION

The end of the Mexican revolution can be seen as a watershed in Mexican film culture. As the scholarship on Mexican national production has shown, the preoccupations of Mexican filmmakers shifted from political events to narrative feature-length films, including *El automóvil gris* (Rosas, 1919), a docudrama serial that would break box office records for a national production. The end of the revolution also coincided with the ascendance of the U.S. film industry as a global force. Whereas in the 1910s and 1920s American films had been more of a novelty than anything else—especially in comparison to the art films being produced by European filmmakers—by the 1920s the Mexican market was dominated by American film companies.

These companies, primarily the producer-distributors that constituted the recently founded Motion Picture Producers and Distributors of America, worked hard to establish a hold on the Mexican market. Though more profits (even the somewhat paltry profits offered by the Mexican market) were always desirable, American studios also wanted control over a market that they saw as the gateway to other parts of Latin America and a hotbed of film piracy.

When *Magazine Fílmico*, the weekly cinema supplement to the popular magazine *Revista de Revistas*, listed its editorial staff's favorite films of the year in 1926, all were American except for one.[135] The top film, *Ben Hur*—perhaps not coincidentally starring the Mexican-born Ramón Novarro—had grossed an unprecedented 50,000 pesos (roughly $25,000 in 1925) during a two-week exclusive run at the Cine Palacio, an upscale theater on the Avenida San Francisco in the center of Mexico City.[136] The *yanqui* invasion had arrived and, it would seem, conquered.

The invasion metaphor was potent, especially given Mexico's fraught relationship with the United States, but it was also somewhat misleading. In the late 1910s and early 1920s U.S. film companies entered territory that had, like the United States itself, been dominated by European films—films that the Mexican cultural elite associated with art and that Mexican filmmakers sought to emulate.[137] Thus, the invasion was more of a displacement of one foreign power by another than the sullying of a pristine national cinematic landscape.

The arrival of *yanqui* film companies followed broader shifts in the global film market—namely, the shift from third-party distribution to authorized exchanges and finally the opening of branch offices abroad by producers and distributors. It also sparked changes in film exhibition and distribution in Mexico. Whereas Mexican nationals had served as the intermediaries between European film studios and Mexican exhibitors, foreign-born representatives of film companies now became a permanent part of the Mexican distribution and exhibition scene. Film company executives often made common cause—for example, over the issue of piracy—with Mexican entrepreneurs anxious to prove that Mexico was a stable place to do business. Once established, film companies studied the Mexican market carefully in order to better tailor their offerings to local conditions. The textual malleability of silent films met audiences preoccupied by periodic political unrest, the religious calendar, and, in the mid-1920s, an armed conflict that pitted Mexicans against each other once more. In addition, the racist assumptions about Mexico's level of development that permeated American business culture often clashed with the realities of the audiences that film companies courted and the Mexican nationals on whose labor their profits depended.

American film companies believed that they were not only exporting entertainment but also raising the level of Mexico's entertainment culture, spreading American political values, and cultivating a new market of potential consumers for American products. But Mexican audiences, film industry entrepreneurs, and government officials had their own ideas about the social function and cultural meaning of consuming American films. Despite the widespread use of the invasion metaphor, American cinema found itself encircled by Mexico's postrevolutionary nation-building project. Nationalism surfaced not only in the form of labor activists intent on ensuring that foreign capitalists respected their rights as workers and thus as citizens, but also in the form of the exhibition practices that framed American films and the social meanings given to the habit of moviegoing in nationalist terms.

2 AMERICAN MOVIES, MEXICAN MODERNITY
The Cinema as a National Space

En México, al caer la noche, es enorme el público que se dedica a "pelicu-
lar" [At nightfall in Mexico, the public that dedicates itself to "going to the
movies" is enormous].
—CARLOS GONZÁLEZ PEÑA, "LA INSPECCIÓN DE LOS CINES,"
EL UNIVERSAL, FEBRUARY 7, 1917

The cinema uncovers the culture of the country that produces the film, not
of the country where they [*sic*] are exhibited.
—MANUEL BAUCHE ALCALDE, "NOTAS EDITORIALES,"
BOLETÍN MUNICIPAL, SEPTEMBER 2, 1924

In 1919, Germán Camus, a film distributor and sometime producer,
opened the Cine Olimpia on Avenida 16 de Septiembre, just around
the corner from Mexico City's main plaza, the Zócalo. That same
year, Camus sold the theater to Jacobo Granat, proprietor of (among
others) one of the city's oldest and toniest cinemas, the Salon Rojo.
Once Granat, with the help of one of his brothers, took over the Cine
Olimpia, he embarked on an ambitious project: constructing Mexico's
first *cine-teatro*, modeled after the movie palaces proliferating in the
United States.[1]

Granat and his architect, Carlos Crombé, designed the 4,000-seat
theater to be more than just a place to view motion pictures.[2] It would
include the latest advances in theater design: fixed seating, a specially
outfitted projection booth, and well-lit exits and walkways. In addition to the main auditorium, there would be a *salon de te–cabaret* (tea
and cabaret room); a smoking room; multiple, well-appointed lobbies for waiting patrons; modern bathrooms; and other multipurpose
rooms that could be used for social gatherings and meetings. Barto-

FIGURE 2.1 Advertisement for D. W. Griffith's *The Idol Dancer* (1920), the feature shown at the premiere of the Cine Olimpia, in Mexico City. *Excélsior*, December 9, 1921. From the collections of the Hemeroteca Nacional de México.

leme Galloti Ceroni, the Italian artist who had executed the neo-Italianate interior of Mexico City's Palacio de Correos (post office) during the Díaz regime was to decorate the interior with subtle Aztec motifs.[3]

With construction about half done and additional capital needed, Jacobo Granat formed a corporation with the American investors R. P. Jennings and Richard and Irving White. Shortly thereafter, however, Granat was forced to flee the country, one step ahead of criminal charges that stemmed from a mysterious conflict between him and his three new associates.[4] Rumors circulated that the charges had been fabricated to keep Granat from reentering the film exhibition business. Some people speculated that he had embezzled funds from the company. Regardless, the result of Granat's sudden departure

FIGURE 2.2 The exterior of the Cine Olimpia on the Avenida 16 de Septiembre, surrounded by other commercial establishments, circa 1928. Posters advertise Emil Jannings in Josef von Sternberg's *The Last Command* (1928) and William Wellman's *The Legion of the Condemned* (1928). © (121099), CONACULTA.INAH .SINAFO.FN.MÉXICO.

was that the Cine Olimpia (along with many of the Granat brothers' other holdings) quickly became the property of a consortium of American-based investors.[5]

On December 10, 1921, three years after Granat had purchased the building, the American-owned Cine Olimpia opened with a gala screening of D. W. Griffith's *The Idol Dancer* (D. W. Griffith Productions, 1920), a film set in the South Seas that touched on the scandalous themes of alcoholism and interracial marriage. The press said little about the film or the elaborate live prologue that accompanied it, but the daily newspaper *Excélsior* devoted a multipage spread to the theater itself on opening day. The *Excélsior*'s reporter admitted that the Olimpia's exterior façade was unremarkable, which was unsurprising given the theater's location in a preexisting space. The interior, however, was another story. "Everything that architecture has introduced in relationship to this type of building," the reporter gushed, "had

FIGURE 2.3 Interior of the Cine Olimpia, with its elaborately decorated box seats, circa 1920s. © (85660), CONACULTA.INAH.SINAFO.FN.MÉXICO.

been made the most of to give the Teatro Olimpia elegance and sumptuousness [and] the public complete comfort and security." Jennings and his associates had taken the "advantages" of "the grand New York and European cinemas" and used them to build a theater that conformed to the unspecified "needs and customs of [Mexico]." The lengthy article, accompanied by several photographs, focused on the auditorium's perfect sight lines, rich décor, and indirect lighting; the theater's enormous pipe organ; and the elegantly appointed dance hall and foyer. Mexicans, the unnamed reporter proclaimed, should take pride in the fact that "there are impresarios that concern themselves with giving the public what it deserves."[6]

With the opening of the Olimpia, a new era in film exhibition had arrived in Mexico. The theater's owners were determined to import only the very best of U.S. film exhibition practices to Mexico. In addition to the theater's design and furnishings, the owners discarded standard Mexican exhibition practices. Rather than offering a continuously running program with *permanencia voluntaria* (in which patrons could come and go as they pleased, just as they had done during the nickelodeon era in the United States, and as they continued to do in Mexico through at least 1926), the Olimpia offered patrons a feature film preceded by both a full concert and a thematically appropriate prologue.[7] Ticket prices reflected the complexity of this new exhibition strategy. On opening night, a *luneta* (orchestra) seat cost 2.50 pesos and an upper balcony seat 1.20. Since the average daily wage of female urban industrial workers at the time could be as low as 75 centavos per day and other theaters charged between 30 centavos and 1.20 pesos for orchestra seats, and between 10 and 30 centavos for the upper balcony, the Olimpia's management clearly did not conceive of cinema as a democratic art.[8]

Mexico City did not have a large enough middle class to fill the theater's three daily functions at such high prices. Even when enticed by special presentations, those who could afford to go to the Olimpia seemed dissatisfied by the feature presentation model. In response, ticket prices were lowered, and the theater added *noches festivas* (promotional events) that combined film screenings with talent contests, special appearances by both foreign and domestic entertainers, and raffles in order to attract a wider, and implicitly less highbrow, audience.[9] The theater also hosted dance contests, concerts, children's matinees, and meetings of private social clubs. Perhaps most tellingly, though, the theater reverted to the program format that Mexican audiences were accustomed to: a newsreel, a comedy, and two or more features with musical accompaniment but no formal prologue. *Permanencia voluntaria* was reinstated; audiences could once again come and go as they pleased.[10]

Though the Olimpia failed to transplant U.S. exhibition practices to Mexico City, it represented an ideal not only in terms of its design, but also in terms of the experience of spectatorship that its owners hoped that design would foster. Luxuriously appointed and at least initially oriented toward showcasing feature films, the theater was modeled on the American movie palace, which in turn borrowed from elite practices of theatergoing to encourage spectatorial absorption in the narrative world of the film. In 1922 Hipólito Amor, a municipal cinema inspector, approvingly deemed it "the only correct cinema in the city."[11] His praise suggests the ways in which cinemas and the social practices they housed were framed by discussions about modernization and progress in postrevolutionary Mexico.

As the story of the Olimpia illustrates, a film culture built on the consumption of imported fare could play an important role in Mexico's project of proving itself civilized and modern. Indeed, movie theaters, as both a business and a social space, brought American cinema and Mexico's vigorous postrevolutionary nationalism into the same orbit. The best-documented site of these dynamics, Mexico City, arguably functioned as a model for provincial governments, which framed their own cinema-related regulatory schemes on that of the capital. The business of film exhibition was acknowledged as being more important than film production to the country's economy. And cinemas—particularly new, purpose-built ones—became concrete symbols of Mexico's development and progress in both the capital and the states. Nationalism shaped film exhibition practices, especially the performative aspects of that practice, and informed advertising strategies, while movie theaters became sites for staging nation-building rituals and educational programs—such as those targeting venereal disease—designed to expose Mexico's citizenry to modern notions of hygiene, health, and behavior.

The cinema and its patrons also became the object of class-inflected reform. Municipal authorities sought to make cinemas modern spaces in terms of safety and aesthetics while monitoring the behavior of patrons in an attempt to make the cinema a space for the production of modern subjects. In the process, what might be best characterized as an ideal spectator emerged: not the middle-class woman who so preoccupied American exhibitors and film producers, but the family of any class, as long as it was what inspectors termed "honorable." This focus on families fit neatly into postrevolutionary rhetoric about the revolutionary family as well as into efforts to bring Mexico's indigenous population and working classes—which were sometimes seen as one and the same—into modernity by encouraging them to adopt middle-class family structures and middle-class norms, including habits of consumption.[12]

At the same time, and sometimes in conflict with this ideal, the municipal government found itself defending cinema patrons' rights to see the film that had been advertised, be spared long delays between reels, and find a seat once they had bought a ticket. The reformist project that made cinema a symbol of Mexico's modernization thus also had to balance the rights of citizens with the goals of the state. Ultimately, the narratives on the screen—mostly American in origin—were just one component of a broader cinematic experience that included the space of the theater itself, a range of sonic and performative elements, promotional strategies, and regulatory regimes, all of which cast the cinema as a national space.

HONORABLE SPECULATION

In December 1924 the head of the Departamento de Productos Manufacturados (Department of Manufactured Products) of the Secretaria de Industria, Comercio, y Trabajo (Secretary of Industry, Commerce, and Labor) compiled an extensive report on the cinema industry in Mexico. The Mexican government, the report noted, had worked to "foster and establish this industry that enjoys, like no other, the double object of intellectual and moral advancement." The film industry, he continued, was the ideal mechanism to promote a goal held dear by the revolutionary government: "progress in the [country's] populations."[13] In other words, the film industry was identified as a potent weapon in the revolutionary state's struggle against the vice, ignorance, and immorality that many believed had beset the country under Porfirio Díaz.

The report began with a celebration of the efforts of national producers. It declared that "14,600 feet of Pro-Mexico film" had been produced, without specifying the time period in which this production took place or the types of films that were produced. In short order, however, the report turned to the "commercial part of the matter": exhibition. The cinema industry in Mexico had reached an "extraordinary peak" not through the production of national films, but through the construction of "magnificent and well-conditioned halls [theaters]." The fact that film "formed one of the most important lines of Mexican life" could be proved, according to the report, not by the popularity of Mexican stars or movies, but by the amount of taxes generated by the exhibition of (foreign) films. Forced to admit that "the production of films in Mexico is really quite meager," the report concluded by acknowledging "the importance of imports and . . . the amount of money invested in them."[14] In sum, exhibition—not production—drove the Mexican film industry in the 1920s.

As the report suggests, before it turned its attention to supporting film production, the Mexican government saw film exhibition as an important part not only of national culture, but also of the national economy—so much so that the previous year, the newly reorganized Departamento de Trabajo (Department of Labor) conducted a national census of the cinema sector, by which it meant cinema exhibition. The census was part of a larger project to gather information about business and labor conditions in important or growing employment sectors such as printing, bricklaying, and textile manufacturing. Collected data were published periodically in the department's monthly bulletin, alongside detailed information on the cost of living in each Mexican state.[15] An analysis of the extant manuscript census material offers a snapshot of the material conditions of cinema exhibition in the early 1920s, suggesting the ways in which the film industry was seen as part of the government's larger project of economic development and allowing us to set recent research on regional exhibition in, for example, the Yucatán and Chihuahua in a broader industrial framework.[16]

Though cinema exhibition had been a thriving business—especially in Mexico City—since the turn of the century, the Mexican government had never before systematically gathered information about cinemas. Thus Department of Labor employees had to appeal to film distributors for help in compiling a list of all the motion picture venues in the country. Piecing together those lists from the distribution arms of U.S. studios, independent Mexican distributors, and the management of the largest cinema chain, the Circuito Olimpia, generates a total of 521 reported venues across Mexico.[17] A trivial number compared to the number of theaters in the United States or some European countries at the time, but still remarkable when one considers that only fifty-five of those theaters were in the country's principal urban center, Mexico City.[18]

It is unclear why the Department of Labor chose to include cinema in the studied industries. Perhaps it was because of the very visible labor organization of cinema workers in the capital. Or perhaps it was because of a more general association between motion pictures and modernity. Regardless of the reason, the department felt that cinema exhibition was going to be an important part of Mexico's economic future. Given this, what sort of information could cinema owners and managers offer to support the revolutionary government's project of addressing "arduous socioeconomic problems" and setting in motion "frank social and industrial benefits"?[19] The survey asked cinema owners how much capital they had on hand; the number, gender, marital status, and nationality of their employees; their staff members' weekly salary or hourly wage; whether or not their workers were literate; what hours they worked; and whether or not they belonged to a union—all questions central to understanding changing labor conditions in Mexico's industrializing sectors. However, as responses to the survey indicate, they may have been less relevant to the business of cinema exhibition.

Indeed, many cinema owners seemed flummoxed by the Labor Department's request and had to be prodded into replying.[20] One exhibitor, who claimed that he had never received the survey, succinctly defended his contribution to national economic life: "The Cine Serralde, which I rent and for which I pay very high contributions [taxes], shows the best releases in Mexico. The prices are very low and the public leaves satisfied."[21] In part, this reluctance to respond seems to have stemmed from the disconnect between the Labor Department's framing of exhibition as an industry and most cinema owners' experience of exhibition as a small business that depended on foreign manufacturers for the product it sold.

The census data suggest that although film exhibition offered patrons a quintessentially modern experience, made use of modern technologies such as projectors and electricity, and participated in the dissemination of modern social norms, it nevertheless differed markedly from other modern industries—in terms of both scale and organization. Most provincial cinemas, for example, operated with approximately 1,000 pesos ($500) on hand, and in many cases much less. Unlike their counterparts in the cigarette or tex-

FIGURE 2.4 The exterior of the Cine Allende in Guadalajara, Jalisco (foreground left), 1920. In the rear is visible the city's Hospicio Cabañas, which was a hospital, workhouse, poorhouse, and orphanage founded in the late eighteenth century. From the collection of Manuel Palomina Aroja.

tile industries, cinema workers rarely worked an eight-hour day. Instead, their work schedules were often irregular, and their earnings limited by the cinema's hours of operation. Indeed, some cinemas barely generated enough income to justify their existence.

Even as cinema exhibition in the United States was becoming increasingly standardized, the returned survey responses and lists of cinemas demonstrate the persistent heterogeneity of the Mexican exhibition industry. Venues ranged from theaters that shared physical space with other businesses to traveling open-air cinemas, opera houses that occasionally showed motion pictures, and theaters attached to workers' mutual aid societies. Regardless of their size or structure, venues for film exhibition emerged as part of a complex of modern activities. For example, in the small Zapotec town of Teotitlán del Camino, Oaxaca, fifteen miles southeast of the state capital, the motion picture exhibitor Ignacio Negulcio operated a *molina de maiz* (an electric mill that ground corn for tortillas, the staple dish of most of Mexico), a newly central institution in most small Mexican towns, which every Sunday doubled as a venue offering "cinematic exhibitions."[22] It is unclear what relationship that assuredly small, informal venue had to the Teatro Velasquez, a larger theater that also operated in town—perhaps the theater charged more and thus attracted a different crowd or perhaps it showed films only periodically—but the *molino*-theater (a combination also found in the town of Ojulpan, Puebla) demonstrates cinema exhibition's intimate relationship to other sometimes very localized manifestations of modernity.

Cinemas were often just one of a handful of business interests held by their owners, and similarly cinema-related employment often constituted just one part of workers' economic survival strategies. In smaller towns, many theaters operated just one or two days a week, with their employees holding other jobs in order to make ends meet. For example, the three cinemas owned by José Jury in Morelia, Michoacan (population 68,467 in 1921), employed twenty-five people (twenty-one men and four women). The three projectionists earned 3 pesos for each six-hour shift, their assistants 1 peso. The ticket sellers (the four women) and doormen each earned between 1 peso and 1.25 pesos a day. The musicians who provided the accompaniment for each showing earned the most: a generous 2 pesos an hour, or 12 pesos for a six-hour shift. Lest the Labor Department wonder how people could survive on such meager wages when the cinema was open just two days a week, Jury explained that the members of his staff were "artisans and government office employees, having this as an extra job."[23] Likewise, at the Cine Olimpia in Nogales, Veracruz, the proprietor Mauro Jiménez and his staff of two all held jobs in the textile factory that employed most of the town (which had been the site of one of the bloodiest labor uprisings that preceded the revolution).[24] Following a well-established pattern, other cinemas were family-run businesses. The Cine Opera in Zamora, Michoacan, for example, consisted of a "very old ruined jacalón [shack]" that was attended to personally by Miguel Anaya and his wife.[25] The Teatro Marquez in Papantla, Veracruz, and the unnamed cinema in Ajalpan, Puebla, were also, their owners reported, operated by family members who drew no salary.[26]

Ana López argues that the diffusion of early cinema into the interior of Latin American countries followed the "level of development of railroads and other modern infrastructures."[27] The 1923 census offers evidence that this pattern continued to shape the development of the exhibition industry in Mexico throughout the silent period. As documented by the census, cinema's spread followed the growth of manufacturing, extractive industries, and export agriculture. Put another way, the spread of cinema exhibition throughout Mexico coincided with regional and local integration into the capitalist economy and the spread of wage labor. States with primarily agricultural economies and rural populations had fewer cinemas. For example, the entire state of Aguascalientes—once a prosperous silver-mining region—had only three theaters, all located in the capital. In contrast, the industrialized state of Nuevo León in the north, with its steel, beer, and cement factories, had twenty-six cinemas that together could accommodate at least

13,500 patrons, or 4 percent of the state's population, at any one time. The small but wealthy state of Yucatán, meanwhile, had approximately sixty cinemas that together could hold around 35,000 people—or almost 10 percent of the state's residents.[28] Moreover, exhibition in the Yucatán roughly followed the rail lines that accompanied the spread of henequen (agave fiber used to make twine) plantations in the late nineteenth century. Likewise, film exhibition in Coahuila (another state with numerous cinemas) appears to have spread along with the development of carbon mining and the accompanying proliferation of railroad stations.[29]

Theaters flourished alongside wage labor and one of its side effects, debt peonage, which remained common in Mexico into the twentieth century—when it sometimes took on the guise of wage labor tied to company towns. On the Hacienda Tixencal Quintero in the Yucatán, a proprietor named Ramon Rivera operated a "cinematographic apparatus" specifically for the "recreation of the workers."[30] (The existence of other "cines" associated with haciendas suggests that this was an amenity easily provided by *patrones* eager to create a more pliant workforce.)[31] In an explicit statement about the way that cinema fit into corporate paternalism, a manager of the Phelps Dodge Mining Corporation, which operated a copper mine in Pilares, Sonora, claimed that the movie theater built in the nearby company town of Nacozari would make workers "willing to stay with the Company," thus "reducing labor turnover and inevitably increasing efficiency."[32] This strategy reflected an expansion of tactics employed by factory owners in Mexico City like the cigarette company El Buen Tono, which as early as 1904 had offered motion picture exhibitions to their primarily female workforce.[33]

Even when not run by the company or hacienda owner, exhibition practices were shaped by local labor conditions. For example, S. Maranón's small theater in Río Blanco, Veracruz (another historically important textile factory town), operated only on Saturday, Sunday, and Monday because "all the people of this place are workers and Saturday is payday."[34] Other cinemas, especially in small towns, reported offering functions only on Sundays, indicating that their primary audiences were workers who had little leisure time during the six-day work week.[35] Thus, even before Mexico's surge in industrialization in the 1940s, flows of international capital and the spread of wage labor created audiences of workers with increasing, if uneven, access to commodified leisure.

Although these audiences of laborers consumed mainly American films, the staging of that consumption, even in remote locations, was cast as part of the country's economic development and modernization. Local economic conditions shaped exhibition practices, limiting days of operation and profits, but the mere existence of a cinema could signal a community's status as civilized and hence modern. For example, when the Teatro E. Durand in Matehuala, a small town in central Mexico, was threatened with closure in the late 1910s, the editors of a local literary, political, and cultural review, *Matehuala*, took the city government to task for "damaging the culture of the city."[36] Likewise, in response to the survey, Rafael Cabrera reported that his theater (one of two in Ajalpan, Puebla, a small town of 3,000 people) often barely made enough to cover the cost of film rentals. Cabrera attributed his business's lack of success to the fact that the majority of the town's residents were "Indians who don't attend this class of diversion," implying that cinema was the reserve of the supposedly civilized mestizo population.[37] Even when a small town had no cinema, talk of motion pictures and theaters by residents returning from trips to larger towns or cities accompanied discussions of other technologies and social practices.[38]

The Mexican popular press participated in the framing of cinema as the realm of the cultured and civilized by disseminating images of provincial cinemas alongside photographs of local schools, public buildings, hospitals, and factories—all of which promoted the country's modernization. Photographs of the Teatros Lírico, Alcázar, Zaragoza, and Juárez in Nuevo León were featured prominently in the June 13, 1920, issue of the popular weekly *Revista de Revistas* as examples of "entirely modern" cinemas.[39] The up-to-date publication *México en Rotograbado* likewise gave provincial cinemas nationalist and national import, especially when it praised the owners of the Cine Alcázar in Chihuahua, Chihauhua, for their "patriotic labor": providing Northern Mexican audiences with "the constant benefits" of quality U.S. films shown in a comfortable, modern setting.[40] Though not typically proclaimed in the national press, motion picture theaters everywhere, from small towns to the capital, were also used for workers' meetings, fund-raisers, and political rallies, thus becoming a site for the production of modern political identities.[41] As economic engines, beacons of civilization, and parts of a network of institutions that lifted small towns closer to the metropolis while providing spaces for political engagement, cinemas performed symbolic labor similar to that of other modern buildings upheld proudly in the Mexican popular press and celebrated by the revolutionary government.[42]

CINEMA IN THE CIUDAD DE PALACIOS (CITY OF PALACES)

Nowhere were the nationalist dimensions of the symbolic labor of cinemas more clearly enunciated than in the capital. The upheaval of the revolution had led to an increase in the number of potential audience members for motion pictures in Mexico City. In addition to the soldiers who passed through the city, hundreds of thousands of people had come to the capital from the countryside and provincial cities to escape the chaos of war and its aftermath. Mexico City's population almost doubled between 1900 and 1921, from 541,000 to 906,000.[43] As the city's population swelled, its cinemas flourished, along with other forms of commercialized leisure such as cabarets and *salones de baile* (dance halls), which brought popular music and dancing out of the bordello and into relatively respectable public spaces. What is more, the click of the camera, the tapping of the typewriter, the mechanized voice of the radio, and the whirl of the projector became part of the everyday sounds heard by Mexico City's residents, rich and poor alike.[44]

Residents of the capital could see films in a variety of venues—as part of variety shows in legitimate theaters, in repurposed colonial buildings, and in tents, for example—but increasingly film exhibition was dominated by new, purpose-built cinemas. The information gathered during the 1923 census confirms the continued growth of motion picture exhibition in the capital. Thirty-eight active theaters in Mexico City and seventeen in the surrounding suburbs could seat a combined total of approximately 80,000 patrons. These theaters ranged in size from the four-thousand-seat Olimpia to theaters in the suburbs with five or six hundred seats. Most cinemas in Mexico City had an average of 2,000 pesos ($970) in capital on hand, though this figure does not include the value of real estate or equipment. In contrast to the provinces, motion picture exhibition in the capital was more likely to be a big business (many more theaters reported being incorporated entities) that approximated the structure of the American film industry's exhibition branch, with chains of theaters owned and operated by large corporations.[45]

Examining the workforce and operations of two different types of theaters in the capital helps illustrate the ways in which exhibition in the capital differed from and resembled that in the provinces. The Cine Olimpia, which became the flagship venue of the thirteen-theater Circuito Olimpia, had a staff of twenty-nine: three foreign nationals who probably held management posts, seventeen Mexican men, and nine Mexican women. The Olimpia's uniformly literate employees—doormen, scenery builders and operators, projectionists, organ players, ticket sellers, usherettes, and general staff members—all worked seven- to eight-hour days, usually from 4:00 to 11:00 PM, and received one day off per week. Their earnings ranged from 12.25 pesos per week for the five general helpers (49 pesos per month) to 100 pesos per week (or 400 pesos per month, most likely a managerial salary).[46] In general, primarily because many cinema employees were single, these salaries constituted a livable wage. The Circuito Olimpia employed over 150 people and operated with more than 1,000,000 pesos in capital. Most of the

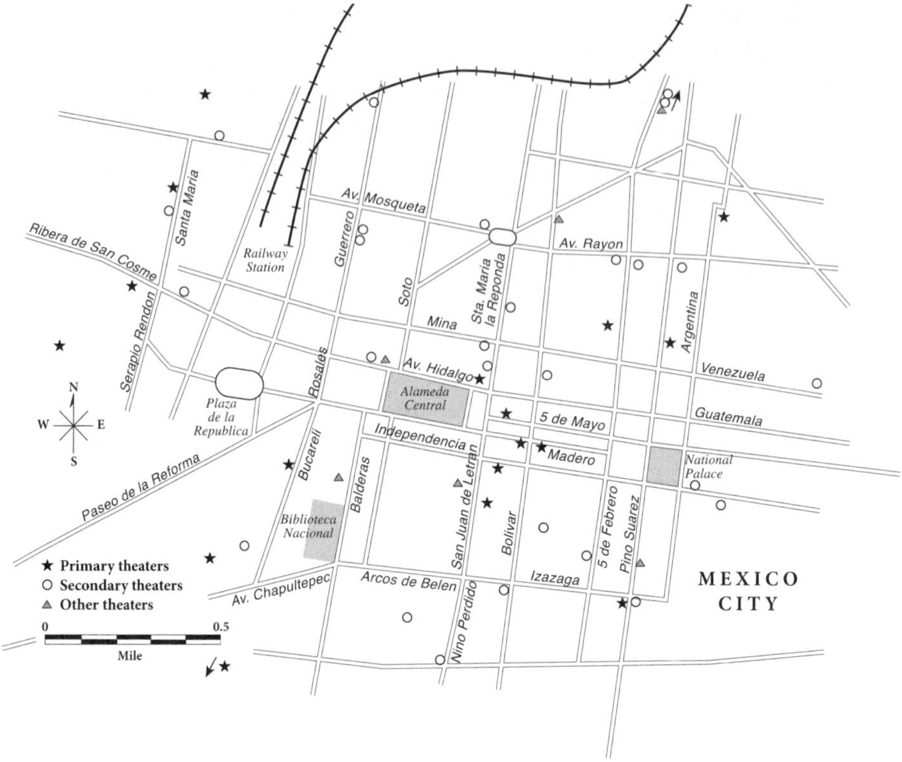
Ribera de San Cosme
Santa Maria
Railway Station
Av. Mosqueta
Guerrero
Soto
Sta. Maria la Reponda
Av. Rayon
Mina
Argentina
Serapio Rendon
Rosales
Av. Hidalgo
Alameda Central
Venezuela
N
W
E
S
Plaza de la Republica
5 de Mayo
Guatemala
Independencia
Madero
National Palace
Paseo de la Reforma
Bucareli
Balderas
San Juan de Letran
Biblioteca Nacional
Bolivar
5 de Febrero
Pino Suarez
Izazaga
★ Primary theaters
○ Secondary theaters
▲ Other theaters
Av. Chapultepec
Arcos de Belen
Nino Perdido
MEXICO CITY
0
0.5
Mile

MAP 1 Distribution of first-run (primary), second-run (secondary), and third- or fourth-run (other) theaters in Mexico City, circa 1923.

Circuito's skilled and semiskilled workers were members of the Sindicato de Empleados Cinematografistas (Union of Cinema Employees)—the union affiliated with the increasingly powerful Confederación Regional de Obreros Mexicanos (Regional Confederation of Mexican Workers)—though in responding to one of the survey questions, the management feigned ignorance about the exact number.[47]

In contrast, the Cine Iris, a theater with just 800 seats in the suburb of Tacuba, had a mere nine employees. Four of them formed a jazz quartet (piano, violin, banjo, and drums) that provided musical accompaniment and entertainment between films. Guadalupe Escalante, who sold tickets in the box office, was the lone female employee. Though the theater was much smaller than the Olimpia, its employees' reported salaries were competitive. The theater's *papelero* (poster hanger) and *ayudante* (general helper) earned 75 and 60 pesos per month, respectively. Only one employee at the Iris was married; almost half of the staff, like many workers in Mexico City, were from elsewhere—in this case Morelia, Michoacan, and San Luis del Río, Durango.

Though the returned survey does not indicate the theater's hours and days of operation, other suburban theaters reported that they were open only one or two days a week, typically on Saturdays and Sundays. The theater's manager, Rafael Bermúdez Zartrain, helped organize one of the major cinema-related unions in 1921, making it likely that his employees were also union members.[48] Working at a cinema in the capital more closely resembled the conditions of labor in other industries. Theater workers were—like workers in factories—young, mobile, and increasingly politicized. And, as in the provinces, exhibition in the capital followed the rhythms of wage labor. Cinemas in the city center were open all evening for workers whose shifts had just ended, while suburban theaters opened on the weekends, when workers were more likely to be home and seeking entertainment options nearby.

Just as in the provinces, Mexico City's purpose-built cinemas functioned as monuments to Mexico's progress. The postrevolutionary government, as had the Porfirian regime that preceded it, perceived the public space of the city as a canvas for painting its version of Mexican modernity.[49] Public art projects, most famously the modernist realist murals painted by revolutionary artists such as Diego Rivera and Jose Clemente Orozco, graced government buildings. New schools, hospitals, and community centers were constructed. Elaborate celebrations of the revolution's triumph, such as the 1921 centennial (the hundredth anniversary of Mexico's independence from Spain) that positioned the revolution as merely the most recent episode in a long political struggle, were complemented by more quotidian—but no less symbolic—practices, such as renaming streets after revolutionary heroes.[50] At the same time, government officials, reformers, and the urban population in general struggled with the question of how to define acceptable behavior in the city's new public spaces, especially as different classes came into increasing contact with each other in a less rigidly stratified society.[51] The cinema participated in both of these processes: as concrete evidence of postrevolutionary modernity and as a site where the state attempted to mold a modern citizenry.

To many, moviegoing seemed to be a singularly egalitarian form of entertainment. Cultural commentators observed that the motion picture's ability to immerse audiences in other worlds, coupled with its relatively low cost, had made it one of the most popular leisure activities of rich and poor alike. In the words of one cinema owner, moviegoing had become "an indispensable necessity" for "the different social classes" that went to the cinema with regularity.[52] Another observer, this one a journalist, called the cinema an "entertainment of salvation, distraction, useful, pleasurable, economical—within reach of everyone's pocketbook—and whose varied program is within

FIGURE 2.5 The interior of an unidentified cinema, with an audience representing a cross section of Mexican society, 1915. Note the projection booth in the back. © (87101), CONACULTA.INAH.SINAFO.FN.MÉXICO.

the reach of every taste and intellect."[53] According to this view, the ability of the cinema to entertain and educate through its various genres gave it an appeal that crossed class boundaries. Indeed, many of the movie theaters in the capital's downtown (among them the Cines America, Los Flores, and Garibaldi) were reported to have attracted audiences from "all the social classes" or from "the lowest classes to the middle classes."[54]

Though nominally serving the public at large, even theaters that catered to a range of social classes managed to separate patrons through ticket pricing. Orchestra seats and box seats cost more than the simple chairs or wooden benches, or *palcos*, of the balcony. A sketch published in the *Revista de Revistas* in 1926 describes the social geography of the movie theater: in the galleries, "humble silhouettes [the poor] copy the attitudes of Novarro and Pola Negri." In the theater's dance hall, "frivolous couples intertwine in the turns of modern dance." And outside the theater, *el fordcito* (the little Ford car), a marker of middle-class prosperity, waits while a young couple bids farewell under the watchful eye of a chaperone.[55] As this impression of a night at the cinema suggests, patrons from different social classes occupied the same imaginative and physical space, but they did not necessarily interact across class lines.

FIGURE 2.6
The Cine César
in Mexico City,
a simple brick
structure with a
banner promising
the delights of a
Jackie Coogan
film, circa 1927–
28. © (2789),
CONACULTA
.INAH.SINAFO
.FN.MÉXICO.

The location of cinemas also, to some extent, reiterated the class separations that marked the city. A close look at municipal records indicates
that the most of Mexico City's theaters were in poorer neighborhoods and
were frequented by workers and a group referred to as "gente pobre" (poor
people).[56] Cinemas in working-class neighborhoods offered their patrons
few amenities, and many of them were cavernous open spaces with slightly
graded floors. For example, the Cine Titán, which served the barrios Obrero
and Hidalgo—neighborhoods that housed the garages of the city's electric
trolleys and were populated by skilled and semi-skilled artisans—is described by the architectural historians Francisco Salazar Alfaro and Alejandro Ochoa Vega as a large, sparse, brick structure with two arched entryways,
a gabled roof, and a pair of false towers.[57] A simple sign painted on the brick
façade and a large electric sign that read "cine" announced the building's
function. Similarly, the Cine Mexico, in the center of the city just south of

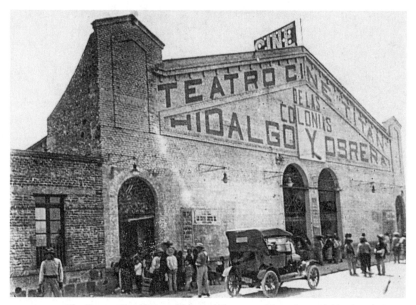

FIGURE 2.7 The Teatro Cine Titán, which served two working-class neighborhoods in Mexico City, circa 1920s. Collection of the author.

the Parque Alameda, was constructed out of wooden boards on the site of a former blacksmith's shop, between stables and a mechanic's shop. There, patrons' cinematic experience was enhanced by the smell of horse dung and smoke.[58] Though less luxurious than other theaters, these cinemas still bespoke modernity in neighborhoods with dense populations and scarce public services.

More elegantly appointed, purpose-built cinemas in the city center or in the commercial districts of wealthier neighborhoods presented more complicated façades and relatively luxurious interiors. Most employed a modified classical style. The Cine Odeon, which was built in the downtown area in 1924, is a good example. It featured a columned entryway, topped by a balcony covered by a grand arch and windows. A third level offered a row of decorative windows, each with its own small arch. An electric sign much more elaborate than that of the Cine Titan graced the right side of the façade. Inside, the theater had a gallery that accommodated 1,500 and orchestra seats for 1,000.[59] Cinemas like the Odeon might seem restrained and ordinary when compared to the elaborate picture palaces being built in the United States, but its vaguely art deco motifs, paned windows, imposing height (relative to buildings from the colonial era), row of exterior electric lights, and multiple photographic displays lining the entryway to the box office all signaled modernity in the Mexican context.

FIGURE 2.8 The Cine Odeon, one of Mexico City's finest purpose-built theaters, circa 1935. © (86862), CONACULTA.INAH.SINAFO.FN.MÉXICO.

The sonic environment of many of Mexico City's upscale theaters was similarly coded as modern. Though vendors called out to patrons sotto voce as they walked through the aisles selling *tortas* (sandwiches), and local performers brought popular Mexican music, puns, and topical themes onto the stage, the big draw in most theaters was a jazz band. At the Cine Royal, the Dorman Royal band accompanied the featured films and provided entertainment during intermissions. The Odeon had the Jazz Band León, while the Parisiana had the Antigua California Jazz Band.[60] The Capitolio had the Capitol Orchestra, which offered a "selection of the latest fox-trots imported from New York."[61] And the Cine Progreso Mundial was home to no less than three jazz orchestras. Though some theaters, like the Cine Bucareli, integrated regional Mexican music into their programs with a marimba group or other traditional musicians, jazz music—which was brought to Mexico via live theater, recorded music, and, perhaps most important, American films like the 1923 hit *Jazzmania* (a Tiffany Film production that took the capital by storm in January 1924)—was perceived to be a key element of the cinemagoing experience in Mexico City. Via jazz music, audience members could participate in a cosmopolitan leisure culture and accrue the cachet that accompanied the consumption of imported cultural products.

The Mexico City press praised these cinemas as symbols of the country's economic and social progress. When it opened, the Odeon, with its

FIGURE 2.9
The Cine Olimpia's
jazz band, circa
1920. © (197689),
CONACULTA
.INAH.SINAFO
.FN.MÉXICO.

American-style seats, was heralded as "meeting all the necessary conditions modern cinemas demand."[62] Alfonso de Icaza, a municipal cinema inspector, was quick to deem the theater "proof of our [Mexico's] progress," particularly in comparison to older cinemas like the Cine Santa Maria, which he called "a cavern."[63] The Cine Bucareli, inaugurated in 1924, was praised for its "decent and attractive" atmosphere.[64] The Cine Majestic, with its ladies' and smoking lounges, state-of-the-art ventilation system, ice cream counter, and adjoining dance hall, was deemed "a true cinema."[65] The Cine Goya, called the "most beautiful cinema in Latin America," featured seating for 6,000, a jazz band, and an orchestra that played "Mexican favorites."[66] And on and on.

Although some of these descriptions were surely promotional hype, cinemas—like new residential subdivisions and public buildings—had become distinctly modern elements in Mexico City's cityscape. They countered images of Mexico as a poverty-stricken country full of adobe structures or mired in its colonial past and gave audience members, many of whom had no running water or electricity at home—the opportunity not only to see modernity on screen but also to experience it by inhabiting, even if only temporarily, one of its representative spaces. The political labor that cinema performed—and in a culture obsessed with progress, it was indeed political labor—found visual expression in the architectural rendering of the Cine San Hipólito, published in the journal *Arquitectura*.[67] The impressive, American-designed building with its multiple colonnades was depicted with a sculpture of the eagle and serpent atop its pediment, flying the flag as proudly as any government building.

REVOLUTIONARY NATIONALISM AT THE MOVIE THEATER

Mexican cinemas "flew the flag" in myriad ways. At the turn of the century, the nation had appeared onscreen in the person of President Porfirio Díaz.[68] During the revolution, competing visions of the nation flashed before eager audiences' eyes in the form of footage of battles, generals, and military parades.[69] But where could the nation be found now that the *yanquis* had once again invaded Mexico City? As Mexican audiences became avid consumers of serials, dramas, comedies, and action films produced in the United States, the nation filled the space around the screen, and advertising, programming, and exhibition practices wove those films into the state's nation-building project.

The way that film was used during patriotic celebrations helps illustrate this point. Perhaps no other single event showcased the cultural aspects of the revolutionary state's nation-building agenda than the centenario of 1921. The ostentatious celebration included official events such as healthcare forums, flag ceremonies, and a commercial parade—all used by the government to "present its image of the revolutionary state and society."[70] An elaborate celebration in the Bosque de Chapultepec, "Noche Mexicana," celebrated *mexicanidad*, and an "Exhibition of Popular Arts" promoted indigenous culture "as meritorious, inspirational, and uniquely Mexican."[71] Thus, in compact form the centenario articulated the liberal social and economic agenda of the revolutionary government, in which progress was tied to the promotion of what was authentically Mexican—even as that notion of progress was, as the historian Michael Gonzales argues, highly contested.[72] The events of the centenario were designed to showcase Mexican modernity in its most spectacular form, but many workers and the poor were unable to attend those events, either because no spaces were reserved for them or because admission prices were prohibitively expensive.[73]

As Gonzales notes in his comprehensive description of the centennial, motion pictures were featured prominently in the celebrations. Some of the screenings were of locally produced footage of the celebration's numerous events. The centenario and its participants were the subject of a film produced by Ediciones Camus, which was the production unit run by the distributor and exhibitor Germán Camus. But advertisements for that film, which depicted events such as the parade of allegorical cars, a horsemanship contest, and the inauguration of the Parque Mexico in the tony Condesa district, seem somewhat lost amid announcements of the popular screenings that had been arranged by the centenario's executive committee. These screenings featured the typical slate of American films offered at reduced prices, with gallery seat tickets available for a mere five centavos. The program for Friday, September 16, which took place at various theaters owned by the Granat family, included Mae McAvoy in *Valle prohibido* (*Forbidden Valley*; J. Stuart Blackton Feature Pictures, 1920), a tale of family feuds set in the Appalachians; Blanche Sweet in *Redes del delito* (*The Girl in the Web*; Jesse D. Hampton / Robert Brunton Productions, 1920), a convoluted drama about debt, crime, and false accusations; Herbert Rawlinson in *Cuerpo y alma* (*Man and His Woman*; J. Stuart Blackton Feature Pictures, 1920), which treated drug addiction and love triangles; and Jane and Katherine Lee in the World War I home-front romance *Sonrisas* (*Smiles*; Fox Film Corporation, 1920).[74] Nothing in these features spoke to Mexican history, culture, or identity, yet they were offered as a gesture of political largesse to the public at large, as well as to residents of the city's prisons, hospitals, and poorhouses.

Even the celebration of María Bibiana Uribe, the winner of the *India Bonita* (beautiful Indian woman) contest—sponsored by the magazine *El Universal Ilustrado* and the Mexican government as part of the centennial celebration—found its way back to the cinema. Though many of Mexico's elite considered indigenous beauty a contradiction in terms, the contest's celebration of it participated in the government's project of bringing Mexico's indigenous population "into the national fold."[75] Government officials feted her at elegant, formal functions. Shopkeepers named their stores after her. Composers wrote musical pieces, including a fox-trot, in her honor.[76] For their part, the Cines San Juan de Letrán, Venecia, Trianon Palace, and Lux celebrated her with a series of special screenings sponsored by Paramount Films. The (probably exhausted) Bibiana appeared at each screening of a "select program" that included *Se llamaba Maria* (*A Girl Named Mary*; Famous Players–Lasky, 1919), starring Marguerite Clark; *¿Porque cambia de esposa?* (*Why Change Your Wife?*; Famous Players–Lasky, 1920), with Gloria Swanson and Tomas Megan; and *Culpa de amor* (*Guilty of Love*; Famous

FIGURE 2.10 Paramount Pictures joins forces with the Cines San Juan de Letrán, Venecia, Trianon Palace, and Lux to present *La India Bonita*, Bibiana Uribe, September 12, 1921. From the collections of the Hemeroteca Nacional de México.

Players–Lasky / Artcraft, 1920), starring Dorothy Dalton.[77] Bibiana—who was supposed to epitomize rural, native innocence—seems the antithesis of the long-lost heiress, spurned wife, and wronged lover who were the (white) heroines of these films, yet there she was. In fact, the owners of the city's major cinemas, theaters, and tents had contributed 4,407 pesos of the cash prize that Bibiana received.

Funciones populares (low-priced screenings) like those that celebrated the centenario became part of the capital's yearly rhythm, as cinema owners, who were exempt from municipal taxes on holidays, made a habit of offering reduced ticket prices on both secular and religious holidays and for special events. In gestures deemed "patriotic" and "disinterested," the owners gave away tickets to schoolchildren and public employees and sponsored special events that tied moviegoing to national celebrations.⁷⁸

In September 1923, for example, the Cine Majestic and the newspaper *Excélsior* hosted a special event in honor of the young women from the two neighborhoods that the theater served, Santa María and San Rafael, who had been nominated to run for queen of the upcoming *fiestas patrias* (the celebration of Mexico's independence). Each patron who cast a vote for either of the young women was eligible for a free ticket that included "the debut of a magnificent film, a tea dance, a variety show, a military band, and a raffle."⁷⁹ The event mobilized Mexican nationalism as a framework for texts and performative elements drawn from both Mexican and American popular culture. That evening patrons saw newsreel footage of the boxing match between the Argentine Luis Firpo and the American Jess Willard, along with three "jewels" from Universal: *Peso de menos, El despreciado* (*The Fox*), and *El delincuente*. Patrons laughed at the comic antics of the Trio Berreteaga, learned the latest dance steps from "Profesor Rubio," enjoyed the sounds of the Lone Star jazz orchestra, and took in U.S. vaudeville performer Baby Russell's "pantomime-dance."⁸⁰ Extra-filmic events like this, whether state-sponsored or part of an exhibitor's marketing effort, consecrated the public's mania for moviegoing under the auspices of national ritual by tying popular entertainment to a national holiday.

Officially sanctioned programs aimed at educating and uplifting Mexico City's poor and working classes likewise offered attendees a mixed program of American popular culture and Mexican nationalism. For example, in 1923 the Departamento de Bellas Artes (Department of Fine Arts) (a subagency of the Secretariat of Public Education) sponsored a series of weekly *festivales culturales* billed as "fun and instructive" events for working-class families.⁸¹ The event, which was held the week of October 14 at the Cine Díaz de León, located in an impoverished neighborhood north of the city center, featured a concert performed by students from the National School of Music, a one-act play, a lecture on Mexican art, and the American-produced short *Leon y leona* (*Lion and Lioness*; Edison, 1904), a film that was surely pulled out of storage. That same week, another cultural event combined a program of unspecified American films with a talk by one of Mexico's premier poets (and an avid filmgoer), Salvador Novo.⁸² A year later, in 1924, a fund-raiser for a state-sponsored school for delinquent children, which was held at the prestigious Cine Olimpia, offered the children and their benefactors Mexican performers, a Mexican newsreel, *Excursión al Popocatépetl* (Excélsior, 1921), and a slate of American films: an animated short, *Un día agitado* (*One Exciting Day*; Century Film, 1923); a comedy short, *Los traviesos* (*Our Gang*, 1920);

and two romantic dramas, *Nido de amor* (*The Love Nest*; Commercial Traders Cinema Corp., 1922) and *Tres almas de pena* (*The Mastermind*, also known as *Sinners Three*; Associated First National, 1920).[83] In 1920 Colonel Norberto Olvera added twice-weekly cinema exhibitions to the educational program offered to soldiers stationed in Mexico City.[84] Even conservative Catholic women's groups, highly critical of moviegoing in general and American motion pictures in particular, used movie nights as rewards for the laborers and their children who attended catechism and as a treat for seminarians.[85] Similar programs, which fused the consumption of American films with instruction in Mexican national and cultural identity, could be found throughout the decade at community-based educational centers, schools, prisons, and mental hospitals.[86]

Public health initiatives provide a particularly salient example of the relationship between government-sponsored educational programs and the cinema. As the historian Claudia Agostini shows, in the decade after the revolution, government functionaries and public health officials believed (as had their counterparts during the porfiriato) that "only through the popularization of health education would it be possible to transform the urban and rural populations into a modern, healthy, and industrious citizenry."[87]

Cinema's cross-class appeal made movie theaters an ideal site for educating people about public health issues, ranging from preventing the spread of contagious diseases to the importance of vaccinations. In 1922 a subsecretary of Mexico City's Department of Cleanliness and Transportation suggested that cinema lobbies were ideal places to hang signs that gave patrons graphic instructions on cleanliness and proper hygiene, though we have no evidence that such signs were in fact displayed in theaters. In 1923 a staff member in the same department ordered cinemas to project slides "in favor of hygiene" at the beginning of every program, placing them squarely before the eyes of the viewing public who might have overlooked such information if it had had to compete with lobby cards, posters, and photographs.[88] Such efforts probably yielded some changes in behavior. From 1925 to 1928, the federal Departamento de Salubridad Pública (Department of Public Health) had been given an expanded mandate under Plutarco Elías Calles, then Mexico's president. The department continued the practice of circulating slides displaying information about public health topics—ranging from rodent control to tuberculosis—throughout Mexico City's movie theaters. Later, "moving lighted machines" projected key phrases from the department's current campaigns onto the walls of cinema foyers.[89]

Though these types of strategies made public health campaigns part of a theater's environment, the department's office of education and propaganda

FIGURE 2.11 A crowd, mostly male, at the Cine Excélsior in La Barca, Jalisco, gathered for a screening sponsored by the Departamento de Salubridad Pública in 1928. Reproduced from Departamento de Salubridad Pública, *Memoria de los trabajos realizados por el Departamento de Salubridad Pública, 1925–1928* (Mexico: Ediciones del Departamento de Salubridad Pública, 1928).

also created its own films (none of which are extant). Those films—*Aprended a cuidar a vuestros hijos* (Learn to care for your children), *Listos para vencer* (Ready to conquer), and *Falso pudor* (False modesty)—dealt, reportedly graphically, with the dangers of venereal disease.[90] These films were shown in local schools and eventually in cinemas in Mexico City and the provinces. The department also screened *The End of the Road* (1919), which had been produced by the U.S. War Department's Commission on Training Camp Activities, to the indigent women and prostitutes being treated for venereal disease at the Hospital Morelos, as well as in other institutions.[91]

In 1927, with the cooperation of cinema owners across the republic, the department launched the National Antivenereal Disease Campaign, which took its venereal disease education program on the road.[92] Exhibiting the department's films to primarily male but sometimes (as evidenced by photographs of various audiences published in the department's 1928 annual report) mixed audiences was a key component of the campaign that began in the state of Mexico but eventually traveled to key cities in seventeen states. In places where health educators were unable to give elaborate talks, they simply screened the department's educational films in the middle of the regularly scheduled program. Despite their potentially controversial subject matter and being "outside of the [regular] program," the department reported that these films were surprisingly well received by provincial audiences.[93]

Building on this successful campaign, the department introduced a series of matinees in the capital's cinemas. Supported by the city's "cultivated elements," the matinees screened films that "show[ed] the dangers of syphilitic and venereal diseases and [gave] instructions about how to prevent or cure them."[94] Admission was completely free, which probably increased attendance. There is no way of knowing how many attendees—reportedly in the thousands at the first event—came out of prurient interest, the promise of a free movie regardless of its subject, or a genuine desire to be educated. Regardless, the crowds at these screenings confirmed the Mexican government's belief that cinema—along with radio and print media—could be enlisted in its efforts to shape modern subjects. Indeed, in the early 1920s in particular, the government turned its attention to regulating the physical and social space of the cinema itself in its attempts to discipline and modernize Mexico's heterogeneous and often uncooperative public.

REFORMING THE CINEMA

As the above examples suggest, the Mexican government conceived of the cinema as an educational space. And although the cinema could facilitate the diffusion of messages about Mexican culture, patriotism, and citizenship, it also became the object of reform itself. To that end, the state—in the form of Mexico City's municipal government—sought to shape people's everyday experience of the social space of the cinema and encourage audience members to become attentive spectators, a subject position that would provide evidence of their civilization and modernity. Officials instituted regulations to protect citizens' health and safety and sought to teach patrons, who were often unruly, how to conduct themselves in a movie theater. In doing so, officials encouraged the adoption of middle-class norms of behavior: disciplining one's body and focusing on the screen rather than on any other activity going on in the theater. Put another way, municipal authorities promoted modes of viewing that more closely approximated the contemplative mode demanded by the fine arts. In many ways, their concerns echoed those of reformers in the nickelodeon era for whom the space of the theater and patrons' behavior in that space was of paramount concern.[95] In an attempt to realize the ideals of the revolution, municipal authorities promoted a particular social formation, the family, as the ideal spectator—an ideal that existed in tension with the patrons' rights as consumers, which were likewise promoted as an extension of the revolutionary rhetoric around workers' rights and citizenship.

Cinema exhibition had been regulated since its introduction in Mexico City. Concerned about the risk of fire, municipal authorities modified regulations governing theaters to include guidelines for the construction of fire-resistant projection booths and the proper handling of nitrate film. Outbreaks of typhoid and other diseases that spread quickly through the closely packed audiences of cinemas led the Consejo Superior de Salubridad (Public Health Committee), which at that time oversaw public health in Mexico City, to recommend that cinemas sweep their premises with a solution of mercury bichloride and install ventilation tubes that ran from the roof to the auditorium and supposedly increased air circulation. It remained difficult, however, to make sure that regulations were enforced; the Consejo Superior de Gobierno del Distrito, the city's governing body, had named only two cinema inspectors.[96]

In 1921, as part of a wide range of reforms that included the establishment of federal agencies such as the Secretariat of Public Education, the city council revised the regulations that governed public diversions (cinemas, theaters, puppet shows, tent shows, mechanical rides, and so on). Tasks that had formerly been the province of the police or Salud Pública were made part of the work of the Departamento de Diversiones Públicas (Department of Public Diversions). A cadre of at least twenty municipal inspectors was formed and charged with visiting cinemas every day—a demanding task, to say the least.[97] These inspectors ensured that cinema owners followed health and safety regulations, sold tickets and ran their programs according to established guidelines, and monitored audience behavior. The inspectors approached their tasks with firmly middle-class notions about culture and the social functions of cinema. Though not a censorship body—a separate office, of which only the barest traces exist in the historical record, undertook that work—the inspectors who worked for the Department of Public Diversions regularly commented on the films being shown in the various theaters they visited. Their comments reveal their class-based belief that films should serve as a vehicle of education and uplift.

Unsurprisingly, the inspectors dismissed the majority of films being screened in the capital, as did many of their peers. Debates in the press deemed the portrayals of love triangles and divorce that animated many American films, crime dramas, and action films responsible for a wide range of social ills. The specific behaviors that critics thought films might encourage included criminal activity and sexual experimentation. Though they rarely named specific films, as early as 1916 critics blamed motion pictures, especially serials, for outbreaks of crime.[98] Middle-class women became particularly vocal about the effects of indiscriminate moviegoing on children, which, they argued, could lead to "maladaptation."[99] *El Hogar*, a women's magazine, called "art" films (dramas) "true schools of punishable acts" that taught children "how to mock virtue, laugh at innocence and acquire goods by fraudulent means."[100] One Mexican theater critic, interviewed in *Cine-Mundial*, opined that the cinema was "identified with the morbid inclinations of [Mexico's] youth" and was a "curse and enemy" of parents and educators.[101] These suspicions about the deleterious effects of viewing such films were confirmed when newspapers publicized confessions from gangs of thieves claiming they had imitated cinematic crimes.[102]

Although they rarely elaborated on the potential effects of viewing such fare, Mexico City's cinema inspectors concurred with such pronouncements. One inspector decried the "lurid tale of jealousy" found in the Metro Pictures' western *La revancha de Duncan* (*Revenge*, 1918).[103] Another declared that the free Sunday matinee programs at the Cine Fenix, located in a poor neighborhood near the city's railroad station, featured fare — "robberies, murders, assaults, and all manner of crimes" — patently unsuitable for children.[104] But inspectors saved their strongest disapproval for American-produced serials, which were wildly popular in Mexico. For example, Armando Domínguez praised the Cine Granat but pointed out one small defect: the theater presented "only American films, mostly serials that are not instructive in any way and much less moralizing."[105] His colleague, Heliodoro Vargas, noted with no small degree of exasperation that the working-class audience at the Cine Tlaxpana reveled "to the point of delirium" in the "truculent scenes" of the "'kilometric'" Antonio Moreno serial film *Los crimenes misteriosos* (possibly *The Veiled Mystery*, 1920).[106] Vargas was particularly vocal about the social effects of serial watching on the members of the criminal class, whom he and others claimed were partisans of the form: "robbers and killers of the metropolis do their apprenticeship through them [serials] . . . turning the cinema into a magnificent school of criminal training."[107] Their concerns were aligned with a general anxiety about criminality and attempts to identify and classify criminals — usually seen as members of the poor and working classes, and often seen as migrants — that the historian Pablo Piccato describes in his account of the social construction of criminality in early twentieth-century Mexico.[108]

Though we have no reports from the audience about why these types of films appealed to them, inspectors noted that such fare — typically combining action, adventure, mystery, and crime — caused "joy" among patrons sitting in the gallery (that is, the poor and working classes).[109] As scholarship on the genre's reception in the United States has demonstrated, serials offered their audiences the thrill of seeing protagonists engaged in daring escapades, escaping brushes with death, and confronting the social and physical environment produced by modernization.[110] Mexican moviegoers—especially those who had come from rural areas and for whom traffic, mechanically produced noise, and other aspects of modern urban life were both jarring and fascinating, as well as the working poor, for whom crime was an everyday reality over which they had little control—might well have recognized elements of their experience in these narratives.[111] Serials, especially the fate of their female protagonists, echoed the sensational news presented in visual form by printmaker José Guadalupe Posada in the late nineteenth century and first decade of the twentieth century. Posada's images, like the melodramatic stage productions that Ben Singer identifies as a primary subtext of serial melodramas, presented struggles between good and evil in the form of sensational crimes involving family members, lovers of all classes, and the aristocratic elite and often thematized the dangers of technologies that the elite in the era of Porfirio Díaz considered emblems of progress, such as the electric trolley car.[112] Women, it is important to note, appeared as protagonists in these stories in numbers far greater than would be expected, given their actual rates of criminal activity as documented in the public record.[113] Posada's images had addressed the same working-class public that frequented Mexico City's second- and third-run theaters' exhibitions of serials. Serials and their sensational story lines were believed to encourage behaviors and attitudes that Mexico's elite wanted to reform and educate out of existence.

If films could school audiences in the ways of crime, they could also instruct audiences in the values the state wanted to nurture—thrift, sobriety, and middle-class morality.[114] Hence, inspectors recommended films based on literary classics or those animated by conservative gender politics and clearly delineated social relationships. They celebrated European art films that more closely resembled their idea of high culture, despite the fact that these films were increasingly rare in Mexico. For example, José Paullado applauded the exhibition of *Hamlet* (either a 1917 German production or a 1921 Italian version), with its "European contours" and "artistic inspirations that are so far from imitating American films."[115] Other European films singled out for praise included *Les misérables* (1921), starring Asta Nielsen, which engendered "feelings of commiseration and piety," and the realist drama *Hedda Gabler* (1920), featuring the diva Italia Almirante-Manzini.[116] Likewise, inspectors uniformly applauded the almost exclusively European offerings of the Cine Cinco de Mayo, which was associated with Germany's Ufa studio.

American films could be suitable fare, when their narratives conformed to the inspectors' middle-class sensibilities. U.S.-produced films applauded for their morally instructive qualities included *Viviette* (1918), *Jubilo* (1919), and *Su deuda* (*His Debt*, 1919). Though these points were not elaborated on in the inspectors' reports, these films share a certain sentimental view of romantic love, a valorization of marriage, and an emphasis on firm social hierarchies. In *Viviette*, a coquette and her impulsive male counterpart become serious and sober married people. In *Jubilo*, a good-hearted hobo becomes a hardworking family man. And, though it lacks a happy ending, *Su deuda*, a vehicle for international star Sessue Hayakawa, reinforces social stratification when the protagonist, Goro, sacrifices his desire for revenge to his love for a white woman, though that love can never be reciprocated because of taboos about miscegenation. Other films—those deemed "worthy of being shown in cultured countries"—were praised for their "teachings" and "moral lessons."[117] In short, inspectors approved of films that displayed a certain moral orientation, religious sensibility, and sentiment rather than sensationalism and physicality.

Inspectors' hopes that commercial cinema would become an instrument of social uplift proved somewhat quixotic. The men could and did recommend that the municipal censors review a particular film, but they could not force exhibitors to show a film, particularly when exhibitors were motivated by audience preferences and constrained by distributors' offerings. Though the inspectors continued to grumble about the quality of the cinematic fare being offered in Mexico City, they focused their attention on elements of the cinematic experience that they could influence.

Concerns about the material conditions of the city's movie theaters emerged as particularly important. A comprehensive inspection of the city's cinemas undertaken in early 1922 revealed that many were dirty and lacked appropriate sanitation facilities—or any sanitation at all. Chipped paint, broken seating, and roofs in need of repair plagued other cinemas. One inspector wrote that at the Cine Victoria, "part of the ceiling was coming down," "the walls were dirty and peeling," and the auditorium looked "more like a storeroom than a movie theater."[118] In some theaters, bathrooms were shared by both sexes, which many inspectors considered an invitation to immoral behavior, and lighting throughout the theater was insufficient either to prevent misbehavior or to safely guide patrons to exits in the event of an emergency. These ills were intensified by the persistence of "traditional" commercial practices in the form of street vendors who set up shop in front of, or inside, theaters, interrupting foot traffic and creating a "bad appearance."[119] Sometimes inspectors merely complained about what they considered bad taste; one theater's green and white auditorium was deemed "common."[120] Big and small, from the perspective of the chief of the Department of Public Diversions, these problems—practices that cheapened the cinematic experience—threatened "the culture of our population."[121]

Thus, the department began a campaign to induce cinema owners to upgrade their facilities to meet modern standards of hygiene—an enterprise that meshed with other efforts to modernize the city's markets, drainage system, and streets.[122] This pressure stemmed from the belief that environment and behavior were intimately linked. Well-behaved patrons, the inspectors reasoned, frequented well-appointed, clean theaters; conversely, well-appointed, clean theaters encouraged appropriate behavior. Thus, Ernesto Dow praised the Cine Casino: "This center of entertainment, which the *best society* of that part of the city attends, is in perfect condition in terms of hygiene."[123] Another inspector reported that the Cine San Rafael, "one of the cleanest cinemas in the capital," appealed to "the best society of the neighborhood."[124] Lower-class clientele, in turn, could be found in dirty theaters. The manager of the Circuito Olimpia, which ran the Cine Obrero, a theater in desperate need of repair, asserted as much, complaining that the "social class that attends it [the theater]" made it impossible to keep the theater clean.[125] The Cine Tlaxpana, on the Ribera de San Cosme at the poorer edge of the San Rafael neighborhood, was the favorite haunt of "gangsters" and thus, according to its manager, likewise doomed to perpetual griminess.[126] Proof of the effects of environment on behavior could be found in the Cine Cervantes, where after major "material improvements"—it was possible to detect "a certain grade of morality among the public that goes there that contrasts with the disorder that one saw before."[127]

Improving the physical plant of cinemas was just one prong in the municipal government's efforts to guide audiences toward middle-class norms of behavior. The relative democracy and anonymity of the movie theater invited a range of disruptive behaviors, most often ascribed to audience members in the gallery and hence to the lower classes. Inspectors lamented "the riffraff" who kept their hats on and smoked in their seats; rural migrants who carried their guns in with them; boys in the gallery who threw "rocks, pieces of wood, fruit peels, and other objects" on unsuspecting patrons below; patrons who refused to sit even when seats were available; and ne'er-do-wells who passed the hours "causing scandals."[128] Though these were not all criminal behaviors, municipal inspectors were careful to take note when individuals had been arrested and frequently complained about the lack of a police presence.[129]

Beyond specific acts, inspectors identified a mode of spectatorship—active and engaged with fellow moviegoers, like that of nickelodeon audiences in New York a decade earlier—that disrupted the cinematic experience. The moviegoers at the downscale Cine La Paz "demonstrated" the "morals reigning among its attendees" in the form of "constantly stamping their feet and the series of whistles they use to ask for music." Similarly, the public in the Buen Tono "hit the seats, whistled, and kicked" the back of the seats in front of them, in expressions of delight and disgust.[130] Roberto Castellot declared that the "crowd, principally that of the Gallery" at the Cines Garibaldi, Santa Maria la Redonda, and the Monte Carlo "exteriorized their satisfaction with laughter and applause."[131] Working-class and poor audience members, often recent migrants to the city, simply did not understand how to behave in theaters, inspectors asserted. Rather, such patrons seemed intent on engaging in distracting forms of spectatorship, in which the activities of the audience competed with the narrative on the screen.

Inspectors reserved special concern for the numerous couples who committed "immoral acts" or participated in what one inspector referred to euphemistically as "unedifying scenes" in the dim light of the theater.[132] Movie theaters across Mexico City were full of couples "who do not go to the cinema to watch the films."[133] In fact, one popular cabaret song of the time elaborated on the pleasures of the cinema's dark interior.[134] Cinema inspectors regularly reported discovering patrons engaged in "immoral acts," which seem to have ranged from masturbation to perhaps even intercourse, especially in theaters frequented by the poor and working classes.[135] Indeed, an unnamed journalist claimed that "the most immoral films aren't those that unfold on the screen; they are those that play out in the auditorium."[136]

Some of these reports may have referred to the activities of prostitutes and their clients—the Salon Rojo, despite its appeal among Mexico City's smart set, for example, was infamous for being "host to some of the most repugnant sexual activity in the metropolis," and the Majestic was plagued by prostitutes.[137] But the problem was cross-class; even "discreet" young ladies and married women, inspectors noted, took advantage of the darkness, often in cinemas in lower-class neighborhoods, to engage in "amitié amouresse [amorous friendship]."[138] The public space of the cinema opened up new spaces for sexual activity outside the confines of marriage for individuals across the class spectrum. Thus, preoccupations with adequate lighting and the purported need for sex-segregated bathrooms stemmed in large part from a desire to police the desires of theater patrons, many of whom saw the theater as an ideal place to find privacy in public. Inspectors framed these concerns as part of a desire to protect women and girls from the unwelcome advances of men. Just as often, as will be discussed in chapter 4, these efforts to safeguard female virtue sought to protect women from themselves.[139]

"Dancings"—or public dances, which became a popular adjunct to moviegoing in the early 1920s—likewise roused the ire of theater inspectors. Held in adjacent rooms or even on the main stage of the auditorium, "dancings" and dance marathons gave young people the opportunity to practice the steps they had "learned from the movies": the Charleston, the foxtrot, and the shimmy.[140] Described in the press as "hysterical convulsions," "anti-aesthetic cramps," and "lecherous tremors," these dances embodied fears about sexuality run amok.[141] Inspectors considered these dances "completely immoral" and inappropriate, especially for Mexico's upper classes or "society."[142] As the historian Katherine Bliss recounts, one inspector claimed that "ten shimmies had been performed in a space [the Salon Rojo] that had at one time been the meeting place of high society and where parents took children to ride the electric stairwell the owners had installed."[143] Other inspectors wrote of "inappropriate manifestations" on the part of onlookers influenced by the sexually suggestive dancing that took place.[144]

Discussions of dancing and the jazz music that accompanied it consistently invoked hierarchies of race and civilization. Intellectuals espoused theories of *mestizaje* and celebrated Mexico's romanticized indigenous past, but conservative observers likened watching couples performing the shimmy to "finding oneself in the middle of Africa, where a group of whites have lost all sense of civilization."[145] (Mexico's Secretary of Education, José Vasconcelos, would refer to the "songs popularized by Hollywood movies" as "syncopated, mechanized vulgarity" and to popular dances as "negroid.")[146] Though "dancings" provided the most blatant example, all of this behavior—behavior that reveled in the nonfilmic visual, aural, and tactile pleasures of the cinema—was seen as "discrediting" the cinemas in which they took place.[147] Between the activities of couples in the semidarkness and on the dance floor, cinemas had become part of the pernicious social environment that could lead to precocious sexuality and even prostitution, hence requiring the monitoring of Mexico's reformers.[148]

Audiences used their bodies to express not only their pleasure with particular films or exhibition practices, but also their displeasure. Scratched films, too many advertising slides, extended intermissions, illegible intertitles, and films patrons simply did not like could provoke outbursts of protest.[149] To cite one example particularly rich in detail, audience members at the Cine Olimpia, no less, protested the theater's insertion of El anillo de boda (a film I have been unable to identify by its original title) in between La moderna magdalena (An Innocent Magdalene; Fine Arts, 1916) and El conde vagabundo (The Vagabond Prince; NYMD / Kay-Bee, 1916) by "hitting the ground with their canes, with their feet, yelling No! No! No!" and breaking the backs of chairs.[150] The Cine Venecia's decision to present *El pequeno Lord Fauntleroy* (*Little Lord Fauntleroy*; Mary Pickford Productions / UA, 1920) as a premiere when it was in fact two years old provoked a similar scene.[151] Even cultured audiences could engage in such behavior: devotees of European art film at the Cine Cinco de Mayo caused a "not-recommended spectacle" when protesting the fact that the "magisterial" German film *Ana Bolena* (*Anne Boleyn*; UFA, 1920) was being accompanied by the "profane sounds of some vulgar fox-trot."[152] Mexico City audiences, in all their diversity, clearly had specific ideas about what they expected from an evening at the cinema.

Unruly spectators offended inspectors' sense of proper decorum and behavior. Such audiences also disrupted the pleasurable viewing experience of the social unit that inspectors (with their reformist goals and sensibilities) saw as comprising the most desirable cinema patrons and the most desirable citizens. During the transitional era, as noted above, in the United States women were sought after as audience members who could confer respectability on the cinema. The respectable woman's counterpart in Mexico was the family.[153] In the municipal records, the host of rowdy spectators in the galleries—single men and women, boys, poor people, and working-class people—are frequently contrasted with families. When performers engaged in off-color banter with audience members, it was "educated people and their family members" who suffered.[154] Men who insisted on smoking in the Cine Las Flores caused "great annoyance" to the families there.[155] Many families, inspectors reported, no longer went to the Cine Royal because of its "lack of order."[156] Most important, unruly patrons paid no mind to the "countless families" who went to the theater "to *see* the movies."[157]

Families, whose members implicitly knew how to control their bodies, were by definition productive members of Mexican society—having been cast in opposition to those who caused scandals, broke laws, and made spectacles of themselves in public. (As Piccato notes, the socially unattached— that is, those without family ties—were often suspected of criminal behavior.)[158] Cinema inspectors upheld families as the right sort of spectators, whose tastes and behavior were divested of the vice, immorality, and ignorance that the revolution hoped to wipe away.[159] Indeed, cinemagoing, even if it meant watching American films with "no merit," represented a modern alternative to the traditional (some would say antiquated and degenerate) pleasures of the *pulqueria* (a bar that sells *pulque*, an alcoholic drink made of fermented agave), the cantina, the brothel, and the distressing social environment of popular living spaces such as the *vecindad* (a multi-family dwelling found in poor neighborhoods), all of which threatened "proper family life" and Mexico's economic potential.[160] Thus, the discourse around cinema audiences can be seen as part of the state's effort to enforce public order and morality, efforts that included other reformist projects like public health education or the regulation of prostitution and commercial activities.[161]

At the same time that inspectors sought to redeem an audience primarily composed of workers and poor people by cultivating a family-friendly atmosphere of middle-class respectability, they also imagined the cinema as a site for the realization of constitutional guarantees of individual liberties and the rights of workers broadly construed. The Department of Public Diversions framed its work in part as an effort to protect the interests of the cinema's heterogeneous public as consumers. In their reports, inspectors were sympathetic to audiences unhappy about excessively long intermissions, films that were literally falling apart or so scratched they were unviewable, excessive advertising, last-minute changes of program, and overly crowded theaters. Deficiencies, like the Salon Rojo's not having the requisite number of public phones or the Cine Mina's poorly placed projection booth, were deemed failures to provide the "good service the public. . . . has a right to expect," another means by which the interests of capital "defraud[ed] the public."[162] Changing films at the last minute meant that audiences who paid to see a Chaplin film might find themselves watching something else altogether—and perhaps not for the first time.[163] When one disgruntled patron, Manuel Carino, wrote to the mayor about the fact that the film *La ciencia y el amor* (most likely *Doctor Neighbor*; Universal Film, 1916) had been advertised as a new release, he argued: "I am of the opinion that even though it involves second- or third-run theaters, a production that no longer has a market, not even in the five-cent theaters in the United States, should not be exhibited as a premiere. . . . [I]t constitutes a deception of the public."[164]

Certainly the zeal with which cinema inspectors handed out fines for a range of infractions—including delayed starting times, changes of program, and oversold theaters—stemmed from Mexico City's desperate need for funds.[165] The submission of daily programs for approval by the department—called *sellando*, which literally means stamping or sealing—was the municipal government's way of tracking the taxes that needed to be collected on box office receipts. But once a program was approved, the public had the right, as consumers, to see the films that had been advertised. Inspectors held exhibitors and distributors—who took prints from one theater to another by bicycle despite the city's poor transportation infrastructure, seeking to squeeze every last cent out of old and damaged prints—responsible for the public's displeasure. The "public," defined in this context as workers who had paid their hard-earned money to be entertained, deserved to be treated with respect by exhibitors, "if only for the fact that they've paid."[166]

CONCLUSION

Cinemas—the physical spaces where motion pictures were seen, as well as the set of institutions and practices that surrounded the consumption of films in Mexico—were explicitly linked to modernity. The cinema gave Mexican audiences representations of modern life, as well as providing them with opportunities to witness new technologies in action and to engage in new forms of sociability. These modern spaces, including the *cine-molino* described above, not only coexisted with Mexican postrevolutionary nationalism—with its emphasis on the history, forms of artistic expression, and popular culture that made Mexico distinct—but also became part of that nationalism as a setting for rituals of nation building and reformist education.

The Mexican government considered cinema exhibition an important national industry, regardless of the country of origin of the films presented. The newly created Department of Labor's study of the exhibition industry drew it into new, scientific techniques of constructing Mexico's labor force as citizen workers and entrepreneurs as partners in the creation of a new Mexico. Indeed, it was precisely the growth of wage labor that allowed the cinema to flourish, as the establishment of movie theaters followed the path of industry and capital. Photographic representations and textual descriptions of the most up-to-date theaters in the country were offered, via the technologies of photographic representation and increasingly affordable printing processes, as material proof of Mexico's progress.

In their day-to-day operations, cinemas became sites for both official and unofficial nation-building activities. Special programs at popular prices were offered to audiences to celebrate national holidays; nonfilmic programming such as contests and live performances likewise often tied film exhibition to Mexican popular culture; and cinemas sometimes incorporated indigenous motifs into their interiors and exteriors, establishing subtle connections to a broader discourse on the popular arts.

Cinemas became a key vehicle in the revolutionary government's reformist, and implicitly nationalist, activities. The Departamento de Salubridad Pública strategically mobilized the public's enthusiasm for moviegoing to educate audiences about the dangers of venereal disease and other public health issues that were essential to the project of modernization. At the same time, the cinema itself became the target of reform. Until 1928, when Mexico City's municipal regulatory scheme underwent a wholesale reorganization, cinema inspectors prodded exhibitors to modernize their theaters as well as their exhibition practices.[167] Good lighting, comfortable seats, appropriate sanitation facilities, truth in advertising, and professional presentation of daily programs, they believed, would turn the country's cinemas into spaces that fostered middle-class morality and decorum and encourage appropriate modes of spectatorship.

In contrast to the focus in the 1910s in the United States on making the cinema a safe space for a desirable female audience, Mexico City's cinema inspectors invoked the family as the ideal cinema audience. A heterogeneous public of single men and women, children, migrants, and longtime urbanites—who were, as inspectors' reports convey, excitable, loud, unruly, and often engaged in social activities that had little to do with what was on the screen and who reveled in the thrilling emotions and action-packed narratives of American serials—was asked to conform not only to norms of narrative absorption but also to a normative social structure that celebrated the family as the essential building block of Mexican society. In theaters that more closely resembled the idealized Olimpia, families could focus on uplifting and instructive narratives that promoted romantic visions of heterosexual pairing, extolled the virtues of marriage, and reaffirmed social stratification as an unremarkable part of life. This ideal audience, like the cinema (exhibition) industry and cinemas themselves, became a symbol of a desired modernity. Increasingly, however, audience members demanded their rights not as part of a family unit but as consumers—another identity that modern Mexicans were encouraged to take on—with their own ideas about how to engage with film culture.[168]

IN LOLA'S HOUSE
Fan Discourse in the Making of Mexican Film Culture

Mucho se ha discutido, mucho se discute aún acerca del *happy ending* de las películas norteamericanas [There has been much discussion and there will be much discussion yet about the happy endings of North American films].
—CELULOIDE [JAIME TORRES BODET], *REVISTA DE REVISTAS*, 1925

In 1928, *Cinelandia*, a Spanish-language fan magazine published in Hollywood, featured a two-page advertisement for Metro-Goldwyn-Mayer featuring "Lola, la chica de Hollywood." Lola is a raven-haired, light-skinned beauty who bears more than a passing resemblance to Dolores del Rio, who was frequently and affectionately called Lola by the Spanish-language press. Wearing a short skirt and fashionable heels in the advertisement, Lola smiles coquettishly at the camera, which has caught her in the act of hanging a photograph of William Haines next to portraits of John Gilbert and Ramón Novarro. A copy of *Cinelandia* lies open on a chair. The caption beneath the image reads: "In Lola's house you'll find the walls adorned with photos of these MGM stars . . . they are her favorites." Her preference for these stars, the rest of the ad copy asserts, derives directly from MGM's ability to showcase them in the "best" films. This advertisement suggests the way in which the press bridged the public space of the movie theater and the personal, private space of the home. In this example, it links Lola's fictional home, the public space of cinema in which films and stars circulated, and the home of the reader, who might have read her copy of *Cinelandia* while seated in a room like Lola's.

The intersection of these three spaces produces Lola as the ideal Latin American consumer of American films, a consumer defined by particular characteristics. First, it positions Lola as a member of

FIGURE 3.1 Metro-Goldwyn-Mayer's advertisement featuring "Lola, la chica de Hollywood," *Cinelandia*, September 1928, 36–37. Billie Rose Theatre Division, the New York Public Library for the Performing Arts, Astor, Lenox and Tilden Foundations.

the middle class; the desk, chair, books, upholstered sofa, wallpaper, and rug speak of education and material comfort. Second, Lola exemplifies the female consumer as modern subject. She looks to the offerings of the market-place—in this case, moving images—to satisfy her personal tastes and desires. And third, Lola is a fan. She not only goes to the cinema, but she also immerses herself in the extra-filmic discourse to be found in fan magazines and the popular press, creating her own collection of images and objects that signify her investment in film culture.[1]

Perhaps intentionally, the advertisement leaves Lola's national identity ambiguous, which allows MGM to employ her in appeals to multiple Latin American constituencies through periodicals like *Cinelandia*, which circulated throughout the Spanish-speaking world. At the same time, the advertisement mobilizes an oblique association with Mexico's most famous star, Dolores del Rio. The tension in this image between the universal and the particular is a tension that marked the film culture in Mexico—where, as elsewhere in Latin America, the U.S. industry's rhetoric of cinema as a universal space was continually negotiated by spectators who brought their own local experiences of modernity, a growing attachment to cultural nationalism, and ideas about the United States to their encounters with American cinema. As Miriam Hansen observes, "the dynamics of the star cult as an industrial-commercial public sphere also entailed a certain amount of real unpredictability and instability and thus harbored potentially alternative formations."[2] It is this instability and its productive possibilities that can be seen at work in the Mexican popular press's discourse on films and fandom. Indeed, in encouraging spectators to develop a critical sensibility about films and a personal taste in stars and genres, the popular press opened up a discursive space in which the values and ideologies promoted by U.S. cinema could be evaluated and contested. Although film companies like MGM were instrumental to the circulation of fan discourse, the popular press also became a space in which Mexican critics, journalists, and fans created a national film culture.

Gaylyn Studlar challenged film scholars to consider fan magazine discourse a "privileged" rather than an impoverished site for understanding the way cinema addressed its female audience in the 1920s.[3] Since, scholars have turned to the popular press in order to track how Hollywood addresses female, racially or ethnically marked, and/or queer audiences and, in turn, to map even if only partially those audiences' response to films and film culture. This chapter mines the Spanish-language press—fan magazines, newspapers, and popular magazines—for evidence of how Mexican audiences on both sides of the border made sense of American cinema, and as a window onto the variety of discourses about cinema that circulated in postrevolutionary Mexico. The Mexican popular press, both in Mexico and in Mexican communities in the United States, served simultaneously as the most efficient disseminator of U.S. film culture and as a public sphere in which the politics of that film culture were debated and critiqued. That is, on the one hand, the popular press made the cosmopolitan world of Hollywood accessible to Mexican audiences by promoting films, stars, and the idea of Hollywood; instructing audiences in the practices of fan culture; and showcasing those elements of consumer culture—such as fashion and beauty products—that accompanied the cinema. On the other hand, journalists and critics modeled the appropriate critical stance toward film for their readers, providing examples of the use of personal judgment and the exercise of agency. In encouraging audiences to develop their critical sensibilities and personal tastes—hallmarks of modern subjectivity—the press opened up a discursive space in which the values and ideologies promoted by American cinema, including its racism, could be critically evaluated and contested.

In and through the Mexican popular press, American cinema and its avatar—Hollywood—were recast as Cinelandia (film land), as it was referred to in the Mexican press. That is, Mexican audiences created a new cultural space, translating, adapting, and appropriating American cinema in ways that bridged its supposed universal appeal and the local and national contexts of its reception in Mexico. The construction of Cinelandia resonates with uses of the term *gringolandia* to describe the social space—"fabricated out dynamic and multiple social relations and interactions"—of Mexican experiences of and in the United States.[4] Rather than having cinema—as a complex of texts and practices—imposed on them as a foreign cultural force, Mexican audiences on both sides of the border engaged with those texts, or read them, from the shared point of reference of *mexicanidad* (even as that imagined community was being constructed out of local and regional experiences), while using their identification with films and stars and their participation in consumer culture to produce their own modern subjectivities.

CINEMATIC NOTES

In March 1923 the entrance to the Cine Olimpia was described as being occupied by "trees sustained with wood ribbing, a paper and wood arbor, a decoration simulating a cabin that covers the ticket booth completely . . . an apparatus of wood and cardboard with the physical dimensions of a known actress and two vitrines [glass cases] with women's shoes to be given as prizes [on display] . . . various tripods [easels] with photos of cinema actors [and] numerous posters."[5] Other descriptions of movie theaters and photographs from the period indicate that exhibitors, especially in the capital, used as much of their entryways as possible, along with the wall space outside their theaters, to advertise upcoming attractions and hint at the pleasures (like those shoes) to be found inside.[6] Clearly, American films were not confined by the boundaries of the screen. Instead, extra-filmic material—most notably images—spilled out into public space, forming a significant part of Mexico's visual culture. Perhaps most important, images of stars, scenes from films, and advertisements circulated widely in the pages of the growing popular illustrated press, another increasingly important public space.

As the art historian Julieta Ortiz Gaitán explains, in the late nineteenth and early twentieth centuries, improved printing technology enabled Mexican publications to increase the number of photographs and graphic illustrations in each issue.[7] Publications like *El Universal, El Imparcial, El Mundo Ilustrado,* and *Revista Moderna* began to be "conceived of as an industry with the goals of informing and entertaining."[8] Primarily addressed to the educated elite, they offered a select reading public images in pictures and prose of progress that were being promoted by the regime of Porfirio Díaz. Less lavishly illustrated daily papers, which could be obtained for one centavo, offered the working classes articles and illustrations (such as the engravings produced

FIGURE 3.2 Exterior of the Cine Royal in Mexico City with posters and lobby cards, advertising *He Who Gets Slapped* (1924), circa 1925. © (89771), CONACULTA.INAH .SINAFO.FN.MÉXICO.

by José Guadalupe Posada) depicting contemporary events as well as forums for the articulation of political views opposing the Díaz regime's policies.[9]

Most of these publications perished in the chaos of the revolution. In their place emerged well-illustrated daily newspapers, many informed by partisan politics, and weekly magazines that emphasized a modernity based on technology, Mexico's liberal (though one-party) democracy, and consumer culture. Two important postrevolutionary dailies, *El Universal* and *Excélsior*, were in fact modeled on U.S. newspapers like the *New York Times*. During the 1920s these Mexican newspapers increased the overall number of advertisements—particularly from foreign companies—published in each issue.[10] Illustrated weeklies offered humorously presented domestic political and economic news alongside features that highlighted Mexico's cultural, material, and social progress; original and translated fiction; and photographs and articles about current entertainment trends and international events. Popular weekly magazines like *Revista de Revistas*, which was printed on cheap paper and cost thirty centavos an issue, along with more elaborately designed weeklies like *El Universal Ilustrado* and *Zig-Zag*, appealed primarily to Mexico's middle and upper classes (as well as to those aspiring to join those classes).

The press might well be considered an institution that served a very small slice of Mexico's population, as literacy was by no means widespread in Mexico in the 1920s—though Mexico City had a higher literacy rate than the rest of the country. The historian Armando Bartra estimates that only 5 percent of Mexico's population of fourteen million read newspapers in the late 1920s, while Anne Rubenstein asserts, with caution, that the national literacy rate had reached 33 percent by 1930.[11] Given estimates like these, Joanne Hershfield argues that the visual became a key register of modernity.[12] It is also likely that the city's circulated newspapers and magazines were shared, read aloud, or picked up by others (like the domestic help) once discarded by the original reader.[13] What is more, images in particular were most likely to have had multiple lives, since photographs and advertisements required minimal literacy.

Two examples, one drawn from the press and the other from literature, suggest the way in which images from the press circulated outside of their original contexts and became part of working-class visual culture. In the first, a journalist describes the daily life of a young, female factory worker who had been chosen to participate in *El Universal*'s "Obrera Simpatica" contest. In the journalist's description, "traditional" feminine piety coexists with a fascination for modernity—which this worker, like Lola, expresses by collecting images of film stars: "She's dark skinned; dark, profuse braids fall over her shoulders in two bunches. . . . She wakes up at dawn, when the rooster crows; arranges her room adorned with photographs of cinema artists, and makes sure that the little lamp placed on a shelf that is a manifestation of love for the Virgin Mary, never goes out."[14] The second example, a 1934 poem by the poet Salvador Novo, similarly suggests the place of popular, as opposed to official, visual culture in the lives of workers: "Él no ha visto esos muros, y en su choza / cuelga un viejo almanaque de los productos Báyer / o el retrato de Miss Arizona en traje de baño / que cortó de un rotograbado dominical." (He has never seen those walls [the murals of the Mexican modernists], and in his hut / he hangs a Bayer products calendar / or a picture of Miss Arizona in a bathing suit / that he cut from a Sunday magazine.)[15] Some might protest that the press had little to do with the lives of working-class Mexicans, but these examples suggest that photographic images and advertisements related to the cinema constituted part of a visual landscape shared across social groups.

Throughout the period there was no shortage of film-related images to be had; cinema had become a major preoccupation of the illustrated press. In 1917 *Cine-Mundial*'s Mexican correspondent declared: "The press in the [Mexican] states, like that of the capital, dedicate special sections to discussions about the art of the silent screen."[16] Ten years later, *La Semana*, an illustrated magazine, confirmed that "the specialized press has contributed in a major way to the 'spread' of the silver screen . . . everywhere we find 'fans' who heatedly discuss to what extent they agree with the opinions that appear monthly in Hollywood's luxurious film magazines."[17] Throughout the 1920s publications of all kinds—including union newsletters, popular magazines, daily newspapers both in Mexico and in Mexican communities in the United States, and fan magazines—provided Mexican audiences with a steady diet of Hollywood gossip, profiles of stars, and film reviews. Self-conscious about their engagement with cinema, these publications actively fostered the development of a vibrant film culture in Mexico.

Unsurprisingly, Mexico City had the most vibrant cinema-related press in the country. In addition to daily advertisements highlighting films currently in the city's theaters, the Sunday editions of all the major newspapers and weekly magazines published article after article about the film industry, printed photographs of stars, and sponsored cinema-related contests. Popular publications sometimes even used their cinema coverage to jockey for readers' attention. *El Universal Ilustrado* boasted that it was "*the* magazine that knows how to treat cinematographic questions."[18] *Zig-Zag* informed readers of its first issue that "seeing the huge interest that cinema questions have been awakening in Mexico, the section destined for this topic [in the magazine] is relatively large."[19] Similarly, in 1926 *La Semana* claimed to have the "most complete" cinema section of all the magazines published in the capital.[20] (Readers certainly noticed when cinema was absent. An anxious reader of *El Continental*, which published short stories in translation, asked its editor: "Why don't you have a special section [about film]?" The editor replied tartly that the periodical "is not a magazine but a 'Magazine' of stories."[21]) The capital was also home to several short-lived specialty publications—*Magazine Fílmico, Semana Cinematográfica*, and possibly others—dedicated exclusively to covering cinema and the local film exhibition scene.[22] Provincial newspapers likewise printed program information, film reviews, Hollywood gossip, and photos, though these were more likely to be translations of articles from U.S. fan magazines or studio publicity rather than original material.

FIGURE 3.3 *Cine-Mundial*'s office in Mexico City. An unnamed employee tends to business, circa late 1920s. © (173324), CONACULTA.INAH.SINAFO.FN.MÉXICO.

Mexican fans could also avail themselves of two types of international publications. First, they could participate in a larger community of Spanish-speaking film lovers via two fan magazines published in the United States, *Cine-Mundial* and *Cinelandia*. As described in chapter 1, *Cine-Mundial* began publication in 1916 as a trade publication aimed at film exhibitors, distributors, and other entertainment and commercial entrepreneurs in the Spanish-speaking world. It published information industry news, information about the business of cinema, and reports on exhibition and distribution in various countries. By 1920 the magazine—in a self-styled shift from "trade appeal to national appeal"—changed its focus and began to publish articles and features that would appeal to film fans, adding fashion spreads, advice columns, and profiles of stars to its reports on the state of the film exhibition industry in different Latin American countries.[23] During the 1920s, the magazine's self-reported newsstand sales rose by 90 percent.[24] In contrast, *Cinelandia* was born as a fan magazine. Published by the Spanish-American Publishing Company, an Anglo-owned enterprise that published material in Spanish, its masthead proudly drew readers' attention to the fact that the magazine was "published in Hollywood."[25]

In addition to these publications, which were marketed to a broad, pan-Latin readership, Mexican audiences could also find a wealth of information about motion pictures and their stars in Spanish-language newspapers published in the United States. The relatively conservative *La Prensa* (San Antonio, Texas) and *La Opinión* (Los Angeles, California), published by brothers Gabriel and Ignacio Lozano, displayed a decidedly nationalist bent and actively encouraged members of Mexican immigrant communities to think of themselves as part of the imagined community of the Mexican nation despite living in the United States.[26] Both newspapers made use of their proximity to Hollywood to offer their readers extensive coverage of film culture. *La Prensa*'s Sunday cinema section was titled "El iman de Hollywood" (Hollywood's magnetism) and was under the direction of Gabriel Navarro — a playwright, author, musician, and the cinema editor of *La Opinion*.[27]

Their readership, however, was not limited to the Mexican migrant community. Just as the large Mexico City dailies and weeklies received correspondence from readers in the United States, so U.S.-based newspapers received letters from readers in Mexico's northern states and, somewhat less frequently, the capital. One could find a poetic tribute to Gloria Swanson by Mariano Viesca Arizipe, from San Antonio, Texas, who signed his work "mexicano" in *Revista de Revistas*, and one could also find queries from readers in Ciudad Juarez, Chihuahua, Torreón, Coahuila, Agua Prieta, Sonora, Tijuana, and even Mexico City in the cinema columns of *La Opinión* and *La Prensa*.[28] These cross-border reading practices, and (as I will discuss below) the discourse they helped circulate, facilitated the formation of a cross-border Mexican film culture.

Collectively, these publications fostered the development of a specialized discourse about cinema. Initially covering films and film exhibition in Mexico had been the province of the chronicler, who focused on explaining the physiological and social effects of the cinema; the paid publicity man, who wrote glowing commentary (called *gacetillas*, or "little cookies") about every film he saw; or theater critics, who often seemed to be at a loss as to how to categorize or evaluate the new medium. Ángel Miquel documents in detail how the boom in publications after the revolution created opportunities for promoters of cinema culture and film critics — such as Carlos Noriega Hope, Rafael Bermúdez Zartrain, and Gabriel Navarro — to practice their craft.[29]

Like literary and fine arts critics, professional film critics in Mexico saw educating readers about film aesthetics as one of their chief tasks. Unlike their predecessors, these critics focused on the specifically cinematographic qualities of films as well as their narratives. For example, in 1916, one reviewer criticized the camerawork in *Maciste bersagliere* (*Maciste the ranger*; Itala Film, 1916) — "poorly focused bits, others that appear gray and fatigue the eyes" — because, he noted, photography had "more importance in the cinema than the typesetting of a book."[30] The following year, another critic wrote of the Pearl White serial *La garra de hiero* (*Iron Claw*; Feature Film, 1916): "The photographic part is truly superb, as is the mise-en-scène, the artistic part being directed in a very happy manner."[31] In passages such as these, critics modeled for their readers how to evaluate a film's cinematography and other plastic qualities. Some magazines even took a programmatic approach to this critical education. In 1920 *El Universal Ilustrado* began publishing articles that explained how films were produced, and in 1922 it introduced a new feature, "Cinematic Notes: the most beautiful scenes of the week," asserting that the feature would "educate the critical sense" of the magazine's readers by offering them models of film criticism.[32] For these critics, film viewing fell squarely within the domain of self-improvement through education that was becoming increasingly important to what the literary critic Danny Anderson describes as Mexico's "new readers and consumers striving to rise socially on the ladder of education and expressions of refined taste."[33]

In addition to evaluating films' cinematographic qualities, reviews made clear the role that the concept of the nation played in film criticism. The Mexican author and critic Martín Luís Guzmán, who lived for many years in Spain, for example, wrote "Each country . . . has its specialty and its signification."[34] French films were known for their "slow digressive pauses," Italian films for their "arbitrary and exaggerated histrionics . . . splendid costumes, furnishings, and scenery."[35] American films were increasingly singled out for their "naturalism," by which most critics meant their mise-en-scène and acting styles, even while such films continued to be criticized for their relentless optimism.[36] But nowhere was the attachment to the nation as a taxonomic category more significant than in discussions of Mexican films, which experienced peaks in 1917 and in the early 1920s. Reviewers lauded the efforts of directors and actors as labor that contributed to the nation's cultural status vis-à-vis global film culture, even as they freely admitted that the Mexican industry was in its infant stage and its products could rarely compete with those of Europe or the United States.[37]

For the Mexican popular press, reception could be just as important an activity as production. Critics and journalists positioned participation in a national film culture, built around the consumption of films produced elsewhere, as part of a set of desirable social practices that demonstrated Mexico's modernity. This meta-goal is on display with notable clarity in *Cine-Mundial*'s monthly "Crónica de México" section, in which cinematic happenings—new releases, national production, and theater openings— shared the page with society events, sports news, and accounts of activity in the live theater. Other publications emphasized that film culture was the hallmark of civilized nations. *El Universal Ilustrado*, for example, emphasized that the "most serious and well-regarded magazines in North America and Europe" had extensive film-related sections.[38] It declared its "best film of 1923" contest a means of "taking the cinematographic pulse" of the nation, implying that within the larger body of worldwide film aficionados, a nationally identified audience existed.[39] During a lull in participation in the contest, one writer scolded the magazine's readers: "In the United States, these contests open annually . . . they [the U.S. press] do not offer a single prize to the public. Why should we be less than the *yanqui* publics?"[40]

QUIERE USTED SER ESTRELLA? (DO YOU WANT TO BE A STAR?)

In order to help the Mexican public reach the same level of sophistication as its North American and European counterparts, the popular press did more than teach readers how to view films critically; it also instructed them in the practices of fandom, encouraging personal investment in the cinema and its stars. Three activities in particular were deemed essential if filmgoers wanted to transform themselves into fans: writing letters to their favorite stars, collecting images of stars, and purchasing and using products and clothing associated both with stars' on- and off-screen lives and with a more generalized notion of material progress.[41]

Magazines and newspapers helped equip their readers to write fan letters with confidence. Write-in cinema columns published stars' addresses and sometimes even phone numbers in order to facilitate fan communication. Film columnists also offered detailed instructions about the mechanics of writing a fan letter. *La Opinión*'s cinema columnist, who went by the confidence-instilling pseudonym "L'homme qui sait" (The man who knows), reminded his readers that as a "general rule" they should accompany their letters with twenty-five cents postage, U.S. or international, when requesting an autographed photograph of their favorite star.[42] *Zig-Zag* encouraged fans to use a typewriter to compose their letters because "in the United States writing with a typewriter is most common."[43] These instructions helped ensure that Mexican fans, like their fellow film lovers overseas, could engage in the direct (if one-sided) communication that characterizes the fan-star relationship.[44]

Indeed, despite the industry's claims that "films speak all languages," cinema columnists regularly helped Mexican fans navigate what was, effectively, the monolingual world of film fandom.[45] "There is no biography of Pearl [White] in Spanish," one of *Cine-Mundial*'s columnists informed a Mexican fan, but "if you want it in English, write directly to her care of 'Fox.'"[46] Fans were not only taught how to write fan letters but were also guided past language barriers with the help of columnists who published templates of fan letters written in English, which readers could simply copy and send to their favorite English-speaking stars. *La Opinión*'s columnist told Elena Dominguez, a Mexican living in Compton, California, that Priscilla Dean possessed a very limited knowledge of Spanish. He advised Dominguez to write to Dean as follows: "I would like to have your picture. I will be very obliged. Thanks."[47] (Dolores del Rio, described as "muy Mexicana" [very Mexican], could be written to without worry in Spanish.)[48] Other columnists explained how to pronounce Anglo-American names: "The English pronunciation of the following names is William Boyd, Güílam Bóid; James Hall, Yéims Jol; Kenneth Harlan, Kénes Járlan."[49]

Photographs, whether requested from stars or clipped from magazines or newspapers, became a tangible expression of fans' personal preferences and investment in fan culture. Hence, virtually all Mexican cinema-related magazines trafficked in stars' images. The cinema columnist of *La Prensa*, "El mago de Hollywood," sent readers portraits they requested from a supply he kept on hand. *Magazine Fílmico* encouraged its readers to send in a coupon indicating which star's photograph they would like to see in the magazine. And the popular monthly *Zig-Zag* was explicit about its goal of facilitating readers' collection and preservation of stars' images. In its second issue, the magazine published a photo of the actress Elsie Ferguson with a caption that read "in *Zig-Zag* number 2 we publish the portrait of this beautiful artist on the cover; but as many of our female readers will want to conserve the photos from our gallery in appropriate albums, we reprint the portrait of Elsie here."[50]

By 1921 the readers of *Zig-Zag*'s triple investment in star images— watching films, buying magazines featuring pictures of their favorite stars, and cutting out and saving those pictures—had grown to the extent that the magazine reported its editors had "resolved to start a special color portrait section of film actors that will form beautiful albums."[51] The magazine reinforced these interlocking practices of consumption when, in the summer of 1922, it collaborated with local exhibitors and film distribution companies to give free photographs to patrons who went to the theater on Wednesday or Sunday evenings. Ten photographs could be exchanged for a one-year subscription to the magazine, which in turn would provide readers with more images and movie-related news to fuel their fandom.[52] In this way, providing the raw materials of fandom to readers cemented the link between global film culture, the Spanish-language press, local exhibition venues, and individual filmgoers.

The gender politics of Mexican fandom during this period is worth parsing. Indeed, fan magazines in Mexico—like those in other countries—

FIGURE 3.4
Elsie Ferguson on
the cover of *Zig-Zag*,
May 6, 1920. From
the collections of the
Hemeroteca Nacional
de México.

cultivated an audience conceived of as primarily female. According to *Zig-Zag*, star photos were most often requested by "female readers." *La Opinión*'s cinema columnist chided one of the rare men who wrote in seeking information about his favorite star, noting that typically "women are the ones who are more interested in knowing about these things [stars and films]."[53] Whether that was true or merely an assumption of journalists, the female audience became the target of appeals that linked the cinema with the consumer culture that was taking root in urban Mexico—where, as in other parts of the world, consumer culture was gendered female.[54]

From the point of view of municipal inspectors, families constituted the ideal spectators, but the popular press emphasized the connection between film culture and modern womanhood. In fact, male participation in Mexico's burgeoning consumer culture was typically coded as effeminate, unproductive, and even degenerate.[55] Despite liberal or socialist rhetoric that lionized class struggle and might have been expected to advocate gender equity, the postrevolutionary state promoted a very traditional set of gender roles. The ideal postrevolutionary man would be hardworking, sober, and scrupulously moral. It was his wife, as Hershfield observes, who would spend the money he earned, ideally wisely, to provision the family and modernize their domestic space.[56] In practice the press promoted the sale of a range of commodities that could serve a new, modern form of femininity: accessories, makeup, clothes, soaps, perfumes, and so on. Of course, cinema itself was a modern commodity that promoted the purchase of other commodities.[57] Advertisements assured Mexican women that they too could share in the glamour and modernity of Hollywood through their practices of consumption.

The cultivation of the connection between cinema and Mexico's emerging consumer culture was hardly limited to industry-specific publications. The popular press was an important ally, as well. For example, in full-page ads the newspaper *Excélsior* offered randomly chosen residents of Mexico City—albeit randomly chosen from the small proportion of Mexicans who owned telephones—the chance to obtain free tickets to the Cine Olimpia's screenings of *La mujer que anda sola* (*The Woman Who Walked Alone*; Famous Players-Lasky, 1922), starring Dorothy Dalton. Residents need only stop by the businesses that had sponsored the promotion—Abel's Cabaret-Restaurant, the American Photo Supply Company, the American Book and Printing Company, the department store El Nuevo Mundo, and Mexico City's Buick dealership—and mention the promotion to receive their tickets.[58] The 1921 "Reina del Cine Contest," sponsored by *El Universal Ilustrado*, became a frenzy of consumer culture, with businesses—including Artistas Unidos S.A.—giving away photographs, phonographs, a gold watch, private film screenings, and even a motion picture camera.[59] In the pages of Mexico's largest newspapers, advertisements for imported beauty products dominated the "women's" sections, anywhere daily cinema news appeared, and weekly entertainment supplements. Similar types of advertisements dotted popular magazines. Finally, the connection between viewing films and the world of consumer goods was further reinforced by the advertising slides for local businesses that exhibitors showed before and after film screenings.[60]

Cinema-specific publications, like general-interest publications, also insistently reinforced the connection between films and the "world of things."[61] As Charles Eckert observes, the studios were acutely aware of the influence of film on foreign trade, though they rarely made this the explicit goal of market expansion, and mobilized fans' desire to emulate their favorite actors and actresses.[62] International publications such as *Cine-Mundial* were open about their role in promoting consumer culture. In addition to selling films and film culture, *Cine-Mundial* promoted the consumption of products ranging from toothpaste and hand lotion to phonographs and breakfast cereal. Indeed, celebratory accounts of the publication's history focused on its success as an advertising outlet in the Spanish-speaking world for brand-name, mass-produced goods.[63]

As in the United States, advertisements for such products, regardless of where they were published, drew on the power of stars' images to appeal to potential customers. For example, Lydia Pinkham, the New England patent medicine company, appealed to Mexican female movie fans' zeal for collecting star photographs to stimulate purchases of its *compuesto vegetal* (vegetable compound), *loción sanative* (healing lotion), and *piladores del higado* (liver pills).[64] In a large advertisement, images of movie stars' photographs frame a description of the products. The copy emphasizes that the photos of actors such as Douglas Fairbanks, Mary Pickford, Wallace Reid, and Pearl White that fans would receive were not prints, but "real photos," each of which came with a minibiography on the back. The "secret to obtaining the portraits," interested readers were informed, was on the back of each product endorsed by the stars, implying that participating in consumer culture was a key to accessing the materials of fandom.[65]

Other advertisers used stars' endorsements (some likely made up) to market their products. The examples are legion: In 1922, *Revista de Revistas* published an advertisement for *Crema Liska* that featured the actress Viola Dana. Meanwhile, Gloria Swanson could be found shilling the mascara "Lash-Brow," and Anita Stewart's image was being used to sell "Camel-line" face cream. (Male stars were very occasionally included in these campaigns—ads for Stacomb hair-styling cream feature a picture of Lon Chaney both as his dapper real-life self and in character as a deranged individual, asking, "Caballero o frascado? [Gentleman or failure?] What will your 'role' in life be?")[66] Associations between stars and products could also be generated through mere proximity, as exemplified by *El Universal*'s placement of advertisements for products such as Palmolive soap, Pepsodent toothpaste, and Kodak cameras alongside its weekly "Hollywood in Images" feature.

Beauty's close cousin, fashion, became the other register in which these connections were reinforced. Hershfield documents the explosion of fashion-related content and advertising in the Mexican press during this period, which she argues constitutes part of the visual construction of *la chica moderna* (the modern girl).[67] As Hershfield notes, Paris had long been the arbiter of fashion for elite Mexican women. Increasingly, though, Mexican women (aided by the popular press) began to look to Hollywood and its

CLARA KIMBALL YOUNG

Nació en Chicago.
Altura 5 pies 6 pulgadas.
Peso 135 libras.
Cabello y ojos obscuros.
Divorciada de Charles Young.
Estrella de Equity Pictures.

EN LA OFICINA

El trabajo de oficina a menudo agrava las enfermedades peculiares de la mujer. Obtenga un alivio permanente tomando el

Compuesto Vegetal
De LYDIA E. PINKHAM

FIGURES 3.5 AND 3.6 A Lydia Pinkham promotional card, like that promoted in Mexico City's *Excelsior*, featuring the actress Clara Kimball Young on the front. Her autobiographical details in Spanish and the Pinkham trademark appear on the reverse. Courtesy the Schlesinger Library, Radcliffe Institute, Harvard University.

FIGURE 3.7 An advertisement for Hinds, featuring the actress Lupe Vélez, in *Revista de Revistas*, May 1931. From the collections of the Hemeroteca Nacional de México.

stars instead. Newspapers and magazines routinely featured photographs of female stars modeling the latest fashions. Photo spreads featured actresses such as Norma Talmadge, Mary Pickford, and later Mae Murray and Aileen Pringle in the latest fashions, while the accompanying text focused on the women's clothing, hairstyles, and homes. *Excélsior*, for example, published a photograph of Mary Miles Minter in an elaborate evening gown with the article titled "Mary Miles Minter talks about future fashions."[68] In the 1920s *Revista de Revistas* began publishing "La moda en Los Angeles" (Fashion in Los Angeles) a feature that explicitly highlighted the clothing worn or modeled by various stars. And *Cine-Mundial* published a section entitled "A través de la moda" (About fashion) that offered readers patterns for clothes similar to those worn by their favorite stars, along with a "detailed

Modas de Hollywood

Compiladas exclusivamente para CINELANDIA por los mejores estudios
Dibujos y dirección artística de Athalie Richardson

Sally Phipps, actriz de Fox, en traje de noche de tejido de plata, con capa del mismo material y profusamente adornado de fondo cuello.

FIGURE 3.8
The actress Sally
Phipps in evening
wear in the fashion
section "Modas
de Hollywood,"
Cinelandia, October
1927. Billie Rose
Theatre Division,
the New York Public
Library for the
Performing Arts,
Astor, Lenox and
Tilden Foundations.

description in Spanish of how to use them."[69] The accompanying photos showed actresses in various elegant gowns posed in rich interiors. By the late 1920s, *Filmográfico* was collaborating with the Mexican women's weekly *El Hogar* to enable women to "dress like the stars" by buying "Patrones Hollywood" (Hollywood patterns) for only seventy cents apiece. Images and texts in such fashion spreads promised that by wearing clothes that approximated those of the stars, Mexican women could "dress with elegance and distinction."[70] These promotions reinforced fans' interest in the on- and off-screen style of their favorite stars and suggested that fans could participate in the glamour of stardom through their own practices of self-fashioning.

Newspapers and magazines sometimes even offered Mexican women opportunities to occupy social spaces constructed to mimic stardom. Special issues of weekly magazines such as *El Heraldo Ilustrado* reproduced portraits of local beauties with hairstyles and clothing inspired by the screen and in poses similar to those found in film studios' publicity materials. Photo spreads and interviews presented these young women both as exemplars of modern Mexican womanhood and as celebrities. Accompanying articles relayed details of their personal lives and achievements as if they were Hollywood stars.

The visual rhetoric that governed the presentation of movie stars in the popular press reigned as well in the coverage of local beauty contests. For example, the beauty queens who were the front-runners of the 1926 "International Queen of the Universe Beauty Contest" (which was actually the promotional vehicle for "The Pageant of Pulchritude," organized by businessmen in Galveston, Texas), could savor seeing their images disseminated, like those of their favorite stars, across national borders. Not only would their photographs appear in the Mexico City newspaper *Excélsior*, but they would also be published in the "biggest *rotativos* [illustrated magazines] in the United States" and displayed in movie theaters in Mexico as well as Galveston.[71] Thus, such contests held out the promise that participants could literally, via their images, occupy the places typically held by their favorite stars.

When *La Opinión* sponsored a "Gran concursio regional de simpatia" (regional beauty contest) in 1927, the presentation of the contestants both contravened and conformed to the rhetoric of Hollywood publicity photos. Contestants, Mexican immigrants or the U.S.-born daughters of immigrants from California and young women from the Mexican state of Baja California, submitted studio portraits of themselves in sleeveless dresses, with bobbed hair and a touch of makeup. These dark-haired beauties, some with thick natural eyebrows and broad features, offered a rebuttal to the never-ending parade of fair-skinned blonde Hollywood starlets that the press typically featured. At the same time, their appearance in the newspaper followed conventions established by the film industry's publicity machine. One group portrait features a handful of the contestants in fashionable dress gathered around a piano (one of the prizes being offered). The two women to the left of the image appear slightly stiff, but the other three present themselves confidently, adopting the body language of the celebrity fashion spread. One smiles coquettishly at the camera. Next to her, another leans seductively against the piano, while a third rests her arms on a decorative pillow on the piano and offers her profile to the camera. Though the participants received no promise of celebrity beyond the migrant Mexican community that read *La Opinión*, the contest draws on the norms of the beauty and fashion culture being promoted through and showcased in the cinema to produce these women as images of modern Mexican femininity.

Of course, not every factory worker who went to the movies religiously would have the good fortune to see herself as a star, but advertising promised that all Mexican fans could share in the glamour of Hollywood through new practices of consumption. Many of these advertisements were translations of appeals targeted at film fans in the United States, appeals that Eckert describes as targeting female consumers who "were not varied as to age, marital status, ethnicity, or any other characteristic."[72] But although American mass media and its partner consumer culture attempted to integrate Mexican fans into a cosmopolitan, if not a Universal, market, it also traded in particular appeals.[73] Those appeals, which mobilized national and nationalist sentiment in the name of profit, dovetailed with efforts on the part of Mexican journalists and critics to lay claim to the modernity represented by the participation in film culture through acts of translation, adaptation, and appropriation.

MAKING *CINELANDIA*

To some extent the extra-filmic material circulated by the studios and distributors consisted of literal translations of centrally produced publicity material. (This is clear in ads that leave some of the text in English.) But even as the popular press served as a Spanish-speaking mouthpiece for both the film industry and consumer culture, it also worked to encourage Mexican audiences to invest themselves in American film culture as Mexicans. That national audience was called into being in two registers: that of capitalism, voiced by studio publicists and marketing departments and that of the public sphere of the imagined community, articulated by critics, journalists, and fans themselves.

Another MGM advertisement—a series of ads presented as letters between Lola "la chica de Hollywood," who is living in Los Angeles, and her best friend back home in Mexico—illustrates the way that appeals to local context could take the form of a corporate marketing strategy. Published in *La Opinión* over ten days in May 1928, the advertisement "letters" are presented in such way as to suggest that they are part of the paper's entertainment news. In her missives, Lola's cinema-fueled fantasies envelop and even obscure her immigrant reality. They recount both her filmgoing and her imaginative engagement with the films she sees and their stars, slipping between the two to textualize the acts of identification that mark women's experience of the cinema.[74] In the imaginative space created by her viewing practices, Lola herself becomes the object of men's visual attention, falls in love over and over again, "borrows" clothes from her favorite film stars, and imagines herself accompanying them in the glamorous pursuits portrayed on screen. In her letters, the line between reality and fantasy is constantly blurred; the activities and emotions she reports symptomatic of the overinvested fan the industry wanted to cultivate.

Lola regales readers with stock-in-trade narratives of romance, social mobility, and glamour. For example, she reports that every week she finds herself "completely entangled in love's trap" with a new man (a male star).[75] A director, she reports, tells her she "deserves to be treated like a great lady and not a vulgar employee," and she discloses that "Antoine cut and styled her hair" while Norma Shearer "permitted her to copy the dress" that she wore in *Despues de medianoche (After Midnight*; MGM, 1927).[76] Lola finds U.S. films and film culture liberating and pleasurable. In fact, motion pictures become her path from traditional culture—she was once a "well behaved *muchacha* who lived sequestered at home"—to modern femininity, signaled here by being "enveloped by a whirlwind of emotions with a heap of suitors courting me."[77]

Certainly, a narrative about the libratory effects of spectatorship was one that the studios were anxious to promote to foreign audiences. But in her epistolary incarnation, Lola highlights the ways in which the film industry collapsed specific national or ethnic identities in its quest to reach international markets. Though published in *La Opinión*, a newspaper targeted toward the Mexican migrant community, idiomatic expressions—for example, calling the United States "America"—mark Lola as not Mexican, but perhaps Spanish. Studio marketing departments probably perceived no difference between Spanish and Mexican audiences since both groups spoke Spanish, but Latin American audiences were keenly aware of the inability of studios to distinguish one Spanish-speaking country from another. As an idealized spectator, Lola retains sufficient ethnic markers to provoke identification even as she lacks historical and cultural specificity.

A similar strategy was employed by the beauty products industry, which regularly tailored its advertising to specific foreign markets.[78] Stars such as Dolores del Rio and Lupe Vélez promoted American beauty products simultaneously as Latin stars and as Mexican stars. Some advertisements referred to Dolores del Rio by the Spanish diminutive "Lola" to create a sense of intimacy with their readers. Others acknowledged that Mexican women might have different needs and preferences than other Latin American women. In one striking example from the late 1920s, the Max Factor cosmetics company offered customers personalized skin analyses (based on customers' self-analysis using descriptive phrases that would have resonated with Mexican women) and emphasized its product line's appropriateness for a variety of skin types and tones. The company ran this series of ads as it entered the consumer market; a typical one featured the Mexican actress Raquel Torres having her makeup done by Factor himself while promoting her latest

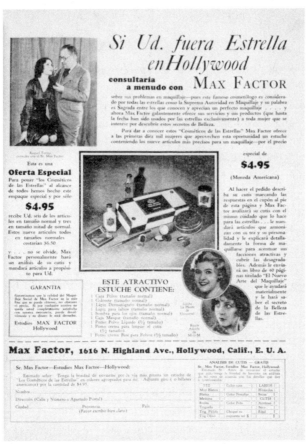

FIGURE 3.9 The actress Raquel Torres in a Max Factor
advertisement aimed at Latina readers, *Cinelandia*, April 1930.
The ad was timed to coincide with the release of *Sea Wolf*. Billie
Rose Theatre Division, the New York Public Library for the
Performing Arts, Astor, Lenox and Tilden Foundations.

film, *White Shadows in the South Seas* (Cosmopolitan, 1928). Acknowledging
Torres's on- and off-screen racial and ethnic difference, the advertisement
suggested somewhat disingenuously that difference could unproblemati-
cally constitute part of what it meant to be a Hollywood star. As the historian Vicki Ruiz points out, most advertisements and fashion spreads in the
Spanish-language press promoted a racialized and class-bound body (white
and middle, if not upper, class) to their readers, and even those ads and
spreads featuring Mexican stars perpetuated the prejudice against dark skin
that decided which Mexicans would be successful in Hollywood.[79]

These ads suggest a strategy of encouraging diffuse associations, but by

FIGURE 3.10
The actor Antonio Moreno on the cover of *El Heraldo Ilustrado*, November 26, 1919. From the collections of the Hemeroteca Nacional de México.

highlighting explicit links between stars and Mexican cultural life, the press also revealed points at which the Mexican public could identify with Hollywood and American film culture. One striking example of this strategy is the proliferation of images that showed stars reading Mexican publications. In 1919 Antonio Moreno was shown reading *El Heraldo Ilustrado*, an image perhaps slightly more plausible than a 1921 cover of *Zig-Zag* that featured the monolingual Gloria Swanson with an open copy of the magazine. Demonstrating that stars are "just like us," which Richard Dyer identifies as one of the key components of the star persona, Agnes Ayres and Walter Hiers were also shown "reading" copies of *Zig-Zag*, which the magazine claimed was a testament to its popularity in Hollywood.[80]

Published interviews likewise emphasized (or invented) the affinities stars had with Mexico. In a 1919 interview with Charlie Chaplin published in the entertainment section of *El Universal*, Chaplin returned again and again to his fascination with Mexico. He declared that he possessed limited knowledge of the land but knew that Mexico was a "grand country, rich, in which the revolutions have not impeded progress." (His interviewer claimed that this was a "true if not direct quote.")[81] Similarly plausible, if not probable, claims were made for other actors as well, such as Mary Pickford, who the Mexican press claimed was learning Spanish, and Marion Davies, who reportedly would have liked to have filmed a motion picture with Pancho Villa. Visits—even projected ones—to Mexico by Hollywood stars were covered in depth in the Mexican press.[82]

Advertisements for upcoming releases demonstrate, in a slightly different way, how local context shaped the way Mexican audiences were addressed. Sometimes framed by titles that suggest a news item rather than an advertisement, short synopses of soon-to-be-released films published in Mexico City's major newspapers spoke directly to the local target audience. Numerous examples include the advertisement for *Amor pirata* (*Homeward Bound*, 1923), which was introduced with the controversy-stirring question: "Can a woman marry without the consent of her father?"[83] Using the first person, the ad declared that even though such behavior was common, "our moral and intellectual education always disapproves." The ad went on to assure readers that the premiere of *El amor pirata* would answer this vexing question for "all Mexican women" in short order. Another example is an advertisement for *El circulo matrimonial* (*The Marriage Circle*, 1924), which was sandwiched between verbiage most certainly taken directly from the studio or distributor. The ad made a direct appeal to Mexican women, whom exhibitors believed to be their primary audience: "The Mexican woman, more than any other, is the right one to admire this veritable jewel of art, which has infinite connections with her passionate psychology."[84] Assumptions about the psychology of Mexican women aside, this ad demonstrates the ways in which films were marketed at the local level by appealing to specific, even if assumed, cultural and national preferences and characteristics.

Appeals generated at the local level also forged links between mass-produced products (films), standardized marketing strategies, and local experiences of cinemagoing. To this end, just as often as they rewarded knowledge of Hollywood cinema, magazines encouraged fans to demonstrate locally specific knowledge as well. For example, the very first issue of *Zig-Zag* announced a contest: "Which actress's eyes are these?" Identifying the actress in question required that readers be knowledgeable about the preferences of Mexican audiences, given that "the actress to whom this beautiful pair of eyes belongs is very well known in Mexico, where her work has been received with genuine applause."[85] In 1926, *Revista de Revistas*' "Cinematic

Novel" contest challenged readers to write a short story based on the plot of a film that had recently opened in Mexico City.[86] These sorts of contests rewarded fans who kept abreast of the local cinema scene—what was playing, what Mexican audiences liked—as well as the latest news from Hollywood.

Although Hollywood liked to market its wares as a cosmopolitan product with appeal that transcended national borders, national identity mattered to Mexican audiences.[87] Readers of Spanish-language fan magazines were constantly being reassured that their favorite Mexican stars continued to consider themselves part of the imagined community of the nation. The Mexican public could proudly claim stars such as Fernando Elizondo, Ramón Novarro, Dolores del Rio, and Lupe Vélez, even as U.S. film studios mobilized their exoticism to tantalize the Anglo-American public.[88] Elizondo, a former railroad worker turned western star, was described in *Zig-Zag* as being "Mexican and very proud of it."[89] Soledad Luna, a *mexicana* living in the Watts neighborhood of Los Angeles, California, learned from *La Opinión* that "Ramon Novarro continues to be as Mexican as you or I, that is, he has not renounced his Mexican citizenship."[90] Novarro reinforced this assertion in a well-publicized interview in *El Universal Ilustrado*, in which he claimed: "I am proud of my country and want my country to be proud of me. That is why I don't want to deny my Mexican nationality."[91] And, as one fan from San Antonio was informed, Novarro had "not forgotten Spanish. . . . [H]e hasn't even completely mastered English."[92]

Other stars' national identity likewise became the object of intense scrutiny by the Mexican public. Mexican readers repeatedly asked columnists to clarify the parentage of stars whose names raised doubts or about whom rumors of Mexican heritage circulated. Columnists repeatedly answered questions about Bebe Daniels, whose mother was Mexican (or Spanish, as some sources would have it); Juanita Hansen, whose name suggested nonexistent Mexican roots; and Antonio Moreno—was he Spanish or Mexican? Either would do, but Mexican would be better. Mexican fans were anxious to identify Mexican stars whom they could claim as "ours," just as "American journalists referring to Mary Pickford, call her 'our Mary.'"[93]

Accordingly, coverage of Latino—primarily Mexican—stars emphasized their shared national identity with Mexican audiences. The Chicago newspaper *México* lauded "Mexicanos que triunfan en Cinelandia" (Mexicans who triumph in Cinelandia).[94] Features about Ramón Novarro published in the Mexican press routinely emphasized his nostalgia for Mexico, though he had left the country at a very young age.[95] In 1923 *Revista de Revistas* proclaimed his career "a Mexican actor's victory in the cinema."[96] Del Rio's rejection of roles that she felt denigrated Mexico or Mexicans was widely discussed in the press, as was her insistence on being identified not as Spanish, an ethnic identity the film industry felt comfortable with, but as Mexican.[97] Her status as "our Dolores" could, one journalist asserted, carry even a bad film in Mexico.[98] Even Antonio Moreno, who was Spanish, was welcomed into the national fold. A photo accompanying the article "Antonio Moreno y su cariño a México" (his love toward Mexico) showed the star in a typical Mexican *charro*, or horseman's outfit. In interviews with the Mexican press, Moreno was cast as an ally of Latino immigrants. "This country [the United States] isn't my scene," he informed readers of *Revista de Revistas*. "My Latin temperament doesn't do very well here."[99] In an earlier interview with the same magazine, Moreno explicitly acknowledged his adoring fans in Mexico and other Latin American countries: "Every day I receive a hundred love letters not only from here [in the United States], but also from Mexico and Argentina."[100] In this way, the Mexican press created affective ties based on national identity between these stars and their Mexican fans. Elaborating and forging these ties so that fans "seemed to be . . . family or intimate friends of these [actors and] actresses" became one of the chief tasks of Mexican journalists covering the U.S. film industry.[101]

Studlar argues that in the 1920s, fan magazines in the United States provided their (assumed female) readers with knowledge about the processes of film production and the "real" lives of stars, while simultaneously perpetuating viewer identification with cinematic images of women. For Studlar, these seemingly contradictory sets of mechanisms add complexity to the traditional accounts of female spectatorship that fix women as passive subjects in their identification with the female object of their gaze, and the women's subsequent desire to possess or be possessed.[102] In the case of Mexican fan culture, journalistic accounts of Hollywood unmasked the industry's inner workings, including its racism, even as they drew Mexican fans further into the imaginative space of Cinelandia. As a result, Mexican fans' desire to be part of the cosmopolitan world of film culture constantly butted up against their knowledge of the ways that film studios exoticized or marginalized Mexicans in films and extra-filmic discourse. Although I consider other responses to the acquisition of this knowledge in chapter 6, here I focus on how journalists constructed a subject position for Mexican fans that is best described as ambivalent fascination.[103]

One common film-related feature, first-person accounts of Hollywood that were part travelogue and part behind-the-scenes exposé, allows us to see this process in action.[104] Examples of this type of literature include "Our Correspondent in Los Angeles and Mexican Stars"; "My Voyage to the Mecca of Cinema"; "In the World of Cinelandia: Oh Hollywood, a Tour through Bohemia"; "From Hollywood," a column published regularly in *Revista de Revistas* throughout 1927; "A Bird's-Eye View of Los Angeles"; and Manuel Ojeda's account of his work at the Ince Studios, which was published in *El Universal*.[105] As a group, these texts map tropes of immigrant displacement onto conventional fan literature's narratives of intimacy with stars and the "unveiling of cinematic truth."[106] They also made typically proud references to Los Angeles's Mexican migrant community as a notable feature of the region and a fact that somehow brought Mexican fans in closer proximity to the film industry.

The writing of Carlos Noriega Hope exemplifies this hybrid genre. A cinema enthusiast who would later become the editor of the popular weekly *El Universal Ilustrado* and an occasional scriptwriter and producer, Noriega Hope traveled to Los Angeles in 1918 for a firsthand look at Hollywood. While in California, he wrote a series of essays that were first published serially in *El Universal Ilustrado* and subsequently collected in *El mundo de las sombras: El cine por fuera y por dentro* (The world of shadows: the cinema inside and out).[107] In these essays, Noriega Hope presents a Mexico-centric account of Hollywood that not only gives his readers a behind-the-scenes look at the industry but that also develops the Mexican spectator as a (here, male) subject with historical, political, and linguistic specificity.

Noriega Hope's account, like much immigrant literature, opens with an arrival scene.[108] The narrator is shaken awake by an African American porter as the train pulls into Union Station in downtown Los Angeles. Over the course of the journey, the "cacti of Arizona and Texas [had] ceded their place to the polychromatic vegetation of the 'land of a thousand wonders.'"[109] Chief among those wonders for the narrator is the order and efficiency of the United States: "The farms were of a complete beauty: the wooden houses, clean, with pointed roofs, the trees, planted in perfectly straight lines, separated by identical spaces." Only the "'Fords' that inundate the United States like an epidemic . . . like strange black beetles" interrupt the grid-like urbanscape.[110]

It is in this new social space that the narrator encounters racial and gender types he had previously encountered only on screen. Arriving in Los Angeles, he realizes that he is missing $15. Influenced by the portrayals of African Americans in U.S. cinema, he immediately blames the porter. But to the narrator's chagrin, it is the porter who returns the money, which the narrator had dropped on the floor. Similarly, on the streets of Los Angeles he is amazed that the thin women dressed in short skirts going about the streets "indifferently" are not movie stars but rather "stenographers, office workers, florists."[111] These moments of cross-cultural encounter hint at the manufactured nature of cinematic reality.

The narrator quickly moves on to a description of the studios and their denizens. In demystifying their star personae by providing readers with accounts of actors at work and at rest, he simultaneously creates the illusion of intimacy between the industry writ large, stars, and their Mexican audiences. As he describes the second take of a scene with the actress Mabel Normand, he emphasizes to his readers that studios "always make two negatives: one for the domestic market and the other for the foreign. . . . American filmmakers who know their business . . . offer films in accordance with the tastes of the consumer."[112] The stars he interviews display extensive knowledge of, and an affinity for, one of these foreign audiences—Mexico. In an interview with May Allen—who, he informs us, "speaks Spanish, reads the Argentine and Mexican press, and is up-to-date on our [Mexico's] film openings"—she tells him authoritatively: "In your country Pearl White is the most popular American actress and Antonio Moreno the male star of the first order."[113] Douglas Fairbanks solicits the narrator's legal advice regarding business transactions in Mexico, Max Linder offers a breezy but complimentary take on the country, and Pauline Fredricks assures the narrator that she has every intention of making a Mexican-themed western in which "Mexicans would not be the eternal bandits of the film." And the Spaniard Antonio Moreno shows the narrator that his daily mail includes "postcards of Mexico showing the streets and buildings of the city" sent to him by "señoritas mexicanas."[114] Though probably embroidered for effect, each of the narrator's interactions with these stars makes the Mexican audience and their lived reality the (momentary) focus of the stars' emotional energy. Various references to the Mexican popular press reinforce this affective bond. Mabel Normand brings the narrator a copy of an interview from an unnamed magazine. She tells him: "I love this piece of paper very much. . . . I see Mexico through these lines . . . written in a language I don't understand."[115] Douglas Fairbanks proudly shows the narrator a signed copy of an image recently published on the cover of *El Universal Ilustrado*. Other mentions of *Cine-Mundial* and *Revista de Revistas* assure the (presumed Mexican) reader that Mexican film culture—fan magazines and fan practices—has currency in Cinelandia.

Finally, Noriega Hope connects the history of Hollywood to the history of Mexican popular culture. Eddie Polo, the narrator says, lived in Mexico for a year and a half while performing with the Bell Family, Mexican circus performers. When Polo mentions the name of Ricardo Bell, the narrator waxes sentimental. "I then felt a strong emotion," he says. "The figure of Ricardo Bell evoked in exotic lands, awoke . . . memories of my life. . . . Perhaps he [Polo] had been one of those robust circus performers . . . who had brightened my childhood—our childhood—beneath the wood roof of the old Circus [Orrin]."[116] Less sentimentally, but no less strategically, the narrator informs his readers that Fairbanks's first riding instructor had been "a charro from [our] country who came to this country with an American circus."[117] In this way, Noriega Hope allows his readers to see Hollywood as a cultural formation that overlaps with and draws on Mexican popular culture. Though some of the rhetorical tropes he employs are typical of all fan features, the strategies of identification I have described work to create a nationally identified spectator and carve out space for Mexican fans in Hollywood's cultural geography.

It would be easy to dismiss Noriega Hope's essays as an accessory to the promotional work of studio publicity machines. However, his text is shot through with an ambivalence that suggests a more complicated dynamic at work. At the end of the narrator's time in "the world of shadows," he boards a train to return to Mexico. Despite having been tempted by the attractions of a bathing-suit-clad Marie Prevost, the charms of Clara Kimball Young, who had learned to "join the Latino with the *yanqui*," and the possibility of working as an extra in movies, he remains determined to go back to his homeland. He decries the United States' automated culture, its cookie-cutter women, and the emptiness of Hollywood's representations of *latinidad*, which consistently and unapologetically confused revolutionaries with gauchos. (In explaining the costuming for Young's next film, Ojeda tells Noriega Hope they were designed by an Argentine: "As it has to do with things Latin, they use the first person who is put in front of them.")[118] And Noriega Hope's affection for Mexico pulls him back, as well. The declaration on the train platform by Ojeda, his compatriot—"I am envying you with all my soul, because you are going back to Mexico and in return you hate me because I have to stay in this town"—can be taken to represent the Mexican audience's ambivalent relationship, somewhere between worship and wariness, with American films and film culture.[119]

ABOUT THAT HAPPY ENDING

The studios' promotion of fans' personal investment in particular stars and journalists' promotion of film culture created a space for fans to exercise and share their own critical judgment. At least one publication, *El Universal Ilustrado*, was quite explicit about its desire to create this space. The magazine's editorial staff saw contests and cinema-related write-in columns as an opportunity to "make known the opinion of average moviegoers."[120] Other publications were not as explicit, but they nevertheless made readers' opinions a significant part of their cinema coverage. Thus, amid the trivia of film-related "news," a discursive space emerged in which Mexican fans offered their own evaluation of the cultural politics of cinema. Even as the popular press documented and promoted the growing popularity of American films and film stars, it demonstrated that for many members of Mexico's transnational audience, Hollywood was not the exclusive owner of cinema.

Film culture's status as a contested domain emerges clearly in the discussions surrounding various film-related contests. In 1920, for example, *El Universal Ilustrado* sponsored a contest called "La reina del cine" (Queen of the cinema), which was explicitly framed as a contest between the Italian divas and the new Hollywood stars, Pearl White, Mary Pickford, and Constance Talmadge. The winner, the Italian actress Francesca Bertini, received 3,650 votes, more than twice the number received by the runner-up, Mabel Normand, and many more than those received by Pearl White, who came in third. In the course of the contest, Mexican fans argued in print about the merits of Italian film and American film and their respective stars. The Italian divas clearly continued to maintain a hold on the public imagination. One reader wrote of Bertini that "her heart guards the secret of all the passions," passions that in this reader's estimation animated the "Latin soul."[121] Likewise, during *El Universal*'s 1923 "Best Film of the Year" contest, some Mexican fans continued to prefer European films. Miguel Santini, for example, wrote that Italian films with their epic themes and swooning divas were better artistically than their American counterparts.[122]

The tide, however, was clearly shifting. Many fans wrote in to laud the naturalism of American films and their stars, echoing Hope's declaration a year earlier that "when someone wants to feel the realism of life, without knowingly prepared poses" he would "recommend a Mary Pickford film."[123] Rafael Fuentes (a reader from Xalapa, Veracruz) echoed Noriega Hope's sentiments, defending art—"the exact representation of life, a mirror of feeling"—as something to be found in American films. "According to what little I know of this life," he wrote, "when women cry or laugh they don't make lustful gestures, make a multitude of contortions, show the whites of their eyes, or any other of the funny faces that are the only weapons of Italian artists."[124] Maria Cristina Arellano wrote: "I vote for the gracious and sympathetic Mabel Normand, who, even though she is not as beautiful and notable as Francesca Bertini, is without a doubt the queen of collegiality and smiles."[125] The definition of art and artistry was contested as new models of femininity captured the Mexican public's imagination. Some even saw

American films as an antidote to the perceived ills of postrevolutionary Mexican society. One reader, for example, voted for *El bruto* (*The Abysmal Brute*, 1923), a film based on Jack London's novel about a prizefighter, as the best film of year. The film's main character, "a vulgar and slightly savage guy," according to the reader, was precisely the type who would stand up to the intellectuals he accused of spending their time constructing "imaginary worlds and utopias" rather than dealing with Mexico's political reality.[126]

Occasionally, someone would feel compelled to defend Mexico's still-nascent film production industry on principle. For example, one reader cast his vote for the Mexican actress and director Mimí Derba as "the queen of cinema" in a "true display of patriotism," despite acknowledging that no Mexican actress could "withstand comparison with Mabel Normand, Francesca Bertini, or la Nazimova."[127] But Mexican cinema usually came up short. In 1921, during a national scriptwriting contest sponsored by *El Universal Ilustrado*, a reader known only as Margarita K. de M. wrote that although she appreciated the magazine's efforts to encourage national production, she found most Mexican films too similar to the "hair-raising dramas" of European cinema.[128] Of course, the press engaged in an ongoing parallel discussion about national production that alternated between celebrating new releases as evidence that the national industry had in fact finally arrived and lamenting the sorry state of an essentially artisanal endeavor that generated films described, for the most part, as "great efforts"—and not much else.

National production sometimes seemed to have little to recommend it, but Mexican fans consistently evaluated American films in the context of the fraught relationship between Mexico and the United States. For example, one reviewer of *Tierras de promision* (*The Promised Land*; Corsay, 1925) wrote that the film's presentation of the United States as a "model of paradise for families" with "accessible prices, hot baths, and water" for everyone was disingenuous and false—a vision of life "the Latino public will not digest quickly."[129] Likewise, a 1917 review of a film titled *Misterios del manicomio* (literally, mysteries of the asylum) began with the terse phrase "American film" and continued by recounting the "improbable, the emotional, the incomprehensible, what is in the end, the psychology of the American film."[130] Another reviewer described films that portrayed "the life of the businessmen of that great country . . . *very* American."[131] Finally, many Mexican spectators (recall Bermúdez Zartrain's review of *La hija del circo* discussed in chapter 1) rejected the narrative conventions of American cinema. Antonio Leal y Romero from Aguascalientes wrote to *Cinelandia*, complaining about U.S. films in which "identical characters all present the same problem. . . ."

An accumulation of false circumstances . . . all end in the same way, with the peachy optimism of a sappy kiss."[132] Where some saw naturalism, others saw "Yankee commerce" and artificially inflated optimism.[133]

On the other side of the border, columnists in Spanish-language news-papers in the United States—where migrants felt pressure to assimilate and the stinging effects of racism and discrimination—often found themselves defending Mexican culture even as they promoted American films and their stars. If Lola used films and film culture to separate herself from a tradition-bound culture, these columnists urged their readers—the Blancas, Magdalenas, Bertas, Sylvias, and Auroras who lived in El Paso, Chicago, San Francisco, San Diego, and Las Cruces—to continue to speak Spanish and to adhere to Mexican cultural values. "El mago de Hollywood," for example, chastised more than one young reader who wrote to him in English, urging them to use their Spanish lest they lose it. He also explained to an aspiring actress named Olivia that becoming successful in Hollywood often involved compromising "what Mexican women value most, their modesty." In his efforts to dissuade her from seeking a career in films, he continued by in-voking "Mexican family tradition" that prohibited defying one's elders.[134] Certainly conservative, these admonitions took their place alongside other criticisms of the lure of the cinema and comments on American cinema's seeming incompatibility with Mexican culture that appeared during this period.

Some publications even articulated a distinctly Mexican version of film history. *Magazine Fílmico*, one of Mexico City's cinema-specific publica-tions, offered readers an alternative history of cinema in Mexico, even as it promoted and celebrated popular American films and directors. Accounts of the Mexican exhibition industry were often filtered through Mexican concerns about economic nationalism—concerns that would structure dis-course on the Mexican film industry in the 1930s—and a desire to give Mexi-can exhibitors and distributors a certain degree of autonomy from the con-cerns and goals of U.S. producers. For example, a two-part feature published in 1926, "Evolucionará el espectaculo de cine en México?" (Will the cinema evolve in Mexico?), began by declaring that "before interviewing 'American experts' located in the capital we would first like our readers to read the opin-ions of Mexican experts."[135]

The comments of the two Mexican experts interviewed, Luis Lezama and Germán Camus, both of whom had been active in the Mexican film distri-bution industry since the early 1910s, reinforced what United Artists had learned through trial and error: success in the Mexican market required an understanding of local economic, political, and cultural conditions. Lezama, for one, did not believe that cinema should be a bastion of equality. Rather, he opined, exhibitors would reap the most profits from setting up circuits modeled after those in the United States that included a range of exhibition venues, from a few first-run theaters to those that served the "pueblo bajo" (lower classes). He advocated presenting "exclusives" in more expensive theaters first, before sending them down the line, instead of showing mixed programs in all theaters. Camus, in contrast, believed that circuits should be composed of similar theaters and should aim to present "good programs" at "extremely economical entry prices."[136] He observed: "Experience has shown me that the [Mexican] public prefers four-hour-long programs. I think that the ideal program would be two so-called art films from distinct genres, a comedy, a travelogue, newsreels, etc."[137] In contrast to Lezama, he did not think exclusives were appropriate for the Mexican market, which comprised mainly audiences of modest means. Both models reflected the particularities of the Mexican market, in which the ability of film exhibitors to fill their houses depended on serving a small audience of some means and a much broader audience of very limited means.

Other features in *Magazine fílmico* likewise reflected Mexican film culture's ambivalent relationship to U.S. cinema. In 1927 Rafael Bermudez Zartrain contributed a multipart personal reflection, "Memorias cinematográficas," to the magazine.[138] Responding directly to Terry Ramsaye's recently published *A Million and One Nights*, he reminded readers that U.S. dominance was not preordained. "Even though our readers today won't believe it," he wrote, "just fifteen years ago no one would have believed in the artistic development [of cinema] in the United States; probably not even the Americans themselves."[139] Perhaps more telling than his assertion that it was "the Europeans, especially the Italians who founded the art of cinema," was the account he offered of the *yanqui* invasion. Instead of ascribing the success of U.S. film companies in Mexico to American ingenuity and business savvy, he made the Mexican distributor, exhibitor, and sometime producer Germán Camus the protagonist of this fundamental shift in Mexican film culture. Camus, Bermúdez Zartrain wrote, "set out to buy American material," which he then introduced ever so carefully in order to see how the Mexican public would respond to it. Before long, Camus had established an office in New York and was bringing Metro and later Goldwyn films to Mexico.[140] (A subsequent installment of Bermúdez Zartrain's personal reflections focused on European export houses). In his account of the development of the cinema industry in Mexico, Bermúdez Zartrain resisted a narrative that centered on American cinema. Instead, he crafted a history in which Mexican entrepreneurs and the Mexican public played as important a role as U.S. studios and their films or stars.

CONCLUSION

Columnists implied that Mexico was culturally distinct, and critics asserted that Mexico had its own film history (albeit one in which production played a minor role). In addition, some Mexican fans used the public sphere carved out by cinema discourse to assert their individuality in the face of pressures to model themselves after stars and live "cinematic" lives. Responding to the question "Which cinema heroine would you like to be?"—posed by a *Revista de Revistas* reporter—Eloidia León acknowledged that the cinema "exercise[d] such an attraction" over its viewers that "the movies . . . impose, even against our will, a mode of thinking and being."[141] Many young women, she continued, chose to "act like Clara Bow in this or that film" rather than being themselves. Hermelina Borbón astutely recognized the role of advertising and publicity in creating a fantasy world for spectators. "If some young girls decide to live a second life," she declared, "the culprit is not cinema itself, but cinema publicists."[142] Antonia Palos averred: "It doesn't interest me to be a heroine from a film. . . . I want to live my own life."[143] Palos's answer, like those of León and Borbón, suggests that Mexican spectators—avid fans though many became—perceived Cinelandia as a space in which they could critique and debate the effects of the *yanqui* invasion on Mexico's modernity.

In postrevolutionary Mexico, the popular press became an important institution for envisioning a modern Mexico. While the country's political, intellectual, and cultural elites were being recruited to the tasks of consolidating a national identity through the arts, for example, the popular press was promoting a modernity based on new practices of consumption. Itself a product of modernization, the press became an important promoter of American films and fan culture, a set of texts and practices that was simultaneously global and local. Journalists modeled an appropriately critical stance toward the cinema. They encouraged audience members to approach films with an eye attuned to the finer points of film production and narrative and to involve themselves actively in debates about the relative quality of films and merits of stars. Furthermore, journalists helped audiences identify even more closely with Hollywood and its star culture by teaching them how to be fans. Advertisements held out consumption as yet another point of entry into this culture, assuring fans that their purchases could help them emulate their favorite stars.

At the same time the press provided a space in which Mexican fans were encouraged to see themselves as members of an audience bound by a shared national identity. In other words, Mexican audiences were encouraged to invest themselves in American film culture as Mexicans. Shared national identity, popular culture, and experiences of racism bound Mexican audiences to stars they could claim as their own. Popular writing that sought to explain Hollywood to Mexican readers was marked by ambivalent fascination, as writers fed audiences' desire for behind-the-scenes knowledge while acknowledging and criticizing Hollywood's racism. As this extra-filmic discourse about stars, fashion, and beauty circulated in the Mexican popular press on both sides of the border, it was translated literally and figuratively into a recognizable local idiom. On one level, this localization demonstrates the flexibility of the American film industry as it sought out global audiences. On another level, the process provides evidence of the way that Mexicans translated, adapted, and appropriated American film culture. Through this back-and-forth the Mexican press produced a new cultural space: Cinelandia. Hollywood, rather than overwhelming or displacing local film culture became the very building blocks of that culture. Hollywood was thoroughly imbricated with the local and national conditions that shaped Mexican experiences of filmic texts and film culture.

In the cultural space created by cinema discourse, Mexican spectators emerge as a national audience marked by language, national identity, and a complicated history of interactions with the United States. Indeed, Mexican audiences' embrace of Cinelandia did not constitute a rejection of mexicanidad. Rather, this new cultural space—part of Mexican film culture—became a site where national identity was contested. Just as they reveled in their participation in global film culture, during this period primarily Hollywood film culture, both the Mexican press and Mexican audiences, in all of their diversity, critiqued and debated how and if the ideologies that were coded as modern, like the new forms of femininity represented by Lola, "la chica de Hollywood," fit into postrevolutionary Mexican society and culture.

BORDER CROSSINGS

A young man, Doroteo Lucero, in front of movie posters in Los Angeles, circa 1925.
Courtesy the Los Angeles Public Library Photo Collection.

4 LA VIRGEN AND LA PELONA
Film Culture, Border Crossing, and the Modern Mexican Woman

The *yankified* Mexican woman is an abominable caricature.
—LEON REY [PSEUD.], *LA DAMA CATÓLICA*, 1923

When they [women] cross the border they change some of their ideas.
—AN UNNAMED IMMIGRANT IN CHICAGO, CIRCA 1931, QUOTED IN
PAUL TAYLOR, *MEXICAN LABOR IN THE UNITED STATES: CHICAGO AND
THE CALUMET REGION*

In the spring of 1923, a curious story appeared on the front pages of
Mexico City's prominent newspapers. A fifteen-year-old girl named
Marina Vega had run away from home in search of Hollywood, determined to meet Charlie Chaplin. (Vega declared that she had fallen in
love with the film star after "seeing him work on the screen in Mexico
City,"[1] and she was convinced that she and Chaplin shared a "spiri-
tual" bond.[2]) Amazingly enough — the press accounts are fuzzy about
the details — the teenager not only made it to Hollywood but also
managed to find Chaplin's Los Angeles home, break in, and hide out
in the star's dressing room. The sources differ about what happened
next. One newspaper, *El Demócrata*, asserted that Chaplin's man-
servant discovered her hiding in the closet. Another paper, *El Universal*, reported that Marina grew tired of waiting for the star to appear
and went downstairs, where she had a nice chat with both Chaplin
and Pola Negri, his then fiancée. In his memoirs, Chaplin remembers
his servant finding a "young Mexican girl" in Chaplin's bed, wearing his pajamas.[3] In any case, the sources concur that in despair after
being discovered, Marina attempted to poison herself. She was taken
to a hospital near Chaplin's home and then sent back to Mexico City
at the star's expense.

But the story did not end there. Apparently not satisfied by the celebrity engendered by her sojourn in Hollywood, Marina returned home and, indulging in a penchant for cross-dressing, stirred up sexual confusion in Mexico City.[4] Having tried on Chaplin's clothes while hiding in his closet, she now roamed the streets of Mexico City dressed like a man and going by the name José Ramos. As José, Marina partook of all the pleasures of the city, becoming a mainstay in its restaurants, bars, and cabarets. He spoke at length about the "beauty of the *tiples* [chorus girls], the temptations of cognac, and the inconveniences of poker," and impressed those around him with his knowledge of English and familiarity with contemporary literature. In sum, José was the perfect modern "gentleman."[5] When not dressed as José, Marina allegedly wore the trademark bobbed hair and short skirts of the *pelona* (literally, "shorn woman"), Mexico's version of the modern girl.[6]

In recounting the discovery of Marina's "true" gender, newspapers put into play a set of narrative conventions that might have been taken directly from the screen itself—a disguise, a mystery hinted at by a set of visual clues, and the voyeuristic pleasures of spying through the keyhole.[7] A nosy chambermaid spied products associated with women's beauty culture—"a lipstick, 'Coty' powder, Rimel [mascara], eyelash pencils, depilatories and we don't know how many other things"—on José's dresser leading to the eventual revelation that José and Marina were one and the same.[8] But Marina's performance of masculinity had been so convincing (or seductive) that even after her discovery, one enchanted young woman refused to believe that "he" was actually a "she."

The press devoted numerous articles to explaining Marina's behavior. Some reports suggested that the avant-garde literary and artistic movement, *estridentismo*, shared some responsibility for Marina's antics.[9] But most Mexican analyses of Marina's adventures in Hollywood and Mexico City framed her aberrant behavior as the corruption of a young, provincial *mexicana* by her exposure to American mass culture.[10] Her rejection of gender norms and likely sexual deviance seemed to be the logical outcome of her indiscriminate consumption of U.S. films and film culture. The press suggested that her behavior would have been unremarkable in the United States, where, supposedly, ordinary women walked the streets of New York in outrageous costumes, young girls offered up their legs for inspection by the urban crowd, and suffragists agitated for women's political rights and the "separation forever of the sexes."[11] In Mexico, however, someone like Marina—"a provincial girl, desiring crazily to be discussed, criticized, admired, [and] analyzed, who forgets all the austere moral education of our

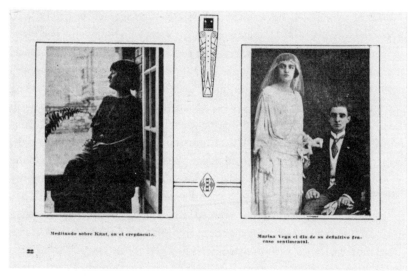

Meditando sobre Kant, en el crepúsculo.

Marina Vega el día de su definitivo fracaso sentimental.

22

FIGURE 4.1 Marina Vega's deepest desires realized in a *Revista de Revistas* photo spread, May 1924. From the collections of the Hemeroteca Nacional de México.

village girls and commits a thousand crazy things"—was, according to newspaper accounts, both disturbingly and fascinatingly anomalous.[12]

Whether they characterized her as a hysterical fan, a perverted soul, or a resourceful and imaginative young woman, Mexican sources concur that Marina hungered for celebrity. *El Demócrata* accused her of creating a "cinematic life" based on the dramas she had seen on-screen and attributed her rebellion against social conventions to "her desire to see her picture in the pages of pictorial reviews and to focus the attention of the public, even if for only an instant, on her expressive eyes, her 'cupid' shaped mouth, and her delicious nape."[13] In other words, Marina sought to become an object of contemplation and sexual desire, like the motion picture stars she admired. She had, the media proclaimed, become infected by the craze for celebrity and attention that fan magazines and news coverage of the U.S. film industry and its stars nurtured. In Mexico, as in other parts of the world, young women's enthusiasm for films and film culture prompted them to pursue in both dramatic and quotidian ways the independence, sexual freedom, and glamour they associated with stardom and modern femininity as portrayed on the screen.

Whether dressed as a man or in the short skirts adopted by modern girls around the world, Vega defied normative models of femininity. She abandoned her husband, traveled alone, and claimed sexual liberty in her pursuit of Chaplin, if not (as later press coverage seemed to imply) in a cross-dressing pursuit of lesbianism. Marina's story highlights the perceived dangers of Mexican women's increasing mobility, presence in public space, and freedom from the strict controls of patriarchal family structures, as well as the figurative and sometimes (as in Vega's case) literal border crossing that these changes in women's status encouraged. Her celebrity took shape at the intersection of postrevolutionary nationalism, changing gender norms, and the transnational circulation of films and film culture. Women's self-fashioning, which Marina engaged in so inventively, was perceived as being at odds with official and unofficial nation-building projects that required women's desires to be strategically mobilized for the benefit of the nation.

Ironically, the Mexican press seemed insatiable in its coverage of Vega's story, fulfilling the very desires they criticized. As the press sought out stories about modern topics, including women's film culture and its perceived dangers, that would attract readers, it both articulated and intensified the dangers of American film culture to the health of the Mexican body politic. What is more, in conjuring up the specter of American fan culture, the Mexican press positioned Vega as the victim of cultural imperialism rather than as a social actor engaged in challenging women's place in Mexican society.

Though the pelona had a male counterpart—the *fifí*, a modern form of masculinity that also took its inspiration from the screen and was likewise associated with deviant sexuality and consumer culture—women's adoption of the styles and behaviors associated with "the modern girl" worldwide, as Vega's story suggests, generated the most public controversy. Thus, this chapter examines the friction between the new model of femininity promoted by American cinema and the demands of postrevolutionary nation building. The pelona—in addition to her negative association with the blurring of gender and social hierarchies, the practices of an emerging consumer culture, and the malevolent forces of American mass culture—became the object of intense public debate. Perceived by many as an "agent of antinationalist subjectivity" who threatened the vision of Mexican modernity promoted by both liberals and conservatives alike, the pelona upset the clearly defined gender roles that many believed were crucial to Mexico's postrevolutionary development.[14] Popular narratives—cautionary tales in the form of fiction, news items, and even press coverage of a beauty contest—demonstrate how Mexican women's fantasies of stardom were understood as desires that needed to be carefully managed in order to support Mexican nation building.

To that end, the press promoted a model of transnational stardom that cast Mexican participation in the U.S. film industry as important political work. As Daisuke Miyao and Yiman Wang have shown in regard to Sessue Hayakawa and the American-born Anna May Wong, respectively, transnational stardom brought with it a set of complex demands.[15] Performers found themselves engaged in a tug-of-war between the demands of Hollywood's racialized economy of representation and the political meanings their performances and personae accrued in their home countries or communities. Ana López develops a similarly complex account of Dolores del Rio's stardom, which she argues had distinct but interconnected meanings in the United States and Mexico and their respective cinema cultures.[16] In Hollywood a figure such as del Rio would, as Joanne Hershfield writes in her examination of the Mexican star's persona, "symbolize the nexus of gender and race," but in Mexico, she and others far less famous or for whom stardom remained an unachieved desire became symbols for the nexus between modernity, gender, and nationalism.[17]

LA PELONA: MEXICO'S MODERN GIRL

By the time Marina Vega's escapades raised eyebrows and became the topic of public discussion, cinema's popularity among Mexican youth of both sexes was both well established and controversial. The debate engendered by the "Reina del Cine" contest—essentially a debate about the merits of the sort of femininity represented by the Italian divas and American actresses—signaled that a new sort of woman—the *chica moderna*[18]—was becoming the exemplar of modern womanhood. Though some described this new woman as natural, unaffected, and "real," others perceived her—as they did Marina Vega—to be sexually adventurous, dangerously liberated, and overly invested in consumer culture.

"A great part of our young women," the editor of the conservative *El Hogar* declared, "try to imitate the heroines of the screen not only in their actions, but also in their liberties."[19] Conservatives decried the romantic plots of films, which provided a "free education" for young women "in the form of the "voluptuous kisses . . . repeated in reel after reel as if it were the most natural thing."[20] Frequent portrayals of divorce and love triangles were singled out as especially dangerous, particularly in concert with coverage of the "details of the incredibly licentious lives of the residents of Cinelandia."[21]

Las Damas Católicas, a conservative women's group, was particularly vocal about the deleterious effects of what it termed "immoral" films.[22] In its monthly magazine, *La Dama Católica*, the group printed monthly reports on campaigns against the pernicious influence of such films. Subcommittees of the group were formed in communities across Mexico—in provincial capitals like Zacatecas, Oaxaca City, and Mérida, as well as in smaller towns like Zaca-poaxtla, Puebla—with designations such as the Committee on Morality and Work, the Committee on Morality and Fashion, and the League for the Pro-tection of Youth. The goal of these groups was to develop alternative forms of recreation for local youth, while pressuring local exhibitors to show what the women called decent films and organizing protests against specific films.[23]

Though the Damas tended to use broad terms such as "immoral films" and "corrupting films," as if their readers knew precisely which films they meant, the few films mentioned by name afford a glimpse of the range of narratives they found objectionable. Specific films the Damas objected to included *Cuerpo y alma* (*Man and His Woman*, 1920), a story about drug ad-diction, romantic intrigue, and betrayal; and *Una noche en Arabia* (*A Night in New Arabia*, 1917), a drama involving a Jewish millionaire, a cross-class ro-mance, and an elopement. The Damas of Mérida made sure that the former film was not shown in that city's theaters, while the Damas of Oaxaca City censored the latter through a word-of-mouth campaign.[24]

Narratives of crime and seduction rankled the religious group's mem-bership, but depictions of the modern girl provoked the loudest protests. In June 1924 the Damas wrote to the editors of Mexico City's two largest news-papers, *El Universal* and *Excélsior*, imploring them in the name of patriot-ism to "repudiate the drugs of the spirit that weaken the race."[25] The "drugs" they referred to were "imported" (that is, American) films that created an "environment of frivolity and foolishness, of indelicacy and corruption."[26] Although their missive spoke generally about Mexico's "moral atmosphere," they referred specifically to a series of advertisements for the upcoming re-lease of *Juventud ardiente* (*Flaming Youth*, 1923), starring Colleen Moore.

In the film, Moore—who would become Hollywood's first flapper star—plays Patricia Fentriss, one of three sisters who want to share in their rich and somewhat debauched parents' pursuit of pleasure—jazz music, bootlegged booze, wild parties, and, most disturbing to the Damas, a range of modern sexual behavior including petting, premarital sex, and adulterous affairs.[27] The film, which was based on a controversial novel released earlier the same year, featured a number of titillating scenes. One showed party guests un-dressing in silhouette, in preparation for coed skinny-dipping. As Sara Ross argues, though the film was controversial when it was released in the United States, it mobilized "melodramatic conventions and moral lessons" in order to "appease more traditionalist audience members, while presenting a strik-ing portrait of modern sexual mores."[28] Most insistently, the film (and the novel, as Ross explains) celebrated heterosexual marriage as the locus of women's happiness.[29]

FIGURE 4.2 *Juventud ardiente* (*Flaming Youth*) advertisement, *Excélsior*, June 1, 1924.
From the collections of the Hemeroteca Nacional de México.

As in the United States, in Mexico the film's promotion focused on the most shocking parts of the story. The newspaper ad that ran in Mexico City highlighted the young woman's "first cigarette," "first cocktail," and "her first red kiss" and used images in silhouette that conjured up the "notorious skinny-dipping scene."[30] In the United States these ads allowed audiences to make connections—ranging from outraged to titillated—between the film's toned-down version of this scene and the more explicit description in the novel.[31] In Mexico the Damas read these images as representative of the characterization of Moore's character in the film, a character they considered the wrong type of role model for Mexican women. "This unhappy protagonist," they asked rhetorically, unmoved by the film's moral lesson, "is what they [Americans] offer as a prototype of the modern woman? This process of corruption is what the women, adolescents, and girls who fill the movie theaters will witness as the model of the day?"[32]

Of course, the Damas must have realized that their alarm about the deleterious effects of American cinema came too late. The pelona could already be found in movie theaters, cafes, parks, schools, and other public spaces, including the pages of the newspapers and weekly magazines. Like Marina Vega, the pelona became the subject of intense media attention; the press discursively produced her for the reading public at the same time that it

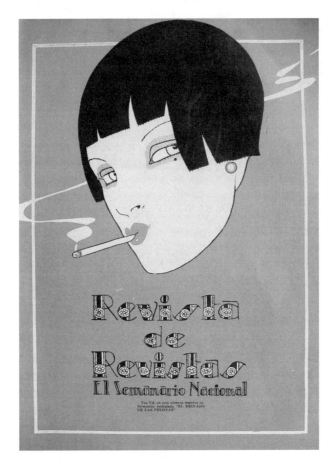

FIGURE 4.3
The "Reign of
the Pelona,"
cover of *Revista
de Revistas*, May
25, 1924. From
the collections of
the Hemeroteca
Nacional de
México.

produced the social dangers she represented. In May 1924 the popular magazine *Revista de Revistas* devoted an entire issue, complete with a modernist rendering of the modern girl on the cover, to the "Reign of the Pelona."[33] At least on the surface this attention was celebratory, but the articles in the issue and others betrayed anxiety about the pelona as they traced her provenance, parsed her relationship to both feminism and the flapper, and puzzled over whether she should be thought of as a symbol of modern Mexico or of cultural imperialism.

According to the press, the pelona, like her counterparts around the world, could be easily identified by her adoption of new modes of femininity, her quest for personal liberation, and her intense engagement with consumer culture.[34] The pelona's attire signaled her embrace of this new vision of modern womanhood. Pelonas, the editor of *El Hogar* declared in horror, dressed with "just one meter of cloth, [and] painted [themselves] from their shadowed eyes to their red and luminous heart-shaped lips."[35] Their knee-length skirts and low-cut necklines likewise scandalized the Damas, who regularly condemned what they called "immoral" fashion.[36] During the First Catholic Women's Congress in 1922, Mexican women joined Catholic women world-wide in condemning girls who wore "unashamed and impudent sleeves and skirts, and transparent stockings."[37] The Damas saved their particular ire for young women who, in imitation of their favorite stars, made liberal use of perfume and cosmetics that had previously been the accessories of pros-titutes and actresses. But it was the pelona's cropped hair that became her trademark. Young Mexican women, like modern girls worldwide, adopted the bobbed hairstyle made famous by Moore in *Flaming Youth*.[38] Although some, including Mexican feminists, defended the rage for short hair with arguments of hygiene and ease, others linked the style to the abandonment of the "womanly" qualities symbolized by the long braids that had become associated with traditional Mexican womanhood.

Although the pelona, "she of short skirts and wide liberties," could be identified by her appearance, it was the behaviors connoted by these fash-ions that were the true source of concern.[39] Girls who had been kept under the watchful eyes of their families were now going out with the "liberty of a twenty-year-old boy," frequenting cafes, movie theaters, and other pub-lic spaces "in the company of male 'friends.'"[40] Being exposed to the gaze of strangers in public was bad enough, but the pelona seemed determined to draw attention to herself through the clothes she wore and the way she comported herself in public. In addition to her short skirts and sleeveless tops, she crossed her legs, chewed gum, talked and laughed loudly, applied makeup in public, and acted excessively familiar with men she did not know. Rather than being demure and modest—which was the middle-class ideal during the late nineteenth and early twentieth centuries as well as being (ac-cording to many) the natural way for "honorable women" to act—the pelona displayed herself, as one anonymous author in a provincial magazine put it, like "those pretty fabrics in the shop windows that are put there to attract the attention of everyone who passes by."[41]

The pelona's willingness to make a public spectacle of herself threatened to blur important social distinctions, including that between respectable women and prostitutes. "Today," wrote Leon Rey, a frequent contributor to *La Dama Católica*, "many honorable women dress and act in a way no different on the outside from lost women [prostitutes]."[42] Late nineteenth-century discourse on prostitution in Mexico had already established a link between questionable morals and public visibility. A passage from Federico Gamboa's novel *Santa* illustrates the relationship between women's public visibility and sexuality.[43] In the novel, Santa, a rural ingénue, has become an infamous prostitute after being seduced and abandoned. At the height of her fame, she learns that her mother has died, and she encounters a group of upper-class women in a church where she seeks solace: "But they had recognized her. . . . [W]ho had sent her to attract fathers, husbands, and sons with the charms of firm and tasty flesh? Who had sent her to exhibit herself in theaters and walks, where married women and young women who, in their air of ignoring Santa in her Olympic disdain of a victor that admits no rivals, had learned by memory her appearance and her name?"[44] In other words, Santa's identity as a prostitute was one produced and confirmed by her public visibility. Like Santa, who frequented public spaces—cafes and *paseos* (promenades)—in the company of her paramours and other prostitutes, the pelona insisted on being seen in cinemas, at "dancings," and on the street—behavior that was perceived as an announcement of her sexual availability.[45] When the pelona appeared on screen in Mexican feature films such as *Mitad y mitad* (Dieli Film, 1921), *Amor* (Ediciones Camus, 1922), and *Amnesia* (Torres Films, 1921), she was cast as a woman "dedicated to the fast life," a "woman of the city," and a "domineering woman whose intense social life led her to neglect her home," characterizations that supported the link between the pelona's public visibility and—if not prostitution—her deviant femininity.[46] As the historian Katherine Bliss explains, after the revolution many women had in fact turned to prostitution as a survival strategy.[47] Thus, the fear that young women might fall into formal or casual prostitution might have been hysterical and class bound, but it was not entirely unfounded.

The pelona's rejection of traditional femininity threatened gender distinctions as well. Often described as "she-men," pelonas were associated with the masculinization of women. One critic interpreted their cropped hair; their clothes "borrowed" from the wardrobes of fathers and brothers; and women's presence in factories, offices, and stores as evidence that women were "trying to join the legions of men."[48] *Revista de Revistas* (the same magazine that seemed to valorize the pelona) published the work of José Elguero, who penned an unflattering portrait of the modern woman that cast her as an emasculating shrew. He insisted that in Mexico "women are still women," but he warned his readers that Mexican feminists, like the pelona, were "copiers of exotic customs."[49] The pelona, by implication, undermined the patriarchal structure of Mexican society.

Perhaps as importantly in the Mexican context, the pelona represented a challenge to the class structure that members of the elite were trying to maintain in the face of the revolution's promises of democracy and equality.

FIGURE 4.4 A young flapper dancing the Charleston in Mexico City's streets, *El Universal Ilustrado*, April 1, 1926. From the collections of the Hemeroteca Nacional de México.

Though the rage for bobbed hair had started among the upper classes, it quickly spread from "the noble class to the classes that live in the *vecinidades* [multi-family housing for the poor] in the *barriadas* [neighborhoods] of Te- pito and San Antonio Abad," and it was even indulged in "by our unchang- ing and loquacious servants."[50] Middle-class observers clucked "in many of the dark faces that carry the imperturbable stamp of the race," the style ends up being "unsympathetic and ridiculous."[51] In designating modern styles as the province of those with fair skin these sorts of comments reinforced Mexico's racial hierarchy, even as upper- and middle-class women—most famously the artist Frida Kahlo—adopted fashions inspired by indigenous traditions that Hershfield calls the "domestic exotic," a trend that had begun during the postindependence period.[52]

Finally, the pelona's fascination with consumer culture was believed to encourage inappropriate practices of consumption. For one, the desire for certain possessions—dresses, jewelry, and other accessories—might prompt working-class and poor women in particular to forget their social status. Their aspirations to live the fabulous on- and off-screen lives of their favor- ite stars (and of the Mexican upper classes) could lead to the unproductive use of their small salaries and, in extreme cases, prompt antisocial behav- ior. Throughout the 1920s, young women who worked in offices, stores, and factories were targeted by advertisements for beauty products and fashion,

FIGURE 4.5 *Flapperismo* spread to the provinces, as demonstrated by the bobbed hair of these young women in Durango, circa 1928. Courtesy the Josefa L. Serna Collection, Chicano Studies Research Center, University of California, Los Angeles.

many of which, as the previous chapter discussed, used stars to sell their wares. At the same time the middle class attempted to make sure that these women spent their money in ways the middle class deemed conducive to Mexico's development and progress—that is, in ways they deemed appropriate.

A 1927 editorial published in *El Hogar* lamented the spendthrift ways of working women.[53] In addition to the increasingly pervasive practices of buying on credit or layaway, women's desires for silk dresses, jewelry, and other luxuries were leading them to neglect the basic necessities of life such as rent and food. Even the "most humble women" were caught up in the vicious cycle of novelty, desire, and obsolescence that characterizes consumer culture.[54] The source of such inappropriate spending was located in two related phenomena: "the windows of the big stores" and motion pictures in which women could see "actresses showing off [those] astonishing 'toilettes.'"[55] Both of these "windows" offered Mexico City's working women, who traversed the city's streets and made up a sizable chunk of the city's motion picture audiences, a "window/mirror"—as Mary Anne Doane calls it—into which they could see both commodities and the identities that those commodities promised to create for them.[56]

At its most extreme, these desires could provoke criminal behavior. Throughout the 1920s a spate of crimes of passion committed by young women described as pelonas jockeyed with political news for space on the front pages of newspapers. Yellow journalists' coverage of the high-profile murder trials of women accused of killing their husbands or lovers that played out in the very public setting of a *jurado popular* (jury trial) dominated Mexico City's news for months. Photographs accompanied detailed, melodramatic accounts of each case's sordid details, and in at least three cases, the sensational events became the subject of hastily produced local films.[57] The prosecution's arguments often asserted that rather than acting to protect their honor, these women had been driven to their crimes by greed for material comfort and social status. The editor of *El Hogar* called them "crazy young women" who were "prisoners of the hallucination of luxury," a characterization that linked their activities to the fantasies offered by the movies.[58]

The case of Esther Borgia Sforza illustrates these connections most clearly. In 1924 Esther was first accused of killing her lover and then, as the details of the case became clearer, of being an accessory to the murder, which (as it turned out) had actually been committed by her half-brother, Moisés Rivera. The crime, called the "crimen de Santa Ursula" after the location where it occurred, garnered more than the usual attention because of the involvement of Esther, a "modern woman, shorn à la flapper."[59] The siblings plotted to murder Ángel Oñate, who worked with Moisés at the accounting firm E. T. Oakley, so they could rob the firm included using Esther to lure Oñate to a spiritualist session in the municipality of Tlalpan, a suburb of Mexico City, her dropping a bracelet in order to have him help her look for it, and her brother's cold-blooded shooting of Oñate in the back. Coverage of the crime focused on the siblings' racial background—Moisés was described as being of "the indigenous race" having a "repulsive aspect" and "crooked teeth," and his sister, though painted as more attractive, was portrayed as sharing some of his racial characteristics.[60]

Neither denied their complicity. In fact, Esther, who had been captured trying to cross the border into the United States with the stolen money, declared in an interview: "I prefer dishonor to misery, [I prefer] to see myself covered in jewels, to live in opulence . . . prostituting myself doesn't matter, nor did taking the life of a man."[61] During the official investigation, the re-creation of the crime meant that "for the second time, as if on the screen of a movie theater, although even more vivid, paraded all the scenes of the crime."[62] The daily newspapers reveled in the lurid details of the case, but *El Hogar* used it as yet another opportunity to admonish its readers about the dangers of the desire for certain lifestyles, luxury items, and celebrity that were provoked by film and film culture.[63] Rather than addressing the social problems—inequality, for example—that might drive women to criminal activity, critics laid the blame for these types of crime at the feet of American mass culture.

Though the flapper and her international avatars generated controversy wherever they appeared, in Mexico discussions about the pelona were inevitably linked to the country's contentious relationship to the United States. These new styles and behaviors were marked as imported customs that clashed with Mexico's traditions and "racial tendencies."[64] "Ask any *'pelona'* friend why she had her hair bobbed," wrote one expatriate American journalist, "and the chances are better than even that she will reply 'because they do it in New York.'"[65] Another journalist called the pelona and her style "blemishes that have been infiltrating the Mexican woman from *yanqui* influence."[66] José Alvarez, a regular contributor to *El Hogar*, reported "burning in indignation" as he watched that "sticky-sweet Valentino, that Italian-American Adonis," corrupt Mexico's young women.[67] The short-lived pan-Americanist magazine *El Heraldo de la Raza*, which was published in Mexico City, included a regular column titled "Los Estados Unidos por dentro" (The United States from the Inside), which connected U.S. cinema with U.S imperialism in no uncertain terms. Frequent topics included girls who used cosmetics or defied their parents and left home to make their own way in the world and, above all else, the "muvimania" that plagued the United States and had created a society antithetical to that of Mexico and other Latin American countries.[68] For critics, the pelona—both as an icon that circulated in the popular press and in her real-life manifestations in the form of women such as Marina Vega and Esther Borgia Sforza—became symptomatic of North American cultural imperialism.

At the height of the press's attention to the pelona, reactions to women's adoption of new forms of femininity leaped off the pages of the popular press and came to life in the streets of Mexico City. "An attack worthy of reproach," announced one headline.[69] "An attack that dishonors the city," proclaimed another.[70] An unspecified number of male students from two of the nation's most respected institutions of higher education, the National School

of Medicine and the National Preparatory School, had attacked several pelonas in the street, dousing them with water and trying to shave their heads.
Pelonas, these young men maintained, were rejecting Mexican "tradition"
by adopting modes of self-presentation coded as American. Hair cropped
"à la bob," they argued—pointing to the bob's cultural kinship with the "taxi-
cab, the 'rapid lunch,' [and] the 'jazz-band,'"—represented a rejection of the
"dark braid" and "discreet nape" that symbolized the "glories" of traditional
Mexican femininity.[71]

The "war on pelonas," as the controversy came to be called, offers a striking example of the extremes to which those who feared the pelona's challenge to gender relations, racial hierarchies, and the social order might go
to curtail women's growing independence and mobility. The historian Anne
Rubenstein points out that as the story developed, women and their status
quickly became a mere secondary theme in the press.[72] Instead, newspaper
accounts and a very heated, public exchange of letters debated the treatment
of women and aggression toward them or in their defense not as a reflection
of women's fundamental rights as human beings or even as fellow citizens,
but as a manifestation of revolutionary Mexican masculinity. The various
male voices that chimed in to express solidarity with the pelonas covered the
political and social spectrum, from military cadets and medical students to
government bureaucrats, laborers, and even trolley car drivers.

A group of students of the National Preparatory School who repudiated
the actions of their peers declared that "the Latin spirit, highly gentleman-
like, rises up in these present moments . . . toward . . . honor and the protection of their women."[73] Some of these students made the rounds of various
girls' vocational and high schools to offer their sincerest apologies in person. While students worked overtime to prove themselves gentlemen, representatives of organized labor seized on the attacks as an opportunity to
strike a blow in the class struggle. Reynaldo Cervantes—a functionary of the
Comisión Nacional Agraría (the National Agrarian Commission), a federal
commission created in 1915 to deal with one of the central issues of the revolution, agrarian reform—wrote to the editor of *Excélsior*, arguing that "the
students have given proof of their absolute lack of morality and culture. . . .
[A]ny worker is more polite and knows how to respect a woman more than
a student, regardless of the books they study."[74] Back and forth, soldiers,
students, and workers took stabs at each others' masculinity, while the film
exhibitors used the incident to assure "peloncitas" that movie theaters were
places where they could be "without danger."[75]

On the surface, this widespread defense of the pelona may have seemed
progressive, even profeminist, but the male public's response to the war on

pelonas was profoundly patriarchal: men turned the debate around to focus not on women and their rights but on which group of men was the epitome of modern Mexican manhood. Some women even called the male response hypocritical. As Paula Gómez, a self-avowed pelona, noted in a letter to the federal prosecutor's office that was published in *Excélsior*, the official response did little to offer more protections to women; instead, it worked to maintain social order and reinforce dominant gender ideals. Men, Gómez asserted, copied North American fashions but were not in any danger of being attacked in the streets, let alone provoking nationwide discussions on their ability to occupy new public spaces of leisure or work.[76] The pelona had become a symbol not only of unease about women's increasingly public role in Mexican society, but also of the conflict between Mexico's nationalist project and American mass culture.

EDUCATING REAL WOMEN FOR THE PATRIA

In Mexico, women's relationship to their families and society underwent profound changes in the 1920s. The chaos of the revolution had split families apart, generated large-scale movements to urban areas, and drawn many young women into paid employment. Although working-class women had always been fixtures of public life in Mexico City, during this period the number of women who inhabited the city's public spaces, educational institutions, public transportation, and commercial leisure establishments increased significantly. What is more, women's participation in the formal labor market grew as more women found work in industries such as garment manufacturing and cigarette making, as well as in offices and shops.[77] These young women, many single and alone in the city, might fall prey to the false visions of glamour, romance, and luxury offered by American films. Conservatives and liberals alike agreed that such women required guidance if they were to fulfill their proper roles as wives and mothers in revolutionary society.

During the porfiriato, women—especially middle- and upper-class women—participated actively in the regime's "developmentalist" project, which the historian Alan Knight defines as "the current of ideas that stressed the need to develop Mexican society and economy, above all by disciplining, educating, and moralizing the degenerate Mexican masses."[78] To those ends, women engaged in activities linked to their domestic role, such as forming beneficent associations and performing charity work. During the revolution, women of all political persuasions and classes—most iconically the *soldaderas* (female soldiers or aides-de-camp that followed revolutionary troops into battle)—had been active advocates for social change. In the revolution's aftermath, women became key participants in the country's nation-building project. After the revolution, women's organizations—conservative, liberal, and radical alike—published periodicals, organized congresses, and cultivated relationships with women's organizations in other countries. Radical feminist groups, particularly in the Yucatán, agitated for female suffrage, but much of women's activism continued to focus on home and family. Yet despite the social upheaval of the revolution, Mexico's postrevolutionary feminine ideal was less a radical break with nineteenth-century gender ideology than a draping of those conventions in revolutionary rhetoric.

The discourse on the pelona makes clear that the cinema and its associations with the pleasures and dangers of urban life were considered by many to be antithetical to the cultivation of the honorable women that Mexico needed after years of internal strife. In *Jueves de Excélsior*, A. B. de Noriega worried explicitly that the mothers of tomorrow would become victims of the "enslaving influence of cinema . . . that invades us."[79] *La Dama Católica* chimed in, asserting that U.S. cinema was a "frivolous and corrupting influence" that produced "vain young women, with cosmetics but without brains, ignorant of modesty, and blind to what constitutes the dignity of life and womanhood."[80] Indeed, critics were convinced that the cinema's encouragement of "deviant" sexuality threatened to prevent the formation of strong heterosexual couples and productive families, social units that would in turn form the basis of a modern nation.

A close reading of a piece of popular fiction describing the effects of motion pictures on the women who were to form the backbone of the revolutionary family sheds light on what many Mexicans thought was at stake. The short story, "75 centavos," was published in *Revista de Revistas* in 1928. It focuses on the fate of Mercedes, the only daughter of a middle-class family that is slowly declining into genteel poverty after the revolution. American films and film culture entrance Mercedes. At home, much like Lola, la chica de Hollywood, she hangs photographs of American actors next to a statue of the Virgin Mary. The "flapper" has convinced her mother to buy a phonograph on credit and spends her time dreaming of a "house in the Colonia Roma [a fashionable new neighborhood in Mexico City] or maybe even further away in Hollywood or New York."[81]

Convinced by the film narratives she avidly consumes that "plebes become princesses," Mercedes longs for a boyfriend like the screen swains who engineer such transformations. Her longing seems to be answered when she meets Roberto Maria, a self-styled "successor to Valentino" with savoir faire and an expensive car—Maria does not know the car is just rented. The couple's first date takes place at a cinema. On subsequent dates, they go dancing at the cabaret on the theater's second floor. Before long, they are "engaged, like in the movies." But the narrator divulges the truth: Roberto is actually an apprentice to a linotypist and earns only seventy-five cents a day. He spins tales drawn from film narratives to impress Mercedes and her family—"a nighttime walk in Venice, a reception with the prince of Wales, a roulette game in Monte Carlo." With each tale he seduces Mercedes further away from her medical student beau and the boring but stable life of a middle-class wife and mother.[82]

In a predictably melodramatic climax, Mercedes marries Roberto after her disapproving mother's convenient death. And instead of a luxurious home in the Colonia Roma, Mercedes finds herself living in a *vecindad* (a multifamily dwelling common in Mexico City's poor neighborhoods) with a deadbeat husband. In the squalor of their one-room apartment, Mercedes realizes that his resemblance to "Yanquis" who used "stacomb" (a hair gel) and wore a "smoking-balloon" (a suit composed of a smoking jacket and wide-legged pants) is an illusion. After one protest "worthy of a film star," Mercedes finds herself taking in sewing, begging, and finally being arrested for circulating counterfeit bills given to her by Roberto.[83] The end of the story finds Mercedes in jail and Roberto seducing other women with the trappings of luxury. Clearly, Roberto is the wrong sort of man, but Mercedes's poor decisions, which prompt her to enter into an unproductive union, are framed as the result of desires awakened by her indiscriminate consumption of motion pictures. Thus, steering girls away from the moral dangers of American cinema by providing alternative models of modern womanhood was, in the words of the Damas Católicas, "constructive, patriotic labor!"[84]

In opposition to Mercedes (or Marina Vega, for that matter), another ideal modern women was taking shape, one who engaged scrupulously with mass culture without allowing herself to "degenerate into grotesque imitation" or fall prey to the cinema's illusions. Such a woman worked not to satisfy her personal desires, but to support her family. She was "strong and sweet" and brought "joy to life, warm[th] to the home [and] vigor to the patria."[85] In contrast to the radical feminism that conservative critics associated with the United States, "true Mexican feminism," as the journalist Margarita Santín Fontoura noted in *El Hogar*, was a maternal feminism through which women advocated on behalf of their parents, husbands, and children.[86] In other words, the ideal modern Mexican woman participated in the necessary work of creating the strong families that constituted the nation's building blocks, literally and figuratively reproducing the revolutionary citizens of tomorrow.

This modern woman can be found in the film *Tepeyac* (Films Colonial,

1917), which presents a version of Mexican femininity the Damas would have applauded. *Tepeyac* takes as its subject the legend of the miraculous appearance of the Virgin of Guadalupe, Mexico's archetypal symbol of femininity and racial mixing, to the Indian Juan Diego in December 1531. The film, which is set in contemporary times, has a simple plot: a young couple torn apart by disaster is subsequently reunited through the miraculous intervention of the Virgin. Briefly, Carlos, the lead male character, leaves Mexico on a mysterious diplomatic mission. His ship is torpedoed, his fate uncertain. His fiancée—Lupita, whose name is a diminutive of Guadalupe—seeks solace in religious devotion, which motivates a flashback to the colonial era and the presentation of the story of the Virgin's appearance. After Carlos returns safe and sound, the couple demonstrate their gratitude by going to the Basilica of Guadalupe on the Virgin's feast day, a trip that closes the romantic narrative. This simple romantic drama frames a retelling of the story of the apparition.

In the film, the Virgin of Guadalupe functions as an appropriate object of a woman's sustained visual attention and emotional energy. Lupita's devotion to the Virgin is cast as the right sort of looking; it is a practice that serves as a generational bond, is coded as an appropriate outlet for her youthful passions, and, in the end, facilitates the achievement of heterosexual partnership, prefiguring the family formation thought to be essential to the advancement of the nation. Throughout, Lupita's identity is circumscribed by the home and its social embodiment, the family.

The identity of other characters is also expressed through their association with particular spaces and the way they are framed in those spaces. The film opens in Mexico's seat of secular power, the Castle of Chapultepec. In a sequence of medium shots, Carlos moves through that space in an automobile to the offices of the Secretaria de Relaciones Exteriores (Ministry of Foreign Relations, or State Department). Beyond associating Carlos visually with these architectural symbols of political power, this sequence establishes that Carlos's natural domain is public space. Carlos is a mobile subject whose movement is facilitated by a series of modern modes of transportation—automobiles, trains, and an ocean liner—technologies that enable him to realize his modern cosmopolitan citizenship.

In contrast, Lupita is shown in the family home. She strays only as far as the liminal zones of a balcony full of potted plants and a lower patio. There, in the interior of the family home—which conspicuously lacks a father figure—the camera moves in closer to its subjects. The living room is cozily decorated with richly carved furniture, flowers, and draperies, emblems of middle-class status. Lupita and Carlos are shown together to the left of the foreground, discussing his eminent departure. They both rise, and she leaves

FIGURE 4.6 Lupita at her home altar with her mother. Frame enlargement from
Tepeyac (1917). Courtesy Filmoteca de la Universidad Nacional de Mexico.

the frame to enter what one suspects is an even more intimate space, returning with a medal of the Virgin that she pins to his lapel. A cut to a close-up
emphasizes both the action and hints at its subsequent narrative importance.
The camera moves back to a close medium shot for the brief and chaste farewell kiss that precedes his exit. The next series of shots, the only example of
crosscutting in the film, shows the couple exchanging affectionate glances
from their respectively gendered spaces.

Lupita is characterized as emotional and expressive, but those qualities
are safely contained within the confines of domestic space and given an
appropriate outlet in religious practice. Two examples convey this characterization. First, when Lupita receives news, information conveyed to the
spectator via a textual insert, of the sinking of Carlos's ship, she crumples a
newspaper in her hands and clutches it to her chest in anguish. That action
is emphasized by light that enters the patio from above and highlights her
body; she is framed by the pillar she leans against. Likewise, when that action
is repeated in the next shot, her mother takes the place of the pillar, and the
doorway serves as a frame. In the sequence that follows, Lupita's emotional
distress is displaced onto a series of objects that she either touches or looks

at: a rosary, the image of the Virgin hanging above the family altar, and finally the devotional book she peruses.

The first part of the contemporary narrative, which sets up the dramatic tension of the film, establishes domestic space and religious practice as key axes of Lupita's subjectivity. In the bookend frame we discern a third axis— her status as part of a heterosexual couple. When the couple visits the Basilica as an expression of gratitude to the Virgin, they are shown as a unit that the camera follows and seeks out when they seem lost in the crowd of indigenous bodies in front of the church. In the film's final sequence, the couple climbs the hill to the spring that marks the site where the Virgin is supposed to have appeared and look out over the church and the city below. An intertitle informs us of what each is thinking as they gaze out onto the city. Carlos recalls the "sacred sign" that became a potent political symbol, Lupita her religious devotion. Their "unending happiness," and that of the nation, depends on their appropriately gendered acts of looking at the nation and its past. *Tepeyac* produces a type of femininity and gendered practices of looking that are diametrically opposed to the sort engaged in by Marina Vega, the pelona, or the fictional Mercedes.

Tepeyac provided audiences with a fictional example of appropriate viewing practices, but public discourse about events like the shorthand and typing contest sponsored by the newspaper *Excélsior* in 1922 celebrated another type of young woman for contributing to Mexico's modernization and positioned these women visually as important protagonists in the nation's development. The 350 women who participated in the contest were described as "pretty," "hardworking," and "virtuous."[87] In addition to receiving prizes— which included medals; cash; and an evening's entertainment of music, theater, and dancing—the contestants had their photographs published in the newspaper, and the contest itself became the subject of a short film produced by Germán Camus and Cia.

That film, a newspaper description tells us, "begins with a 'close-up' in which appear [first] the hands of four young women that lightly glide over the keyboard of the machines." "Later," the description continues, "you see the full bodies of the typists, pretty, able, and cheerful." This was followed by wider shots that showcased the "beautiful scene" of the women, the government officials present, and the architecture of the colonial-era building in which the contest was held.[88] This description of the Camus film, now considered lost, suggests a representational strategy that used the cinema to connect these young women's productive mastery of technology to official nation-building projects.

Other public events were more straightforward about their goal of teach-

FIGURE 4.7
Employees of
M. E. Raya &
Company posing
with a Royal
typewriter, 1920.
© (165859),
CONACULTA
.INAH.SINAFO
.FN.MÉXICO.

ing women in appropriate ways to engage with film culture. For example, the *1928 Vestido Ecónomico* (economic dress) contest, sponsored by *El Universal*, a rival of *Excélsior*, was framed explicitly as a remedy for the problem of excessive or inappropriate consumption. Young women, divided into the categories of factory workers, secretaries and other office workers, and vocational school students, would compete to make the most stylish, well-designed dress for less than fifteen pesos (approximately seven 1928 U.S. dollars).[89]

Helping women dress economically would, the contest's promoters asserted, prevent them from becoming slaves to the "too-real-to-be-true hallucinations of the screen," while educating the working classes in a "[pure] concept of elegance."[90] In support of the latter goal, one contestant, described as an attractive blonde typist, expressed her hope that the contest would prevent the future recurrence of the scandal of seeing "girls who show off their crass ignorance, dressed for an evening party with generous décolletage at eleven o'clock in the morning, or who go to the theater or parties in suits."[91] Perhaps most important, the contest would help working women become the "companions of [their] future husbands" by teaching them how to "exercise true economy."[92] Learning how to make attractive and inexpensive clothes would prevent fights between husbands and wives over excessive spending and, by "educating women for the home," arm them with the skills necessary to contribute to Mexico's advancement.[93]

Although framed as a reaction to the perceived corrosive effects of the cinema, the contest drew heavily on the elements of cinematic culture in order to appeal to potential participants. Meeting the challenge required ingenuity, creativity, and imagination, and it promised publicity. The contestants participated in rounds of competition modeled on fashion shows, and the winning designs, modeled by their designers, were featured on the newspaper's front page. Unlike cinematic discourse—where dressing well became a source of personal pleasure, romantic possibility, and social mobility—the contest focused on fashion as a source of national pride and a means of demonstrating the "economizing and the purest simplicity" that should form the foundation of the Mexican family.[94] Even though, as the images circulated from the contest suggest, young women had not left their taste for bobbed hair and short skirts behind, these types of programmatic public events sought to frame women's engagement with film culture and their desire to adopt the styles and personae they saw on screen in ways that would benefit Mexican society.

CHINAS POBLANAS IN CINELANDIA

Despite the circulation of these alternative models of modern Mexican femininity, mexicanas, like their counterparts across the world, were seduced by the "growing cult of celebrity" that characterized the early Hollywood film industry.[95] If the comments of journalists are to be believed, many women—young and not so young, well off and poor—contemplated leaving Mexico in hopes of becoming cinema heroines. Writer and film critic Carlos Noriega Hope reported receiving numerous "blue and red [envelopes] that smell of cheap perfume and young flesh" from young women—"Carmen, Josefina, Maria, Enriqueta, Dolores, and Esperanza"—asking for the addresses of Hollywood film studios.[96] These young women, he wrote, were eager to leave the "numbing mediocrity" of their lives, in order to "throw themselves into the world to live the intense life of serial films."[97] Similarly, the editor of El Hogar described receiving voluminous correspondence from young women who wanted to "abandon the tranquil homes of their parents" for Hollywood.[98]

Many of these letters pointed to the biographies of film stars published in magazines as the chief source of these dreams.[99] As in the United States, the rags-to-riches fantasy of arriving in Hollywood from some small town and becoming the latest star was a potent part of Mexican fan culture, spread in large part through the fan discourse that was translated, reprinted, and circulated in the local press. In addition to the numerous articles that translated features from the American press about the lives of female stars, their career trajectories, and the latest Hollywood gossip, by the late 1920s accounts of Dolores del Río's meteoric rise to fame were widely publicized and avidly consumed by Mexicans on both sides of the border. This proliferation of texts that narrated stars' rise from anonymity fueled the desires of Mexican girls who were, like aspiring starlets from the Midwest, a mere train ride away from Los Angeles and who did not need to speak English to imagine themselves on screen.

As often as profiles and features celebrated stardom and proffered enticing tales of a rise from obscurity to fame, Spanish-language magazines and newspapers on both sides of the border warned girls of the dangers in store for the majority of aspiring starlets.[100] Even Noriega Hope—a cinema enthusiast if ever there was one—called the movies a "fatal mirage" and urged women to resign themselves to their workaday lives.[101] In December 1926 La Opinión, Los Angeles's largest Spanish-language daily, elaborated on Noriega Hope's warning. Under the alarming headline "Huge Exodus of Mexican Women," the paper informed its readers that women, some as young as fifteen, were—like Marina Vega—abandoning their homes in droves and marching across the border toward Hollywood.[102] The explanation that followed offered a Mexican twist on the familiar cautionary tale about Anglo-American women and the moral dangers of the longing for stardom, which has been explored by Shelley Stamp and Heidi Kenaga.[103]

According to the article, scores of young Mexican women were abandoning hearth and home and marching off to Cinelandia in the hope of becoming movie stars. And as the article put it, the Mexican government, which was "justifiably alarmed by the growing exodus," had every intention of halting this wholesale desertion by stopping any young woman trying to cross the border without her husband or another "honorable" (male) member of her family. As it turned out, the article's interpretation of recent changes to Mexican migration regulations proved to be misinformed—girls were, from the perspective of Mexican officials, as free to travel as they had ever been—but the explanation for this phantom restriction illuminates the anxiety provoked by the desire of young women to see the world and to see themselves objects of public adulation around the world.

The article in *La Opinión* offered the story of the "latest frustrated escape" as an explanation for the government's purported actions. Two young girls from "honorable metropolitan families"—perhaps adolescents, although the article is vague on this point—had left their homes for Hollywood, determined to become film stars. They financed their journey by stealing a variety of valuable objects from their homes. However, the girls' plan fell apart, according to the article, when they failed to take into account the "astute vigilance of the secret police that guard the train stations daily." Officials had become suspicious of the two girls traveling alone, reading their rosy faces as either a sign of youthful health (and exposure to the morning air) or as evidence of their fugitive status. The newspaper reported that under interrogation, the girls broke down in tears and confessed that they had indeed been "preparing themselves to leave in the direction of Hollywood." Shamed, the two would-be-adventuresses marched off "sad and repentant with their parents to receive the punishment warranted by their failed deed."[104]

La Opinión's sensational and potentially titillating story of young girls on the lam echoes other stories published in Mexican newspapers in the early 1920s. A representative example, published in *El Demócrata* in 1923, related how two sisters had assembled their best dresses and personal effects (including jewelry that had been purchased for them by their clearly well-off families) in preparation for their journey to Hollywood, which they mistakenly thought was in San Francisco. To the girls' chagrin, an observant parent—instead of an agent of the state—foiled their dreams of meeting Rudolf Valentino and Antonio Moreno and experiencing "tremendous adventures in California's wide open spaces." Their father's presentation of the facts of the case at the local police station—his daughters' intention of abandoning the family home and his suspicions about the perverse intentions of a neighbor, the girls' abettor—was motivated by his desire to put a stop to the "vice that had extended throughout Mexico in such a manner that love could only be obtained at such high prices." It is unclear whether the "love" referred to was that of girls for their movie stars or of parents for their children, but clearly fandom had, at least in the eyes of respectable *padres de familia* (parents) become another danger of contemporary life.[105]

In the first narrative, it is implied that the girls' desire for "adventure" was prompted by their habits of moviegoing—a cautionary tale that mirrors Marina Vega's. In the second narrative, the girls had been led into deceiving their family by a "friend" who had exposed them to "American 'magazines,' the supplementary pages of newspapers, [and] books with anecdotes from the lives of movie stars."[106] Clearly, film culture incited desires that threatened the educated, middle-class household, the building blocks of postrevolutionary Mexico. These stories offered models of parental control and family-state cooperation that promised to contain women's desires for mobility, autonomy, and sexual freedom. The continuous and ever-increasing influx of U.S. films and film culture, however, made checking girls' desire to go to Hollywood as unlikely as stopping the flood of Mexican laborers crossing the border. Girls' desires for the liberation that stardom represented would need to be channeled so that they could be used for rather than against Mexico's nation-building project.

Much of the discourse about cinema circulating in the Mexican popular press presented the cinema as a powerful tool that could calm antipathies and foster cultural rapprochement. Actors who could represent Mexico in Hollywood and on screen were central to this project. A 1927 editorial in *La Opinión* staked this claim baldly: Mexican stars working in Hollywood would "destroy existing prejudices." Since cinema could reach both "the grand metropolis" and the "smallest village" simultaneously, American feature films starring Mexican actors would ensure that "all the publics would form a better conception of Mexico."[107] Thus, under the right circumstances, becoming a star could be important political labor.

The textual construction of stars Dolores del Rio and Lupe Vélez in the Spanish-language press—both in Mexico and in the United States—emphasized the patriotic dimensions of their rise to stardom. The fan magazine versions of their lives contained important lessons about the need to square the quest for celebrity with the needs of the nation. For example, the radical nature of the aristocratic Del Rio's decision to pursue a career in Hollywood was invariably tempered by the fact that she went to Hollywood accompanied by her mother and with the blessing of her husband. The press praised del Rio for her insistence on being identified as Mexican rather than Spanish, while scolding Vélez for perpetuating stereotypes though her popular character, the Mexican Spitfire, even as she was celebrated for representing Mexico on screen. Each actress was asked to make her stardom serve the nation, reinforcing ideas about stardom as a patriotic act.[108]

In the spring of 1923 this patriotic service took the form of a beauty contest star search jointly sponsored by Paramount Pictures, the liberal daily *El Demócrata*, and the American-owned Circuito Olimpia, which was one of Mexico City's largest theater chains. At the end of the contest, the young woman who had garnered the most votes from an audience composed of "workers, students, drivers, truckers, military men, and office employees" would win a trip to Hollywood, the opportunity to star in a Paramount Pictures production, and the chance to "meet and live with famous Paramount stars."[109]

FIGURE 4.8 A ballot coupon for *La Estrella del Sur* contest, positioning the winner between Los Angeles (Hollywood) and Mexico, *El Demócrata*, April 1, 1923. From the collections of the Hemeroteca Nacional de México.

Its promoters proposed that the contest would achieve two goals at once. First, it would provide an appropriate outlet for young women on the verge of being ruined by American mass culture. *El Demócrata* described the contest hyperbolically as a cure for young girls—"virgins," was the word it used—to whom the cinema offered "crazy panoramas through which their juvenile anxieties are shipwrecked, spurred by the enslaving horseman of temptation." And second, it would be an important tool of diplomacy, improving Mexico's international reputation through what had become the most powerful disseminator of images and ideologies: Hollywood films. The triumph of the contest's winner in Hollywood would be "for the glory of Mexico"; the winner's success and the nation's would be one and the same.[110]

The ballot coupon published in *El Demócrata* depicted this nationally sanctioned immigration fantasy in visual terms. The image pictured "Mexico" in the form of a stylized colonial church and Los Angeles as a cluster of skyscrapers. In the center is a glamorous young woman, her face half covered by her flowing head wrap. A cameraman and a director in the act of directing the woman's activities in front of the camera appear in the midground to the left, aligned visually with Mexico. Appropriate relationships between the two countries and the appropriate crossing of national borders, the image implies, might be possible in the person of the modern woman, provided that she remain in the middle of the two countries. Training her focus on the needs and demands of the nation (letting them "direct" her), the image implies, will ensure that she does not cross over completely to the American side.

Throughout the months of front-page news coverage devoted to the competition, aspiring actresses' desire to become "la estrella del sur" (the star of the South), and the public's participation were explicitly framed in nationalist terms. One contender proclaimed her desire to "make films in favor of Mexico, films that will be 'pro' Mexican civilization and increase the prestige of *la raza*." Another declared that the winner's stardom would "put the name of her homeland in its proper place in the United States."[111] The contest was represented in the press as a nationally unifying activity, as entries came in from all over Mexico. In the capital, groups of laborers picked their own favorite would-be starlet and campaigned on her behalf (with telephone workers and truck drivers favoring the contestant Adela Sequeyro (who would go on to become Mexico's first female film director). In June 1923, as the competition drew to a close, *El Demócrata* presented vivid accounts of the tallying of the votes, framing a typical Hollywood publicity scheme as an exercise in democracy.[112]

The media frenzy surrounding the naming of the winner, Honoria Suárez, reinforced the nationalist dimensions of the contest. *El Demócrata* assured its readers that she would be the "vanquisher of prejudices and erroneous concepts in the heart of *yanquilandia*." The press avidly followed Suárez's journey to Hollywood, declaring that her triumph had been the "fruit of popular justice," which assured her success.[113]

In the end, though, Honoria Suárez's sojourn in Hollywood was not the success that many had hoped for. She was given a screen test and small roles in two Paramount shorts. One of them, *Honoria Suárez en Hollywood* (considered lost), showed Honoria being shown around Paramount Studios by Antonio Moreno, watching several films being shot, chatting with Cecil B. DeMille, and finally appearing in a short "try-out" with the Italian actor Geno Corrado. All of these efforts received poor reviews. Other Mexico City newspapers criticized *El Demócrata* for thinking that the democratic process could dictate celebrity, with Honoria herself eventually admitting that she had been a failure in Hollywood. For the next few years, she shuttled back and forth between Mexico City and Los Angeles, attempting to revive her career. But unlike the contest's runner-ups, she was never put under contract for any national production, and in October 1926 she died alone and penniless in Los Angeles. She was not yet twenty-five.[114]

FIGURE 4.9 Honoria
Suárez remembered
four years after
her death as one
of Mexico's stars
in Hollywood, *El
Universal Ilustrado*,
February 23, 1927.
From the collections
of the Hemeroteca
Nacional de México.

Honoria Suárez
dora "estrella'
en un concurso,
Hollywood...

In death as in the initial golden glow of her victory, Suárez was treated
as a national heroine by the Mexican government. Her body lay in state at
the funeral home of Cunningham and O'Connor in downtown Los Angeles,
where, as one reporter declared, she appeared to be still "under the influence
of a dream." The local Mexican community's elite held a requiem mass in her
honor at the Temple of Our Lady of Los Angeles, the first church established
in the city and the center of Mexican immigrant religious life. The Mexican
consul in Los Angeles arranged for a temporary interment at Calvary Cemetery in East Los Angeles before her body was shipped back to Mexico for
permanent burial. Honoria's dream of becoming a star never came to fruition in life, but her personal aspirations for fame, wealth, and independence
continued to be marshaled in the service of Mexican nation building even
after her death.[115]

CONCLUSION

The contradictory public discourse about the Mexico-to-Hollywood journeys of Mexico's frequently anonymous female movie fans illuminates the gendered dimensions of the intersection between American films and film culture and Mexico's postrevolutionary nationalism. The embrace of American film culture by Mexican women, an embrace materialized in the figure of the pelona, alarmed both the conservative elite like the Damas, who longed for the social order that the revolution had sought to overcome, and the liberal elite, which sought to manage the emerging social order—including gender norms—to consolidate its political power. For example, José Vasconcelos, the head of the Secretaría de Educación Pública (Ministry of Public Education) from 1921 to 1924 and one of the chief promoters of modernization through secularization, sided with the Damas in their complaints against *Juventud ardiente*, though he surely took issue with their religious convictions. "I am entirely in agreement," he wrote to the organization in response to their public letters of complaint, "with the point of view that you express." He agreed with the Damas not only in regard to the particular film in question, but also in regard to their assessment of the "damage the cinema causes." All films, he opined, were "infinitely vulgar and in poor taste."[116]

Vasconcelos might have made an exception for *Tepeyac*, had he seen it. That film presented an ideal version of modern Mexican womanhood in which women were seen in the context of their roles as daughters, wives, and future mothers, and when they looked outside the confines of the domestic sphere they had eyes only for the nation. In contrast, the looking practices of movie fans like Marina Vega focused on objects of desire, whether movie stars or the latest fashions, and produced the desire to be seen as objects of desire themselves in the public sphere. This new modern sense of self—intimately tied, as Hillary Hallett has argued to new forms of sexuality that accompanied the spread of film culture—was at odds with Mexico's nation-building project.[117]

A range of social groups attempted to direct women's practices of looking and to manage women's desire to be looked at. For Paramount, the Estrella del Sur contest was likely just another publicity stunt designed to draw attention to the studio's films and stars. In Mexico, however, the contest presented an alternative Mexico-to-Hollywood migration, in which young women's desire to cross borders could contribute to the well-being of the nation. Implicit in the discourse surrounding the event was the belief that U.S. film culture—and stardom, in particular—could be used to nationalist ends, although doing so required guidance from Mexico's cultural and intellectual elite. In the Mexican cultural imagination, Honoria—failure though she was—and other Mexican actresses who had secured bit parts in Hollywood productions and would go on to participate in the national industry that emerged in the 1930s took their place alongside Dolores del Rio (who was dubbed "our artistic ambassador in the Hollywood studios") as representatives of the nation in the global media culture being created by the American film industry.[118] In this way the pernicious influence of American mass culture, as women's fandom was characterized, could be corrected and women's desire for autonomy and self-determination could be channeled not toward social change, but to shoring up the nation-state and reinforcing its patriarchal structure.

5 DENIGRATING PICTURES
Censorship and the Politics of U.S. Film in Greater Mexico

Who will restore the truth to its just dominion, when the industry in Hollywood, teacher par excellence of the North American people, writes history like this?
—"TÓPICOS CINEMATOGRÁFICOS: LOS PELIGROS DE LA PANTALLA
COMO MEDIO DE PROPAGANDA Y EDUCACIÓN COLECTIVA,"
LA OPINIÓN, JANUARY 3, 1928

We fear that "Why Worry" is being regarded altogether more seriously than it warrants.
—LETTER FROM COURBET BROTHERS TO MANUEL TÉLLEZ,
MEXICAN AMBASSADOR TO THE UNITED STATES, 1923

The fifth most popular film in the United States in 1923 was Harold Lloyd's farcical comedy *Why Worry?*[1] In the film, Lloyd plays a wealthy hypochondriac, Harold Van Pelham, who visits an "island paradise" somewhere in Latin America for a "rest cure." But instead of rest, he encounters a revolution, a revolution he initially believes has been staged for his personal entertainment—not unlike the way many Americans in the Southwest seemed to have perceived the Mexican Revolution.[2] Once Van Pelham realizes the revolution is real, however, he and a giant named Colosso defend themselves against a band of buffoonish soldiers, all to comic effect. Initially, there seems to have been some confusion about where exactly the film's story was set. One review in the *New York Times* claimed that the film "revolves around a miniature revolution in South America," while a second review, published just a few days later in the same paper, locates the action in "Paradise, somewhere in Mexico."[3] This confusion formed the crux of the controversy that the film engendered between its producer, Hal E. Roach Studios, its distributor, Pathé Exchange, and the Mexican government.

Though popular with U.S. domestic audiences, *Why Worry?* was decidedly unpopular with Mexican moviegoers. One Mexican viewer, most likely a diplomat, who saw the film at New York's Strand Theater offered Mexico's consul general in New York a detailed analysis of the film's offensive qualities, which he sent along with the theater's printed program and other advertising material. The film portrayed Mexico, he wrote, as a country "composed exclusively of poor peons of the lowest order" and the Mexican army as a gaggle of "busybodies."[4] Despite its being set in the "Republic of Paradise," the locale could only be understood to be Mexico. The writer pointed to the ubiquitous presence of a tricolor flag (complete with the national symbol of an eagle devouring a serpent), adobe buildings, and the sombrero, headwear associated worldwide with Mexico. Twenty minutes into the film, he reported, the giant plays a game of ninepins with Mexican soldiers. Other scenes of this type could be found throughout the film, culminating in an elaborately staged battle scene, which depicted "thousands" of Mexican soldiers fleeing a hailstorm of first tomatoes and then coconuts "like cowardly puppets."[5]

Why Worry? generated a flurry of other complaints. The Mexican consul in Milwaukee wrote to Lloyd himself, asking the star for his "co-operation in helping to eliminate characterizing the Mexican as an indolent person and the country as being run-over by revolutionists and bandits."[6] In San Francisco the matter wound its way to the city's office of censorship, which determined that the film violated a municipal ordinance forbidding the exhibition of films that encouraged "race hatred."[7] When one of the city's local theaters refused to stop showing the film, however, a staffer at the Mexican consulate filed a suit against the theater. A judge subsequently found that the film could not be considered denigrating, given its location in the "utopian country of 'Paradiso,'" but ordered the exhibitor to make cuts wherever the Mexican flag appeared. When the theater refused, its manager was arrested — an act that precipitated *Why Worry?*'s departure once and for all from San Francisco's movie theaters.[8] In the wake of these complaints, Manuel Téllez, the Mexican ambassador to the United States, exchanged a series of letters with Lloyd's lawyers, who opined that they felt the film, a comedy, was "being regarded altogether more seriously than it warrants."[9] Téllez replied with a short history of the U.S. film industry's representation of Mexico and Mexicans and declared that he had "a list of hundreds of pictures produced during the past twelve years in which the Mexican people [had] been so unjustly or maliciously depicted," which he was happy to send along.[10]

FIGURE 5.1 Harold Van Pelham (Harold Lloyd) and his sidekick, the giant Colosso (John Aasen), triumph over members of Paraiso's military. Still from *Why Worry?* (1923). Courtesy the Harold Lloyd Trust.

As the flap over *Why Worry?* illustrates, the U.S. film industry's representation of Mexico and Mexicans became the source of political conflict between the two countries. Indeed in the early 1920s, the Mexican government attempted to censor U.S. films not because of their moral content, but because they were rife with stereotypes that undermined the government's desire to project an image of Mexico as a modern nation. In contrast to other countries where moral concerns shaped the development of official censorship programs, in Mexico representations of the nation, by both domestic and foreign filmmakers, became the focal point of domestic censorship efforts, although those efforts were resisted by exhibitors who perceived them as an obstacle to the growth of the exhibition industry. In large part, the urgency of this task stemmed from the fact that many of the very symbols being mobilized to create a cohesive, postrevolutionary national identity—the *charro* and the revolutionary, for example—were being used in Hollywood's racist depictions of Mexico.

In 1922 an embargo against films produced in the United States (engendered by the controversy over films like *Why Worry?*) led to a series of talks with representatives of the newly formed Motion Picture Producers and Distributors of America (MPPDA) and, ultimately, the employment of a range of formal strategies designed to obscure settings and the national origins of characters that U.S. filmmakers hoped would appease the Mexican government. Negotiations with Mexico were just one of the tasks taken up by the MPPDA, which was attempting to control the industry's public image in the wake of a series of star scandals and to fend off efforts to censor films at the state and local level.[11] Those talks established a framework of negotiation and appeasement through which, as Ruth Vasey explains, the MPPDA would negotiate with various foreign governments about their complaints.[12] For the U.S. film industry the embargo constituted a barrier to profits abroad of just the type it was trying to avoid and, perhaps, a minor public relations controversy, but for the Mexican public (at home and abroad) the embargo brought to the fore conflicting popular interpretations of what it meant to be a citizen.

The literature on censorship during the silent and early sound era has shifted from accounts of the institutions and individuals who acted as censors, imposing a set of rules or regulations on specific film texts, to a consideration of the productive forces of censorship. For example, Annette Kuhn argues that censorship does not merely act on film texts but, out of a set of relationships between different institutions and social groups, produces "cinema as a public sphere of a particular kind" that includes a certain type of film consumer, categories of films that can or cannot be censored, and even ways of reading films.[13] Lee Grieveson, in turn, traces the way that regulatory bodies and the film industry's negotiations around not just content, but also the social function of cinema—education or entertainment—produced the fictional narrative as the dominant film form in early twentieth-century America.[14] Focused on sexuality and its relationship to class in the first case, and to a broad range of sensational or otherwise controversial films in the second, this research has established that censorship generates types of films, narrative forms, audiences, categories, and so on rather than simply regulating what images can and cannot be seen on screen.

In terms of censorship in Mexico, the state's perception of cinema as an industry that could contribute to the country's economic growth ultimately led to the development of a collaborative, rather than adversarial, relationship between U.S. film studios and the Mexican government. Taking advantage of the "Open Door" established by the MPPA that, as Vasey explains, allowed "specific lobby groups to influence aspects of motion picture production," the Mexican government focused on influencing the content of U.S.-produced films that took up Mexican themes or narratives rather than curtailing the circulation of films within its borders or even in other Latin

American countries.[15] This détente—which conformed to the role that the MPPDA and its Studio Relations Committee had established for special interest groups in the production process—was not, however, the most significant outcome of attempts to censor American films; indeed, at the end of the 1920s Mexico seemed to wield only slightly more influence than it had at the beginning of the decade. Rather, whether for or against the government's embargo, Mexican audiences on either side of the border united in viewing U.S. films through the lens of an emerging postrevolutionary nationalism. That is, the Mexican government's censorship policies and the discourse about them made the nation the primary lens through which films, domestic and foreign, could and should be seen, even as what constituted the nation and the national was negotiated by different stakeholders: diplomats, cinema owners and workers, and migrants to the United States. The category "national cinema" emerged from this dynamic as more than a reference to the site of production or thematic content. Instead, in the debate over censoring denigrating films, the national dimensions of cinema emerged as a set of ideas about the role cinema should play in international relations and domestic nation-building projects and how Mexicans, as Mexicans, should read film texts.

DENIGRATING FILMS: A SHORT HISTORY

Racist images of Mexico and its citizens abounded in American silent films.[16] Taking their cue from a long tradition in U.S. popular culture of portraying of Mexico and Mexicans, filmmakers mobilized stereotypes of Mexicans as sneaky, savage, hypersexualized, or simply primitively picturesque.[17] Mexican themes had a place among the filmed vaudeville acts and scenes from foreign lands that populated the earliest motion picture productions. For example, the Edison Kinetoscope catalogue from 1895 included an entry for the film *Pedro Esquirel* [Esquivel] *and Dionicio Gonzales—Mexican Knife Duel*, which featured cast members from Buffalo Bill's Wild West Show. The film, advertised as "full of action, exciting and interesting," appealed—as the title indicates—to audiences' perception of Mexicans as primitive and violent.[18]

As the "cinema of attractions," as Tom Gunning and others have described early cinema, gave way to films with more complex narratives, Mexican characters became stock figures in early westerns.[19] Scholars such as Arthur Pettit, Gary D. Keller, and, most recently, Charles Ramírez Berg and Rosa Linda Fregoso have documented the ways in which American films with western or border themes employed the Mexican "greaser" as a convenient foil for the white protagonist's heroic reestablishment of the diegetic social order.[20] Films such as *The Greaser's Gauntlet* (Biograph, 1908), *Ah Sing and the*

Greasers (Lubin, 1910), *Tony, the Greaser* (Méliès, 1911), *The Greaser and the Weakling* (American Film, 1912), and *The Girl and the Greaser* (American Film, 1913) flattened out the complicated history of Mexico's presence in the U.S. Southwest as they supported imperial visions of relations between the two countries.[21]

During the 1910s, the Mexican Revolution became a multimedia spectacle, bringing the greasers of the screen to life. U.S. citizens gathered information about the revolution from journalistic accounts that ranged from the sympathetic coverage of John Reed to the yellow journalism of William Randolph Hearst's newspaper empire, as well as from postcards and photographs that presented images of the conflict and its actors that were skewed by racist perceptions of Mexicans.[22] The revolution provided an endless source of fascination for U.S. newsreel and feature film producers. These films, which helped shape public opinion, reflected the U.S. government's stance toward the war (which changed over time, though it was always self-interested) and, even when sympathetic, relied on Americans' long-held racial stereotypes.[23]

After the revolution ended, early Hollywood features continued to use Mexican characters and themes, portraying Mexican men as violent and barbarous, lazy and weak, or buffoonish and inept, depending on the demands of the narrative.[24] All the while, the sultry señorita continued to sway her hips and bat her eyelashes. More than anything, these characters assured Anglo-American audiences of their racial superiority at a moment of massive and controversial Mexican immigration to the United States—immigration that was invoked to justify discrimination and even violence, while providing a rationale for American economic imperialism and intervention in Mexico's internal affairs. This proliferation of fantasy *mexicanidad* coincided with Hollywood's increasingly global reach. As the film studies scholar Andrea Noble puts it, Mexico had an "image problem."[25]

Although it is difficult to determine with certainty how many Mexican-themed films produced by U.S. companies were ultimately screened in Mexico, those that were seen by Mexican audiences on either side of the border routinely caused outrage. For example, in 1913 a travelogue/newsreel called *A Trip through Barbarous Mexico: Madero versus Díaz* (aka *Barbarous Mexico*, America's Feature Film Co.) elicited complaints from the Mexican consul in Chicago. The film featured footage of horse races, bullfights, and the floating gardens of Xochimilco (an attraction for domestic and international tourists alike), as well as footage of the revolutionary leader Francisco Madero's inauguration, an uprising against Madero led by one of his generals, and the ensuing destruction in Mexico City. In truth, the Mexican consul could find nothing objectionable in the film itself. Rather, he objected to the film's marketing, which sensationalized its subject matter. One advertisement published in the trade publication *Moving Picture World*, for example, promised readers images of "actual warfare," encapsulating the rhetoric that concerned the consul: "Mexico as she really is today, mingling together its beauties and its terrors. A country full of wonderful scenery, interesting pleasure reports, and amusements that have not changed since the days of Nero."[26] The consul demanded that the State Theater in Chicago's Loop district remove the word "barbarous," which he found a "public offense to my country," from all advertising.[27] The city's authorities made a desultory effort at appeasing the consul by agreeing to paint over the word "barbarous." When the consul next visited the theaters in the Loop, he saw that the film's sensational advertising campaign had continued uninterrupted.[28]

Other films did contain offensive content. A film identified by *Excélsior* as *El verdadero México* purportedly showed scenes of the markets of Texcoco (a small town north of Mexico City) "with two dozen semi-nude *indios*" selling wood, followed by an intertitle reading "productive businesses."[29] Another scene showed one of Mexico City's largest streets, Avenida San Francisco, deserted except for two or three mules carrying loads of coal, with the title "the most aristocratic avenue of the capital."[30] This particular film had been shot by an unnamed American businessman who had requested permission from the Mexican government to film a "series of views" to "present Mexico abroad."[31] Mexican critics noted that these types of films worked against Mexican efforts to present the country as modern and civilized, instead portraying it as the "most backward country on earth."[32] Missing were any scenes that, as an unnamed journalist wrote in *Excélsior*, "demonstrate our material advances . . . our modern avenues, public buildings, the promenades, our flowering industries . . . all that represents Mexico today and is our pride in front of the rest of the world."[33] Indeed, as the Mexican press noted, "when they [American filmmakers] want to present something truly bad and cruel in their films, there is nothing better than a Mexican bandit."[34] Whether faux travelogues or Hollywood feature films like *Why Worry?*, stereotypical representations of Mexico and Mexicans were recognized by the Mexican government as explicit, if unofficial, anti-Mexican propaganda.

FILM CENSORSHIP IN MEXICO:
PROTECTING THE NATION'S IMAGE

In contrast to the United States, where concerns about morality and the impressionability of vulnerable audiences shaped early censorship, in Mexico censorship policies were structured by the exigencies of nation building and the fact that the film industry in Mexico relied on imported films. Though the history of film censorship in Mexico, like that of the United States, began as a concern over regulating the spaces of film exhibition, by the 1920s concerns about content focused primarily, though not exclusively, on the way that Mexico and its citizens were portrayed.

When motion pictures were introduced in Mexico City in 1896, exhibition was governed by the municipal code that regulated live theater productions. In 1908, when the municipal government issued a new regulation of public entertainments, it made specific provisions for film as a medium. Municipal inspectors were charged with ensuring that movie theaters conformed to safety standards, with little regard for the films that were being shown—despite periodic protests about the racy narratives of some European films. The revolution brought the content of films to the fore as municipal authorities became more concerned with films' capacity to model antisocial behavior or, in the case of domestically produced films, to promote a political position. When Madero came to power in 1911, the municipal government of Mexico City modestly increased the number of motion picture inspectors and began to develop a formal censorship policy. Inspectors and the police were empowered to halt programs they considered "opposed to correctness and moral conventions."[35] A new set of regulations issued during the brief regime of General Victoriano Huerta (1913–14), who toppled Madero in a violent coup, set up guidelines governing the depiction of crime and its consequences and forbade "insults to *buenas costumbres* [moral conventions], peace, and public order"—meaning, among other things, that criminals had to receive their just punishment by the end of the film—mirroring similar concerns in other countries and reflecting anxieties about the social unrest that plagued the capital city.[36] This type of censorship worked obliquely to affirm the status of the revolutionary faction in power and to contain cinema's power to stir up unrest or incite popular action.[37]

Explicit mechanisms for censorship did not emerge, however, until after the revolution. President Venustiano Carranza (1917–20) was keenly aware of the potential of cinema to advance or retard the interests of the state. He did little to promote domestic film production, but in 1919 he promulgated a censorship code that included a first-ever provision for the creation of a *Consejo de Censura* (Censorship Council), to be made up of three citizens "known for their honesty."[38] The new regulations affirmed the social function of cinema as a moralizing force but made national concerns preeminent, over and above individual morality. The council was charged first and foremost with ensuring that all films shown in Mexico "contained nothing denigrating for the country, whether in the scenes, the legends, or for whatever other reason."[39] Moral concerns receive no mention until the code's second chapter. There, the regulation alludes vaguely to the representation of criminal behavior and those narratives that might "inspire sympathy for the person or immoral habits of the [criminal] protagonist."[40] Representations of this nature, along with "immoral" scenes, were to be repressed or modified at the council's recommendation.[41]

The new regulations caused an uproar among film distributors and exhibitors. Not happy with the prospect of the government telling them what films they could or could not screen, they were even less enthusiastic about paying a revision fee for the privilege of having the films they had acquired censored. This additional expense came hot on the heels of an increase in municipal taxes on gross ticket sales, from 6 percent to 8 percent; and exhibitors saw only diminishing profits in the government's new censorship program.

Initially, exhibitors and distributors simply refused to bring their films to the censorship council's office. "As of now," the Mexico City newspaper *Excélsior* reported in early February 1920, "not a single film has been presented for censorship."[42] Refusing to cooperate led to even more problems: if exhibitors and distributors failed to submit their film stock for revision, there would be nothing to show on the capital's movie screens. But if they submitted their films, they would have to raise ticket prices to cover the cost of the revision fee, essentially putting prices out of the reach of their audiences. Using the same rhetoric that the government used to claim exhibition's importance as a national industry, exhibitors and distributors argued that putting them out of business would only harm the working classes, while severely setting back the development of the Mexican film industry.[43]

By summer the government had reached the limits of its patience. The secretary of the interior issued a circular demanding the compliance of exhibitors. Members of the industry made one last collective appeal for a repeal or modification of the regulations. In their letter to the municipal president, they complained that the new rules made no provision for the timely revision of films or the protection of the prints being reviewed, potentially jeopardizing the substantial investments they made when renting films. Censors in the United States, they argued, had already reviewed films being imported into Mexico. Moreover, the government's censorship regulations constituted a violation of the right to free expression that had been written into the constitution of 1917.[44]

Miguel Alonzo Romero, then *presidente municipal* (mayor) and the man whose job it was to enforce the new regulations, offered a quick rejoinder. An official press release stated that it was the government's duty to "defend" censorship out of concern for the "higher interests of society" and to "protect the public against the unbridled search for profit."[45] Without acknowledging the heated debates and particular contours of each case, he asserted that other "civilized" countries, such as England, the United States, and Germany, exercised censorship. Mexico would become more like these developed countries if it too censored motion pictures. Finally, with a bureaucratic sleight of hand, Romero defended Mexico's censorship regulations by claiming that the council was not charged with exercising "censura previa," that is, prior restraint, but rather evaluating films after they had premiered. That small detail saved the office, he asserted, from violating the constitution.[46] The capital's exhibitors gave in, folding the additional costs of film revision into their vanishing profit margins. The conflict over the council and its charge made it clear that although the government saw itself as protecting the image of the nation and safeguarding Mexican audiences from cinematic representations of crime and immorality, exhibitors perceived the government's censorship as an impediment to the development of the film industry, which they understood as patriotic labor.

The council was ultimately and somewhat mysteriously disbanded in 1922, with its duties—covering everything from preventing the exhibition of films that demeaned Mexico to protecting children from so-called immoralities—eventually taken up by the municipal office responsible for licensing and inspecting cinemas.[47] However, regardless of these bureaucratic shifts, protecting the nation's image remained a primary concern of the Mexican government under the leadership of President Álvaro Obregón. The minister of foreign relations observed: "The cinema—and almost exclusively the cinema of the United States—was the most efficient vehicle for the discredit with which Mexico is presented to the world."[48] Accordingly, the Mexican government turned its attention to stopping the exhibition of denigrating pictures abroad as well as at home.

THE 1922 EMBARGO AGAINST DENIGRATING FILMS

In February 1922 Mexico's tolerance for stereotypical representations appeared to have reached its limit. Obregón had notified the newly formed MPPDA that Mexico would forbid the importation and exhibition of films it considered denigrating to Mexico if American film companies did not remove certain offensive titles from worldwide circulation immediately.[49] Yet even after this dramatic declaration, consular staff in Tucson, New York, San Francisco, Boston, and Los Angeles reported that such "denigrating" films as *Moran of the Lady Letty* (Famous Players–Lasky, 1922), *The Golden Gift* (Metro, 1922), and *North of the Rio Grande* (Famous Players–Lasky, 1922), *The Man of Courage* (Aywon, 1922), and *Fool's Paradise* (Famous Players–

Lasky, 1922), most of which were being distributed by Paramount Pictures, continued to be shown in theaters.[50]

In fact, such films were even making their way into Mexican theaters. In March a Mexico City cinema inspector wrote to his supervisor that in the course of his rounds the day before, he had seen an "offensive North American" film, *Los Mosqueteros de la maniagua* (literally "Musketeers of the swamp"; possibly *The Musketeers of Pig Alley*; Biograph, 1912).[51] In the film, he reported, one of the main characters wore the "national suit of the charro." This outfit, the rest of his appearance, and his "racial characteristics" (that is, his physiogonomy) gave this character "the appearance of a genuine Mexican."[52] According to the inspector, viewers could not possibly mistake the character for either an Argentine gaucho or an American Plains Indian. And, predictably, this particular character played the villain of the film. The inspector wrote to his superior, he said, out of his sense of "duty" as a "Mexican, citizen, and municipal employee." He found the exhibition of such films "depressing," "sad," and "extremely embarrassing," noting that even the foreigners in the audience criticized the fact that it was allowed to screen in Mexico.[53] Similarly, the February 1922 minutes of the meeting of the municipal council of Guanajuato, the capital of the state by the same name, recorded the protests of a Sr. Rivera, who had witnessed a film that "denigrated Mexico by dishonoring her."[54] The film "showed people dressed in typical national dress who were dedicated to committing all sorts of depredations, while those entrusted with defending against them wore typical American costume."[55] The presidente municipal and the city council agreed that this was an outrage, but beyond reminding theater owners to select their material more carefully, there was little they could do.

Clearly, as with earlier Mexican complaints about U.S. films, Obregón's threat had fallen on deaf ears. So in April 1922 Obregón issued a presidential decree forbidding the importation and exhibition in Mexico of the film *Her Husband's Trademark* (Famous Players–Lasky, 1922) and all other films distributed by Paramount.[56] In the subsequent months, the Mexican government banned the products of Aywon Films, Metro Pictures, Educational Films, Christie Comedies, and Warner Bros. until they "retired denigrating films from worldwide circulation."[57] The decrees represented the culmination of years of complaints but also reflected Mexico's sense of itself as an important Latin American market for U.S. films.

In rationalizing the embargo, Mexican officials focused on the effect that "denigrating" films might have on other countries' willingness to invest in Mexico and engage in commerce with Mexican companies. In 1922 Mexico's business agent in Toronto, Ontario, wrote that an unnamed Paramount Pictures film would result in "industry and business men resist[ing] doing business with Mexico due to the fact that Paramount paints it [Mexico] with the most barbarous colors."[58] Other staff members from Mexican consulates around the world concurred, attesting to film's ability to "impede the development of commercial relations" between countries.

Indeed, denigrating films were seen as bad for business, not only by Mexican diplomats, but also by U.S. businessmen in the Southwest whose interests were intimately linked to Mexico's. When the chambers of commerce of New Orleans and San Antonio initiated a campaign to improve relations with Mexico, they made one request of other chambers: pressure local authorities to forbid the exhibition of films that might offend Mexico, in order to foster a "true rapprochement between the people and commerce of the two nations."[59] In 1923, when the president of the chamber of commerce of Nogales, Arizona, wrote to Obregón on behalf of Goldwyn Pictures, which wanted to film in Mexico, the chamber's request was couched between an acknowledgment that U.S. cinema not only "disoriented public opinion, creating a bad atmosphere for Mexican citizens," but also "sowed the lively antipathy of cultured Mexicans toward the North American people." The chamber's president, however, went on to defend Goldwyn as the "company that has been the least guilty of showing pictures objectionable to the Mexican people."[60] Nogales's chamber of commerce, composed of like-minded businessmen across the American Southwest, had vested interests in eliminating barriers, cinematic and otherwise, to lucrative commercial relations between the two countries.

The Mexican government's awareness of the importance of business proved critical in its campaign against denigrating films. The writer of an anonymous letter to the Mexican consul general seethed that it was "time to teach these 'film-men' a lesson, causing them to lose the most money possible. This is the ONLY way to make them understand."[61] Indeed, the film industry's perception of Mexico as a growing market and an important gateway to other lucrative markets in Latin America set the stage for Mexico to respond to U.S. studios' representations of Mexico and Mexicans in a language that the American film industry understood: the language of commerce.

Obregón's decree caused the U.S. film industry no small amount of anxiety about its bottom line. In June 1922 Jack S. Connolly, the MPPDA's representative in Washington, wrote to Secretary of State Charles E. Hughes, upset about the embargo against Metro Pictures and Famous Players–Lasky. He emphasized that the "two American companies involved are most representative, and should this ruling be carried out they will lose more than

$200,000 a year."[62] The U.S. Department of Commerce reported that the value of films exported to Mexico in 1921 was $132,625.[63] Industry reports indicate that Mexico accounted for 2 percent of U.S. film companies' international gross receipts throughout the 1920s.[64] International receipts, in turn, accounted for 35 percent of total gross receipts.[65] In other words, Connolly was worried about a very small slice of the studios' foreign revenues, which by the late 1920s reached $200,000,000 per year.[66] Revenues from Mexico, however, were primarily profit, part of the foreign income that capitalized the production of prestige pictures in Hollywood.[67]

The motion picture industry was even more fearful of a possible ripple effect through Latin America. Pan-Latin solidarity could seriously injure the interests of U.S. producers—Argentina and Brazil, for example, had many more theaters per capita than Mexico and together constituted a large percentage of revenues from Latin America, a market that was attractive to U.S. producers because of the lack of competition from domestic producers, though it was consistently less lucrative than European markets.[68] The U.S. consul general in Mexico declared that "the Mexican government is not only looking out for itself but is using opportunity to attract Latin-American sympathy."[69] Concerns about hemispheric solidarity were warranted. Looking back on the embargo, Enoch Pariagua, a member of the diplomatic corps, would report that "for sympathy and racial affinity almost all the Latin American Republics likewise boycotted those companies . . . diminishing considerably their sales abroad."[70] Although the State Department had not yet recognized Obregón's government, the U.S. government considered film companies in Mexico "important commercial interests" and urged George T. Summerlin, U.S. special envoy in Mexico, to "resolve the situation 'informally' if possible."[71]

Backed by Summerlin, the MPPDA resorted to "private" diplomacy, mobilizing its own agent, B. T. Woodle, to engage in negotiations on its behalf. When he arrived in Mexico, Woodle presented a letter signed by Will Hays, the MPPDA's newly installed president, declaring the industry's desire to establish "mutually satisfactory relations" with Mexico and emphasizing "the real gain possible to Mexican exhibitors of motion pictures through opening up this outlet for American films."[72] Throughout its negotiations with Mexico, the MPPDA focused on commercial relations, including film piracy, and avoided broader questions of representational practices that promoted prejudice and negative stereotyping—questions that had already been raised by other countries, such as France.[73]

After five weeks of talks, the Obregón government signed an agreement with the MPPDA that consisted of a series of vaguely worded measures designed to end Hollywood's stereotypical portrayal of Mexico and Mexicans and reopen the Mexican market to U.S. film companies.[74] The MPPDA agreed that its members would cease making films that might offend Mexico or any other Latin American country. In turn, the Mexican government promised to lift its bans and work even harder to counter film piracy within its borders.

The industry hoped to maintain its position in the Latin American market, while the Mexican government hoped that the agreement would end Hollywood's "hateful anti-Mexican campaign."[75] Ultimately, however, the MPPDA's signing of the agreement did little to alter Hollywood's representational practices. Although foreign markets were important, the domestic audience continued to be the industry's primary source of revenue, and that audience had few objections to stereotypical representations of other nations or cultures.[76] Moreover, the rationalization of the production process made the industry reluctant to discard tried-and-true formulas. Since the official agreement forbade the overt representation of national types, Hollywood directors and producers simply moved the action of their films into historically or geographically vague locations, while relying on well-worn visual clichés or textual indicators that did little to keep the audience from guessing the ethnic/national identity of the villain or where the action might be occurring.

The practical application of this strategy began before the agreement was signed. *Her Husband's Trademark*, one of the films that had touched off the embargo, became the subject of negotiations as its producer, Famous Players–Lasky, attempted to assuage the concerns of the Mexican government. As originally produced, *Her Husband's Trademark* tells the story of a love triangle between James Berkeley (Stuart Holmes); his wife, Lois Miller (Gloria Swanson); and his college chum, Allan Franklin (Richard Wayne). Initially torn between the two men, Lois marries Berkeley, who keeps her in furs, gowns, and jewels that attest to his upper-class status even as his business ventures flounder. When Franklin, an engineer, obtains an oil concession from the Mexican government, Berkeley attempts to get in on the venture by using his wife's charms. He and Lois accompany Franklin back to Mexico, where Lois realizes she really loves Franklin. In the final reel, Mexican bandits attempt to kidnap Lois. During the ensuing battle, Berkeley is killed, and the two lovers escape the bandits by fleeing over the border into the United States.[77]

American audiences appear to have received the film as a regular program picture, notable perhaps for Gloria Swanson's numerous costume changes (the *New York Times* acknowledged its release but did not bother to review it), but Mexican viewers took umbrage at the film's portrayal of Mexico as a lawless place overrun with bandits. The film prompted com-

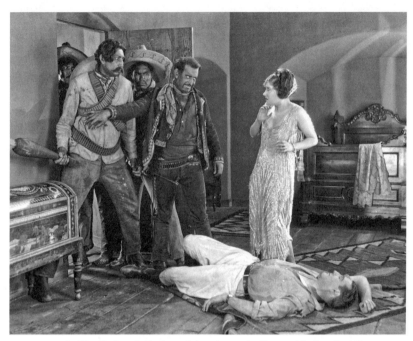

FIGURE 5.2 In *Her Husband's Trademark* (1922), nominally non-Mexican bandits attack the film's protagonists, Lois Miller (Gloria Swanson) and Allan Franklin (Richard Wayne). From the Collections of the Margaret Herrick Library.

plaints from members of the Mexican diplomatic corps in San Francisco, New York, Philadelphia, Portland, Los Angeles, Chicago, Rio de Janeiro, and even Tokyo.[78] Armed with these complaints and the pressure of the embargo, the Mexican government pressured Famous Players–Lasky to make substantial changes to the film less than two months after its release.

In April 1922 the story's setting was changed from Mexico to "Cristobana." One company executive wrote to Mexico's secretary of foreign relations, insisting that "this is not a simulated change, such as writing the name Mexico backwards or selecting a name that suggests that of Mexico, but a real and effective change."[79] At the same time, the company agreed to change nineteen of the film's dialogue and expository titles, changes that attempted to alter the way that audiences read the film's images.[80] Revised intertitles insisted that the action was taking place somewhere in South America by substituting the words "Cristobana" or "South America" wherever Mexico had been mentioned. Added intertitles further emphasized the film's changed setting. For example, the trio's voyage to Mexico, which in the original was accomplished via train and took just four days, was transformed via titles into a steamer voyage of two weeks. These changes to *Her Husband's Trade-*

mark asked viewers to believe what they read rather than what they saw. Since no additional scenes were shot, the film's costuming and sets remained the same.

The final sequence of the film became the subject of the most radical alteration of meaning. In its original form, the film portrayed Lois and Franklin fleeing across the U.S.-Mexico border to the safety of an American military camp. The screenplay synopsis summarizes the end of the story: "After a battle, [Franklin] gets Lois safely over the American border, and they find happiness in their love for each other."[81] The continuity script renders this series of events with a title that reads "Sunrise on the Rio Grande," followed by a series of shots of Lois and Franklin fleeing toward a military camp, with the Mexican bandits in hot pursuit. The final shot was to show Franklin and Lois embracing on the northern side of the Rio Grande.[82] In the list of changes made to the film, however, the final intertitle was altered to read "Al amanecer en Rio Blanco" (Sunrise on the Rio Blanco).[83] Because the action was supposed to take place in Cristobana, which presumably shared no border with the United States, the Mexican government asked Famous Players–Lasky to add a title to the penultimate sequence that portrayed the struggle between the Mexican bandits and Franklin at his hacienda. The final title that was accepted read: "Si podemos llegar a Rio Blanco estamos a salvo. El gobierno Cristobana tiene allí un patrol." (If we can get to Rio Blanco we're safe. The government of Cristobana has a patrol there.)[84] Thus, the revised titles labored to transform American soldiers into Cristobanian soldiers and the Rio Grande into just another obstacle to the characters' safe haven. It is doubtful, however, whether such textual sleights of hand were effective in altering spectators' reading of the film, given the way its visual logic conformed to standardized representations of the U.S.-Mexico border. (A similar strategy was employed with other films such as *I Can Explain* [1922], which was set in the mythical South American country of "Orinomo," though the film's intertitles identified the villains as "greasers.")[85]

The Mexican government insisted that *Why Worry?* be altered as well, despite its fantastical setting. In correspondence with Mexican officials, Lloyd insisted that he too was concerned about the "tendency of other producers to fail to consider the feelings of other nations" and promised to remedy the situation.[86] Lloyd and the film's distributor, Pathé Exchange, eliminated all references to South America in copies of the film destined for the Latin American market, even substituting the generic "a fantastic island" for "the Island of Paradiso" in all the intertitles that referred to the film's setting. In a letter to Mexican Ambassador Téllez, Lloyd's lawyers explained the steps that had been taken: "Our client has inserted into the action of the play a

FIGURE 5.3 Visual proof that the Isle of Paradiso is far, far away from Mexico. Screen shot from *Why Worry?* (1923).

map of the Western Hemisphere with a progressive dotted line showing that the ship which takes the principals of the play from the US to the Island of Paradiso passes beyond Mexico and goes into the distant Pacific far west of the Chilean Coast. In this way there is an *affirmative ocular demonstration* that the Island of Paradiso is as distant from Mexico as possible."[87]

Yet Mexican diplomats deemed the revised version of the film unacceptable, noting that the film's publicity continued to use the term "Mexicans," and asked Central and South American governments to ban the film and all the products of its distributor, Pathé Exchange, from entering their countries.[88] Mexico succeeded in banning the film within its own borders and managed to place an embargo against its distributor, although sometime later—presumably after the uproar over *Why Worry?* had faded—the embargo was lifted (the archive is unclear about precisely when this happened).[89]

Threats of embargo proved less and less effective as the 1920s wore on and the industry persisted in its disingenuous strategy. For example, the Mexican press deemed *La paloma* (*The Dove*; Norma Talmadge Productions, 1927), a border drama starring Norma Talmadge and distributed by United Artists, a "mystification" of the agreement between the film industry and Mexico.[90] One reviewer, Baltasar Fernandez Cue, noted that the film's producers had failed miserably in their attempts to avoid offending Mexico. The mythical country of Costa Roja bore a striking resemblance to northern Mexico, and the narrative (in which a Spanish-speaking villain named Lopez struggled with a "noble young man" named Powell for the favors of a mixed-race heroine, "the Dove") followed the conventions of the border western.[91] For all presumed efforts to prevent any identification of the film's setting as Mexico, Cue concluded that "the public would . . . see the film as Mexican."[92] By 1932, when the controversial sound film *Girl of the Rio* (RKO, 1932), with Dolores del Rio, premiered in Mexico, banning a film had become a symbolic gesture. *Girl of the Rio* was banned in Mexico City and, in a gesture of solidarity, in Panama and other Latin American countries, but it was screened in other cities across Mexico without a murmur.[93]

TRANSNATIONAL AUDIENCES: VIEWING THE NATION

Bans and embargoes may have ultimately proved ineffective in altering the industry's representational practices, but they were effective in uniting Mexican viewers on either side of the border in their defense of the nation. The negotiations between the MPPDA and the Mexican government had been the topic of extensive diplomatic correspondence and were well publicized in both the Mexican press and the Spanish-language press in the United States. Mexican citizens at home and abroad stood ready to report violations of the agreement to Mexico's Foreign Ministry. In their letters, these citizens offered close readings of films that violated either the embargo or, later, the spirit (if not the letter) of the agreement, as well as some films that seemed to flagrantly disregard the agreement altogether. Such letters proved Mexican moviegoers to be equally adept at parsing the language of film and gauging the political work that language performed.

Throughout the early 1920s communiqués from consular staff members poured into the offices of the Ministry of Foreign Relations, describing the "denigrating" films that continued to be exhibited in the United States, often quoting correspondence they had received from members of the Mexican community. In their reports, consular staff members homed in on three primary elements common to "denigrating" American films. First, they complained that American films provided a one-sided view of Mexico as a nation of impoverished peasants, completely given over to their baser instincts. One writer opined that the film companies seemed "content to portray our country as composed solely of unhappy peons of the poorest kind, not even as people but as a mass of broken pottery."[94] Others observed that films such as *North of the Rio Grande* portrayed Americans—in this case, Val Hannon (Bebe Daniels)—as the bearers of hygiene, and thus civilization.[95]

Second, viewers complained that the films made a mockery of national institutions, depicting the army as corrupt, buffoonish, or at least inept. Being painfully aware of the balance of power, members of the Mexican diplomatic corps were infuriated by the constant assertion of U.S. imperial aspirations and arrogance. A consular staff member described one film's American hero as a "Napoleon" who did not even consider the Mexican characters in the film worthy of punishment but rather "herded them out of town like sheep."[96] J. Garza, the consul in San Francisco, observed that in *North of the Rio Grande*, the bandits—who were dressed in "nothing less than our army's uniforms"—were armed with weapons that they meekly gave up at the "mere presence of a horseman played by Jack Holt."[97] Not only did American films mock the Mexican army, but they also made light of the recent revolution—a conflict that, as Mexican Ambassador Téllez reminded Paramount's lawyers in 1923, like "the American Civil War . . . cost the Mexican people untold costs and sacrifices."[98]

Finally, the very symbols being mobilized to create a cohesive national identity in Mexico were also being used by the U.S. film industry as visual stand-ins for savagery and cultural poverty. The mise-en-scène of denigrating films linked these national symbols with the negative stereotypical qualities ascribed to Mexican characters. For example, in describing the plot of the film *I Can Explain*, the Mexican consul in Salt Lake City noted that the buildings in the movie were decorated with flags that, "to judge by the position of their colors, simulate ours."[99] Similarly, the consul at El Paso noted that in *Quicksands* (Agfar, 1923), "individuals wearing the hat typical of our country, with the clothing of our lower classes," were depicted "hitting women, getting drunk, and dedicating themselves solely to vice and prostitution."[100] Report after report observed uses of mise-en-scène and costuming so obvious that, as the consul in Salt Lake City wrote, "even a school-child" could connect the dots that equated the charro, the sombrero, and the tricolored flag with "villainy" and "moral degeneracy."[101]

It is important to bear in mind that the images and symbols that consular staff members pointed to—symbols that we still readily associate with Mexico today—were in the process of becoming part of the national imagination thanks to the efforts of Mexican state bureaucrats, intellectuals, and artists.[102] Practices and objects that originally had regional connotations—the charro and other examples of folk costume, adobe buildings, dances such as the *jarabe tapatio*, and folk art—were promoted by the state domestically and exported to the United States via the work of anthropologists, journalists, and artists.[103] These symbols, as consular staff members observed, had come back to Mexico as part of the American film industry's construction of a cinematic mexicanidad.

The attention that members of the Mexican diplomatic corps paid to the ways in which the U.S. film industry's representational practices threatened Mexico's nation-building practices could be considered part of the diplomats' work as representatives of their nation. Individual citizens who wrote to report the exhibition of "denigrating" films likewise saw themselves as representing Mexico. They typically prefaced their remarks with phrases like "as Mexicans and citizens interested in the good name of our country," "as a Mexican I feel it is my duty," and sometimes simply, "as a Mexican."[104] That is, they brought their complaints about U.S. films to the attention of Mexican government officials based on their understanding of a shared national identity.

This identification with the nation could be complex. Individuals tended to evaluate denigrating films and the government's efforts to suppress them according to the ways in which those films, and the social relationships they reflected and created, affected their everyday lives. Very often, citizens who wrote to express their position against the embargo couched their opinions in the same nationalist vocabulary used by those who supported the measure. Both during and after the embargo, for example, Mexico's president received letters from movie theater owners across the republic asking for clarification of the policy. Describing themselves as conscientious citizens, they asserted that the embargo or its misinterpretation endangered their business interests and thus their ability to contribute to the national economy. During the embargo, the management of the Circuito Olimpia, the biggest theater chain in Mexico City, was quick to point out to the municipal authorities that it had returned its copy of the offensive film *Los Mosqueteros de la maniagua* to the distributor (after it had been shown once by mistake). The company assured the municipal authorities that despite being an American-owned business, they would never show "a film that in the least bit [was] offensive to the people or government of Mexico."[105] During the embargo, other theaters complied with the ban—for example, withdrawing *Su Majestad* (*His Majesty the American*; Douglas Fairbanks Pictures, 1919), with Douglas Fairbanks, from exhibition, even though that caused "great displeasure" to the public.[106] Miguel T. Gonzalez, who represented a chain of cinemas in Mérida, Yucatán, wrote asking that the customs office at Puerto Progreso be ordered to release two films from the distributor Paramount. The customs officials had seized the films even though they had already been shown in Merida, "as well as in other important cities in the state of the Yucatán," over the course of the prior two years.[107] The government received similar letters from cinema owners or their representatives in the cities of Acapulco, Ciudad Chihuahua, Mazatlan, and Orizaba, all claiming that the overzealousness of customs officers and municipal authorities had brought them "numerous damages due to the expense" they had incurred in acquiring the films in the first place.[108] Not only were the films already in the country, they argued, but they were "far from causing dishonor to our country, they are highly moral and instructive."[109]

The line between patriotism and self-interest was often blurred. For example, B. Trasviña reported from Tampico, Tamaulipas, that the Cine Alhambra—owned, he emphasized, by Spanish nationals—refused to comply with the embargo.[110] In another case, citizens of Mexicali, Baja California, asked the municipal president to take action against a local theater that was owned by "individuals of Chinese nationality," which allegedly exhibited "denigrating films." The theater was closed, more likely because of the anti-Chinese sentiment that ran rampant in northern Mexico than because of the gravity of the charges.[111] Luis Lezama, an independent film distributor, may have had his own interests in mind when he reported that films produced by Selznick Pictures, which had been banned after the agreement had been signed, were being marketed under the trademark of First National, making a "joke out of the government's policy."[112]

Workers in the cinema industry also balked at the embargo. Representatives of the Sindicato de Empleados Cinematografistas (Cinema Employees Union) wrote to President Obregón to inform him about the "real situation of the [Olimpia] circuit's employees."[113] The chain's closure, looming because of the embargo's restriction on films coming into Mexico, would leave "around 200 families without the sustenance they earn through their work." As "a genuine representative of our race," the union representative assured the president that the films in question were in no way denigrating.[114] For the employees, whose livelihoods depended on the exhibition of U.S. films, the embargo represented a government policy that interfered with their ability to contribute to the Mexican economy and thus fulfill their patriotic duty as citizens.

Reports about denigrating films came from the other side of the border, as well. Mexicans living in the United States proved particularly attuned to the way that stereotypical portrayals of Mexicans could affect their everyday lives. The Mexican consul in San Diego appealed to the mayor to remove the Harry Carey film *The Kick-Back* (R-C Pictures, 1922) from the city's theaters. The consul drew the mayor's attention to the numerous complaints that had poured into his office from the city's Mexican residents.[115] Perhaps

San Diego's large Mexican community, whose members had to contend with the common perception of Tijuana as a haven for criminals and a hotbed of vice, objected to scenes comically depicting a Mexican jail and easily duped soldiers.

Though rare, examples of the complaints of individual Mexican migrants demonstrate the connections they made between representational practices and their lived experience. Just after the agreement with the MPPDA was signed, Miguel Castillo, a Mexican citizen living in Chicago, informed the Mexican secretary of the interior that he had read about the controversy in Chicago's Spanish-language press. "I do not know," he wrote, "if the agreement included all the companies, but the case is that yesterday I was at one of the principal theaters of this city and witnessed one of many [denigrating films]."[116] He went on to provide the secretary with details about *One Week of Love* (Selznick Pictures, 1922). "This [film] is set in California," he wrote, "and the part that I'm referring to takes place in the desert in Baja California, two Mexicans of the humble class appear, whom one of the protagonists calls 'Greasers.'" Castillo hoped that his report "will serve in the campaign undertaken against films that denigrate *our nationality* in this way."[117] Another example is a letter from Dionisio Torres, a Mexican citizen living in Galveston, who wrote to President Obregón in June 1924 to inform him about a denigrating film, *Hell's Fury Gordon* (Canyon Pictures, 1919), starring Franklin Farnum, that was being screened at a theater near his home.[118] In simple language, Torres reported a typical scenario in which one American overwhelmed six men, who were identified as Mexican because of the charro suits they wore. The audience, he wrote, broke out into wild applause, prompting Torres to observe that scenes such as this were "extremely embarrassing for the Mexicans present, since our *neighbors* think us entirely savage and lacking in any notion of culture."[119] Torres pointed to the ubiquity of such films and their potential to affect his and other Mexican migrants' relationships with their Anglo neighbors.

Even as these Mexicans living in the United States acknowledged the particular ways in which cinematic representations of Mexico and Mexicans affected them, they thought of themselves as part of the imagined community of "Mexico."[120] Torres considered himself one of "her [Mexico's] sons."[121] In Laredo, Texas, Mexican nationals working as projectionists in the Strand Theater passed along clips from offending films to consular staff members, out of "patriotism."[122] The actions of these projectionists, like the complaints of Torres and Castillo, suggest that immigrants considered themselves part of a larger, transnational Mexican audience.

Immigrants' critical sensibilities and sense of national belonging continued to be honed over the course of the 1920s. In May 1930 the mayor of Mexico City, Manuel Puig Casauranc, received a curious letter from the Confederación de Sociedades Mexicanas (Confederation of Mexican Societies) in Los Angeles.[123] Members of the confederation asked the mayor (though it is unclear as to why they appealed to him and not the secretary of exterior relations) to inquire if a Committee for the Supervision of Film, comprising members of the confederation and representatives of the city's Mexican consulate, could be created in Los Angeles. Hollywood, the letter asserted, continued to flout the 1922 agreement. Studios produced offensive films even "when the companies know beforehand that they will not be able to exhibit them in Mexico."[124]

Ironically, in their letter, the members of the confederation chose to focus on a film that was specifically intended for exhibition in Mexico and other Spanish-speaking countries. *The Bad Man* (*El hombre malo*; First National / Warners, 1930), a sound version of the 1920 play by Emerson Browne Porter that had already been made into a silent film, offered plenty to criticize.[125] *La Dama Católica* reported that the earlier version's "shameless type of Mexican bandit," despite the film's being advertised as having been "made especially for Mexico," had raised the ire of the Mexican community in the United States, generated protests in the Mexican press, and led some Mexican exhibitors to take the film off their weekly programs.[126] The confederation skipped over the way in which the new version's Pancho Lopez character, played by Wallace Beery in brownface, epitomized Mexican stereotypes. Instead, they turned their attention to the politics of film production.

The Bad Man, according to the confederation's members, was being produced in both English and Spanish, presumably as part of the studios' efforts to cultivate Spanish-speaking audiences for sound films. The members argued that the Spanish-language version's production values reduced Mexican audiences to second-class status: "The first version, in English, was mounted at all cost and luxury, even when the costuming is absolutely inappropriate and makes Mexico look ridiculous. . . . In contrast, the Spanish-language version is more or less all right in costuming, but as it is for the Mexican public they spent only a hundredth of the cost, which is to say that for the producers, the Mexican public does not merit the same consideration as the American [public]."[127] Exacerbating this slight were the industry's racially biased hiring practices. The confederation's members drew the mayor's attention to the fact that, in general, "Spanish-language films and films with a Mexican setting that are being filmed now feature only two or three Mexicans, the rest of the roles are given to Jews, Italians, Americans, Spaniards, and other races." Government intervention, they suggested, could force film companies to "employ Mexicans and at the same time prevent them from continuing to exploit thousands of Mexican extras."[128] Indeed, their suggestions emerged in the context of a struggle in Los Angeles between members of the Mexican community, other Latin Americans, and Spaniards over which accent or group would be used in Hollywood's Spanish-language productions.[129]

The members of the confederation argued from their multiple subject positions as part of Hollywood's global audience, historical subjects who considered themselves Mexican citizens, and potential participants in the processes of film production. Indeed, these Mexicans living in the United States saw themselves as transnational subjects who were particularly well positioned to look out for Mexico's interests abroad. They sought expanded representation in the industry not only to help eradicate stereotypes, but also to improve opportunities for Mexicans to obtain work in the film industry.

CONCLUSION

When the Spanish-language version of *El hombre malo*—starring one of Mexico's favorite actors, Antonio Moreno—was finally released in September 1930, it received mixed reviews. *Cinelandia*'s reviewer said that although the writing and acting were so-so, the cinematography was first-rate. He predicted that the public in Mexico and other Latin American countries would love the film because it had a "popular rather than high society theme."[130] Furthermore, First National Pictures had been particularly careful to remove any elements of the film that would have been offensive to Mexican viewers; the Mexican consul in Los Angeles, Alfonso Pesqueira, had personally reviewed the script.

Indeed, the year before, Pesqueira had written to executives at First National Pictures to tell them that they could count on members of the consular staff to supervise the production and edition of the new, sound version of the film *El hombre malo*.[131] The consul had already "taken a good look" at the script on which the film was based, but First National executives had requested additional Mexican input to ensure that the film would not be subject to any censorship by the Mexican government. A consular communiqué said that once Mexico's Ministry of Foreign Relations approved the film, "there would be no difficulties exhibiting the film in our country [Mexico]."[132]

As nationalism increasingly guided Mexico's domestic and international politics, the Mexican government had entered into a cooperative relationship with the U.S. film industry. Latin American markets had grown significantly throughout the 1920s. As a result, the MPPDA declared, "our companies can't afford to ignore these things" and urged studios to take the reaction of the Mexican government into account when buying film rights or developing production plans.[133] For its part, instead of banning films or issuing embargoes, the Mexican government sought to intervene in the preproduction process. Members of the diplomatic corps stationed in Los Angeles took the lead in this endeavor. Though their suggestion that the consulate there be empowered to "approve definitely, in the name of the Mexican government, films that have met all suggestions and requirements" never received official approval, they developed close relationships with studio executives.[134]

In fact, diplomats like Pariagua, whose extensive 1929 report had detailed the offenses committed against Mexico by the U.S. film industry, celebrated the success of the Los Angeles consulate in clearing up misconceptions about the country held by the film industry, including the idea that Mexico was a dangerous place to do business.[135] In this way, the Mexican government was able to ameliorate some of the worst stereotypes perpetuated in U.S. films while fostering the growth of the Mexican film industry, which in the early 1930s included offering incentives such as tax breaks or exemptions from regulations on the temporary importation of equipment and personnel to U.S. film companies to encourage them to shoot on location in Mexico. Suggestions to U.S. film makers about the content of their Mexican-themed films such as *Tampico* (an MGM property based on the novel of the same title by Joseph Hergesheimer) consisted primarily of requests that the studio "show that in Mexico, as in any other country, we have both good and bad."[136] Mexico's censors would, as the national industry gained steam, increasingly monitor how Mexican filmmakers portrayed the nation, while focusing on the moral content of foreign films.[137]

Though this rapprochement signaled a less antagonistic relationship between the Mexican government and Hollywood film studios, U.S. filmmakers continued to mobilize stereotypes when making films about Mexico or Mexicans (in the United States or on the U.S.-Mexico border) until the exigencies of the good neighbor policy in the 1940s made it inconvenient to do so. The Mexican government's attempts to censor such films, then, might be perceived as having failed. However, the state's efforts to shape foreign film companies' portrayals of Mexico proved extremely successful in another register.

In the course of negotiating what were and were not acceptable representations of the nation in imported films, the Mexican government had made the nation a key lens through which cinema could and should be seen. In fact, in the late 1920s an unnamed MPPDA official wrote: "Whether they call

it the 'Isle of Proviso' or 'Land of Paradise,' doesn't make any difference—
the fact that the costumes and scenery are distinctly Mexican is enough to
stamp the picture as Mexican in the eyes of their nationals."[138] That is, as responses to the 1922 embargo illustrate, Mexican viewers approached American cinema as spectators versed in the visual vocabulary of Mexico's emerging post-revolutionary nationalism. Whether as diplomats who perceived
film, even if produced in another country, as a key component of Mexico's
program to portray itself as a civilized and modern nation; film exhibitors
who saw the ability to fill their programs with little or no governmental inter-
ference as key to their performance of citizenship; or Mexican migrants in
the United States who viewed U.S. films through the prism of their local,
everyday interactions with their Anglo neighbors, Mexican audiences saw
cinema as a set of texts and practices intimately intertwined with the postrevolutionary project of unification around a set of symbols and icons that
collectively represented the nation and, ironically, were some of the same
symbols used by American filmmakers to signal Mexico's lack of modernity.
The category of "national cinema," therefore, was generated out of a set of
viewing practices, an audience defined by its membership in the imagined
community of the nation, and firm ideas about the role of cinema in producing national identity.

6

AL CINE
Mexican Migrants Go to the Movies

The Moving Picture Theatres provide a great deal of amusement for the
Mexicans.
—WILLIAM MCEUEN, "A SURVEY OF THE MEXICANS IN LOS ANGELES"

I dreamed of being a movie star in my youth and one day I came to
Hollywood. . . . Goodbye to my life's dreams, goodbye movie stars.
I return to my dear fatherland poorer than when I left.
—"EL LAVAPLATOS" (CORRIDO), CIRCA 1931

In 1928 the Los Angeles–based Spanish-language newspaper *El Heraldo de México* published in serial form *Las aventuras de Don Chipote: O, cuando los pericos mamen* (The Adventures of Don Chipote:
Or, When Parrots Breastfeed), a picaresque novel by the journalist
Daniel Venegas. The novel recounts the misadventures of Don Chipote, a Mexican immigrant to the United States, as Mexicans and
Anglos alike take advantage of his naïveté. From his comical attempts
to cross the U.S.-Mexico border to his experiences working in the
fields prior to his arrival in Los Angeles, Don Chipote is portrayed
as a classic rube. Ultimately, the novel functions as a cautionary tale,
warning migrants of the dangers of crossing the border and suggesting that the only good that could come of migration was a renewed
appreciation for the comforts of home and homeland.

Tellingly, the novel's climactic showdown takes place in a movie
theater on Main Street in downtown Los Angeles, where American
films and local Mexican talent—the latter singing Mexican songs, performing risqué dances, and galloping through comic skits that poke
fun at new arrivals—entertain new migrants and long-time residents
of Mexican Los Angeles alike. The narrator's description of Don Chi-

pote's first encounter with the "sho" contains all the elements of the oft-repeated and, as some scholars have argued, apocryphal accounts of early audiences' encounters with motion pictures.[1] When the figures on the screen begin to move, Don Chipote is petrified, certain that he is face-to-face with the devil himself. Slowly, though, Chipote relaxes and joins in the laughter of those around him. Before long, he has become a regular attendee, showing off his new clothes—"an aquamarine suit with lots of buttons, yellow shoes . . . bell shaped slacks and tail coats"—and courting his flapper girlfriend.[2]

In *Las aventuras* the cinema functions as a symbol of both American decadence and the deformation of *mexicanidad* that immigration engenders. Moviegoing seals the protagonist's rejection of what the novel defines as Mexican values—religiosity, tradition, and family. After her own arduous journey from Mexico, Don Chipote's wife finds him at the movie theater and drags him back to their small village in Mexico. The novel's humorous ending, the literary critic Nicolas Kanellos writes, "reestablishes the social order," with Don Chipote abandoning the hostile and shallow United States in favor of his homeland.[3] In this way, the novel reiterates a trope common to many Mexican cultural narratives about the cinema, which present the motion picture show and its attendant social practices and cultural formations as antithetical to traditional Mexican values.

The widespread diffusion of cinema culture in urban and urbanizing Mexico makes it difficult, however, to assume that migrants had no familiarity with the cinema or its attendant ethic of consumption before they crossed the border. Indeed, migrants' exposure to cinema probably increased during their journey to the United States. Small towns or *rancherias*, where itinerant exhibitors might have made infrequent appearances, perhaps offered only rumors of an intriguing new entertainment. Company towns or towns close to mines or factories, as the 1923 census showed, were likely to house at least one cinema that people could stand outside of trying to catch a glimpse of what was on screen, even if they could not afford a ticket. Larger Mexican towns, typically one of the many steps toward the border, were also more likely to have at least one motion picture theater, and major border-crossing points, as I will discuss, provided plenty of opportunities for inexpensive moviegoing. Once in the United States, migrants had even greater access to motion pictures. Studies of migrants in the United States have noted that in cities large and small, Mexicans attended movie theaters in their own neighborhoods or in downtowns accessible by public transportation.[4] Even rural migrant communities in the United States had at least periodic access to motion pictures. For example, the historian Devra

Weber observes in her study of cotton workers in California that "a small *mutualista* [mutual aid society] in rural Imperial Valley boasted among its few assets a 'motion picture machine.'"[5]

As Douglas Monroy notes, studies produced by sociologists, economists, and U.S. government agencies have pointed out that for all but the poorest, cinemagoing was a basic expenditure in the budgets of Mexican families in the United States.[6] In a survey conducted by the economist Paul Taylor in Los Angeles in the late 1920s, 72 of 104 Mexican families reported going to the movies more often than other activities like attending church, going to the playground, or playing sports.[7] Accordingly, a large percentage of family budget allocations for leisure was spent on movie tickets. A 1933 study of Mexican families in Los Angeles found that 90 percent of them spent an average of $22 per year on moviegoing, even though the average annual family income at the time was only $1,204. These Mexican families spent as much on recreation in general, and movie tickets specifically, as their white counterparts did.[8]

Mexican migrant moviegoing has, thus, like that of Eastern and Southern European immigrants in the Northeast at the beginning of the twentieth century, become a topic of investigation for historians. Vicki Ruiz, Douglas Monroy, and George Sanchez, for example, have taken up the practice of moviegoing as part of Mexican migrants' culture in Los Angeles in the period between the two world wars.[9] Similarly, Mario García has examined moviegoing in El Paso, Texas.[10] In these historical accounts, moviegoing constitutes part of a broader set of cultural activities including sports, other forms of entertainment, participation in consumer culture, and—in the case of Monroy and Ruiz, whose analyses extend into the early sound period and the years just before World War II, respectively—new patterns of courtship and sexual behavior.

To a large extent, the same opposition that structures Venegas's novel animates this body of scholarship: Mexican tradition versus American mass culture. Drawing on sociological studies, oral histories, and the Spanish-language press, this research documents the importance of moviegoing in larger Mexican immigrant communities and situates it in the context of narratives of acculturation. For example, Ruiz discusses young Mexican American women's engagement with the cinema as part of their acculturation into an American "ethic of consumption"—an ethic that she argues goes hand in hand with their resistance to traditional Mexican family structures.[11] Monroy, in turn, casts motion pictures as "a bridge to americano culture."[12] Garcia likewise asserts that American films exercised "an acculturating influence" on Mexican audiences in El Paso by exposing them to "American material and cultural values and mores."[13] Sanchez takes a more nuanced view, asserting that the American film industry helped Mexicans living in Southern California to "retain old values" but that it also "played a role in cultural change."[14] In keeping with the general trajectory of the historiography of immigration in the United States, this opposition frequently takes the form of generational conflict, in which young people become more Americanized—to the chagrin of their traditional parents.

The evidence clearly indicates that generational conflict profoundly marked Mexican families in the United States. Thus, I seek neither to reassess this dimension of the immigrant experience nor to dismiss it, but rather to offer another way of interpreting Mexican migrants' encounters with American mass culture in the 1920s. Many historians have seen the movie theater as a site of cultural discontinuity, offering radically new pleasures and, as the assessments of the historians cited above indicate, perils.[15] But in many ways the experience of moviegoing in the United States showed the ways in which members of Mexican migrant communities—even as they grappled with the disorienting and very often disconcerting aspects of life in a new country, and sometimes because of that rupture from the old ways of life—shared experiences, including that of a growing sense of national identity, with their counterparts at home. Drawing on anthropological, sociological, and economic studies as well as archival sources and the Spanish-language press, this chapter traces how Mexicans' racial status shaped their moviegoing practices in the United States in ways that drew them closer to, rather than farther from, audiences in Mexico proper.

How can we understand this apparent love of moviegoing in the context of the transnational circulation of American films and film culture across the U.S.-Mexico border? Like their peers in Mexico, Mexican migrants in the United States most frequently saw American films shown with translated intertitles, but they responded with enthusiasm to infrequently screened Mexican productions or the appearance of Mexican actors and actresses in starring roles. As was the case with their counterparts in urban Mexico, moviegoing became a central part of their experience of modern life and its new models of gender and social relationships, from which they could fashion their own subjectivities. What differentiated their experiences from those of audiences within Mexico's borders was the way in which race shaped their engagement with films and film culture.

Informed by scholarship on African American audiences by Gregory Waller, Mary Carbine, Jacqueline Stewart, and others, I have focused on the space around the screen in which ideas about class, racial hierarchies, and entrepreneurship circulated and established the conditions of reception for on-screen representations of race.[16] In the United States, migrants were more likely than their counterparts in Mexico to find themselves face-to-face with on-screen bandolier-draped bandits, sultry señoritas, and buffoonish revolutionaries who made them cringe. Seeing racist images of themselves in the United States—while simultaneously struggling with anti-Mexican racism in their day-to-day lives—gave new meaning to these images. In this way, Mexicans on the U.S. side of the border experienced even more acutely the contradiction of being part of a mass market for the U.S. film industry's products and part of its (racist) racial imaginary. For these Mexicans, racism not only structured the narratives on the screen but also shaped where they saw films and the meanings ascribed to their moviegoing practices.

As it had for African American audiences, segregation and discrimination in the movie theater fostered the creation of a parallel film culture. That film culture, part of the broader transnational Mexican film culture I have described, combined U.S.-produced films with Mexican entertainment, nationally inflected promotional and exhibition practices, and a critical sensibility that emerged from a shared sense of national identity. Though in some respects Mexican immigrants' engagement with U.S. film culture taught them how to be American—as it did their compatriots in urban areas of Mexico—in other important ways it nurtured nationalist sentiments, linking Mexican migrant audiences to audiences in Mexico.

Research on Mexican audiences in the United States has primarily focused on Los Angeles, a city for which there is particularly rich documentation of everyday Mexican life. As Rosa Linda Fregoso notes in her evocative account of her own family's involvement in the film-exhibition business in south Texas, we know far less about Mexican communities and their moviegoing practices in other parts of the country.[17] Here, I have put Los Angeles in comparative context with other parts of the country, especially the El Paso–Juárez region, which in the 1920s was the primary point of entry for Mexican migrants to the United States. In examining El Paso–Juárez, I focus on exhibition practices that linked Mexican communities in the United States to Mexican audiences in Mexico through discourses of nationalism and modernity. My consideration of film culture in Mexican Los Angeles, a community much closer to the film industry, concentrates on the way that critical practices nurtured nationalist sentiment even as Mexicans, like many other people around the world, experienced Hollywood's lure as a vehicle for social mobility.

After the Mexican Revolution, at least a million Mexicans crossed the U.S. border in pursuit of a better life for themselves and their families.[18] This huge wave of migration had been long in the making. The social inequality of the porfiriato displaced millions of Mexico's rural poor. These uprooted peasants, sometimes referred to as the country's *población flotante* (floating population), first began moving across Mexico—to bigger towns, sometimes the capital, or to other regions of the country where industries that required wage labor, like large-scale agriculture, were growing apace.[19] The social upheaval of the revolution also pushed people, including political exiles, toward the United States, which dovetailed with the growing demand for Mexican labor in the fields of the American Southwest—a demand that was exacerbated by restrictions on immigration from Europe and Asia.[20]

As Sanchez and others have documented, during this first wave of immigration few Mexican migrants expected to make the United States their permanent home.[21] The two countries' close proximity meant that migrants could quickly return in response to downswings in the U.S. economy or other factors. Many migrants chose not to apply for U.S. citizenship out of loyalty to Mexico or, as Gabriela Arredondo has shown, a perception that regardless of their official citizenship status, they would continue to experience discrimination.[22] Indeed, most Mexican migrants in the United States faced substandard living conditions, lower-than-expected (or promised) pay, and social discrimination that dampened their enthusiasm about becoming U.S. citizens.

The elite of both countries perceived this massive influx of Mexican migrants as problematic, though for different reasons. Mexican politicians and intellectuals saw migration as a drain on the country's stock of able-bodied and industrious workers. In the 1920s the Mexican government responded to these trends by initiating an extensive propaganda campaign to deter laborers from leaving Mexico, instituting more systematic repatriation programs, expanding its consular corps, and beginning a review of migration law under the guidance of a national advisory commission.[23] Some intellectuals and politicians drew on the language of eugenics to pronounce Mexico's migration "suicidal" and "sterilizing."[24] Gustavo Durón Gonzalez, a member of the Mexican Congress, labeled the losses due to emigration "shameful."[25] The Mexican press held three groups responsible for Mexico's growing levels of migration: American labor contractors, who were accused of deceiving Mexican workers; the Mexican government, which one editorial called a "defective social and political order"; and migrants themselves.[26]

Migrants, the Mexican press asserted, were being lured across the border by misperceptions about the United States as a "land of promise, of well-being, of gold in fabled abundance and stupendous living facilities"—precisely the images of the United States being circulated by American films.[27] Unrealistic dreams of wealth and consumer goods, journalists asserted, drove some migrants to crime, forced others to live in squalor, and prompted still others to seek repatriation.[28]

Repatriated migrants, in turn, were believed to have a deleterious effect on the nation. Some commentators argued, dramatically, that repatriates brought back with them "insanity, vice created in desperation, a bitter [illegible] for everything and against everything . . . a lack of will, a moral weakness [that] nullifies our proletariat and withers all enthusiasm and desire."[29] Francisco Naranjo, a Mexican journalist based in Los Angeles, observed: "Immigration to the United States suits neither Mexico in general nor Mexicans in particular . . . they [Mexicans] don't adapt to the customs of this country [the United States] but instead learn everything bad."[30] Whether they blamed cultural incompatibility or negative experiences in the United States, Mexican journalists saw migration as weakening rather than strengthening Mexican society.

The anthropologist Manuel Gamio, whose 1927 study of Mexican migration to the United States had been sponsored by the Social Science Research Council, viewed the situation less pessimistically.[31] Gamio agreed that living and working in the United States changed Mexicans, but he believed that their experiences could prove useful, even crucial, to the economic and social development of the Mexican nation. Gamio included exposure to modern agricultural and industrial techniques, secularization, increased literacy, and a heightened sense of national identity as among the positive aspects of migration to the United States.

One way that Gamio measured migrants' exposure to American culture was to tabulate the consumer goods brought back by returning migrants. Gamio interpreted their mass-produced clothing (which was brought back in particularly high quantities), phonographs, and automobiles as evidence of the "collective taste . . . acquired by the Mexican immigrants in the American environment."[32] It is likely, as Sanchez suggests, that migrants had some level of exposure to these technologies and objects in Mexico, but their sojourn in the United States meant intensified exposure to the practices and culture of urban and industrial society.[33] The acquired "collective taste" would, as Gamio argued, lead the "masses" to "compare their own living conditions, their existence under tyranny, and their great misery with the liberty and the intellectual and material well-being of the American masses."[34] In other words, exposure to American mass culture—including cinema, though this was not indicated explicitly—could motivate the Mexican working classes to be economically productive and politically engaged.

Of course, the positive effects of migration could accrue to Mexico only if Mexican migrants returned, an idea reiterated in popular representations of border crossing. The film *El hombre sin patria* (Contreras Torres, 1922), for example, told the story of the wealthy and dissolute Rodolfo, who journeys to the United States after his father expels him from the family home. After running through his money, Rodolfo finds himself working on the railroad. In a racially motivated confrontation, he murders his supervisor. Chastened by the reality of migrant life, Rodolfo returns to Mexico, where he "finds gainful employment and a woman who loves him."[35] Although this film, which is considered lost, puts the migrant experience in cinematic form, other popular texts used journeys to Hollywood as stand-ins for migration.

The journalist Carlos Noriega Hope drew on his own observations of Hollywood to craft the novella *"Che" Ferrati, Inventor*, which was published in 1923 as part of the magazine *El Universal Ilustrado*'s *novela semanal* series.[36] The plot of the story is simple: a man named Federico Granados journeys from Mexico to Hollywood, where he finds work as a lowly extra while nurturing fantasies of being discovered in the movie theater he attends with his American girlfriend. When a major star dies, special makeup allows studio executives to use Federico in his place. However, the eventual transformation soon drains Federico, because he cannot be his authentic, Mexican self. At the end of the story, he returns to Mexico disenchanted by Hollywood and the United States.

The story is both an analysis of the racial economy that structured the American film industry and a cautionary tale that celebrates Mexican nationalism in the face of Hollywood's racism. Like the journalists who attempted to show would-be migrants the truth about the United States, Noriega Hope's text unmasks Hollywood as a fantasy world of cosmopolitanism. Each of the story's main characters—Federico Granados, a Mexican migrant who arrives in Hollywood with fifty cents in his pocket; Che Ferrati, the Argentine artistic director; and Hazel Van Buren, Federico's flapper girlfriend—operates under the spell of the cinema. The studio of "Superb Pictures Corporation" is initially described as a site of happy, ethnic coexistence, mixing "Arabs of the desert with white burnooses and un-shirted '93ers; cowboys and women dressed for a 'soirée'; natives from India . . . all of history, all epochs."[37] But in truth, as Federico discovers, Hollywood operates on the principle of "absorption," drawing in actors from various countries and essentially removing their particularity to make them palatable to "global" (that is, white American) audiences. (The narrator compares the career trajectory of the famous actor Henri LeGoffic to those of the actress Pola Negri and the director Ernst Lubitsch.)

Federico's racial identity shapes his interactions in the United States. His girlfriend must convince herself that he has "Spanish blood, like Tony Moreno" and that he had been "born among bullfights, flowers, warm sun, and stabbings in the street"—basically, transforming him into a cinematic version of *latinidad* before accepting him as a romantic partner.[38] Studio executives call him a "Mexican boy," diminishing his masculinity and racializing him in the same breath. Most pointedly, the special makeup that allows him to be mistaken for Le Goffic Europeanizes his features. When Federico returns to Mexico, his *tierruca* (little homeland), he leaves behind this racism, which he finds soul killing, but—like Gamio's ideal—he repatriates his "gringo education" and the substantial amount of capital he accumulated during his sojourn in Cinelandia.[39]

White American social workers, social scientists, and politicians also thought about Mexican migrants' encounters with cinema in racial terms. Many people in the United States reacted to the influx of Mexicans with alarm. Mexican immigration became a hot topic in the popular press, which blamed immigrants for crime and the deterioration of neighborhoods. Journalists and social scientists alike ascribed a set of characteristics—laziness, filthiness, immorality, and low mental functioning—to migrants, declaring them racially unfit for citizenship.[40] At the same time, Americanization programs sought to educate Mexicans into readiness for citizenship, often (as with other immigrant populations) using film as a tool of acculturation.[41]

Sociological studies, master's theses, and reports generated by social welfare organizations on the topic of Mexicans in the United States, many of which focused on Los Angeles, fused observations about Mexican migrants' leisure habits, especially those of Mexican youth, with ideas about Mexicans' racial characteristics. These investigators shared with other social scientists a concern about the relationship between young people and mass culture. A series of studies of the effects of mass culture on young people emerged in the 1920s, culminating in the famous Payne Studies of the 1930s.[42] Film historians, most notably Garth Jowett and Kathryn Fuller, have taken up those studies as evidence of the way that social scientists constructed a youth audience for motion pictures.[43] The ways in which certain modes of film viewing and moviegoing practices were linked to delinquency and generational conflict for Anglo American youth were magnified in considerations of racialized communities such as Los Angeles's Mexican enclave.

In his 1914 master's thesis, William McEuen reported with little approval that the social life of Mexicans in Los Angeles centered on three institutions: "the Plaza [downtown], the Moving Picture Theatre and the Pool Hall."[44] (When McEuen completed his study, the cinemas on Main Street were primarily attended by men, though by the early 1920s, more families patronized both those theaters and smaller movie houses in Mexican neighborhoods.) Another master's student, Evangeline Hymer, noted that of the sixty-five Mexican night-school students she surveyed, most preferred going to the movies than to concerts. This predilection caused her concern, but it worried her less than their taste for jazz music—a taste developed, she believed, out of "[their] experiences on Main street [sic], where cheap [movie and vaudeville] theaters hold forth with cheaper music."[45] Other studies of Mexican boys and girls invariably found that moviegoing counted among the respondents' favorite leisure activities, only ceding first place to dancing.

Among the problems that sociologists and others foresaw emerging from the movie-viewing habits of Mexican migrants were financial irresponsibility, delinquency, and promiscuity. Researchers lamented the fact that even in "the families where economy is practiced and where thin pallid faces tell of hunger, the members will be able to discuss the latest movie feature."[46] Alice Culp observed that seven of the thirty-five families she studied went to the movies frequently, "although only two of them [could] afford to spend money so foolishly."[47] Other researchers found that Mexican boys had internalized the movies' glamorization of crime. One sixteen-year-old boy arrested for pickpocketing declared excitedly in one study: "I got caught last night and they chased me just like in the movies!"[48] Sociology student Mary Lanigan held "crime pictures" responsible for glorifying illegality in the mind of this young man, while blaming other suggestive films, like *It*, for turning nice girls into "cheap flirts."[49] Others surveying Mexican youth and their leisure habits noted disapprovingly that many, though not all, Mexican boys and girls started going to the movies with members of the opposite sex at very young ages. Though this would seem to align this population with the rest of American youth, researchers were careful to point out that Mexican girls matured earlier than Anglo girls, implying that such habits could prove dangerous.[50] Cinema, it seemed, exacerbated the racial characteristics that social scientists were ready to ascribe to Mexicans.

Indeed, whether they viewed American cinema as a corrupting or a potentially educational influence, these sorts of studies reinforced associations that many white Americans made between Mexican migrants and pathological family structures, crime, and potential deviance. McEuen, for example, found that Mexican tastes in movies ran toward the "melodramatic and exciting in the extreme . . . not infrequently suggestive and more or less immoral."⁵¹ Culp concurred: "The type of picture desired by these people is very melodramatic and thrilling one."⁵² She offered as evidence the serial *Daredevil Jack* (Astra Film, 1920), the boxing film *Fighting Fate* (Vitagraph, 1921), and the provocative-sounding *El escandalo* (*The scandal*; Cía. Manufacturera de Películas, 1920), a Mexican drama.⁵³

One social worker attributed migrants' delinquency to the "constant inflaming of the baser elements of nature by unspeakably improper novels, moving pictures, and familiar dances."⁵⁴ Emory Bogardus, a sociologist at the University of Southern California, linked the problems experienced by migrants to their immersion in new urban environments. After studying the Mexican population in Los Angeles for years, Bogardus concluded that American values remained foreign to Mexican migrants, who were thus "guided more by what appeals to [the] senses."⁵⁵ No pleasure of modern life appealed more to the senses than the cinema, a pleasure that had to be monitored in order to achieve the desired educational effects.

Among the studies claiming that cinema could actually serve an educational purpose for migrants was Rena Peek's 1929 study of Mexican girls who were served by the All Nations Foundation in Los Angeles. Peek found that, in general, these girls liked films that "have a good story plot, contain an element of suspense and plenty of excitement, but not necessarily any great amount of 'sex appeal.'"⁵⁶ Similarly, the actors that the girls reported liking best, Charles "Buddy" Rogers and John Gilbert, both seemed to Peek relatively innocuous, since Gilbert was "not exactly the 'sheik' type of actor" and Rogers tended to star in films "which 'the whole family can enjoy.'"⁵⁷ Peek concluded that, except for the small number of very young girls who reported going to the movies alone or with boys, motion pictures posed no serious threat to the girls' social adjustment. In Lanigan's study, one boy reported: "There are movies that can do good, too. I know another girl who made quite a success of her home by going to shows and seeing some beautiful homes that she could only have seen in the movies."⁵⁸ Lanigan, like Peek, concluded that "movies as a form of recreation in general does [*sic*] not seem to be harmful. For the ideas gained that are harmful, there are balancing sets of ideas which are stimulating and good."⁵⁹ Their observations supported Alfred White's contention that in terms of Mexican migrants' acculturation, "less damage would be done by the crude type of moving picture show if we would but open our community centers to well chosen shows, legitimate motion pictures . . . amusement . . . of the right kind."⁶⁰

Though perhaps not a lesson that reformers anticipated, one of the first things that Mexican migrants might have learned while in the movie theater was their place in the U.S. racial pecking order. That lesson could have been taught in two ways: through the action on the screen, or in the social space of the cinema itself. For Mexicans in the United States, race typically determined which theaters they could enter and where they could sit. Some theaters explicitly stated that Mexican patrons were unwelcome. In Texas, for example, segregation was particularly acute. In a study of Mexican communities conducted in 1920, a researcher reported that many of the "better" movie theaters in Fort Worth had signs that read "Mexicans not wanted."[61] Similar warnings appeared at theaters in other Texas cities, such as Dallas and Austin. Some theaters discouraged Mexican patronage by assigning seating based on appearance or class status, or by relegating Mexican patrons to the same galleries occupied by African Americans. In 1926 the Commission on International and Interracial Factors in the Problem of Mexicans in the United States, led by the Reverend George L. Cady, reported that in Texas "it frequently happens that motion picture theatres have one side exclusively for Mexicans, and even educated, cultured Mexicans are sometimes roughly ordered to stay on their side."[62] In the Winter Garden District in south Texas, a local resident interviewed by Taylor confirmed that the local movie theater had "a place for the Mexicans" and that a movie theater being built would have a "balcony for them."[63] Similarly, in Marfa, a small town in southwestern Texas, local custom relegated Mexicans to "a certain place" in the theater.[64] Such practices could also be found in small towns in Kansas and Missouri, where—as the Mexican consul in Kansas City put it—"they don't admit Mexicans equally."[65] Annie Watson, a social worker at the International Institute in San Antonio, explained the rationale for such separations: "It is partly a matter of appearance and conduct, but even if a Mexican is clean most Americans would not want a dark Mexican to sit side of them."[66]

Though apparently with less zeal, Chicago-area movie theaters also segregated Mexican patrons. Taylor noted that in the summer of 1928, only a couple of movie theaters in the Chicago-Gary region of Illinois segregated Mexican audience members.[67] More commonly in the upper Midwest, the ater managers forced Mexican patrons to sit in the gallery with African American patrons or simply denied them entrance based on phenotype or dress. Darker patrons were least welcome. In Gary, Indiana, a Presbyterian preacher reported that one community member, Miss Solis, "never had trouble," explaining that "Miss Solis is as light as any of you but I am dark."[68] Taylor noted that one of the theater owners he interviewed justified such discrimination on the ground that other audience members, whose patronage he valued, objected to the presence of Mexicans. Those patrons objected to Mexicans who were "not clean" or who came to the movies dressed in their work clothes, but it was easier to let "nationality" serve as the criterion for discrimination. According to Taylor's informant, only "high class" theaters practiced such discrimination, which suggests that theaters in working-class neighborhoods might have been more accepting of ethnically mixed audiences.[69]

Mexican audiences bristled at white racism that manifested itself as segregation in theaters. Consuls regularly fielded complaints about Mexicans' not being admitted to theaters on an equal basis with other moviegoers. In Kansas City, members of the Mexican community started to provide "free shows" in a community center to protest the Pennway Theater's segregation and sometimes outright barring of Mexicans.[70] In Marfa, Texas, Annie Watson had seen Mexican patrons protest passively by refusing to move "when they were asked to leave."[71] In Luling, Texas, one young man reported that his father had stopped attending the local movie theater ever since it started separating Mexican and Anglo patrons.[72]

But Mexicans also jockeyed for status—distancing themselves from African Americans, for example—in a racial landscape that evaluated Mexicans based on class and appearance. For example, in Gary, Indiana, a Mr. Valles bought a ticket to see a film at the Palace Theater and was told: "Colored upstairs." The manager relented after Valles explained: "I am not colored, I am Mexican."[73] Another immigrant resented being "seated . . . with the Negroes" during the time he spent working in Oklahoma.[74] In Nueces County, Texas, Mexican patrons collectively protested being seated with African Americans. "When one of the movie theaters [in an unnamed town] began to seat Mexicans with Negroes," Taylor reported, "the matter was discussed by one of the mutual benefit societies, and the members agreed to not patronize the theater so long as the practice was continued."[75] In another town in Texas, a resourceful community member handed out fliers protesting a theater that had directed Mexican patrons to the gallery. The theater responded by handing out fliers indicating that Mexican patrons would not be discriminated against.[76] At other times, audience members challenged other ethnic groups' claims to whiteness. In Illinois and Indiana, Mexicans reacted with incredulity at being seated with African Americans when Polish immigrants, whom they considered "not the real 'Americans,'" were allowed to sit with other white patrons.[77]

Sometimes, however, reactions to discrimination in the social space of the theater put intragroup conflicts on display. One of Taylor's Chicago respondents, a Mexican migrant, noted that "some Mexicans have given cause for criticism by going to shows with dirty clothes and unbathed. Anyone with a clean suit of clothes would object to that."[78] Another young man told

Taylor: "Once my father was not admitted to a theater in Chicago when he went in his working clothes. He said clothes do not make the man. I think he should have worn his good clothes."[79] Though some immigrants criticized fellow Mexicans who did not conform to class-based notions of respectability, others expressed solidarity with fellow immigrants who experienced discrimination. A light-skinned young Mexican man living in Chicago recounted how his father had urged him and his siblings not to patronize movie theaters that discriminated against Mexicans, even though they were not the target of such practices since they could pass for white.[80] Another man criticized a mutual aid society that had negotiated a nondiscrimination policy for its members. "They [the society]," he declared, "are supposed to be working for the homeland and should not accept special privileges."[81] In the United States, the cinema became a "theater of racial difference" where the prevalent racial pecking order was put on display and often resisted, and where American ideas about race both affected community solidarity and nurtured the emergence of a parallel film culture that served Mexican audiences in the United States.[82]

MEXICAN MOVIE THEATERS IN EL PASO

When the actress Pola Negri stopped in El Paso on her way from New York City to Los Angeles in April 1927, both the *El Paso Herald* and *El Continental* (the region's leading Spanish-language newspaper) covered her brief visit.[83] *El Continental* was thrilled to offer its readers an up-close glimpse of one of their favorite stars in the form of an interview; the *El Paso Herald* described how the star's dark-haired fans (probably including many Mexican and Mexican-American women) lined up along the railroad tracks, anxious to catch a glimpse of the star whom the article deemed "a justification for dark beauty."[84] The bilingual publicity buzz around Negri's brief visit demonstrates that Mexican audiences along the border were as invested in film culture as their Anglo counterparts, but it also suggests the existence of separate though parallel film cultures.

The crystallization of separate cinematic spaces for Anglo and Mexican audiences can be linked to changes in the population in the El Paso–Juárez region that began in the late nineteenth century. With the arrival of the railroad, which coincided roughly with the introduction of motion pictures, El Paso experienced an industrial and commercial boom. The growth of mining, construction, and agriculture, as well as the ancillary industries that served them, created a huge demand for laborers—a demand met by Mexican peasants seeking economic opportunities. In the 1910s, the Mexican Revolution led to a further influx of political and economic refugees. El

Paso's Mexican population almost doubled between 1910 and 1920, going from 367,510 to 700,541.[85]

The fact that El Paso's Mexican population was much larger than the Anglo population did not translate into political or economic power. Instead, El Paso was structured, according to Garcia—as a "class system tainted with racial prejudice."[86] Mexicans worked primarily in low-paying blue-collar jobs, while Anglos dominated the skilled trades and white-collar sectors. What's more, Mexicans were usually paid lower wages than their Anglo counterparts, even when they performed the same jobs. In terms of housing, Mexicans were almost completely segregated from Anglos. Both long-time Mexican residents and new arrivals found housing in several barrios—the area just over the border known as Chihuahuita, another barrio to the east near the cemetery, and two smaller communities to the north. De facto (rather than de jure) segregation applied in schools and commercial establishments, such as stores, restaurants, and theaters. In the early years of the twentieth century, El Paso's Anglos expressed concern about the city's growing Mexican population, which they feared would lead to increased levels of disease. Anti-Mexican sentiment rose as Americans in Mexico and their property were threatened or actually attacked by revolutionary forces. The revolution seemed poised to spill over the border, and increasing numbers of refugees flooded the area. When the revolution ended, patterns of racial discrimination, segregation, and barely concealed ethnic tensions combined with an ongoing influx of migrants, as El Paso became the primary entry point for Mexicans coming to the United States—all of which set the stage for the emergence of a parallel film culture.[87]

Early film culture in the El Paso–Juárez region had been somewhat fluid. The region was positioned on the outermost rings of the distribution networks that spread out from the American northeast (and later the West Coast) on the U.S. side, and from Mexico City on the Mexican side. Reports suggest that an audience drawn from both sides of the Rio Grande watched the first moving picture exhibition in El Paso in 1896.[88] Likewise, El Paso's earliest movie houses—the Crawford, the Grand, the Little Wigwam, and the Bijou—apparently did not explicitly exclude Mexicans.[89] During the first decade of the twentieth century, Mexicans from either side of the border also attended motion picture exhibitions mounted by itinerant Mexican film exhibitors who toured cities, towns, and rancherias along Mexico's northern border.[90]

The first movement toward separate film cultures came in 1903. Moving pictures started to be exhibited on a regular basis in Juarez when the City Council agreed to underwrite the construction of a theater, in part to persuade *juarenses* to spend their leisure dollars in town rather than across the border in El Paso.[91] Teatro Juárez, which hosted not only theater but also *zarzuela* (light opera), concerts, official meetings, civic celebrations, and film exhibition, became a central part of public and community life in Juárez. By the end of the decade, however, as movie exhibition had overtaken almost every other use, the building became known simply as Cine Juárez. Two different companies, one managed by a local businessman named Silvio Lacoma and the other a company called the Empresa Cinematógrafo y Variedades, rented the theater for stretches at a time to offer motion picture programs. Shortly after the Battle of Juárez (1911), one of the key border conflicts in the early years of the revolution, two additional cinemas, neither as luxurious nor as well designed as the Cine Juárez, sprang up in Juárez— the Cine Azteca (built in 1912) and the Cine Anahuac (built in 1913).[92] These theaters often combined the showing of motion pictures with the staging of *zarzuela* and light theater to appeal to audience members who were already fans of the Spanish-language variety and theatrical troupes popular across the Southwest.[93]

During the first two decades of the twentieth century, investment in Juárez increasingly expanded into tourist venues like saloons, curio shops, and a bullring, which—combined with increasing political and economic instability—served to stymie investment in movie theaters.[94] Mexicans increasingly looked to El Paso to fill their motion picture needs. The accumulation of "Mexican" theaters in El Paso had accelerated during the revolution, perhaps due to the large numbers of displaced Mexicans—wealthy expatriates and poorer refugees alike—living in the area. Particularly important among these theaters were the Teatro Cristal (built circa 1913), Silvio Lacomo's Teatro Estrella (circa 1913), and Felix Padilla and Pedro Maseo's Imperial Theater (1915) in East El Paso. Mexican workers living in Smelter Town, the company town of the local lead processing plant, could attend the Smelter Theater, which operated off and on between 1914 and 1926, or an unidentified theater owned by a local proprietor that apparently operated only in 1916.[95] By the close of the revolution, the two cities' Anglo and Mexican populations occupied separate, clearly marked cinematic spaces.

The numerous theaters that sprang up in Mexican El Paso in the early 1920s joined other establishments that were owned by a mix of Mexican and European immigrant merchants and provided goods and services to Mexican residents of both El Paso and Juarez, as well as the migrants who came through the city. Most of the theaters were located in the blocks closest to the international border crossing in Chihuahuita.[96] Residents from either side of the border (many residents of Juárez came to El Paso to take advantage of

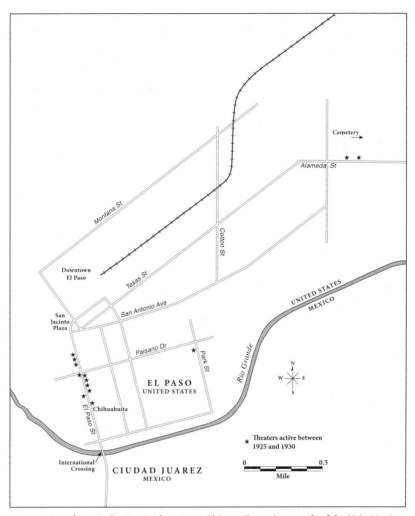

MAP 2 Map of movie theaters in downtown El Paso, Texas, just north of the U.S.-Mexico border that served Mexicans from both sides of the border.

lower prices or to work), as well as a steady stream of migrants en route to the United States, supported eleven movie theaters in El Paso as well as the handful in Juárez. Local Spanish-language newspapers provided extensive and consistent coverage of cinema-related news. Moviegoing had become part of the fabric of Mexican life in the border cities.

Scattered evidence indicates that during the 1910s the U.S. film industry had taken notice of the importance of motion pictures to Mexicans in the Southwest. In 1918 *Moving Picture World* declared that "the peace which reigns from Matamoros to Juarez" was nurturing a "good trans-border trade."[97] The manager of the Vitagraph film rental exchange in Dallas, Texas, was singled out for his attention to what the company's weekly publication called a "unique territory" that consisted of "theatres on the Mexican border which cater strictly to Spanish audiences."[98] The regional manager who ensured that advertisements for Vitagraph films in Spanish were featured prominently in the *Rio Grande Herald*, a south Texas publication whose readers Vitagraph's house organ claimed had "peculiar needs," likewise won high praise.[99] This "peculiar" audience required a particular approach if American film men were to turn a nice profit. As Samuel Schwartz, the manager of the Aztec Theater in Eagle Pass, Texas, reported, "should a border town house run a film which in the least reflects upon the Mexican people, he's [sic] immediately in trouble." The Mexicans, as Schwartz referred to them, "are entitled to be equally proud of their nativity."[100] Not only were Mexicans on the U.S. side of the border becoming loyal ticket buyers, but Mexican exhibitors from northern Mexico were coming to Texas to buy supplies and rent films, and American entrepreneurs were investing in theaters on the Mexican side of the border.

Unlike other parts of the Southwest, the El Paso–Juárez region was increasingly served by a group of ethnic Mexican entrepreneurs, who considered themselves Mexican nationalists but whose business interests spanned the border. They owned and operated theaters that played multiple roles for the Mexicans in El Paso and Juárez: they offered a space of leisure removed from the discrimination that characterized mainstream theaters in El Paso, and they became a social space—part of a larger regional film culture—in which nationalist discourse circulated and connections to Mexico were nurtured and affirmed. Their owners formed part of a transborder, transnational commercial culture. Like their Anglo counterparts, they counted commercialized leisure culture as a hallmark of civilization and progress. They perceived their cinema-related activities as part of a broader program of regional and national uplift.

The activities of the Calderón brothers, Rafael and Juan, and of their associate Juan Salas Porras, exemplified these characteristics. Before entering the motion picture business, the Calderóns had owned El Nuevo Mundo, a department store in Ciudad Chihuahua, about 206 miles south of Juárez, that specialized in dry goods imported from Europe and the United States.[101] Salas Porras was the store's manager.[102] The three men realized that there was a profit to be made in mass entertainment. Allegedly, they took a trip to San Antonio, Texas, to learn how the business operated, and they bought their first projector. Beginning in 1916, they proceeded to acquire a set of cinemas in Ciudad Chihuahua: the Alcázar, Apolo, Ideal, and Estrella, as well as the

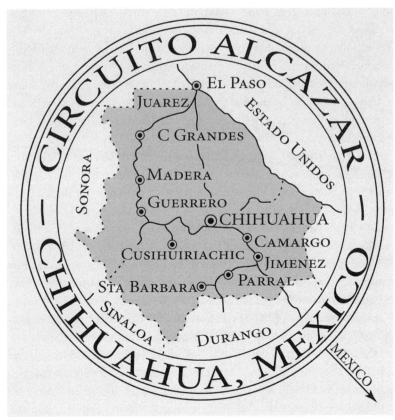

FIGURE 6.1 The Circuito Alcazar logo shows the extent of the Calderóns' cinematic holdings in northern Mexico, circa 1930. Courtesy the Bancroft Library at the University of California, Berkeley.

Teatro Centenario, a former live-stage venue that had been adapted for use as a cinema.[103] In the ensuing years, they would buy or build theaters across the state of Chihuahua and in El Paso. They used their circuit of theaters, the Circuito Alcazar, and the distribution arm of their business, International Pictures (also known as the International Amusement Co.), which they formed with Juan de la C. Alarcón, a former newspaperman, to minimize expenses and maximize profits.[104]

Alarcón headed the distribution arm of the business until it came under the complete control of the Calderóns in 1921, and he was explicit about the cinema's role as an agent of modernity.[105] He claimed to have sent an employee on a "market research" trip through Mexico to get "exact information as to what the people want in picture shows, how much they will pay, and so on."[106] Alarcón declared in an El Paso newspaper that chief among his purposes in entering the movie exhibition and distribution business was the "education and democratization of the Mexican people by means of film." He confidently claimed that in terms of education, which was "what the Mexican people need," cinema was in a position to do "something . . . worth while—more than the government perhaps." Its democratic space, in which the "lower, middle, and higher classes" could mix, would expose the "peon" to members of the "better class," thus inspiring the working-class moviegoer to "take more pride in himself, dress better and more cleanly."[107]

Though Alarcón seemed to be concerned primarily with audiences in Mexico proper, his activities and those of the Calteróns spanned the border. In the 1920s the Calderóns would open two important theaters, one in Juárez and the other in El Paso. Each demonstrated how Mexican filmgoing on either side of the border was tied to the ritual production of nationalist sentiment and was inserted into a discourse on development and modernization. In January 1927 the New Cine Alcázar opened on the Main Plaza in Ciudad Chihuahua with great fanfare. The theater had been constructed according to the latest principles of design, with padded seats, security lights, emergency exits, sanitary facilities, a candy counter, and automated projectors. Its inauguration featured the monumental epic *Ben-Hur: A Tale of the Christ* (MGM, 1925), starring the Mexican native Ramón Novarro, and a speech by Manuel Roche y Chabre, a respected local poet and literary critic. Although the text of his speech is lost to us today, we can imagine that before MGM's silent masterpiece rolled across the screen, Roche y Chabre might have celebrated the modern theater, praising yet another example of the region's development, culture, and contribution to the country's overall economic development. Indeed, the illustrated monthly *México en Rotograbado*, published in Mexico City, lauded the project as a "patriotic act . . . in favor of cultural diffusion."[108]

The gala opening of the Alcázar showcased the way that the Calderón-Salas Porras circuit combined the exhibition of American films with performative elements that nurtured nationalist sentiment. All of the circuit's theaters featured Mexican vaudeville performers, touring stock theater companies, and occasional appearances by renowned Mexican actors, writers, and playwrights. Stylistically, the theaters adopted a particularly Mexican aesthetic that integrated the country's indigenous past with markers of American modernity like jazz bands. The Cine el Azteca, built in Ciudad Chihuahua in 1929, is a case in point. The 1,600-seat theater featured pre-Columbian and modernist design motifs inside and out. The sounds of the Aztec Jazz Boys accompanied the theater's offerings, linking the country's indigenous past to its modern present.

Just a few years before the opening of the new Cine Alcázar, the Calderón brothers and their associates had acquired the Cine Colón on what is today South El Paso Street, just a few minutes' walk into the United States from the international border crossing. Originally built in 1919 by the proprietors of two smaller El Paso theaters that also served the Mexican community, the Colón had been conceived of as a modern space that made use of the "newest ideas in theater construction."[109] It was also conceived of as an explicitly Mexican space. Its seating plan followed that of the "best class theaters in Mexico," and it offered entertainment "by artists of the Latin races."[110]

As part of the Calderón–Salas Porras circuit, the Colón became a central institution in Mexican El Paso. By 1927, the year the New Alcázar opened, Spanish-language journalists on the U.S. side of the border were describing the Calderón brothers with laudatory adjectives similar to those used by the Mexican press, such as "active" and "wise." Their business was praised for bringing "not only good films, but also spectacles worthy of the Mexican colony [in El Paso]."[111] A description of their exhibition practices noted the care with which they selected the films ("always the latest and most notable productions of the big studios") and live entertainment (including musical numbers that would help patrons "remember the absent homeland") that they presented to their audiences.[112] The theater was praised for selecting films that featured the biggest Mexican stars working in Hollywood, such as *La edad de la inocencia* (*The Plastic Age*; Schulberg Productions, 1925), starring Gilbert Roland (né Luis Alonso)—a native of Juárez. But the theater also showed Mexican films like newsreel footage documenting the funeral of the Mexican aviator Emilio Carranza in 1928, whose death was marked as a national tragedy.[113] In this way the Colón became the "favored center of diversion" for the Mexicans living in El Paso and their counterparts in Juárez, a place that would later be remembered as a "work of the Maderista revolution."[114]

Other theaters serving the Mexican population in the region likewise balanced American films and film culture with expressions of Mexican nationalism and community building. In 1927, for example, Mexican residents of El Paso were urged not to miss William Duncan, "the king of courage," appearing in *El torbellino* (*The Whirlwind*; Allgood Pictures, 1920), "the last word in dramatic series," which would be screened with the three reels of film taken during the recent Mexican Independence Day celebrations—presumably in Juárez—which featured "all the Mexicans" at the Circuito Alcázar's Alcázar theater in Juárez.[115] The Teatro Julimes in Canutillo, Texas, slightly northwest of El Paso, not only showed motion pictures but also doubled as a community center that hosted events, like the 1924 "Theatrical Benefit for the Hispanic American Alliance," which featured local talent dancing, singing, reciting poetry and prose, and a "beautiful" (unnamed) seven-part film.[116] Until the advent of Mexican cinema's Golden Age, the consumption of American films and the production of national identity could be compatible and in fact reinforced each other.

Mexican film exhibitors like the Calderóns were not simply active participants in the border region's transnational commercial culture, filling a market niche neglected or only cursorily attended to by Anglo proprietors. They were also agents of modernity, providing Mexican audiences with entertainment in spaces specifically coded as modern and as agents of nation building. Like their counterparts in Mexico, they made the movie theater a space to celebrate and build national identity. In El Paso, cultural nationalism served to oppose white racism. El Paso was not unique in this regard. Movie theaters served a similar function in Los Angeles, where tens of thousands of Mexican migrants created a vibrant parallel film culture during the 1910s and 1920s.

MEXICANS AND THE MOVIES IN LOS ANGELES

In 1910 Los Angeles had the third largest Mexican population (behind San Antonio and El Paso) in the United States. That population grew as more and more Mexican migrants made Southern California their final destination. By 1920 almost 30,000 Mexicans lived in Los Angeles, a number that would triple by 1930.[117] Mexican workers, as social historians have documented, were critical to the region's growth, laboring in agriculture, the railroads, and construction; they indirectly supported the development of the cinema industry.

As in the border region, discrimination in housing, employment, and social life contributed to the maintenance of a sense of group identity that was nurtured by mutual aid societies, social clubs, elaborate patriotic celebrations of Mexican national holidays, and leisure activities that ranged from church socials and family dances to moviegoing. In the 1920s, though new barrios were emerging in semi-urban areas like East Los Angeles, the center of Mexican community life remained near the historic plaza downtown, previously referred to by many Anglos as Sonoratown. Retail stores that featured foods and other products from Mexico, music stores that sold recordings of Mexican favorites, and the Spanish-language press all played a role in nurturing a sense of community. Growing economic stability in the area gave migrants more purchasing power, facilitating their participation in new forms of commodified leisure. Mexican migrants went to dance halls catering to a mixed clientele of Mexicans and Filipinos, while Spanish-language theaters presented everything from classic Spanish dramas to contemporary plays, and vaudeville theaters combined live performance with film shorts.[118]

By the 1920s movie theaters catering to Mexican migrants lined Broadway and Main Street, south of the plaza. As Jan Olsson notes in his brief essay on ethnic audiences in Los Angeles during the nickelodeon era, this pattern had appeared as early as 1905, when ethnic spectatorship emerged "as an unavoidable side effect of location."[119] That is, the nickelodeons in that part of town drew their audience from the Mexican workers who lived in the plaza area. Olsson argues that by 1911, exhibitors in Los Angeles were seeking to cater to specific audiences.

His assertion is borne out by McEuen's 1914 survey of Mexican Los Angeles. McEuen found that along North Main Street, theaters offered programming designed to appeal to Mexican immigrant audiences. He collected samples of handbills and posters displayed outside of the Hidalgo, Electric, Metropolitan, Plaza, and New Federal Theaters. This advertising material promoted a quintet of Japanese acrobats to Mexican and Italian audiences, a "Fakir" who would, it was promised, "stick daggers in different parts of [his] body," a set of actuality or newsreel films about the Mexican Revolution, and a film denoted solely as "The Devil." McEuen's reformist sensibilities labeled this advertising "lurid and disgusting." If we look beyond McEuen's likely class-bound reaction, the material he gathered tells us that Main Street exhibitors combined live entertainment with motion pictures and that they programmed films that appealed to audience members' ties to Mexico and their desire to keep abreast of current events.[120]

McEuen goes on to describe the character and patronage of the five theaters frequented by Mexican audiences. All offered audiences musical accompaniment in the form of a piano player (McEuen describes three of them as "poor"). The Hidalgo, the largest of the five theaters, employed not just a piano player but also an orchestra, a luxury reflected in its ten-cent admission price. According to the survey, most of these theaters served predominantly male Mexican audiences. Indeed, McEuen documents the persistence of male-oriented exhibition practices—the area (Main Street) also offered Mexican men sexually charged, possibly pornographic, "reel views" and "moving picture machines," which were probably individual viewing machines. The Hidalgo, though, appears to have served a more diverse audience composed of women and young adults and children of both sexes.[121] Thus, in 1914 McEuen describes a film culture in transition from one serving Los Angeles's transient male Mexican migrant population to one serving a broader community.

By the beginning of the 1920s, theaters that, in the words of a Univer-

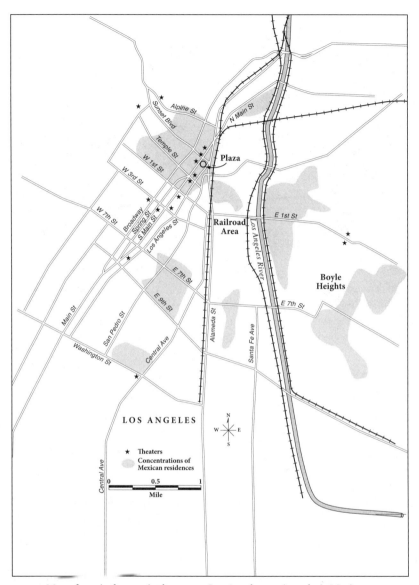

MAP 3 Map of movie theaters in downtown Los Angeles serving ethnic Mexican communities. The shaded areas show concentrations of Mexican residents in the downtown area during the late 1910s and 1920s.

FIGURE 6.2 The Hidalgo Theater, one of the Mexican community's primary motion picture venues, on North Main Street, Los Angeles, circa 1930. Security Pacific National Bank Collection / Los Angeles Public Library Photo Collection.

sity of Southern California researcher, catered "exclusively to these people [Mexicans], having the advertisements written in Spanish as well as English," included the México, Hidalgo, Novel, Capitol, and California Theaters.[122]

Such theaters regularly advertised in *La Opinión*, a Spanish-language daily with a strong (Mexican) nationalist orientation. I found just one example of segregation in a Southern California theater, though such practices might not have been uncommon in other California municipalities.[123] At least downtown, it seems that Mexicans were welcome in theaters that catered to Anglo audiences as well. For example, the Hippodrome on Main Street, the Million Dollar Theater on Broadway and Third Street, the Boulevard, the Broadway Palace, the Metropolitan, the Egyptian, the Rialto, and Grauman's Chinese Theatre all advertised in *La Opinión*. It may have been that Mexican migrants felt more comfortable in exhibition spaces run specifically for migrant audiences—like the theater described in *Las aventuras de Don Chipote*.

When asked, many Mexican migrants who lived in Los Angeles reported going to the movies regularly. Luis Aguinaga, a native of the Mexican state of Zacatecas who lived in Los Angeles at the time, declared: "I like everything about this country, the traffic, the cinema, the parks, [and] the work, because

FIGURE 6.3 Musicians who performed at the Hidalgo, as their fellow jazz musicians did in Mexico City, circa late 1920s. Shades of L.A. Collection / Los Angeles Public Library Photo Collection.

you earn good money."[124] José Roche, originally from Guanajuato, Mexico, did not care to go to the cinema himself, but "I take my wife, she especially likes American cinemas."[125] Indeed, his wife reported that the cinemas were the only thing she liked about Los Angeles.[126] Another migrant, María Rovitz Ramos, described a typical evening out with her American husband: "We go out to the cinema or a dance hall or just for a ride in the car."[127] Other migrants reported that although they had little leisure time, they tried to go to the movies when they could.[128]

As in Texas, in Los Angeles films and film culture were important sites for the cultivation of Mexican identity and sense of community. Curtis Marez has described the way that the performative space of Mexican cinemas in Los Angeles, particularly the sonic elements, reinforced ties to Mexico and Mexican culture.[129] In the space of working-class Mexican movie theaters, films produced by U.S. film studios shared the program with local singers and performers, who brought audiences popular music from Mexico and topical comedy sketches that often reflected on immigrant life. Special events that featured Mexican stars also affirmed the cinema as a space of community building. For example, in October 1927 Lola del Río (as La Opinión affectionately referred to her) had been named queen of the *Fiesta de la Raza* celebration sponsored by the Associación Deportiva Hispano-Americana (Hispanic American Sports Association) which had been formed by *La Opinión* to promote athletics within the Mexican community in Los Angeles.[130] The newspaper advertised the celebration as a transnational event—it reprinted a congratulatory telegram from the Mexican bullfighter Juan Silveti, for example—and emphasized its importance by announcing that the director Edwin Carewe had halted the filming of *Ramona* (1928) so that del Rio could attend.[131] Del Rio played hostess to Mexican journalists sent to cover the event and received top billing in a list of stars that included Gilbert Roland, Clare Windsor, and Ruth Roland (no relation to Gilbert).[132] Such events afforded Mexicans in Los Angeles the opportunity to celebrate their history and culture, while enabling them to feel connected to the glamorous world of Hollywood.

The oppositional nature of these spaces comes into high relief when compared to the ways that racist stereotypes could spill off the screen and into the performative space of mainstream theaters. In 1928 *La Opinión* reported the controversy over the "Fiesta de Mexico," a gala program mounted in honor of Mexican actress Lupe Vélez, who appeared in the Douglas Fairbanks film *El gaucho* (*The Gaucho*; Elton, 1927). *The Gaucho* was a typical Fairbanks action vehicle that mixed themes of popular religiosity and dictatorial politics with adventure and romance. In the film, the gaucho, played by Fairbanks in brownface, rides to the rescue of a mountain town that has been taken over by the troops of an illegitimate dictator. He is accompanied by "Mountain Girl," played by Lupe Vélez. The film mobilizes virtually every stereotype about Latin Americans that could be gathered into a single story line. The gaucho is brutal and physical. Mountain Girl is sexy and hot tempered. The usurper is cruel. The Robin Hood–like narrative— the gaucho is spurred to good deeds by the ethereal spirituality of the "Girl of the Shrine," played by Eve Southern, and a miraculous cure for leprosy—is somewhat confusing. But none of this concerned *La Opinión's* editorial staff. Such stereotypes had become standard fare, and at least the female lead was played by a Mexican actress.

La Opinión focused instead on how race emerged in the space around the screen. The film exhibition impresario Sid Grauman had developed a spectacular prologue, "Noches Argentinas" (Argentine nights), to accompany screenings of *The Gaucho* at Grauman's Chinese Theatre in Hollywood.[133] Characterized simultaneously by "tropical ardor" and "Argentine passion," "Noches Argentinas" featured tango numbers and flamenco dancers, with over a hundred performers in all, including the vaudeville performer

FIGURE 6.4 Advertisement for a screening of *El gaucho* featuring the prologue "Noches Argentinas," *La Opinión*, December 5, 1927.

Borrah Minevitch and his harmonica players, renamed the Argentine Rascals.[134] Though seemingly confused about where, precisely, the film was set—the tropics, the pampas, or the Andes—Grauman and United Artists used the film's Latin theme as an opportunity to court the Mexican public and promote the newly discovered Vélez. At the end of the film's exclusive run in Hollywood, Grauman organized a special event that he called "Fiesta de México," ostensibly to honor Vélez, who had just signed a five-year contract.

The event was held on a Monday night, traditionally the slowest night in the theater business. Grauman circulated invitations to the crème de la crème of the Mexican immigrant community, including members of Mexico's diplomatic corps, educators, and the owners of *La Opinión*. In addition to the numbers that made up "Noches Argentinas," the performers were to present "special numbers dedicated to Mexico," and the cinema's vestibule was to be decorated with "Mexican and American symbols" in a "gesture of international amity."[135] The theater announced that the Mexican national anthem would be performed to mark the occasion, although the Mexican vice consul had hinted that "this was not the appropriate occasion for such a thing."[136]

Despite Grauman's best intentions (we can assume that, if nothing else, he at least wanted to attract the Mexican community's entertainment dollars), the gala was a public relations disaster. To the surprise of the assembled luminaries, the entrance of Lupe Vélez, identified by *La Opinión* as an "ex-chorus girl from the Lírico" (a cabaret in Mexico City), was accompanied by the Mexican national anthem. Vélez's association with the racy world of cabaret made her a problematic candidate for the position of cultural ambassador and an unlikely official representative of the Mexican government. "Never, not even in the most backward country," the newspaper protested, "has this patriotic symbol been played as an homage to a person who is not the legitimate representative of a nation."[137]

Adding insult to injury, the specially prepared version of Grauman's prologue offered an additional and even more keenly felt insult to Mexican national pride. When Minevitch announced with a flourish that "a Mexican would play the harmonica," instead "a poor comical Negro came out on the stage doing pirouettes and making hysterical gestures."[138] The racial sleight of hand performed by the bandleader—"that a Negro could be taken as a point of comparison" for a Mexican—did not amuse the audience.[139]

La Opinión's staff grounded their critique of Grauman's show in a rather selective interpretation of Mexico's liberal political tradition. They reminded the paper's readers that, unlike the United States, Mexico had outlawed slavery practically at the moment the nation was formed. In Mexico, as an article published shortly afterward explained, "the Magna Carta promulgated by the Constitutionalists of 57 [1857, Mexico's first independent constitution] specifies, we are all free and sovereign, a slave, just by stepping on Mexican territory, ceases to be a slave."[140] Thus, Mexico considered "the Negro to possess all the rights of the white man," whereas in the United States, "racial differences still exist." Grauman's "joke," the article's anonymous author continued, "had the intention of making the American audience laugh at the cost of two races: Mexicans and blacks." Thus, *La Opinión* simultaneously distinguished the community it served from African Americans and made common cause with them, as they rejected the racism that surrounded the cinema.

Mexican migrants not only enjoyed going to the movies, but many also aspired to work in the industry. The son of a bootlegger in Arizona informed a researcher that he wanted to be neither a bootlegger nor, as the researcher had helpfully suggested, a lawyer; rather, he wanted to be a movie star "like Rudolph Valentino."[141] The little boy was familiar enough with film culture to know that stars "do not have to work very hard and get paid a great deal."[142] Some migrants to Los Angeles likewise reported that they had hoped to find work as extras. For example, Margarita Alvarez de Castillo, who worked as an actress in Spanish-language variety theater, wanted to work in the movies but found gaining entrée "very difficult," in addition to facing the disapproval of her family.[143] Twenty-three-year-old Juana Martínez had journeyed alone from Sinaloa to Los Angeles after separating from her husband on hearing that there were "good opportunities to earn money, to work as 'extras' in the movies."[144] In spite of the publicity that surrounded Mexican stars working in the industry, Mexican immigrants found their opportunities in Hollywood—like those of many Anglo women and men who had come from other parts of the United States—limited to work as low-paid laborers or extras.[145]

Anglos contested Mexicans' participation in even these low ranks. To cite one example, after World War I a group of white veterans, soldiers, and seamen approached a company called the Cinema Exchange, looking for work as "extra men." The veterans signed a contract that guaranteed that they would receive $3.00 a day and lunch, with twenty cents deducted as the exchange's commission. Unfortunately, their foray into the film business did not end well. In addition to lodging complaints with the city about being overworked, not receiving water during the lengthy filming of a battle scene, and low pay, they complained that "a bunch of Mexicans" were being paid $5.00 a day.[146] Mexicans being paid more than white veterans? This seemed patently unfair to the veterans, who expected to be treated preferentially based on their race, citizenship, and military service. The archive leaves no trace of the Mexican extras' opinions on the subject. They were likely thrilled to be earning so much, even if only for a few days. It is also likely that they had experienced racial prejudice in the broader labor market; the white veterans' reactions were, sadly, nothing new.

La Opinión's coverage of the rise in anti-foreign sentiment in Hollywood in the late 1920s demonstrates the way that community leaders used discussions about cinema to critique the racial politics of American labor both inside and outside of Hollywood. The question of immigrants working in Hollywood was only one of many issues underlying the industry's labor troubles during this period, but it was one that *La Opinión* chose to focus on.[147] In doing so, the newspaper's editors made common cause with émigré actors, directors, and technical staff members, while analyzing Mexicans' particular place in the racially stratified U.S. labor market.[148]

As is well documented, during the interwar period, talent had come primarily from Europe to the United States, seeking opportunities in American film studios, which had begun to dominate the global film market. Many observers viewed this development positively. However, as the industry went through periodic economic downswings—like the one that struck in 1926, when many studios tried to economize by reducing actors' salaries—complaints about the influx of foreign nationals grew.

La Opinión followed the rise in anti-foreign sentiment in Hollywood in the fall of 1926 closely. The newspaper approvingly called Hollywood "the new tower of Babel," where "each train that arrives . . . brings us the surprise of a new representative of theater or cinema from faraway lands."[149] Unfortunately, "certain 'genuinely' American individuals" in Hollywood increasingly harbored "a feeling of hostility against the 'invaders.'"[150] The paper's entertainment editor noted that the debate over foreign artists was becoming increasingly strident in ways that paralleled the debates over Mexican migrant labor in the United States. Opponents of the "foreign atmosphere" in Hollywood used inflammatory language similar to that used by opponents of Mexican and Asian immigration to the United States. Beneath the headline "Foreign Directors and Artists Out! War against the Invader!," *La Opinión*'s readers learned that an editorial in *Filmograph*, a film industry weekly, had asserted that by hiring foreign actors and directors, the studio heads were engaging in anti-American behavior. *La Opinión* translated and reproduced in their entirety the even more inflammatory comments made in *Filmograph* by the actor and Hollywood labor activist Aubrey Blair.[151]

Blair began his piece by describing in economic terms the effects of the "foreign invasion" on "Americans" working in Hollywood. "The income generated by the cinematic 'failures' that have been made in the majority by those imported directors," Blair argued, "can not be compared with the profits obtained by the productions of American directors." He accused the industry of placing American artists on "hunger rations," when they were in fact the industry's most productive workers. Throughout the piece, he drew parallels between the actors' situation and that of the laboring classes, using the language of organized labor.[152]

The day after Blair's comments were published in *La Opinión*, the newspaper offered its interpretation of Blair's nativist rhetoric. Acknowledging that "the position of the intellectual worker, the artist, differs notably from that which the manual laborer occupies," the unnamed author mobilized a strategy that mirrored Blair's—equating the virulent attacks on foreign directors, screenwriters, and actors with those on Mexican laborers. Complaints about foreign labor in the studios came, the article claimed, from "the 'jingoists' . . . the same people that constantly ask for . . . expulsion of Mexican workers in California." The author described the comparison drawn by Blair between the plight of manual laborers and actors and directors as "infantile." After all, the U.S. film industry was the most powerful in the world.[153]

The "war against foreigners" faded into the background for almost a year. Then, in December 1927, the paper revisited the topic, reporting that native-born white American actors (most of whom *La Opinión* deemed "second-rate") had formed the "Society of North American Actors" to represent their views. Complaints made in relatively modest tones the year before were now being shouted: "Hollywood is being invaded by a true legion of actors from other countries that have no right to be in the United States." The society laid the blame for this state of affairs at the feet of film czar William Hays and the "influence he . . . has with the immigration authorities."[154]

La Opinión considered the issue so important that it devoted an editorial to the subject. Acknowledging that "the topic that we are going to discuss might fit better in the entertainment section rather than the editorial page," which was typically reserved for "items of orientation and utility for our readers" and for "Mexican interests," the editorial asserted that the issue "includes a part that affects us."[155] The news that the Society of North American Actors was planning an anti-immigrant campaign prompted a warning to all Mexicans: "without full preparation and without previous contacts, do not attempt to break in [to the movie business]."[156] Beyond this rather run-of-the-mill warning about the perils of pursuing fame and fortune, the editorial also offered a critique of American racial ideologies. Foreign actors, including Mexican extras, the editors of *La Opinión* declared, represented fundamental American values. "The American people," they wrote, "have made axiomatic the saying that 'success is for the most qualified.'" Since the foreigners who have "come to invade Hollywood are the most qualified (not to mention the cheapest)," it would be difficult if not impossible to expel them. The same sort of logic, the editorial continued, made Mexican labor indispensable to the greater U.S. economy.[157]

Despite putting forward critiques of the racial politics of labor in the United States—and despite warning Hollywood hopefuls about the perils of pursuing their dreams of stardom without adequate preparation and good industry contacts—*La Opinión* nevertheless continued to assist Mexican men and women looking for work in an industry that promised relief from the low-paid, backbreaking work that characterized most immigrant lives.

The paper consistently gave almost as much attention to any expression of interest in local talent on the part of the industry as it did to Mexican stars, and informed its readers about periodic opportunities at the studios.[158]

For example, in February 1928, just months after its coverage of the "war on foreigners," *La Opinión* reported that the major studios were in the process of hiring thousands of extras to fill the needs of an industrywide production increase. This hiring bonanza promised opportunities for Mexican aspirants who were, the paper noted, "favorites of Central Casting." In addition to needing Mexican and "Spanish" extras to perform in films set in Spain or Latin America that required "their type" in crowd scenes, extras "with dark skin and black hair" were needed to play "horsemen," as well as to act in films set in the South Seas and to perform in scenes that required them to be "semi-naked at the risk of contracting deadly pneumonia."[159] Of this last specialty, *La Opinión* observed that Mexican extras, like "workers in the lettuce camps of Arizona and the construction sites of urban Los Angeles," occupy "those jobs that the Americans disdain to perform because they are dangerous or poorly paid." Work as an extra offered daily pay that far exceeded what one could earn in other industries, and in "these times of crisis in which they talk about repatriation of braceros" it was certainly better than no job at all, but *La Opinión* remained skeptical about Mexicans' long-term prospects for employment in the film industry.[160] The paper's editorial staff members remained keenly aware of the contradictions of this state of affairs, with Mexicans being sought after as part of a larger audience of ticket buyers and sometimes as a cheap source of labor that added local color to feature films, while at the same time being excluded from the possibilities for social mobility promoted by the popular, and indeed international, discourse on Hollywood as a land of promise and possibility.

CONCLUSION

From December 1926 to April 1927, *La Opinión*'s sister newspaper in San Antonio, *La Prensa*, published a novel in weekly installments by the Los Angeles–based orchestra leader, writer, and cinema columnist Gabriel Navarro, titled *La ciudad de irás y no volverás* (The City of No Return).[161] The story recounts the misadventures—tragedies, really—of Laura Canedo, a young *mexicana* who travels from Guadalajara to Hollywood in hopes of becoming a star. The novel contrasts Laura's fantasies about the life of a star with the realities of immigrant life. The first installment opens with Laura in a luxuriously appointed room being waited on by servants. She is greeted by three of the male stars whom Mexican audiences idolized—Antonio Moreno, John Gilbert, and Ramón Novarro—who proclaim their admiration for the "Mexican beauty." Laura wakes from this dream in a cheap hotel in Los Angeles, where taxi drivers take advantage of her, studio receptionists take one look at her non-Anglo features and rudely turn her away, and industry hangers-on eye her lecherously.

The story's plot combines romance—Laura meets an attractive fellow aspirant and immigrant Raymundo—with the sensational extra-filmic discourse about Hollywood and its stars that circulated in the 1920s (among other things, Laura falls prey to a smarmy talent agent). Unable to get a toehold in Hollywood, Laura finds herself pushed to the margins of the entertainment industry, working at a theater on Main Street in downtown Los Angeles, which offers live entertainment and "adventure films" to an undiscerning immigrant audience. Throughout the novel, Laura negotiates not one but two unfamiliar worlds, that of Hollywood and that of immigrant Los Angeles life. In this way the story is as much an immigrant tale as it is a film-world fable, exploring the tenuous position of *mexicanos* in Hollywood (a topic also addressed by the diplomatic tussles of the 1920s), and the place of cinema in Greater Mexico's process of modernization and urbanization, a process to which immigration was central. Yet unlike *Las aventuras de Don Chipote*, *La ciudad de irás y no volverás* does not posit the existence of an idealized, traditional, peasant Mexico. Rather, Laura's fascination with cinema emerges as the logical result of the diffusion and growing ubiquity of certain cultural formations—especially the novel and the motion picture— along with the actual technologies of movement, such as the railroad and steamships, which physically crossed borders. What's more, Laura uses the cinema as a resource for self-fashioning, and although her story is heartrending at times, she is never the stock character that Don Chipote becomes. That is, Laura, like the Mexican youth interviewed by Lanigan in 1932, yearned for a "better form of living . . . the finer things the world has to offer," and found a model, if not satisfaction, for those desires in American cinema.[162]

Throughout the 1920s, Mexican migrants engaged with U.S. films and film culture as a source of pleasure—motion pictures were a central leisure activity for many migrants and their children—and a source of consternation, as they were forced to negotiate the racial ideologies that shaped American film on- and off-screen. Both Mexican and American observers perceived race as a critical component of Mexican immigrants' experience of American mass culture. Although wary of the way that mass culture could lead to alienation, Mexican commentators saw immigrants' encounters with the racism that shaped American cinema as a potential catalyst for solidifying national affinity. Alternatively, from the point of view of American social scientists and reformers, cinemagoing was most often, though not always, another factor contributing to Mexicans' perceived criminality, out-of-control sexual behavior, and lack of thrift. At best, the right kind of films could help steer Mexicans away from their natural tendencies and toward Americanization. The question of race not only governed how Mexican moviegoing practices were perceived but, in many parts of the United States, dictated where Mexicans could go to the movies. Particularly in Texas, Mexican movie theater patrons were segregated from their Anglo peers and, to the chagrin of immigrants who astutely read the racial hierarchy that governed social life in the United States, grouped with African American patrons.

Out of these contradictions, Mexican audiences in the United States created a parallel film culture and gave cinema a space in community life that included but exceeded generational conflicts. In El Paso participation in the film distribution and exhibition business allowed ethnic Mexican entrepreneurs to become agents of a transnational modernity, while exhibition practices reinforced immigrants' ties to Mexico's film culture. El Paso's Mexican theaters constituted part of a regional Mexican film culture that included theaters on both sides of the border and was proof not of acculturation per se, but of northern Mexico's participation in the country's larger modernizing project. In Los Angeles, where many immigrants hoped to gain a foothold in the film industry, and where work as an extra seemed relatively easy compared to the hard labor many migrants were accustomed to, Mexican critics engaged film culture as both a cultural force and a potential source of employment. *La Opinión*'s coverage of the way that American racism shaped not only on-screen narratives but the performative space of mainstream motion picture theaters and the regional labor market allows us to see how the community's literate elite used Mexican engagement with cinema as an opportunity to critique the racial politics of not just Hollywood, but also the United States more broadly.

In sum, on the U.S. side of the border anti-Mexican racism shaped Mexican migrant moviegoing and set the conditions for the emergence of a parallel film culture. There the cinema became a site not of Americanization—or at least not exclusively one of Americanization, and then only somewhat more so than in Mexico's own urban areas—but of participation in Greater Mexico's cross-border film culture. The transnational circulation of film texts, film culture, and film audiences meant that exhibition and critical practices could foster national sentiment even as the images on the screen and star texts exposed Mexican audiences to new forms of self-presentation, gender relations, and sexual practices, producing distinctly Mexican versions of modernity.

CONCLUSION

The cinema, with the coming of sound, has taken a 180-degree turn
toward its nationalization.

— "POSIBILIDADES CINEMATOGRÁFICAS DE MÉXICO,"

EL NACIONAL REVOLUCIONARIO, AUGUST 17, 1931

In the spring of 1929, Mexican President Emilio Portes Gil (1928–30)
received a letter from the Paramount Pictures office in Mexico City
inviting him to attend a gala celebrating the installation of the first
Vitaphone system in Mexico. Paramount's representative in Mexico
City, Victoriano Medina, assured the president that the system installed in the Cine Olimpia was "similar in every way to those in the
high class theaters in the United States," signing his letter "for the
good of the Mexican family, that is, the good of the fatherland."[1] With
this Medina framed sound cinema as a national good. The adoption
of the new technology was cast not as a form of cultural imperialism,
but rather as yet another step toward modernity. Indeed, this was the
view of many. In the capital, *El Universal* noted that Vitaphone films
were being "exhibited in the same form and with machines identical
to those in New York theaters," putting the country on par with other
developed nations.[2] In El Paso, *El Continental* announced that the
Teatro Colón, the Mexican community's favorite cinema, had been
remodeled to "acoustic perfection."[3]

The introduction of sound films also engendered both loud protests by influential segments of Mexico's intellectual and cultural elite,
as well as leftist political activists, and a flurry of excitement among
critics and audiences about Hollywood's Spanish-language production. More significantly, however, the transition to sound encouraged
national film production as Mexican directors and producers sought

FIGURE CONC.1 The Teatro Colón in El Paso, Texas, unveils its sound on-disc system, 1929. Courtesy Viviana García Bresne.

to satisfy audiences' desires to hear Spanish, see narratives that spoke to their realities, and be touched by stars they could claim as their own. Indeed, by the 1940s no other national cinema, as contemporary commentators seemed to be aware, was better poised to serve the hemisphere's Spanish-speaking audiences. Excitement about the possibilities engendered by the emergence of sound grew in the optimistic atmosphere created by Mexico's national-ization of major industries under Lazaro Cardenas, Mexico's president from 1934 to 1940. With strong state support, a nascent Mexican studio system emerged during the 1930s, and Hollywood-trained actors and other person-nel returned to Mexico to work in those new studios. The stage was set for the development of a strong industry in the 1940s, whose products would win Mexico acclaim internationally and box-office success at home and throughout the hemisphere.

Narratives of Mexican cinematic history have marked this moment as the beginning of an established national film culture and the production of a recognizable national imaginary. The striking visuals of melodramas such as *Maria Candelaria* (Films Mundiales, 1942), one of many productive col-laborations between the director Emilio "el indio" Fernández and the cine-matographer Gabriel Figueroa, and the folk culture portrayed in the *come-dia ranchera* cycle that began with Fernando de Fuentes's 1936 comedy *Alla en el rancho grande* (Bustamante and de Fuentes), became the calling card of Mexican cinema around the world.[4] At the same time, the faces of actors such as Dolores del Rio who resumed her career in Mexico, María Félix, and Pedro Infante became icons across Latin America. The prolific output of the studio system that became Mexico's third largest industry has inspired a prolific body of scholarship in both Spanish and English, the latter with particular enthusiasm since the 1995 publication of Paulo Paranaguá's *Mexican Cinema*, an edited volume that surveys Mexican cinema, in English translation.[5] Despite a surge in interest in Mexican cinema, particularly from the 1930s to the present, the silent period has received scant attention in English-language scholarship. The period between the end of the revolution and the emergence of Golden Age cinema has been characterized as a moment of anticipation in which the future Golden Age can be seen in exemplary films such as *El automóvil gris* (1919) and the activities of Mexican directors and actors. Focusing on national production in this way links the remarkable documentary tradition of the revolutionary era to the sound feature film production that consciously sought to present national stories.

The products of the few, ephemeral Mexican studios of the 1920s were often lost among the large number of films imported from the United States, but this does not mean that Mexico lacked a national film culture. On the contrary, my research complicates the equation of national cinema with national production. Saturnino Cedillo dreamed that his people would have motion pictures, and indeed they did. Across urban Mexico, and in many rural areas as well, all but the very poor went to the cinema with regularity. Regardless of the country of origin of the films being shown, the very fact of their exhibition and the complex of performative, promotional, and cultural practices that accompanied cinemagoing were perceived as being part of Mexico's own modernity. Indisputably, the U.S. film industry came to dominate the Mexican market. With that dominance came windows onto new models of gender and social relations and the world of consumer culture that many Mexicans took up with enthusiasm. American films and film culture also brought American notions of race that pushed Mexicans away as insistently as advertising called them to the ticket booth. Out of these contradictions, Mexican audiences—heterogeneous but increasingly united by a notion of what it meant to be Mexican—translated, appropriated, and adapted American cinema in the service of not only Mexico's postrevolutionary nation-building project, but also the production of modern Mexican identities.

When U.S. film producers turned their attention to Mexico in the late 1910s, Mexican exhibitors and many Mexican filmgoers welcomed them. At the same time, some commentators viewed their activities as part of the ongoing U.S. imperial designs on Mexico. American film studios sought control over the rampant piracy that affected their profits in the rest of Latin America and worked in concert with the U.S. State Department to improve the United States' public image south of the border. Mexican audiences and film critics celebrated expanded opportunities to participate in global film culture. The *yanqui* invasion, as some referred to this influx of American films and American stars, appeared to have been successful, but as North American film companies expanded their reach into the Mexican market, they pursued but did not necessarily impose their own agenda. Rather, they contended with local tastes, business culture, and politics. Representatives of the producers and distributors that came to dominate the American film industry brought with them racist notions about Mexico and Mexicans. They were met by an active labor movement that advocated for Mexican cinema workers' rights in an industry increasingly dominated by foreign capital.

The upheaval and chaos of the revolution, which brought peasants and others into urban areas as migrants or soldiers, expanded the Mexican audience for motion pictures. The Mexican Department of Labor as well as the press considered film exhibition an important industry that attested to Mexico's industrial development and civilization. Within this framework, purpose-built motion picture theaters became tangible evidence of the country's development and the setting for both official and popular nation-building rituals.

Cinema audiences became the object of reformist projects that sought to mold Mexico's masses into a modern citizenry. Municipal regulators, especially in Mexico City, urged exhibitors to provide an atmosphere that would encourage patrons to adopt middle-class norms of behavior and morality. Honorable families, ostensibly from any social class, rather than middle-class women as in the United States, were sought out as ideal patrons who would bestow legitimacy on motion pictures. At the same time, municipal authorities found themselves defending cinema patrons as consumers, a new identity that the state also sought to cultivate as part of a modern society.

In its coverage of film culture, the Mexican popular press sought out and even produced filmgoers as consumers with their personal opinions and preferences. With a reach that extended beyond the literate public, the press disseminated American film culture across urban Mexico. In the pages of daily newspapers, popular magazines, and internationally circulated fan magazines, journalists and critics initiated Mexico's moviegoing public into the practices of fandom, showed them the link between the movies and consumer culture, and encouraged moviegoers to develop a critical sensibility that would mark them as sophisticated viewers equal to those of developed countries. In one register, these publications preached the gospel of Hollywood as the locus of a cosmopolitan, universal film culture. In another very important register, they addressed Mexican audiences as a separate audience shaped by language, culture, and a history of conflict with the United States. It was in this space that Mexican journalists, critics, fans, and everyday moviegoers recast Hollywood as Cinelandia, a distinctly Mexican cultural space. Through acts of translation, adaptation, and appropriation, American cinema became a resource for both Mexico's postrevolutionary nation-building project and individual fans' production of modern subjectivities. Whereas Hollywood fan culture invited complete identification, in Cinelandia Mexican audience members found a space to negotiate Hollywood's values, ideological assumptions, and anti-Mexican racism.

As the debate over the *pelona* demonstrates, the social effects of the Mexican public's consumption of American films became a source of anxiety for many members of the middle class as well as the conservative and liberal elite. The pelona's yearning for autonomy, social mobility, and sexual liberation, often framed as a desire for cinematic stardom, prompted some young women to cross figurative and sometimes literal borders. The pelona's critics deemed her manner of dressing, public behavior, and longing for celebrity to be anti-Mexican, offering her up as proof of U.S. cultural imperialism. Conjuring up the specter of foreign influence, rather than addressing the emergence of the modern girl as a product of Mexican society, directed attention away from women's dissatisfaction with the place assigned to them in postrevolutionary society. Since women's longing for stardom, or the lifestyle it represented, seemed impossible to temper, the press produced narratives of frustrated journeys to Hollywood, which had been thwarted by concerned parents, avatars of the state, and transnational stardom that cast Mexican participation in the U.S. film industry as a form of diplomacy. In this way, women's adoption of new modes of self-presentation, activities in the public sphere, and participation in consumer culture could be channeled to support rather than undermine Mexico's nation-building project.

Young Mexican women (and many men) dreamed of stardom, but many Mexicans viewed Hollywood's on-screen representations of Mexico and Mexicans with wariness. Much to their dismay, the political elite saw national symbols that were being mobilized to unite a diverse population, such as the revolutionary and the *charro*, become the stuff of stereotypes and a distinctly unmodern image of Mexico that was circulated worldwide via American films. In 1922 their unhappiness prompted an embargo against the U.S. film companies that produced such films. The solution the Motion Picture Producers and Distributors of America lighted on—to shift such narratives to fantastical locations—ostensibly dealt with the government's complaints. But many Mexican viewers proved savvy in discerning the studios' obfuscation. In the end, the Mexican government moved away from overt censorship and the use of embargos and other measures to influence the studios, instead offering advice to studios in the preproduction phase of films related to Mexico. Mexico emerged with only slightly more influence over on-screen representations of Mexico and Mexicans than it had possessed at the beginning of the 1920s. Though this seems like a failure, the state's attempts to exercise censorship over Mexico's cinematic image did have a productive function. Although different social groups—diplomats, cinema owners and workers, film distributors, and the public—viewed embargos differently, some seeing them positively and some negatively, all of them perceived cinema as having an important place in Mexico's modern nation-building project.

The responses by Mexicans living and working on the U.S. side of the border to what they referred to as denigrating films attest to the fact that the racial regime that governed silent cinema affected Mexican immigrants more acutely than their peers in Mexico. Racism not only shaped the narratives they saw on the screen, but it also became the frame through which American reformers and social scientists viewed Mexican moviegoing. Perhaps most critically, in many parts of the United States, de facto segregation determined the conditions under which Mexican immigrants could see films. This pervasive anti-Mexican racism established the conditions for the emergence of a parallel film culture akin to that formed in African American communities. As the case of El Paso demonstrates, cinemas serving Mexican audiences, particularly in south Texas, constituted part of a trans-border, regional economy. Positioned as part of northern Mexico's film culture, their exhibition practices—including the presence of Mexican entertainers—promotional strategies, and articulated role in the community encouraged patrons to link moviegoing with the cultivation of Mexican national sensibilities. In Los Angeles, where similar exhibition practices held sway, critical practices nurtured nationalist sentiment even as they critiqued the racial hierarchy that governed not only filmic narratives but also Hollywood's labor market. The parallel film culture that emerged in Mexican communities on the U.S. side of the border was a site of generational conflict, but it was also part of a Mexican film culture that had been established through the circulation of American films in urban Mexico.

In the 1930s many Mexicans on both sides of the border looked to a new culture industry—Mexican cinema—to satisfy their desires to see themselves on the screen. Mexican film fans found new objects of affection in the form of national film stars and new opportunities for identification in narratives conceived of as "100 percent Mexican."[6] Though the aspiration to speak to or for all Mexicans would prove as fictional as the American film industry's claims to universality, the Mexican government began to see film production—rather than participation in the U.S. industry, exhibition, or even movie-going itself—as a "way of spreading [Mexico's] progress and artistic expression."[7]

U.S. film companies did not, of course, disappear completely from Mexico. Rather, as Seth Fein has shown, they retreated backstage into the business of international distribution and continued to export hundreds of films a year to Mexico, which now shared screen space with domestic productions.[8] Theaters serving Mexican communities in the United States began to offer audiences films in Spanish, first Hollywood's Spanish-language productions and then Mexican films. They continued, as Colin Gunckel and Desiree Garcia explore, to be sites for community building and the solidification of transnational ties to Mexico.[9] Mexican national cinema was deeply transnational in nature, bringing together Mexican audiences on either side of the border; playing a role in the formation of Mexican-American and, eventually, Chicana/o identity on the U.S. side of the border; and addressing a broader, pan-Latin audience throughout the hemisphere.[10]

It is in the 1920s, between the reign of European films and the emergence of Mexican sound cinema, that the contours of Mexico's national film culture emerge: the discourse on cinema made the nation the shared point of reference for audiences in the process of becoming Mexican. American film companies brought to Mexico what they considered the latest in modern entertainment but had to contend with local preferences, political upheaval, and an organized labor force in Mexico's cinemas. Newly constructed theaters, designed to showcase imported films, became icons of Mexico's modernity. Film journalists presented Hollywood through Mexican eyes, and would-be stars became national ambassadors. Mexican viewers declared their outrage at Hollywood's stereotypes and sometimes at the Mexican government's attempts to suppress them, and Mexican migrants went to the show to revel in both the fantasies offered by Hollywood and Mexican nationalism. In these ways, the circulation of silent-era films across the U.S.-Mexico border proved to be more than mere entertainment and less than an inescapable vehicle of Americanization. Mexico's diverse audiences made their own meanings out of their encounters with American cinema as they translated, adopted, and appropriated American films and film culture to create a distinctly Mexican cultural space, Cinelandia. There the nation was confirmed as the primary lens through which Mexicans should see cinema, both domestic and foreign.

ABBREVIATIONS OF FREQUENTLY CITED SOURCES

NEWSPAPERS AND MAGAZINES

CM	*Cine-Mundial* (New York)
EC	*El Continental* (El Paso, TX)
ED	*El Demócrata* (Mexico City)
EH	*El Hogar* (Mexico City)
EPH	*El Paso Herald* (El Paso, TX)
EPT	*El Paso Times* (El Paso, TX)
EU	*El Universal* (Mexico City)
EUI	*El Universal Ilustrado* (Mexico City)
EX	*Excélsior* (Mexico City)
LDC	*La Dama Católica* (Mexico City)
LO	*La Opinión* (Los Angeles)
MPW	*Moving Picture World* (New York)
RR	*Revista de Revistas* (Mexico City)

ARCHIVES

AGN, DGG	Archivo General de la Nación, Fondo Dirección General de Gobierno
AGN, DT	Archivo General de la Nación, Fondo Departamento de Trabajo
AGN, POC	Archivo General de la Nación, Fondo Presidentes Obregón-Calles
AHDF, A, DP	Archivo Histórico del Distrito Federal (formerly Archivo Histórico del Antiguo Ayuntamiento), Fondo Diversiones Públicas
AHDF, A, M	Archivo Histórico del Distrito Federal (formerly Archivo Histórico del Antiguo Ayuntamiento), Municipalidades
AHDF, A, SG	Archivo Histórico del Distrito Federal (formerly Archivo Histórico del Antiguo Ayuntamiento), Secretaría General
AHDF, J	Archivo Histórico del Distrito Federal, Justicia
AHSRE	Archivo Histórico de la Secretaría de Relaciones Exteriores

NOTES

PRÓLOGO (PROLOGUE)

1. "Frente a la pantalla," *El Universal Gráfico*, February 11, 1926.
2. "Frente a la pantalla."
3. Tierney, *Emilio Fernández*, 6.

INTRODUCTION

1. Quoted in Robert Haberman, "Bandit Colonies," *Survey*, May 1, 1924, 148.
2. Haberman, "Bandit Colonies," 148.
3. Though the term "American" refers to the entire continent, for the sake of brevity I employ it throughout this book to refer to people or things from the United States, as this was one of the primary ways it was used in my sources.
4. On this effort and various arguments about what aspects of the film industry's organization and strategic planning made this possible, see Thompson, *Exporting Entertainment*; Trumpboar, *Selling Hollywood to the World*; De Grazia, *Irresistible Empire*, 384–85; Jarvie, *Hollywood's Overseas Campaign*. On Hollywood's spread into France, see Ulff-Møller, *Hollywood's "Film Wars" with France*, which charts the emergence of protective quotas. On Germany, see Saunders, *Hollywood in Berlin*, which examines the German film communities' response to American films. On Latin America, see Usabel, *The High Noon*, which looks specifically at the activities of United Artists from the 1920s to the 1950s.
5. For example, in July 1919 the United Shoe Machinery Company of Mexico sponsored a reportedly well-attended showing at the Cine Santa María la Redonda in Mexico City of a sponsored film about shoe manufacturing in the United States ("Película interesante y instructiva," *Excélsior* [hereafter EX], July 2, 1919). The distribution and reception of nontheatrical fare in Mexico during this period begs for its own extensive study.
6. U.S. film exports to Mexico increased from 197,835 feet fiscal year 1913 to 3.3 million feet fiscal year 1922 (U.S. Department of Commerce, Latin American Division, *U.S. Trade with Latin America in 1922*, 34).
7. Amador and Ayala Blanco, *Cartelera cinematográfica, 1920–1929*, 465–69.
8. García Riera, *Historia documental del cine mexicano*, 1:11.
9. On *El automóvil gris*, see Ramírez Berg, "*El automóvil gris*." On Mimí Derba,

see García Rodríguez, "Mimí Derba and Azteca Films"; Miquel, *Mimi Derba*. Though they have not been the subject of their own study, we know through Aurelio de los Reyes's meticulous research that a number of Mexican companies were formed in the 1920s to produce national newsreels. The Sociedad Anunciadora Mexicana produced *Actualidades de México*; the Ehler sisters, who make a brief appearance in chapter 5 of this book, founded *Revista Ehlers*, which they produced from 1922 to 1931; and the newspaper *El Demócrata* also produced a regular newsreel. See Reyes, *Filmografía del cine mudo*, 123, and *Cine y sociedad en Mexico*, 2:243–44; Ciuk, *Diccionario de directores del cine mexicano*, 224–25.

10. In describing the career of the distributor and sometime film producer German Camus, *Magazine Fílmico*—a Mexico City weekly aimed at local distributors and exhibitors—declared that he had decided to focus on the distribution side of his business precisely because filmmaking required large investments of capital and, in Mexico, promised limited returns (Rafael Bermúdez Zartrain, "Memorias Cinematográficas," *Magazine Fílmico*, November or December 1927, n.p.).

11. A list of theaters and information about other venues was compiled from census material found in AGN, DT, 620, 5, and 641, 5. I discuss this study in greater depth in chapter 2.

12. "*El hijo de la loca*: Película nacional," EX, October 14, 1923. Others used some variation of this phrasing.

13. Thompson, *Exporting Entertainment*, 49.

14. On relations between the United States and Mexico during the revolution and the postrevolutionary period, see Ulloa, *La lucha armada*; Gonzales, *The Mexican Revolution*; Womack, "The Mexican Revolution"; J. Meyer and Bethell, "Revolution and Reconstruction in the 1920s." See also Rodríguez O., *The Revolutionary Process in Mexico*. For an analysis of the Mexican government's willingness to negotiate with the United States about resource ownership and reparations for damage to American-owned property during the civil war, see L. Meyer, "La institucionalización del nuevo régimen"; Matute, *Historia de la revolución mexicana*; Meyer, Krauze, and Reyes, *Historia de la revolución*; M. Meyer, Sherman, and Deeds, *The Course of Mexican History*. The literature on the treatment of Mexican immigrants in the United States is, rightly, substantial. A classic perspective can be found in Acuña, *Occupied America*. See also Cardoso, *Mexican Emigration to the United States*; Guerin-Gonzalez, *Mexican Workers and American Dreams*; Sanchez, *Becoming Mexican American*; Gonzáles, *Mexicanos*.

15. The historian Alan Knight describes this process in "Popular Culture and the Revolutionary State." He refers to the drive to "nationalize and rationalize" Mexico's citizenry (426). Claudio Lomnitz explores the more recent history of the discursive production of nationalism by the Mexican intelligentsia from an anthropological perspective in *Deep Mexico*.

16. Benjamin, *La Revolución*, 13–23. The essays in *The Eagle and the Virgin*, edited by Mary Kay Vaughan and Steven Lewis, take up the nation-building projects engaged in by the postrevolutionary government in collaboration with artists, intellectuals, reformers, and educators. The Mexican elite focused on "ethnicizing" the

nation by making Mexico's indigenous past central to Mexican identity and celebrating the popular arts. The literature on *indigenismo*, as this movement is referred to, is quite expansive. The key text in terms of the philosophy of *mestizaje*, or racial mixing, as the basis of Mexican society is Vasconcelos, *La raza cósmica*. In terms of the popular arts, for an excellent account of the interplay between indigenous artisans, intellectuals, and the state, see López, *Crafting Mexico*.

17. These dual and sometimes seemingly conflicted projects of ethnicization and modernization often met with resistance from people who were attached to local identities or who conceived of themselves as members of broader communities of interest, such as Catholics—whose discontent with the government's secular vision of the nation erupted in the violence of the Cristero Rebellion, 1926–28. On this project and its complications, see Vaughan, *Cultural Politics in Revolution*; Rubenstein, *Bad Language*; Bliss, *Compromised Positions*; Knight, "Popular Culture and the Revolutionary State."

18. On the "revolutionary politicization" of private life, see Bliss, *Compromised Positions*, 13.

19. On the exchange of high culture and Mexican popular culture between Mexico and the United States in the 1920s, see Delpar, *The Enormous Vogue*.

20. Aurelio de los Reyes gives the most attention to the presence and influence of American cinema in his magisterial two-volume social history of silent cinema, *Cine y sociedad*. Scholarship on Mexican silent cinema in Spanish is vibrant. Filmographies include Reyes, *Filmografía del cine mudo* (three volumes); Reyes, *Los orígenes del cine*; Ramírez, *Crónica del cine mudo mexicano*; Dávalos Orozco and Vázquez Bernal, *Filmografía general del cine mexicano*; G. García, *El cine mudo mexicano*. On the careers of prominent directors, particularly those active during the revolutionary period and early 1930s, see Miquel, *Salvador Toscano*; Pick, "Jesús H. Abitía"; Vega Alfaro and Torres San Martín, *Adela Sequeyro*. For the history of film criticism in Mexico City, see Miquel, *Por las pantallas*; González Casanova, "Por la pantalla." For its history in Guadalajara, see Torres San Martín, *Crónicas tapatías*. Research on regional production includes G. Ramírez, *El cine yucateco*, and a number of the essays in Vega Alfaro, *Microhistorias del cine en México*. There are several important compilations of criticism and press coverage of cinema during this period, including Garrido, *Luz y sombra*; Reyes de la Maza, *Salón Rojo*; Almoina, *Notas para la historia del cine*.

21. Reyes, *Cine y sociedad*, 1:269–70.

22. Ramírez Berg, "El automóvil gris," 5.

23. Higson, "The Concept of National Cinema," 37.

24. Monsiváis, "All the People Came," 150.

25. Chase, *Mexico*, 198.

26. Chase, *Mexico*, 198.

27. Icaza, *Así era aquello*. Other memorias of Mexico City in the early twentieth century likewise privilege the emergence of motion picture venues and the act of filmgoing. See, for example, Flores Rivera, *Relatos de mi barrio*; Motts, *La vida en la Ciudad de México*. See also the brief mention of cinema in Ramírez Plancarte, *La*

Ciudad de México; the section on cinemas in Pensado and Correa, *Mixcoac*; Novo, *La estatua de sal*.

28. Higson, "The Concept of National Cinema," 52.

29. This broad historical approach to film culture is referred to by the historian Nan Enstad as the "social circulation" of film (*Ladies of Labor*, 12) and by the film studies scholar Yuri Tsivian as "cultural reception" (*Early Cinema in Russia*, 1–3). Lynn Spigel takes this approach in her now-classic study of the introduction of television in the United States, *Make Room for TV*. Eric Smoodin advocates this type of broad, multi-archival historical inquiry as a way of reframing the history of cinema as a history of not only film texts but also the social and cultural space of cinema "beyond the screen" (Smoodin, "The History of Film History").

30. Fein, "Film Propaganda," 403. For a critique of the notion of "dominant ideology" and of the cultural imperialism model, see Sinclair, "Culture and Trade." Sinclair argues that both preclude a consideration of the possible meanings made of any given text by consumers (50).

31. Pratt, *Imperial Eyes*, 4.

32. The transnational as a framing concept has become an important category of analysis in a range of fields. In American studies and related fields, scholars have trained their analysis on the work performed abroad by American culture and the ways in which it has been appropriated in different political and historical contexts. For an early example of this approach, see McAlister's *Epic Encounters*. Other examples include Siegel, *Uneven Encounters*; Foster, *Projections of Power*; and Feeney, "Hollywood in Havana." In Latin American history, focusing on the Americas has been suggested as an antidote to scholarship trained on the nation-state. See, for example, Zolov, *Refried Elvis*; Moreno, *Yankee Don't Go Home!*; Joseph, LeGrand, and Salvatore, *Close Encounters of Empire*.

33. S. Hall, "Encoding/Decoding," 137.

34. Haberman, "Bandit Colonies," 148.

35. Hansen, "Fallen Women," 12.

36. On Mexico's desire for modernity both before and after the revolution, see Tenorio Trillo, *Mexico at the World's Fairs*; Gallo, *Mexican Modernity*; Hershfield, *Imagining la Chica Moderna*.

37. See Vaughan, *Cultural Politics in Revolution*.

38. García Canclini, *Hybrid Cultures*, 3, 1.

39. Knauft, "Critically Modern," 3–4. There is a growing body of anthropological literature on the concept of alternative modernities that seeks to track the spread of capitalism and its attendant cultural forms while avoiding casting the modern and traditional as distinct, rather than mutually constitutive, categories. In addition to Knauft, see Gaonka, *Alternative Modernities*. In a similar vein, Allen Wells and Gilbert Joseph have argued for an understanding of the developmentalist ideologies that shaped nation building in Latin America in the late nineteenth and early twentieth centuries as the product of "local claims to modernity and a shared Western tradition" ("Modernizing Visions," 171).

40. Borge, *Latin American Writers*, 48–73; Duffey, "'Un dinamismo abrasador.'"

On these two often-in-conflict literary groups, the estridentistas and the contemporaneos, see Schneider, *El estridentismo*, and Sheridan, *Los contemporáneos ayer*.

41. Manuel Maples Arce, Germán List Arzubide, Salvador Gallardo, et al., "Manifiesto Estridentista," January 1, 1923, reproduced in Schwartz, *Las vanguardias latinoamericanas*, 198–200.

42. Quoted in Schwartz, *Las vanguardias latinoamericanas*, 91.

43. Novo, *La estatua de sal*, 78.

44. "En una tempestad de pasiones se ahonda el proceso de la Sra. Magdalena Jurado," *El Heraldo de México*, April 7, 1922.

45. "La tragedia de Altavista," *El Universal* (hereafter *EU*), April 1, 1924.

46. "Un robo cinematográfico en la Villa de Tlalpan," *EU*, January 12, 1924. See also José de J. Nuñez y Dominguez, "Los hombres del delito," *EX*, September 1923.

47. "Una 'mocosa' se propuso probar que era muy mujer," *EX*, July 29, 1920.

48. A. López, "Early Cinema and Modernity in Latin America," 53.

49. Peiss, *Cheap Amusements*; Rabinovitz, *For the Love of Pleasure*; Stamp, *Movie-Struck Girls*.

50. Hansen, *Babel and Babylon*, 93–114; Stamp, *Movie-Struck Girls*, 24–32.

51. Hansen, *Babel and Babylon*, 34–86; Stamp, *Movie-Struck Girls*, 7–8. Variations of the acculturation argument, some with caveats about the provisional nature of that acculturation, can be found in Monroy, *Rebirth*, 168–81; M. Garcia, *Desert Immigrants*, 197–232; Ruiz, *From out of the Shadows*, 51–70; and Sanchez, *Becoming Mexican American*, 171–87. The latter two emphasize the give-and-take of tradition and cultural change. Ruiz emphasizes generational conflict to a greater degree than does Sanchez.

52. Limón, "Stereotyping and Chicano Resistance"; Fregoso, *MeXicana Encounters*, 148–68; Marez, "Subaltern Soundtracks."

53. Monroy, *Rebirth*, 202–3. Américo Paredes uses the term "Greater Mexico" to refer to "all the areas inhabited by people of a Mexican culture—not only within the [present] limits of the Republic of Mexico but in the United States as well" (quoted in Limón, *American Encounters*, 215, note 1).

54. Ruiz, *From out of the Shadows*; Monroy, *Rebirth*. Historical research on Mexican migration that takes up the ways in which Mexican migrants had already encountered mass consumer culture and capitalist labor discipline include Arredondo, *Mexican Chicago*; Vargas, *Proletarians of the North*; Sanchez, *Becoming Mexican American*, 17–25; and Durand and Arias, *La experiencia migrante*, 22–40.

55. Pettit, *Images of the Mexican American*; Ramírez Berg, *Latino Images*. See also García Riera, *México visto*, vol. 1; Keller, *Hispanics and United States Film*; Berumen Garcia, *The Chicano/Hispanic Image*. Chon Noriega examines the ways in which Chicano cinema emerged out of protests against stereotypical images on television and the lack of Chicano/as in both the television and film industries. Noriega argues that the independent media that emerged was subject to the regulation of the mainstream institutions that had been the target of protest. Noriega, *Shot in America*.

56. See Thompson, *Exporting Entertainment*.

57. Charles Eckert and Gaylyn Studlar have traced the ways in which the film in-

dustry and fan magazines addressed female audiences in the United States as consumers. Eckert, "The Carole Lombard in Macy's Window"; Studlar, "The Perils of Pleasure?"

58. On the ways that censorship influenced production practices in the United States, see Grieveson, *Policing Cinema*; Jacobs, *The Wages of Sin*. In *Cinema, Censorship, and Sexuality*, Annette Kuhn argues that censorship during the silent period produced categories of films as well as audiences.

59. Stewart, *Migrating to the Movies*; Carbine, "The 'Finest outside the Loop'"; Waller, "Another Audience."

60. On mass culture as a means of maintaining ethnic identity or even forging a national identity in other immigrant communities, see Cohen, "Encountering Mass Culture"; Bertellini, *Italy in Early American Cinema*, 236–75.

1. SOUTH OF THE BORDER

1. Hipólito Seijas [Rafael Pérez Taylor], "La hija del circo," *El Universal* (hereafter *EU*), March 16, 1917.

2. Seijas, "La hija del circo."

3. "La fascinación del cine," *Revista de Revistas*, September 26, 1920, 5.

4. "El hijo de la loca: Película nacional," *Excélsior*, October 14, 1923, 3. José S. Ortiz directed the film referred to in the article's title for the short-lived Mexican production company Netzahualcóyotl Film.

5. Thompson, *Exporting Entertainment*, x.

6. On relations between the United States and Mexico during the revolution and the postrevolutionary period, see Ulloa, *La lucha armada*; Gonzales, *The Mexican Revolution*; Womack, "The Mexican Revolution"; J. Meyer and Bethell, "Revolution and Reconstruction in the 1920s." See also Rodríguez O., *The Revolutionary Process in Mexico*.

7. For more on this period, see Reyes, *Cine y sociedad*, especially 1:53–59; Leal, Barraza, and Flores, *Anales del cine en México*.

8. Mexican critics devoted a great deal of attention to the Italian divas Menichelli, Lyda Borelli, and Francesca Bertini—from whom Mexican stage and early film actresses copied manners, dress, and melodramatic acting style. Their reign in Mexico's public imagination was relatively brief in relation to the amount of attention that it has received in Mexican film historiography. See Reyes, *Cine y sociedad*, 1:199–209; Gonzalez Casanova, *"Por la pantalla,"* 101–8. On the influence of the Italian divas on Mexican stage actresses, see Dueñas, *Las divas en el teatro*.

9. Pick, *Constructing the Image*, 11–12.

10. See Reyes, *Cine y sociedad*, 1:128–41; de Orellana, *La mirada circular*; Pick, *Constructing the Image*, 11–38. The revolution was also an object of fascination for American filmmakers, as de Orellana discusses in detail. Most famously, Pancho Villa signed a contract with Mutual Film, which got exclusive access to him and his troops in exchange for funds. Those reels, as well as some fictionalized footage, were exhibited in the United States in 1915 as *The Life of General Villa*, a film that is considered lost. The Mexican experimental documentarian Gregorio Rocha chronicled

his efforts to find the footage in *Los rollos perdidos de Pancho Villa* (CONACULTA/ FONCA, 2003). Pick reflects on this footage as an archival source in *Constructing the Image*, 57–68.

11. Josefina Bouvi remembered her father's cinemas in Aguascalientes being full of soldiers—whose presence meant that she and her sister were confined to the family's living quarters, which abutted the screening space (Bouvi interviewed by Aurelio de los Reyes, March 18, 1974, PHO (E)/2/7, Archivo de la Palabra, Proyecto de Cine Mexicano, Instituto Nacional de Antropologia e Historia, Mexico City (hereafter Palabra).

12. The number of theaters in Mexico City remained steady during the revolution despite intermittent hostilities (Reyes, *Cine y sociedad*, 1:165).

13. Florían [pseud.], "Impresiones del cronista: La ola del cine salta de su cauce y amaga el arte escénico," *EU*, March 14, 1917.

14. On Mexico City's commercial links to Europe in general and France in particular, see Bunker, "'Consumers of Good Taste,'" 248. Bunker refers readers to Ceceña Cervantes, *México en la órbita imperial*, 72–75.

15. Advertisement for Gonzalo Varela films, *EU*, October 9, 1916.

16. Advertisement for Cinema México, *EU*, October 16, 1916. *Exploits of Elaine* was produced by the U.S. arm of Pathé, whose parent company was French.

17. Miguel Saucedo, "Crónica de México," *Cine-Mundial* (hereafter *CM*), December 1917, 629.

18. Saucedo, "Crónica de México," *CM*, December 1917, 629.

19. José Luis Navarro, "De Guadalajara, México," *CM*, April 1917, 189.

20. Angel Campero, "Crónica de Morelia (México)," *CM*, April 1918, 209.

21. Valente Cervantes, interviewed by Aurelio de los Reyes, February 2, 1974, PHO (E) 2/4, Palabra.

22. "De México," *CM*, April 1917, 188.

23. "De México," 188.

24. Saucedo, "Crónica de México," *CM*, October 1918, 856.

25. For a summary of this literature, see Cooper, "Pearl White and Grace Cunard."

26. Cooper, "Pearl White and Grace Cunard," 190.

27. "El hijo de la loca: Película nacional," *El Heraldo de México*, October 14, 1923.

28. Judex [pseud.], "Notas teatrales," *Matehuala, December 28, 1921, 3.*

29. "Crónica de México," *CM*, September 1918, 579.

30. Silvestre Bonnard [Carlos Noriega Hope], "Vanidad de vanidades," *EU*, November 18, 1919.

31. Pensado and Correa, *Mixcoac*, 67.

32. The Salon Rojo, located in the center of the city, had been in business since 1906 and offered patrons fun-house mirrors, the novelty of an escalator, and a richly decorated interior.

33. Handbills for the Cine Parisiana and Cine la Paz, AHDF (AHA), DP, multas, 824.

34. Cervantes interview, 2/3.

35. "Resumen anual," *CM*, January 1918, 13.

36. In *The Red Rooster Scare*, Richard Abel has examined the way in which American film producers asserted themselves against European studios in the domestic market some years earlier.

37. Rev. George B. Winton, "The Mexican Revolution and Missions," *Missionary Review*, August 1920, 693.

38. "Opportunities for Trade with Mexico Are Increasing," *Americas*, November 1920, 18–19.

39. Index, *CM*, January 1916, n.p. On the history of *Moving Picture World* (hereafter *MPW*), see D'Agostino, *An Index*. Based on my review of *CM* from 1916 to 1920, it functioned primarily as a resource for exhibitors and distributors, offering them descriptions of the latest releases; how-to articles related to marketing and projection; contact information for companies that provided cinema furnishings, equipment, or services such as translation; and industry-related news. Some of the articles were translations, but many were written specifically for Latin American readers.

40. "Exportación de películas," *CM*, January 1916, 409.

41. "Crónica de México: La marcha de cinematógrafo en México," *CM*, February 1917, 87.

42. F. G. Ortega, "Film Export Notes," *MPW*, June 16, 1917, 1768.

43. "Nuestro programa," *CM*, January 1916, 10.

44. F. G. Ortega, "De farándula," *CM*, January 1916, 12. See also Juan Rivero, "La democracia de la pelicula," *CM*, May 1918, 249.

45. See Rosenberg, *Spreading the American Dream*, 99–103. De Grazia expands on Rosenberg's brief observations in *Irresistible Empire*, 284–335.

46. C. Campbell, *Reel America*, 81.

47. The communiqué from Berlin known as the Zimmermann Telegram instructed the German ambassador in Mexico to propose an alliance between Germany and Mexico, which would include "substantial financial support and an agreement on our part for Mexico to re-conquer its former territories in Texas, New Mexico, and Arizona" (quoted in Katz, *The Secret War in Mexico*, 354).

48. The Mexican director Alejandro Galindo remembered in an interview that "intense pro-Allied propaganda made in the United States," including *Armas al hombro* (*Shoulder Arms*, 1918), circulated in Mexico during the war (Galindo, interviewed by Ximena Sepúlveda, July 2 and 9, 1975, PHO/2/29, Palabra.

49. Gaylord Marsh to Secretary of State Robert Lansing, July 26, 1917, 812.4061/9 (National Archives Microfilm Publication M1370, roll 148); Records of the Department of State Relating to the Internal Affairs of Mexico, 1919–29, Record Group 59, National Archives at College Park, MD (hereafter Records).

50. Cassius M. Clay, memorandum to Boas Long, Department of State, January 17, 1919, 812.4061/1, 2, Records.

51. George Woodward to Lansing, 812.4061/3 and 10, Records.

52. Woodward to Lansing, September 20, 1918, 812.4061/10, 1, Records. For more on wartime newsreels and other films, see Mould, *American Newsfilm*, especially 237–39.

53. Quoted in copy of Woodward to Department of State, August 19, 1918, 802.4061/10, Records.

54. Woodward to Department of State.

55. Transcription of "Exhibiciones de una película insultante," in Dispatch 506, 802.4061/10, 20, Records.

56. Woodward to Lansing, August 19, 1918, 812.4061/8, Records. Emily Rosenberg uses the term "the promotional state" to describe the way in which, from the turn of the century through the 1930s, the U.S. government supported the activities of the private sector in order to promote American political and economic interests abroad (*Spreading the American Dream*, 38–86).

57. Zachary Cobb (War Trade Board), memorandum to Lansing, January 16, 1919, 812.4061/1, Records; Clay to Long, 2.

58. Snider, *Selling in Foreign Markets*, 348.

59. Edward A. Dow to Secretary of State, April 2, 1919, 812.4061/1, Records.

60. The industry was concerned about piracy in other areas of the world as well. See "Dupers Wreching [*sic*] Foreign Market," *Variety*, August 19, 1921, 39; "One Million Worth of Stolen Film," *MPW*, February 11, 1922, 608; "Pressure on Film Pirates," *Variety*, September 2, 1921, 62; "UA Satisfied with Clean-Up of Pirates," *Variety*, December 23, 1921, 38.

61. "Otra voz de alerta a los exportadores," *CM*, September 1918, 585.

62. "Cien programas para México," *CM*, September 1918, 547.

63. On the traffic in illicit goods on the border, see McCrossen, "Drawing Boundaries," 28–30.

64. McCrossen, "Drawing Boundaries," 28–30. An article in *MPW* in February 1922 estimated that over $1 million worth of film had been stolen in Mexico since the beginning of the year ("One Million").

65. "Como viene," *CM*, March 1919, 224. The films included the serials *Por venganza y por mujer* (*Vengeance and the Woman*, 1917) and *El sendero sangriente* (*The Fighting Trail*, 1917), as well as a film, *Las joyas de los Romanoff*, which I've been unable to match precisely to any Vitagraph releases for 1919 or earlier years. At least one of them may have been an episode of the Russian-themed serial *The Woman in the Web* (1918).

66. Saucedo, "Crónica de México," *CM*, February 1919, 145. This series of events is also described in "Report to the National Ass'n [*sic*] of the Motion Picture Industry on Film Theft Investigation," January 3, 1919, folder 2, box 18, Roy and Harry Aitken Papers, US MSS 9AF, Wisconsin Center for Film and Theater Research, Madison, WI.

67. "Notas," *CM*, April 1918, 181.

68. "Como Viene," *CM*, March 1919, 224.

69. "Crónica de Méjico," *CM*, May 1920, 501.

70. Grieveson, *Policing Cinema*, 205.

71. George E. Kann to Lansing, January 22, 1919, 812.4061/12, Records. In 1921 Dennis O'Brien, of United Artists' executive offices, wrote to another United Artists executive, Harry Abrams: "Our people in California are very keen to come to a conclusion relative to the distribution of our pictures in foreign territories, particularly

South America, Mexico, Japan and those countries where stolen films are liable to be circulated" (O'Brien to Abrams, August 12, 1921, folder 8, box 201, US MSS 99AN/2A, United Artists Collection, Wisconsin Center for Film and Theater Research, Madison, WI [hereafter UAC]).

72. Kann to Lansing.

73. Nielson to Goldwyn Distributing Corp., May 4, 1922, 812.544/G58, Records. The 1917 Mexican constitution had changed the terms under which U.S. businesses could operate and invest in Mexican industries like extractive mining or petroleum drilling. American citizens felt that in addition to the losses they had sustained as a result of the revolution, their financial interests were seriously jeopardized by the new constitution. They demanded that the U.S. government protect their investments (and opportunities to invest). One strategy used by the U.S. government was a refusal to recognize successive Mexican regimes until treaties and agreements more favorable to U.S. business interests were signed. See Smith, *The United States and Revolutionary Nationalism in Mexico*; L. Hall, *Oil, Banks, and Politics*; Hart, *Empire and Revolution*, especially chapter 3.

74. International American Conference, *Fourth International Conference*, 275.

75. The 1871 civil code, still in effect in 1929, which makes no explicit mention of cinematographic works, is reproduced in H. Rodríguez, *Propiedad artística y literaria*, 91–114.

76. Quoted in "Report on Foreign Markets," *Motion Picture News*, April 17, 1920, 2507.

77. "E. H. Roth, California Exhibitor, Sees Mexico as Land of Film Opportunity," *MPW*, January 15, 1921, 276.

78. "E. H. Roth," 276.

79. José Navarro, "De Méjico," *CM*, August 1916, 350.

80. "Cien programas para México," 546–47.

81. "Exportación de películas, *CM*, January 1916, 409.

82. Paramount Pictures, *The Story of the Famous Players-Lasky Corporation*, 48.

83. "Notas," *CM*, February 1916, 53.

84. "Las películas en México: Lo que dice el Sr. Gutiérrez Urquiza," *CM*, January 1918, 42.

85. "World Wide Advertising Pays for F. P. Lasky: Globe Girdling Campaign Makes Foreign Demand Heavy," *Motion Picture News*, November 1919, 3470.

86. Advertisement for International Pictures Company, *CM*, July 1919, n.p.

87. Thompson discusses the opening of branch offices as a strategy to expand U.S. control of world markets, especially non-European markets, in *Exporting Entertainment*, 71–84.

88. "To Establish Fox Branch in Mexico," *MPW*, March 29, 1919, 1797.

89. "De polo a polo," *CM*, June 1918, 250.

90. "Información general," *CM*, June 1923, 374.

91. "Amusements," *Mexican American*, August 2, 1924, 33.

92. "Amusements," *Mexican American*, June 20, 1925, 27.

93. The complicated history of the industry in this period is succinctly explained in Koszarski, *An Evening's Entertainment*, 64–94.

94. Quoted in "Exportación de películas."

95. "Crónica de México," *CM*, January 1921, 50.

96. "Doce meses en la pantalla cinematográfica," *Excélsior*, January 1, 1922.

97. "Cien programas para México."

98. "Cien programas para México."

99. Balio, *United Artists*; Usabel, *The High Noon*.

100. Little archival material related to studios' foreign offices during this period either survives or is accessible to researchers. This archival gap is the result of archival practices that have focused on the art, rather than the business, of cinema as well as of a general reluctance on the part of studios to share business-related material with researchers. Material related to Artistas Unidos S.A., primarily correspondence exchanged between the company's corporate headquarters in New York and its Mexico City office, survives because of a legal tangle involving the branch's manager. Though not produced to document the day-to-day activities of the Mexico office per se, it is incredibly illuminating.

101. Usabel, *The High Noon*, 18–20.

102. Memorandum of agreement, April 1, 1922, folder 12, box 23, US MSS 99AN/2F, UAC. *A Small Town Idol* was a Mack Sennett comedy that had been distributed in the United States by First National Pictures. In 1929, when Warner Brothers and First National merged their Mexican offices as a result of the former company's complete takeover of the latter, First National's Mexican operation had a board composed entirely of Americans, except for one high-level Mexican employee, the cashier Arturo Alvarez. Technically Warner Brothers bought First National, S.A., for 10,000 pesos. Like its peers, the company entered into a percentage rental agreement with the New York office. The Mexican subsidiary rented films rather than buying them outright. Perkins to Boothby, Danehy, and Blum, memo, December 26, 1928, vol. 1184, p. 384, and Price to Sandy, Boothby, Danehy, and Carlisle, memo, July 5, 1929, vol. 1184, p. 697, Warner Bros. Archives, School of Cinematic Arts, University of Southern California, Los Angeles.

103. Usabel, *The High Noon*.

104. Usabel, *The High Noon*, 58–59. United Artists also changed its profit-sharing agreement with exchanges in Cuba, the Far East, Australia, and Germany, indicating that the Mexican exchange was not the only struggling subsidiary. See Contract, December 3, 1925, folder 8, box 110, O'Brien Files, MSS 99AN/2A, 110/8, UAC.

105. Harvey Sheahan, letter to Dennis O'Brien, December 20, 1921, folder 6, box 216, O'Brien Files, US MSS 99AN/2A, UAC.

106. In *Refried Elvis*, Eric Zolov describes the transnational and local marketing strategies of the music industry in the 1950s and 1960s. As with film companies during this period, U.S. companies opened subsidiaries in countries such as Argentina, Australia, Brazil, Canada, and Mexico in order to gain access to those countries' domestic and adjacent markets. Some companies, like RCA, provided materials for

domestic production as a way of realizing profits in an economic climate shaped by import substitution policies (70 and 206).

107. Letter from Harvey Sheahan to A. W. Kelley, December 9, 1926, folder 5, box 216, O'Brien Files, US MSS 99AN/2A, UAC.

108. Zolov, *Refried Elvis*.

109. "Boicot económico esta produciendo sus efectos," *La Prensa*, August 6, 1926; "Boletín No. 12: Intensificación del Boycott," November 14, 1926, Centro de Estudios Sobre la Universidad, Fondo Palomar y Vizcarro, Serie: LNDLR, Caja 47, Exp. 347.

110. Harvey Sheahan to Arthur Kelly [*sic*], August 6, 1926, folder 15, box 216, O'Brien Files, US MSS 99AN/2A, UAC.

111. George H. Waters, American Vice Consul, Mexico City, to Alexander W. Woodell, Department of State, September 2, 1926, American Intelligence Reports, Archivo Plutarco Elías Calles.

112. "Report Number 5," January 26, 1924, folder 6, box 216, O'Brien Files, MSS 99AN/2A, UAC. See also "Crónica de Morelia (México)," *CM*, April 1918, 339, which reports that some motion picture theaters shut down completely during Lent.

113. S. C. de la Garza, "Artistas Unidos General Report," April 28, 1928, folder 713, box 144-48, O'Brien Files, MSS 99AN/2A, UAC.

114. Sheahan, "Report—Mexico," April 24, 1924; and Sheahan, "Report—Mexico," May 13, 1924, folder 6, box 216, O'Brien Files, MSS 99AN/2A, UAC.

115. Epifanio Soto, hijo, "Crónica de Méjico," *CM*, April 1920, 579. For a history of Judas burnings and their significance during the porfiriato, see Beezley, *Judas at the Jockey Club*, 89–123.

116. De la Garza, "Artistas Unidos General Report."

117. De la Garza, "Artistas Unidos General Report."

118. "King of Kings Foreign Sales and Collections," May 31, 1928, folder 5, box 2, Cinema Corporation of America Collection, Special Collections, Florida State University Libraries.

119. Luz Alba [Cube Bonifant], "Rey de reyes," *Revista de Revistas*, February 16, 1928, 4.

120. Henry Muller to United Artists Corporation, August 28, 1923, folder 5, box 216, O'Brien Files, MSS 99AN/2A, UAC.

121. Muller to United Artists Corporation. *The Mexican American* provides an interesting snapshot of this expatriate culture. Published weekly beginning in 1922, the magazine featured political, business, social, cultural, and travel news of interest to Americans living in Mexico. Officially, the publication advocated the perception of commercial exchange as the route to hemispheric understanding. It was published by Associated Latin American Publications, which also published *The Brazilian American*, *The Panama Times*, *The American Weekly* (Buenos Aires), *The West Coast Leader* (Lima), and *The South Pacific Mail* (Valparaiso). A running theme throughout the magazines, all of which were aimed at expatriates, was the spread of U.S. customs and social practices.

122. Harvey Sheahan to United Artists, New York, September 6, 1924, MSS 99AN/2A, 216/6, UAC.

123. Harvey Sheahan to Foreign Department, January 19, 1927, folder 5, box 216, O'Brien files, MSS 99AN/2A, 216/5, UAC.

124. Special municipal inspector of fiscal agents to the chief of the Department of Public Diversions, February 7, 1922, AHDF (AHA), DP, 811, 1620.

125. "Mundillo cinematográfico," *La Gaceta del Espectador*, July 8, 1928, 3; "Mundillo cinematográfica," *La Gaceta del Espectador*, July 29, 1928, 3.

126. Aurelio de los Reyes (*Cine y sociedad*, 2:343–44) cites a July 1921 labor census conducted by the Mexican Federal Government, which I have been unable to locate. According to Reyes, cinemas in the Federal District employed approximately 319 people, including 47 women—employed as ticket sellers, pianists, and the like—and 20 minors. The Circuito Granat, S.A., which would become Circuito Olimpia in December 1921, employed 264 of the 319 workers.

127. Sheahan to Kelly, December 9, 1936, folder 5, box 216, O'Brien Files, MSS 99AN/2A, 216/5, UAC.

128. The Circuito Maximo consisted of thirteen cinemas: the Salon Rojo and Cinemas Goya, Venecia, Rialto, San Juan de Letrán, América, María Guerrero, Bucareli, San Rafael, Buen Tono, Rivoli, Condesa, and one other cinema that I have been unable to identify.

129. Sheahan to Hiram Abrams, May 14, 1925, folder 5, box 215, O'Brien Files, MSS 99AN/2A, UAC.

130. Film Board of Trade, "Meeting Report," May 1925, folder 5, box 216, O'Brien Files, MSS 99AN/2A, 216/5, UAC.

131. Sheahan to Abrams.

132. This account is drawn from the materials in the United Artists' records. Unfortunately, to date there is little information about the Film Board of Trade and its fate.

133. Beginning in the first decade of the twentieth century, local boards of trade regulated exhibitor-distributor relations in many U.S. cities. The Mexican Film Board of Trade was more akin to these domestic bodies. See Thompson, *Exporting Entertainment*, 118–20.

134. The Sindicato de Trabajadores de la Industria Cinematográfica, an umbrella union for film industry workers, was formed out of the Unión de Empleados Confederados de Cinematógrafos. See García Riera, *Historia documental del cine mexicano*, 1:120; Macotela, "El sindicalismo."

135. "Películas favoritas de 1926," *Magazine Filmico*, January 1927, n p

136. "Películas favoritas de 1926."

137. See Abel, *The Red Rooster Scare*, especially chapters 1–3.

2. AMERICAN MOVIES, MEXICAN MODERNITY

1. On the rise of the motion picture palace in the United States, see Koszarski, *An Evening's Entertainment*, 20–25; Naylor, *American Picture Palaces*.

2. Aurelio de los Reyes (*Cine y sociedad*, 2:307) speculates that Granat and Crombé based the Olimpia's design on Kinsila, *Modern Theatre Construction*, which advocated adapting Greek theater design to the demands of motion picture exhibition.

3. These decorative motifs were described in an unsigned report on the cinema's

inauguration. See Inspector to Head of the Department of Public Diversions, AHDF, A, DP, sección teatros y cines, 853, 317. The interior of the Palacio de Correos, built in the late nineteenth century, had also been designed by Ceroni. With marble imported from Italy and fine metalwork, it reflected Mexico City's efforts to put itself on par with the capitals of Europe. On the relationship between urban planning, civic decoration, and nationalism in the regime of Porfirio Díaz, see Tenorio Trillo, "1910 Mexico City."

4. Reyes (*Cine y sociedad*, 2:307) asserts that Jennings and his associates fabricated the charges against Granat to ensure that he would be unable to rebuild his exhibition empire but either tacitly or explicitly agreed to let him leave the country before he could be arrested.

5. I have been unable to discover much about Jennings and his associates. They soon owned or controlled numerous exhibition venues in Mexico City, which made up the *Circuito Olimpia*, along with theaters in other major cities. Spotty archival records make it unclear what happened to the exhibition empire they created. The Olimpia returned to the hands of the Granat family, though not to Jacobo, in 1925. Another U.S. citizen, William O. Jenkins, the former U.S. vice consul in Puebla who had become a businessman, would hold a virtual monopoly over movie exhibition in Mexico in the 1950s. See Paxman, "William Jenkins."

6. All quotes in this paragraph are from "La Ciudad de México cuenta desde hoy con otro hermoso y elegante coliseo," *Excélsior* (hereafter *EX*), December 10, 1921.

7. The magazine *Mexican Life*, oriented toward American expatriates, describes the "traditional evil of the Mexican picture theater, that of the all-day program" ("In the Realm of the Dumb," June 1926, 4).

8. Reyes, *Cine y sociedad*, 2:307–41. In 1921, $1.00 equaled 2.06 pesos. Thus a ticket costing 2.50 pesos would have cost over $1.00, and a ticket costing 1.00 peso would have cost approximately $0.53. Similarly, 40 and 20 centavos were equal to approximately 21 and 10 cents, respectively (historical exchange rates were taken from http://www.eh.net/hmit/exchangerates/, accessed April 20, 2005). Data for wages in Mexico during the 1920s are limited. Verena Radkau (*La fama y la vida*, 59) gives 75 centavos per day as the average wage for female factory workers in 1919. To give a sense of the range of worker salaries, the Departamento de Trabajo found that average wage for advertisement hangers in 1922 was 3.21 pesos per day ("Promedio del salario que ganan los obreros en la Ciudad de Mexico, D.F.," *Boletín mensual del Departamento de Trabajo* 1, no. 3 [1922]). Susie Porter (*Working Women in Mexico City*, 29) notes that in 1929 men's shirt seamstresses in Mexico earned an average of 1.93 pesos per day. Ticket prices for other theaters were drawn from newspaper advertisements.

9. Prices would eventually drop to 1 peso for a luneta seat and 50 centavos for balcony seating.

10. Reyes, *Cine y sociedad*, 2:339, 341.

11. Report, Hipólito Amor to the Section Head, Public Diversions, July 13, 1922, AHDF, A, DP 812, 1691.

12. Knight, "Popular Culture and the Revolutionary State."

13. "Report," Jefe de la Sección de Productos Manufacturados to Ing. Domingo Diéz, Sria. De Industria Comercio y Trabajo, December 18, 1924, AHSRE, 19-10-8 (1)/ III/8333 (00-72)/1, 1.

14. "Report."

15. For example, see *Boletín mensual del Departamento de Trabajo* 1, no. 3 (1922).

16. See, for example, G. Ramírez, *El cine yucateco*; Montemayor, *Cien años*; de la Vega Alfaro, *Microhistorias del cine en México*.

17. These lists can be found in AGN, DT, 620, 5, and 641, 5.

18. There were approximately 15,000 theaters in the United States in 1919 (Koszarski, *An Evening's Entertainment*, 13). The U.S. population was 106,021,537 in 1920 (U.S. Department of Commerce, *Statistical Abstract of the United States, 1920*, 39), while Mexico's was a mere 14,334,780 in 1921 (Departamento de la Estadística Nacional, *Resumen del censo general*, 193).

19. G. Villalobos to "Sr. Proprietario o Representante del Teatro-Cine," AGN, DT, 620, 5.

20. The manuscript material contains numerous letters threatening legal action against cinema owners who failed to return the survey. It appears that many still chose to overlook the survey, since the number of responses, even if one includes the incomplete responses that were archived, does not approach the total number of cinemas listed in the accompanying materials.

21. Carlos del Castillo to Sr. Director del Departamento de Trabajo, November 7, 1923, AGN, DT, 620, 5.

22. Ignacio Negulcio, response to "Cuestionario para el censo obrero," AGN, DT, 641, 4, 57.

23. José Jury, response to "Cuestionario para el censo obrero," no. 213, AGN, DT, 641, 4, 5. José Simental, who operated the Teatro Corona in Escuinapa de Hidalgo, Sinaloa, likewise reported that all of his workers had other employment: "The projectionist is a carpenter; the doormen are both construction workers; the ticket seller a seamstress, and the publicity boys work at chores in their homes" (Simental to Sria. de Industria, Comercio y Trabajo, August 10, 1923, AGN, DT, 641, 4, 2.

24. Mauro Jimenez to Departamento de Trabajo, AGN, DT, 641, 5, 58.

25. Miguel Anaya, response "Cuestionario para el censo obrero," no. 222, AGN, DT, 641, 4, 27.

26. "Cuestionario para el censo obrero," no number, AGN, DT, 641, 5, fol 81, and 641, 4, fol. 77.

27. López, "Early Cinema and Modernity in Latin America," 51.

28. The statistics in this paragraph are all based on my analysis of the industrial census material that can be found in the Archivo Nacional de México, AGN, DT, 620, 5, and 641, 5, and statistics from the 1921 census. On film exhibition and production in the Yucatán, see G. Ramírez, *El cine yucateco*.

29. According to Departamento de la Estadística Nacional (*Resumen del censo general*, 193), the populations of these states in 1921 were 107,581 (Aguascalientes), 336,412 (Nuevo León), 358,221 (Yucatán), and 393,480 (Coahuila). On the development of industry in Nuevo León, particularly in Monterrey before the revolu-

tion, see Mora-Torres, *The Making of the Mexican Border*. The Yucatán was one of the states featured frequently in early issues of *Cine-Mundial* (hereafter CM). See, for example, "De Yucatán," CM, March 1917, 137, which begins: "In this rich state of the Republic cinema is very developed." On the Yucatán and the henequen industry, an industry intimately tied to the U.S. agricultural sector and American capital, see Joseph, *Revolution from Without*; Wells, *Yucatán's Gilded Age*. As Wells and Joseph note (*Summer of Discontent*, 127–29), the Yucatán had one of the most highly developed rail transportation networks in Mexico, which facilitated the distribution of films to towns both small and large and to haciendas. Historians argue that the system of labor on the henequen plantations remained consistent until the 1930s, though changes in government yielded significant shifts in terms of education and politics. Most historical studies focus on the late porfiriato and the development of a slavery-like debt peonage, which makes it difficult to ascertain when motion pictures first became a fixture on haciendas or in smaller towns. Such information is likely to be found in regional archival sources. On the development of carbon mining and the extension of the railway in Coahuila, see Contreras Delgado, *Espacio y sociedad*, 60–69.

30. Ramón Rivera, response to "Cuestionario para el censo obrero," AGN, DT, 641, 5, fol. 104.

31. Alston, Mattiace, and Nonnenmacher ("Coercion, Culture, and Contracts") examine the coercive nature of wage labor in the henequen industry during the porfiriato. On the rise of industrial labor in modern Mexico, see R. Anderson, *Outcasts in Their Own Land*.

32. A. T. Thompson, assistant to the president, Phelps Dodge Corporation, to J. S. Williams Jr., general manager, Moctezuma Copper Company, May 12, 1918, Phelps Dodge Corporation Corporate Archives, Phoenix, AZ. (I am grateful to my colleague Samuel Truett for sharing this source and others on cinemas in northern Mexican mining towns with me.)

33. Morgan, "Proletarians, Politicos, and Patriarchs," 155. In 1922 the Unión de Empleados y Obreros del Buen Tono acquired its own projector in order to hold screenings for its membership, part of the organization's campaign to provide members with "honest distractions" ("Labor Social Obrera," *Boletín mensual del Departamento de Trabajo* 2, no. 1 [1923]: 23).

34. S. Maranón to G. Villalobos, August 1, 1923, AGN, DT, 641, 5, 54.

35. See, for example, "Cuestionarios," AGN, DT, 641, 5, 106, and 641, 4, 14.

36. "Los espectaculos y el ayuntamiento," *Matehuala*, September 15, 1919, 2.

37. Rafael Cabrera to Secretaria de Industria, November 27, 1923, AGN, DT, 620, 77.

38. For a description of the way this type of knowledge circulated in Luis González, see González y González, *San José de Gracia*, 100.

39. "Teatros y cines modernos," *Revista de Revistas* (hereafter RR), June 13, 1920, 51.

40. "La empresa Calderón y Salas Porras ensancha su campo de acción," *México en Rotograbado*, August 1927, n.p.

41. Galindo to Sria. De Industria, November 29, 1923, AGN, DT, 641, 5, 67. See also the series of letters between Quentin Rosas, manager of the Teatro Mayo in Navo-

joa, Sonora, and the presidential candidate General Álvaro Obregon, August 2 and 12 and September 13 and 23, 1919, legajo 1/2, "Peliculas," exp. 38, Fondo Plutarco Elías Calles, Fideicomiso Archivos Plutarco Elías Calles y Fernando Torreblanca, Mexico City. In that series of letters Rosas, who was also a garbanzo bean farmer, asked Obregon for posters and a film to use "as propaganda in favor of his [Obregon's] candidacy." In Mexico City, political meetings were often held in cinemas. For example, the Departamento de Trabajo reported that a series of conferences for workers, sponsored by the Secretaria de Educación Pública, were going to be held "Sundays in different cinema halls" ("Efemeridades," *Boletín mensual del Departamento de Trabajo* 1, no. 2 [1922]: 79). And the Comité Pro-Huelga de la Liga de Profesores de la Federación de Sindicatos Obreros del Distrito Federal held a special benefit function with the "best art and comic films" at the Cine Granat. "Annuncio: Teatro Cine Granat," *El Universal* (hereafter *EU*), May 15, 1919. Numerous examples can be found in other publications, too.

42. Bunker, "'Consumers of Good Taste,'" 256.

43. Cruz Rodríguez (*Crecimiento urbano*, 62) submits that the capital accounted for 60.3 percent of the country's urban growth between 1910 and 1921.

44. Gallo, *Mexican Modernity*, 22–23. American travelers noted the presence of cinemas in both the capital and smaller cities. See Cleland, *The Mexican Year Book*; Chase, *Mexico*.

45. On the proliferation of movie theater chains in the United States, most of them ultimately part of studio holdings, see Gomery, "U.S. Film Exhibition."

46. "Cuestionario para el censo obrero," no. 550, AGN, DT, 620, 5, 121.

47. Response to "Cuestionario para el censo obrero," no. 550, AGN, DT, 620, 5, 121. Aurelio de los Reyes (*Cine y sociedad*, 2:343–73) offers a detailed account of the development of early cinema unions one of which, the Sindicato de Empleados Confederados de Cinematografo, he points out was formed primarily by the employees of the Circuito Olimpia in response to the management practices of the chain's foreign-born managers. He situates the militant labor organizing among cinema workers in the context of a larger trend toward unionization among Mexican workers.

48. Rafael Bermúdez Zartrain to Departamento de Trabajo, AGN, DT, 620, 5, 175, and Zartrain, response to "Cuestionario para el censo obrero," AGN, DT, 620, 5, 177.

49. On the relationship of renovations of public space and the modernization project during the porfiriato, see Tenenbaum, "Streetwise History."

50. On the relationship between the state and the arts, culture, and education in postrevolutionary Mexico, see Folgarait, *Mural Painting and Social Revolution*; Vaughan and Lewis, *The Eagle and the Virgin*; Gónzalez Mello, "El régimen visual y el fin de la revolución"; Fell, *José Vasconcelos*. On street names as a practice of memory, see Olsen, "Revolution in the City Streets," 123–24.

51. On behavior in public and shifting perceptions of criminality, see Piccato, *City of Suspects*.

52. Rosendo Luengas to D. Marcos E. Raya, presidente del consejo municipal, March 10, 1924, AHDF, A, SG, oficios diversos, 3194, 861.

53. "Cinematofilia," *RR*, September 28, 1924, 31.

54. E. P. Castillo to Head Inspector, June 6 and June 8, 1921, AHDF, A, DP, inspectors, 834, 89. See also "Rifa Buen-Tono en Cine Imperial," *EU*, May 26, 1924.

55. "Siluetas del cinematógrafo," *RR*, May 30, 1926, 38.

56. R. Peraza to Head Inspector Public Diversions, June 4, 1921, AHDF, A, DP, sección teatros y cines, 835, 91.

57. Salazar Alfaro and Ochoa Vega, *Espacios distantes*, 56.

58. Juan Benavente, "Report," June 14, 1921, AHDF, A, DP, informes, 815, 6.

59. J. H. Martinez to Sub-head of the Diversions Section, October 10, 1922, AHDF, A, DP, 812, 1732.

60. The names of bands were drawn from a collection of handbills housed in the Archivo Histórico del Distrito Federal, Mexico City (AHDF, A, DP, multas, 824 and 825) and newspaper advertisements.

61. "Hoy es la solemne inauguración del palacio de la cinematografía. El 'CAPITOLIO' será el cine de moda," *EU*, April 19, 1924.

62. "Cine Odeon," *El Heraldo de México*, May 4, 1922. See also "El Odeon, llamado con razon 'el as de los cines,'" *EU*, March 8, 1924.

63. Head of Public Diversions, quoting from a report submitted by Alfonso de Icaza, June 21, 1922, AHDF, A, DP, 812, 1674. It is not clear whether or not this is the same Alfonso de Icaza who later wrote a memoir of life in Mexico City, *Así era aquello*. The author does not mention working as a cinema inspector, but I suspect they are the same person.

64. "El Cine Bucareli y sus anexos," *EU*, December 4, 1924.

65. Cine Majestic," *El Heraldo de México*, April 15, 1922. When it reopened under the management of the Granat brothers in 1924, the Majestic was lauded for offering a viewing experience that was "perfectly moral, attractive, and entirely adjusted to the needs of the neighborhood" ("El Cine Majestic, vuelve a ponerse de moda," *EU*, April 5, 1924).

66. "El Cine Goya," *EX*, January 31, 1925; "Los planes del Cine Goya," *EU*, January 20, 1925. For descriptions of the Cines Progreso, Parisiana, and Capitolio in the same vein, see "El Cine Progreso Mundial ha contribuido noblemente al incremento commercial del barrio de La Merced," *EU*, March 9, 1924; "El publico mas elegante de México se congrega diariamente en el aristocrático Cine Parisiana," *EU*, February 15, 192; "Hoy es la solemne inauguración."

67. Drawing of Cine San Hipólito, *Arquitectura*, January 1, 1923, 18.

68. On Porfirio Díaz's overwhelming presence in early Mexican cinema, see A. López, "Early Cinema and Modernity in Latin America," 61–62.

69. Reyes, *Cine y sociedad*, 1:118–24; Pick, "Jesús H. Abitia."

70. Gonzales, "Imagining Mexico in 1921," 248.

71. Gonzales, "Imagining Mexico in 1921," 262.

72. Gonzales, "Imagining Mexico in 1921," 262.

73. For workers' complaints about their exclusion from the centennial's official events, see "Las fiestas del centenario-hechos y comentarios," *El Demócrata*, September 23, 1921.

74. Advertisement for cinemas, *EU*, September 16, 1921.

75. R. López, "*Lo más mexicano de México*," 30.

76. R. López, "*Lo más mexicano de México*," 35.

77. Advertisement for Cines San Juan de Letrán, Venecia, Trianon Palace, and Lux, "La India Bonita," *EX*, September 14, 1921.

78. R. G. Gomez to H. Ayuntamiento, May 14, 1921, AHDF, A, DP, 807, 1402. Reports about these sorts of special functions are numerous in the press. See also Head of Public Diversions to Presidente Municipal, July 11, 1921, AHDF, A, DP, 808, 1402; Juan P. Arroyo to Mayor of Tacubaya, May 3, 1922, AHDF, M (Tacubaya), 77, 35. Arroyo asked for an exemption from municipal taxes for a function organized by the students of a company school run by the factory Excélsior. Event proceeds were to benefit a children's hospital.

79. Advertisement for the Cine Majestic, *EX*, September 10, 1923.

80. Advertisement for Cine Majestic, *EX*, July 10, 1923; "El festival en el Majestic," *EX*, July 13, 1923.

81. "Festivales culturales para hoy en diversos cinematógrafos," *EX*, October 14, 1923.

82. "Festivales culturales."

83. "Grandiosa beneficio para la escuela granja del niño en el Teatro Olimpia," *EX*, March 3, 1924.

84. "Los soldados visitarán los museos y tendrán exhibiciones cinematográficas," *EU*, March 9, 1920.

85. See, for example, "San Luís Potosi," October 1922; "Zacatecas," January 1923; "Méjico," June 1923; "Día del seminarista," August 1925, all in *La dama católica* (hereafter *LDC*).

86. Claude Fell (*José Vasconcelos*, 360–66) provides what may be the clearest description of the debate over defining Mexican culture in this period. Because his primary subject is the work of José Vasconcelos, Fell talks primarily about the activities of the Secretaria de Educación Pública and Bellas Artes.

87. Agostini, "Popular Health Education and Propaganda," 52. See also Matute, "Salud, familia y moral social."

88. "La higienización de la capital," *EX*, May 27, 1922. In February 1921 the municipal government was reported to have in the final phase of production 150 public health films that would be exhibited in the city's cinemas ("Películas para hacer campaña de hygiene," *EU*, February 9, 1921). It is unclear if these films were in fact ever shown.

89. Departamento de Salubridad Pública, *Memoria*, 254.

90. Departamento de Salubridad Pública, *Memoria*, 255.

91. Eric Schaefer describes *The End of the Road* in "Of Hygiene and Hollywood," 41. See also Departamento de Salubridad Pública, *Memoria*, 256.

92. Departamento de Salubridad Pública, *Memoria*, 261.

93. Departamento de Salubridad Pública, *Memoria*, 263.

94. Departamento de Salubridad Pública, *Memoria*, 264.

95. Miriam Hansen's discussion of the silent film audience offers a comprehen-

sive overview of reformers' concerns and scholarly debate about the composition of nickelodeon audiences (*Babel and Babylon*, 60–89).

96. This picture of early regulation is drawn from the following material: Jorge Alcalde to Consejo Superior, May 1906, AHDF, A, CS, diversiones públicas, 596, 6; Alfonso [illegible] to Consejo Superior, June 24 and July 3, 1912, AHDF, A, CS, diversiones públicas, 596, 19; Luis J. Amor to Consejo Superior, July 12, 1912, AHDF, A, CS, diversiones públicas, 596, 19; Luis L. Ruiz, "Informe," November 17, 1911, AHDF, A, DP, 807, 131. Of course, the regulation of public entertainment was not new. On the regulation of public entertainment in eighteenth-century New Spain, see Viquiera Albán, *Relajados o reprimidos?*

97. Ayuntamiento Constitucional de México, *Reglamento de Diversiones Públicas.*

98. Parker to Department of State, September 15, 1916, 812.4061/0579 (National Archives Microfilm Publication M1370, roll 148); Records of the Department of State Relating to the Internal Affairs of Mexico, 1919–29, Record Group 59, National Archives at College Park, MD (hereafter Records). See also "La marcha del cinematógrafo en Mexico," CM, February 1917, 87.

99. "Sección de hygiene: Inconvenientes del cinematógrafo para los niños," LDC, March 24, 1926, n.p.

100. "Paralelo generoso," *El Hogar,* June 17, 1925, 5.

101. Quoted in Epifanio Soto, "Crónica de México," CM, April 1919, 290.

102. Piccato (*City of Suspects*, 176) cites a 1914 newspaper article in which a gang of safebreakers claimed they had imitated the Black Glove Gang from Éclair's Nick Carter Films.

103. Armando Dominguez to Head of Public Diversions, June 27, 1921, AHDF, A, DP, sección teatros y cines, 835, 96.

104. C. Avila Donceres to Head of Public Diversions, August 23, 1921, AHDF, A, DP, sección teatros y cines, 853, 345.

105. Dominguez to Head of Public Diversions, June 1921, AHDF, A, DP, sección teatros y cines, 835, 96.

106. Heliodoro Vargas to Head of Public Diversions, June 5, 1921, AHDF, A, DP, sección teatros y cines, 836, 106. It is unclear which of the Vitagraph serials starring Moreno and released in 1919 he is referring to here.

107. Vargas to Head, June 4, 1921.

108. Piccato, *City of Suspects.*

109. Roberto P. Castellot to Head of Public Diversions, June 9, 1921, AHDF, A, DP, sección teatros y cines, 835, 92.

110. Stamp, "An Awful Struggle"; Bean, "Technologies of Early Stardom"; Cooper, "Pearl White and Grace Cunard."

111. Piccato, *City of Suspects*, 3. Ben Singer (*Melodrama and Modernity*) connects the dangers of the city to early audiences' fascination with melodrama, first on stage and later on screen.

112. Frank, *Posada's Broadsides*, 19–37, 167–201. On the visualization of modernity in Posada's work, see also Museo Nacional de Arte, *Posada.*

113. Frank, *Posada's Broadsides*, 21.

114. On the "developmentalist" or reformist goals of the revolutionary government, see Knight, "Popular Culture and the Revolutionary State," 396–97.

115. José Paullado to Head of Public Diversions, July 16, 1921, AHDF, A, DP, sección teatros y cines, 837, 112.

116. Juan Carlos Briones to Head of Public Diversions, June 13, 1921, AHDF, A, DP, sección teatros y cines, 835, 93.

117. Paullado to Head Inspector, Public Diversions, August 8, 1921, AHDF, A, DP, sección teatros y cines, 837, 112; José Cruz Briones to Head of Public Diversions, June 20, 1921, AHDF, A, DP, sección teatros y cines, 835, 93, and Briones to Head of Public Diversions, June 13, 1921, AHDF, A, DP, sección teatros y cines, 835, 93.

118. Alfonso Icaza to Head of Public Diversions, May 24, 1922, AHDF, A, DP, sección teatros y cines, 840, 192.

119. Jefe de la sección to Secretaria del H. Ayunt., February 3, 1922, AHDF, A, DP, sección teatros y cines, 840, 192. See also G. M. Martínez to Administrative Inspector, Head of Diversions, May 11, 1920, AHDF, A, DP, sección teatros y cines, 833, 47.

120. Hipólito Amor to Section Head, December 29, 1922, AHDF, A, DP, 812, 1667.

121. Head of the Department of Public Diversions, Report of Theater and Cinema Inspectors to the Diversions Commission, January 23, 1922, AHDF, A, DP, sección teatros y cines, 848, 233.

122. On the revival of Mexico City as a key component of postrevolutionary industrialization, see Davis, *Urban Leviathan*, 20–62; Cruz Rodríguez, *Crecimiento urbano*, 85–96.

123. Ernesto H. Dow to Head of Public Diversions, August 8, 1922, AHDF, A, DP, seccion teatros y cines, 850, 264.

124. E. P. Castillo to Head of Public Diversions, June 13, 1921, AHDF, A, DP, sección teatros y cines, 834, 89.

125. Manager of the Circuito Olimpia to Ayuntamiento, sección de diversiones, March 20, 1922, AHDF, DP, sección teatros y cines, 809, 1602.

126. Roberto Perera Castellot to Head of Public Diversions, June 16, 1921, AHDF, A, DP, sección teatros y cines, 835, 92.

127. Report, "Cine Cervantes," June 29, 1921, AHDF, A, DP, sección teatros y cines, 835, 93.

128. C. Avila Donceres to Head of Public Diversions, August 24, 1921, AHDF, A, DP, 808, 1406; and Eduardo Abad to Head of Public Diversions, August 16, 1922, AHDF, A, DP, 808, 1702. See also [illegible] to Head, July 24, 1922, AHDF, A, DP, 812, 1694; Report, "Inspectors and Activities of the Office," February 1, 1922, AHDF, A, DP, 815, 4; Gonzalo Varela to Presidente Municipal, March 26, 1919, AHDF, A, DP, infracciones de teatros y cines, 2406, 84. Numerous other complaints can be found in AHDF, A, DP, informes, 814, 815, and 835.

129. Reports of patrons being asked to leave or being consigned to the nearest police station are numerous. See, for example, AHDF, A, DP, 815, various expedientes, AHDF, A, DP, sección teatros y cines, 841, 203, and 845, 220.

130. Juan Benavente, "Informe," February 25, 1922, AHDF, A, DP, 815, 4.

131. Castellot to Head of Public Diversions, June 9, 1921, AHDF, A, DP, sección teatros y cines, 835, 92.

132. Head of Public Diversions to Diversions Commission, July 14, 1921, AHDF, A, DP, 809, 1589.

133. Quoted in Bliss, *Compromised Positions*, 88. See also Report, "Majestic," May 27, 1922, AHDF, A, DP, sección teatros y cines, 845, 222.

134. The song goes: "Vamos al cine, mama (Let's go to the cinema, mama) / Mamá . . . matagrafo (Mama . . . matograph) / Que eso de la oscuridá (Because all of that darkness) / me gusta una atrocidá (I really love)" (quoted in Monsiváis, "All the People Came," 148).

135. This phrase peppers inspectors' reports. See, for example, "Cine Garibaldi," April 18, 1922, AHDF, A, DP, 809, 1597, exp. 4; Felipe Castillo to Head of Public Diversions, March 10, 1922, AHDF, A, DP, 809, 1602, exp. 35; Cinema Inspectors, report, February 3, 1922, AHDF, A, DP, 815, 4; Cinema Inspectors, report, March 13, 1922, 815, exp. 6; and Eduardo Gonzalez, March 13, 1992, AHDF, J, 706.

136. "Cinematofilia," 31.

137. Quoted in Bliss, *Compromised Positions*, 88; see also Report, "Majestic," May 27, 1922, AHDF, A, DP, sección teatros y cines, 845, 222.

138. Roberto Perera Castellot, "Report," June 2, 1921, AHDF, A, DP, sección teatros y cines, 835, 92.

139. Hipólito Amor to Head of Public Diversions, July 13, 1922, AHDF, A, DP, 812, 1691. Juan Carmago describes the way that adults (men, we'll assume) joined young people on the Salon Rojo's escalator in order to manhandle young girls (Carmago to Head of Public Diversions, August 21, 1922, AGN, A, DP, multas, 825, 7).

140. "Otro nuevo modus viviendi," *El Hogar*, November 10, 1926. Reyes (*Cine y sociedad*, 2:239–333) discusses the mania for dance marathons. See also Sevilla, *Los templos del buen bailar*; Dallal, *El "dancing" Mexicano*.

141. Untitled articles, *EUI*, April 1 and 8, 1926.

142. C. Avila Donceres to Head of Public Diversions, undated, circa summer 1921, AHDF, A, DP, sección teatros y cines, 834, 85.

143. Bliss, *Compromised Positions*, 88. Bliss also discusses cabarets as sexually permissive locales in part because of their encouragement of suggestive dances.

144. José Mayora Medina to Head of Public Diversions, August 14, 1922, AHDF, A, DP, sección teatros y cines, 845, 222.

145. "Bailes antiguos y modernos," *LDC*, August 1, 1924, 15.

146. Vasconcelos, *A Mexican Ulysses*, 142.

147. José Mayora Medina to Head of Public Diversions, May 27, 1922, AHDF, A, DP, sección teatros y cines, 845, 222.

148. On how Mexican reformers thought about the environment's influence on the sexual behavior of young people, see Bliss, *Compromised Positions*, 106–14.

149. For examples, see Bliss, *Compromised Positions*, 106–14; Carlos Pliego to Head of Public Diversions, May 1, 1923, AHDF, A, DP, sección teatros y cines, 835, 25; and Head of Public Diversions to Presidente Municipal, June 21, 1922, AHDF, A, DP,

812, 1674. Another report said that the state of various films "caused *disgusto* [displeasure]" among the public (R. Ramos to Head of Public Diversions, April 16, 1923, AHDF, A, DP, sección teatros y cines, 835, 25.

150. Report, "Cine Olimpia," May 26, 1919, AHDF, A, DP, infracciones, 2406, 10.

151. Head of Public Diversions to Empresario del Cine Venecia, August 3, 1922, AHDF, A, DP, 812, 1704.

152. Report (untitled), February 17, 1922, AHDF, A, DP, 815, 4.

153. Stamp, *Movie-Struck Girls*, 10–40.

154. Ciro B. Ceballas to Head of Public Diversions, undated, AHDF, A, DP, 812, 1733.

155. José Cruz Briones to Head of Public Diversions, June 6, 1921, AHDF, A, DP, sección teatros y cines, 835, 93.

156. Report, Head of Public Diversions to ayuntamiento, July 9–10, 1921, AHDF, A, DP, informes, 814.

157. JCB to Head of Public Diversions, June 7, 1921, AHDF, A, DP, sección teatros y cines, 835, 93.

158. Piccato, *City of Suspects*, 165.

159. On the reformist goals of the postrevolutionary state especially with regard to families, see Bliss, *Compromised Positions*, 126–51; Matute, "Salud, familia y moral social"; Blum, "Breaking and Making Families."

160. Quoted in Bliss, *Compromised Positions*, 113.

161. Bliss, *Compromised Positions*, 89.

162. C. Palacios G. to Head of Public Diversions, August 29, 1922, AHDF, A, DP, 812, 1712; Palacios G. to Head, October 18, 1922, AHDF, A, DP, 812, 1665.

163. C. Avila Donceres to Head of Public Diversions, June 30, 1922, AHDF, A, DP, sección teatros y cines, 835, 1575.

164. Manuel Carino to Presidente Municipal, November 3, 1922, AHDF, A, SG, inspectores, 3925, 102.

165. On the dire financial straits of Mexico City's municipal government in the late 1910s and 1920s, see Cruz Rodríguez, *Crecimiento urbano*, 89–96.

166. Izcara, "Report," no date, AHDF, A, DP, sección teatros y cines, 851, 268.

167. In 1928 the governing structure of the capital underwent a complete overhaul. It is unclear from the available archival record how the inspection of cinemas figured in the new organization. Although records are not available for the period between 1924 and 1928, I am assuming that the regulatory regime instituted in 1921 persisted until 1928. See Cruz Rodríguez, *Crecimiento urbano*, 67.

168. On the consumer as an ideal modern Mexican subject, see Bunker, "'Consumers of Good Taste,'" 231.

3. IN LOLA'S HOUSE

1. My analysis of the way that Lola is produced as a fan in this advertisement draws on John Fiske's articulation of the characteristics of fandom ("The Cultural Economy of Fandom").

2. Hansen, *Babel and Babylon*, 248.

3. Studlar, "The Perils of Pleasure?," 8. The use of fan magazines and other popular print sources has become deeply engrained in film and media studies, especially by scholars seeking to historicize the experiences of audiences previously considered marginal to the main trajectory of film history. See, for example, Fuller, *At the Picture Show*; Stamp, *Movie-Struck Girls*; Stewart, *Migrating to the Movies*, especially chapters 4 and 5; Spigel, *Make Room for TV*; Streible, *Fight Pictures*. Although the evidentiary status of the press has been the subject of debate, careful and critical reading of such sources allows scholars to reconstruct the experiences of groups, like Mexican audiences, that are absent from accounts of the audience that rely either on other types of sources—like the reports of reform groups—or on English-language sources.

4. Torres and Momsen, "Gringolandia," 315. The experimental filmmakers Jesse Lerner and Ruben Ortiz Torres use a similarly constructed neologism, Frontierlandia, to describe the hybrid cultural spaces created out of contacts between the United States and Mexico that they highlight in their film *Frontierland/Frontierlandia* (2005).

5. Visiting Inspector Borja Bolado to Head of Public Diversions, March 22, 1923, AHDF, A, DP, 3952, 55.

6. For example, in the provincial capital of Guanajuato, Guanajuato, an exhibitor implored the city council to allow him to hang posters and other advertising materials, "indispensable for the business's success," outside the city's main theater, which he had rented to show motion pictures on a part-time basis. Actos de Cabildo, 1926, Legajo 145, Archivo Municipal de Guanajuato, Guanajuato.

7. Ortiz Gaitán, *Imágenes del deseo*. See also "El periodismo moderno: Cómo se hacen los periódicos diarios," *El Mundo Ilustrado*, January 3, 1904, n.p.

8. Ortiz Gaitán, *Imágenes del deseo*, 41.

9. Díaz, "The Satiric Penny Press for Workers in Mexico."

10. Ortiz Gaitán, *Imágenes del deseo*, 51–52. See also Lorenzo de la Torre, "La evolución del anuncio en México: Los anuncios de otras épocas," *El Universal Ilustrado* (hereafter *EUI*), March 3, 1927, 27.

11. Bartra, "The Seduction of the Innocents," 302; Rubenstein, *Bad Language*, 14–16. Though some, like Bartra, point to the state-sponsored literacy campaigns of the 1930s as the key to growing literacy rates, others, including Rubenstein, argue that higher literacy rates in the 1930s reflect a population increase and the fact that the state collected literacy statistics using a rather generous definition of literacy. See also D. Anderson, "Literary Reading and the Nation."

12. Hershfield, *Imagining la Chica Moderna*, 12.

13. Broadening our definition of readers to include the nonliterate seems entirely appropriate when considering a country like Mexico. My thinking on this topic has been influenced by Kirsten Silva Gruesz, who proposes a more inclusive body of readers for nineteenth-century Latino writing (*Ambassadors of Culture*), and Keith Thomas, who argues for the inclusion of the technically illiterate in early modern interpretive communities ("The Meaning of Literacy in Early Modern England").

14. "Salva a una obrera del suicidio el concurso de 'El Universal,'" *El Universal* (hereafter *EU*), January 9, 1924.

15. Salvador Novo, "Del pasado remoto."

16. "Crónica de México," *Cine-Mundial* (hereafter *CM*), July 1917, 356.

17. "El cine en la semana," *La Semana*, October 15, 1927, 9.

18. Quoted in Miquel, *Por las pantallas*, 89.

19. "Notas del editor," *Zig-Zag*, April 6, 1920, n.p.

20. "Estrenos cinematógraficos de la semana," *La Semana*, May 22, 1926, 12.

21. "Querido editor," *El Continental* (Mexico City), August 1926, 132.

22. The Nettie Lee Benson Latin American Collection at the University of Texas, Austin, contains one very tattered copy of *Semana Cinematográfica: Semanario de propaganda del arte cinema* from January 1917. The editor's note in that issue suggests that the publication was a reincarnation of an earlier effort.

23. Quoted in A. J. Chalmers, "The Story of Twenty Years," *Moving Picture World*, March 26, 1927, 282.

24. Chalmers, "The Story of Twenty Years," 282. *CM* was distributed in Spain and Portugal as well as Latin America, but approximately 85 percent of the correspondence received by the magazine and subsequently referred to in its pages came from the Americas, with the majority of that correspondence coming from Mexico, Cuba, and Argentina.

25. James Irvine Jr., son of the Southern California agriculture magnate James Irvine, is listed as the company's president. An annual subscription to the monthly publication cost $2.50, and individual copies were 25 cents each.

26. The Lozano brothers established *La Prensa* in 1913 and launched *La Opinión* (hereafter cited as *LO*) in 1926. Other Spanish-language dailies had been published in Los Angeles, but *La Opinión* seemed to reflect a new sophistication and broader sense of community, which may have been the result of its being well capitalized and managed by experienced editors with business interests across the U.S. Southwest. For the history of the Spanish-language press in the United States during this period, see Kanellos, "A Socio-Historic Study."

27. Navarro would later move to San Diego, where he was active in the Sociedad Editora Mexicana (Mexican editors society) and the editor of *El Pueblo*, a Spanish-language newspaper published in San Diego.

28. Mariano Viesca Arizipe, "A Gloria Swanson," *Revista de Revistas* (hereafter *RR*), April 27, 1924, 30.

29. Miquel, *Por las pantallas*.

30. Jean Humbolt [pseud.], "*Maciste*," *El Nacional*, May 10, 1916.

31. Raphael Dufilm [pseud.], "Miss Pearl White, Elena en *La garra de hiero*," *El Nacional*, March 26, 1917.

32. See, for example, "Caricaturas de la pantalla," *EUI*, August 21, 1919, 14; "Acotaciones cinematográficas: Las escenas más hermosas de la semana," *EUI*, March 9, 1922, 10.

33. D. Anderson, "Literary Reading and the Nation," 2.

34. Martín Luís Guzman, "Las naciones en el cine," *Semenario de Espana*, 1915, n.p.

35. Celuloide [Jaime Torres Bodet], "La cinta de plata," RR, December 13, 1925.

36. Celuloide, "La cinta de plata," RR, December 13, 1925.

37. A comprehensive study of the critical reception of Mexican films of the 1910s and 1920s has yet to be undertaken. Ángel Miquel's *Por las pantallas* deals with this issue peripherally as he constructs the history of the practice of film criticism in Mexico. Films that have been assigned iconic status appear quite differently in the press than they do in later scholarship. To cite just one example, *El automovil gris* was initially recognized as cinematically innovative and artistically distinguished, but at the time its success was equally attributed to a well-executed marketing strategy. See "'La banda del automóvil' y su magnifica propaganda," EU, September 3, 1919, which notes that "the propaganda for 'La banda del automóvil' rivals that of the principal European and North American houses [companies]."

38. "Cual es la mejor película que ha visto durante 1923," EUI, April 26, 1923, 11.

39. "Concurso de *Zig-Zag*: Numero 1," *Zig-Zag*, April 6, 1920.

40. "Cual es la mejor película," EUI, April 26, 1923, 11.

41. The Mexican state would promote material progress—like the emergence of the movie theater discussed in chapter 2—and democracy throughout the first half of the twentieth century. See Moreno, *Yankee Don't Go Home!*, 112–51; Rubenstein, *Bad Language*, 59–61.

42. "Estafeta de Hollywood," LO, December 22, 1926.

43. "Consultas de cine," *Zig-Zag*, December 22, 1921, 6.

44. On these dynamics and the development of fan culture in the United States, particularly in small towns, see Fuller, *At the Picture Show*.

45. Goldwyn Cosmopolitan used this phrase in its 1923 ads in CM.

46. "Preguntas y respuestas," CM, June 1921, 434.

47. "Estafeta de Hollywood," LO, December 22, 1926.

48. "El cristal encantado," LO, July 21, 1926.

49. "El correo de Hollywood," *Cinelandia*, July 1928, 24.

50. Front matter, *Zig-Zag*, May 6, 1920, n.p.

51. "Consultas de cine," *Zig-Zag*, December 29, 1921, 15.

52. Front matter, *Zig-Zag*, June 22, 1922, n.p.

53. "Estafeta de Hollywood," LO, December 15, 1926.

54. Western societies have historically gendered acts of consumption and exchange from the department store to the accumulation of wealth. See de Grazia and Furlough, *The Sex of Things*, which historicizes and interrogates the discursive relationship between the feminine and consumer society. The contributors to Weinbaum and The Modern Girl around the World Research Group, *The Modern Girl around the World*, note the intertwined nature of new forms of femininity and consumer culture in the 1920s. See also Cohen, *A Consumer's Republic*, 31–41, 133–52, 366–70; Scanlon, *The Gender and Consumer Culture Reader*.

55. Male participation in consumer culture was linked to the decadence of the porfiriato. Urban men who engaged in displays of flashy clothes, makeup, and per-

formative posing in public spaces—like women—were called *fifís* and associated with homosexuality.

56. Hershfield, *Imagining la Chica Moderna*, 33–45.

57. Hansen, "Early Cinema: Whose Public Sphere?," 231.

58. Advertisement promoting *La mujer que anda sola*, *Excélsior* (hereafter *EX*), March 11, 1923. The contest preselected its participants by choosing names from the phonebook, surely a select segment of Mexico City's population and precisely the segment that businesses wanted to target as customers.

59. "Nuestro concurso," *EUI*, July 2, 1923, 8–9.

60. Scattered mentions of such slides can be found in the Mexico City municipal archives, in the form of complaints about there being too many of them.

61. In *The Adman in the Parlor*, Ellen Gruber Garvey describes how, during the late nineteenth and early twentieth centuries, features and fiction were increasingly interwoven with new image-laden advertisements, becoming, she argues, a virtual department store. On the rise of such advertising in Mexico, see Ortiz Gaitán, *Imágenes del deseo*.

62. Eckert, "The Carole Lombard in Macy's Window," 103–5.

63. Chalmers, "The Story of Twenty Years," 282.

64. Cine Olimpia Advertisement, *EU*, August 11, 1923.

65. Lydia Pinkham, advertisement, *EX*, May 6, 1923, section 3, 9.

66. Stacomb hairgel advertisement, *EUI*, August 11, 1929.

67. Hershfield, *Imagining la Chica Moderna*, 56–57.

68. "Mary Miles Minter habla de modas futuras," *EX*, December 21, 1923.

69. Josefina Romero, "A través de la moda," *CM*, January 1921, 27–28.

70. "Patrones Hollywood" advertisement, *Filmográfica*, June 19, 1933.

71. "Concurso," *RR*, February 14, 1926, 23.

72. Eckert, "The Carole Lombard in Macy's Window," 109.

73. This international model of modern femininity and its local permutations as it traveled the globe is brilliantly explored in Weinbaum and The Modern Girl around the World Research Group, *The Modern Girl around the World*.

74. See Doane, *The Desire to Desire* and "Film and the Masquerade."

75. "Lola la chica de Hollywood," *LO*, May 12, 1928.

76. "Lola la chica de Hollywood," *LO*, May 10 and 12, 1928.

77. "Lola la chica de Hollywood," *LO*, May 13, 1928.

78. See Weinbaum and The Modern Girl around the World Research Group, *The Modern Girl around the World*, 26–37.

79. Ruiz, *From out of the Shadows*, 57. See also Ortiz Gaitán, *Imágenes del deseo*, 315–22.

80. Dyer, *Stars*, 43. Photo spread, *Zig-Zag*, February 10, 1921, 28–29.

81. Manuel R. Ojeda, "Charles Spencer Chaplin habla de México," *EU*, December 31, 1919.

82. José Maria Sánchez García, "Mary Pickford," *RR*, July 23, 1922; Sánchez García, "Marion Davies," *RR*, February 24, 1925. For examples of the coverage of star visits to Mexico, see "Tres populares actors de cine en México: Eddy Polo, Billy

West, y Art Acord nos cuentan sus impresiones," *RR*, July 29, 1923; Fernando Arevalo, "Bonnie May filma en México," *RR*, May 25, 1925; "Bebe Daniels en México," *RR* (supplement), May 15, 1927; "Viene a México una gran compañia de cine," *EU*, January 3, 1919.

83. "¿Puede una mujer casarse sin el consentimiento de su padre?" (advertisement for *El amor pirata*), *EU*, April 16, 1924.

84. "La gran exclusiva adquirida a gran costo por el 'Salon Rojo'" (advertisement for *El circulo de matrimonio*), *El Demócrata*, April 24, 1924.

85. "Concurso de *Zig-Zag*: Numero 1," *Zig-Zag*, April 6, 1920, n.p.

86. "Novela de cine," *RR*, March 28, 1926, 3.

87. As Miriam Hansen has argued in "Universal Language and Democratic Culture," the conceit of film as a "universal language" circulated widely and with varying ideological emphases throughout the silent period.

88. All of these stars were born in Mexico. Mary Beltrán calls them the first "Latin invasion" (*Latina/o Stars in U.S. Eyes*, 17; see also 18–39). In addition to Beltrán, who focuses on del Rio, see also Ríos-Bustamante's description of Latina/o activity in silent and early sound film, "Latino Participation." The cultural politics of del Rio's career is well covered in Hershfield, *The Invention of Dolores del Río*, and A. López, "From Hollywood and Back." Neither Ramón Novarro nor Lupe Vélez has been the subject of an academic monograph to date. Essays on the two stars include Chavez, "'Ramón Is Not One of These,'" and Sturtevant, "Spitfire." Elizondo's "star" turn was brief and is rarely remembered today. On the subject of racial or ethnic exoticism and silent cinema stardom, see Hansen, *Babel and Babylon*, 243–68; Studlar, *This Mad Masquerade*, 150–97; Kirihara, "The Accepted Idea Displaced"; Miyao, *Sessue Hayakawa*; Wang, "The Art of Screen Passing."

89. "Un astro mexicano de la pantalla: Fernando R. Elizondo en 'El noveno mandamiento,'" *Zig-Zag*, June 20, 1920.

90. "Estafeta de Hollywood," *LO*, December 15, 1926.

91. Quoted in Julian de Roble, "Crónicas de Los Ángeles: Un señor mexicano," *EUI*, May 3, 1923, 25. As popular as he was with Mexican audiences, Novarro remained an unrepentant classist who had definite ideas about how the Mexican masses should be uplifted and educated. See Soares, *Beyond Paradise*, 107–9.

92. "El cristal encantado," *La Prensa*, September 23, 1926.

93. "Estafeta de Hollywood," *LO*, December 15, 1926.

94. "Mexicanos que triunfan en Cinelandia," *México*, January 1, 1926.

95. Roble, "Crónicas de Los Ángeles"; Rafael Bermudez Zartrain, "Al margen del cine: A Ramón Novarro Samaniegos," *EU*, January 25, 1924; "Pagina cinematografica: Ramón Novarro," *EU*, January 27, 1924; "Come ve Matias Santoyo al gran actor de la pantalla Ramon Novarro," *LO*, May 30, 1927.

96. "La victoria de un actor mexicano," *RR*, August 4, 1923, 7.

97. On the construction of del Rio in the American press, see Hershfield, *The Invention of Dolores del Río*; A. López, "From Hollywood and Back"; Rodríguez-Estrada, "Dolores del Río and Lupe Vélez." See also Ríos-Bustamante, "Latino Participation."

98. Review of *La virgen de las amazonas*, *La Gaceta del Espectador*, May 1928, 6. The precise film to which the author is referring is unclear. See also "Nuestras artistas: Dolores del Río," *México*, June 11, 1927.

99. Quoted in "Antonio Moreno y su cariño a México," *RR*, January 22, 1922, 20.

100. Quoted in Alfonso Busson, "Lo que dijó Antonio Moreno," *RR*, February 8, 1920, 8.

101. "Nuestro concurso," *EUI*, May 27, 1920, 2.

102. Studlar, "The Perils of Pleasure?"

103. Paul Gilroy explores this type of ambivalent fascination in *The Black Atlantic*. In film and media studies, this connection has been addressed most directly in terms of colonial and ethnographic films, on the one hand, and considerations of the representation of blackness on the other. See, for example, Griffiths, *Wondrous Difference*; Rony, *The Third Eye*; Shohat and Stam, "The Imperial Imaginary," in *Unthinking Eurocentrism*; Stewart, *Migrating to the Movies*, especially 1–19.

104. Jason Borge takes up the writings of Mexican journalists in Hollywood in *Latin American Writers*, 48–73. There he contextualizes the work of Carlos Noriega Hope in the context of a broader intellectual engagement with Hollywood by Latin American writers. Borge argues that these journalists were seduced by Hollywood's glamour and cosmopolitanism and only belatedly were able to see the U.S. film industries' imperialist ideology.

105. "Nuestro corresponsal en Los Angeles," *RR*, February 12, 1922, 26–27; "Mi viaje al meca del cine," *RR*, March 12, 1922, 41; "Por el mundo de Cinelandia: Oh Hollywood, una vuelta por Bohemia," *Zig-Zag*, October 13, 1921, 320–23; "Desde Hollywood," *RR*, various issues, 1927; Manuel R. Ojeda, "Los principios de una artista mexicano en Los Angeles, Cal," *EU*, July 27, 1919.

106. Studlar, "The Perils of Pleasure?," 28. Studlar elaborates on the way that fan magazines in the 1920s encouraged women's identification with stars as they simultaneously exposed the "truth" behind the screen and that behind the star image ("The Perils of Pleasure?," 27–28).

107. Noriega Hope, *El mundo de las sombras*. For biographical information about Noriega Hope, see *Carlos Noriega Hope*. Noriega Hope (his mother was a U.S. citizen who married a Mexican) was instrumental in supporting and spreading film culture in Mexico in the 1920s and 1930s. Rumored to be gay, he died young and without heirs at the age of thirty-eight.

108. On the arrival scene in American ethnic literature, see Sollors, "'A World Somewhere, Somewhere Else.'" Sollors calls the prologue to the novel *Call It Sleep*, set on Ellis Island in front of the Statue of Liberty, a "panoramic immigrant arrival scene" (139).

109. Noriega Hope, *El mundo de las sombras*, 15.

110. Noriega Hope, *El mundo de las sombras*, 16.

111. Noriega Hope, *El mundo de las sombras*, 25–26.

112. Noriega Hope, *El mundo de las sombras*, 36.

113. Quoted in Noriega Hope, *El mundo de las sombras*, 67.

114. Noriega Hope, *El mundo de las sombras*, 92, 130, 137, 55.

115. Quoted in Noriega Hope, *El mundo de las sombras*, 32–33.

116. Noriega Hope, *El mundo de las sombras*, 78.

117. Noriega Hope, *El mundo de las sombras*, 92.

118. Noriega Hope, *El mundo de las sombras*, 125.

119. Noriega Hope, *El mundo de las sombras*, 124.

120. "Un servicio a nuestros lectores," *EUI*, April 17, 1921, n.p.

121. "Triunfara la Bertini?," *EUI*, April 22, 1920, 2.

122. "Nuestro concurso," *EUI*, June 14, 1923, 7.

123. "Oh! . . . LAS PELICULAS AMERICANAS," *EUI*, March 7, 1919, 12. See also Noriega Hope's review of *Polly of the Circus* (1917), *EU*, May 7, 1919.

124. "El mejor voto razonado," *EUI*, May 20, 1920, 19.

125. "Triunfara la Bertini?"

126. "Nuestro concurso," *EUI*, August 16, 1923, 9.

127. "La sal de la vida," *EUI*, May 6, 1920, 29.

128. "Nuestro gran concurso cinematográfico," *EUI*, December 29, 1921, 8.

129. "La cinta de plata," *RR*, February 14, 1926, 27.

130. "Por la pantalla," *EU*, March 20, 1917.

131. Review of "El amor pirata," *EU*, April 27, 1924.

132. "La opinion del público," *Cinelandia*, September 1927, 31.

133. "Nuestro buzon cinematográfico," *EUI*, April 29, 1920, 22.

134. "El cristal encantado," *La Prensa*, June 20, 1926.

135. "Evolucionará el espectaculo de cine en México," *Magazine Fílmico*, December 1926, n.p.

136. "Evolucionará el espectaculo de cine en México," n.p.

137. Quoted in "Evolucionará el espectaculo de cine en México," n.p.

138. Rafael Bermúdez Zartrain, "Memorias cinematográficas" (part 1), *Magazine Fílmico*, n.d., n.p. Because this publication is in such bad shape, this issue was missing any identifying material. Based on the appearance of other parts of this feature in subsequent issues it is likely to have been the November or December 1927 issue.

139. Bermúdez Zartrain, "Memorias cinematográficas" (part 1).

140. Bermúdez Zartrain, "Memorias cinematográficas" (part 1); Rafael Bermudez Zartrain, "Memorias" (part 2), n.d., n.p.

141. Quoted in Maximo Bretal, "Que heroína del cine le agradaría ser?," *EUI*, January 25, 1931, 24–25.

142. Quoted in Bretal, "Que heroína del cine le agradaría ser?," 24–25.

143. Quoted in Bretal, "Que heroína del cine le agradaría ser?," 24–25.

4. *LA VIRGEN* AND *LA PELONA*

1. "Una joven mexicana, enamorada de Charlie Chaplin," *El Demócrata* (hereafter *ED*), April 3, 1923. See also Pepe Rouletabille, "Crónicas de Pepe Rouletabille: El caso de Marina Vega, desde el punto de vista filosófico," *El Universal Ilustrado* (hereafter *EUI*), April 12, 1923, 36; Ortega, "La verdadera Marina Vega," *EUI*, May 24, 1923, 23; "Marina Vega, vampiresa del país," *Revista de Revistas* (hereafter *RR*), April 8, 1923, 7.

2. "Una joven mexicana."

3. Chaplin, *My Autobiography*, 302–3. Chaplin remembered that after her suicide attempt Vega—whom he did not refer to by name—was placed in the care of the Welfare League and that he paid for her fare back to Mexico City.

4. Marjorie Garber calls transvestism a "category crisis," which she defines as "disrupting and calling attention to cultural, social, or aesthetic dissonances" (*Vested Interests*, 16).

5. "La tragicomedia de la bella enamorada del *estridentismo*," ED, April 14, 1923. *Tiple*, the Spanish word for treble or soprano, is commonly used to refer to a soprano singer. The word came to refer to the beauties populating the choruses in theatrical productions and cabarets. A *tiple* is also a small guitar-like instrument common in parts of Latin America.

6. Joanne Hershfield refers to the *pelona* as the *flapperista*, a term I have seen only rarely in discussions of *la chica moderna*, the modern girl in Mexico (*Imagining la Chica Moderna*). In colloquial Mexican Spanish, *la pelona* is also a nickname for death, which invites all sorts of gendered associations.

7. Hershfield, *Imagining la Chica Moderna*. The narrative structure of this account borrows liberally from the conventions of both dime novels and the early cinema. Judith Mayne discusses the use of this device in early cinema. Men, she observes, often have to be punished for their voyeurism, while women's looking sometimes leads them to "manipulate the scene" or, to put it another way, make something happen (*The Woman at the Keyhole*, 177).

8. "La tragicomedia de la bella enamorada."

9. The extent of Marina's contact with this avant-garde artistic movement is not clear from the available sources. On the movement, see Schneider, *El estridentismo*.

10. The historian Aurelio de los Reyes concurs with this assessment (*Cine y sociedad en México*, 1:298). He proposes that Marina's models were the spunky heroines who sought out a better standard of living and personal and sexual satisfaction in films such as *Male and Female* (DeMille, 1919). See Enstad, *Ladies of Labor, Girls of Adventure*, 131–203, on the uses of motion pictures, especially serials, by working women in early twentieth-century New York in creating new public identities out of the "realm of fantasy, imagination, and desire" (181).

11. "Una joven mexicana."

12. "Una joven mexicana." U.S. news outlets portrayed Marina as duplicitous and morally compromised, character flaws that were associated with her being Mexican. The *New York Times* focused on her prior divorce at the age of fifteen and her attempts to sneak past Chaplin's staff, perpetuating stereotypes of Mexico as a land of child brides and criminals ("Girl Pursues Chaplin," *New York Times*, April 2, 1923). The *Los Angeles Times* described her as "husky" and "buxom," not at all the image of the glamorous flapper described in the Mexican press ("Loves Chaplin: Seeks to Die," *Los Angeles Times*, April 2, 1923).

13. "La tragicomedia de la bella enamorada."

14. Weinbaum and The Modern Girl around the World Research Group, *The Modern Girl around the World*, 16.

15. Miyao, *Sessue Hayakawa*; Wang, "The Art of Screen Passing."

16. A. López, "From Hollywood and Back." López also argues that del Rio's transnational stardom continues to reverberate in Latino cultural production in the United States precisely because of its hybrid origins and history.

17. Hershfield, *The Invention of Dolores del Río*, ix.

18. Anne Rubenstein uses this term—as does Hershfield, in *Imagining la Chica Moderna*—to describe the modern girl of the 1930s and 1940s in her study of comic books, *Bad Language, Naked Ladies*.

19. "El baile y su influencia social," *El Hogar* (hereafter EH), May 18, 1927, 5.

20. "En la nombre de la moral," EH, August 24, 1927, 5.

21. "¿Hacia donde vamos?," EH, November 26, 1924, 5.

22. The name of the organization is Las Damas Católicas. The name of its national publication is *La Dama Católica* (hereafter LDC).

23. For reports from various local chapters, see issues of LDC from 1920 to 1930. Groups from all over Mexico reported successes and frustrations. In Montemorelos, Nuevo León, the Damas met with the local cinema owner who, they reported, was more than happy to accommodate their requests. In Durango, the Damas reported a successful awareness campaign in 1925. However, the group in San Luis Potosí reported that their projector had been put in storage for lack of appropriate films to show. "Lo que hacen las damas," LDC, March 1, 1924, 3, 28; March 1, 1925, 8.

24. "Mérida," LDC, March 1, 1923, 30; "Moralidad: Oaxaca," LDC, January 1, 1923, 33.

25. "A *El Universal* y *Excélsior*," LDC, July 1, 1924, 2.

26. "A *El Universal* y *Excélsior*," 2.

27. On Moore's flapper stardom, see Sara Ross, "Screening the Modern Girl"; Negra, *Off-White Hollywood*, 38.

28. Sara Ross, "Screening the Modern Girl," 286.

29. This narrative convention is of a piece with the flapper film cycle in general. Lori Landay writes: "On one hand, the narrative of the flapper film explores women's liberation from Victorian restrictions, and seems to represent an emerging alternative or even oppositional culture; on the other, it contains female independence within the traditional confines of romance and marriage" ("The Flapper Film," 225). For a general discussion of the flapper in American culture, see Yellis, "Prosperity's Child."

30. *Juventud ardiente* (*Flaming Youth*) advertisement, *El Universal* (hereafter EU), May 31, 1924. Sara Ross describes the canny use of this image in U.S. advertising ("Screening the Modern Girl," 283).

31. Sara Ross, "Screening the Modern Girl," 283.

32. "A *El universal* y *Excélsior*," 2.

33. Cover, RR, May 25, 1924. Ageeth Sluis connects the *pelona* to what she calls the "deco body." Centering her analysis on the popularity of the *bataclan*, a racy performance genre, Sluis argues that the deco body "ushered in new gender ideals, helped visualize urban modernity, and bridged the gap between two divergent discourses that accompanied revolutionary reform, indigenismo and mestizaje." "Bataclanismo!," 469.

34. This definition of the modern girl is borrowed from Weinbaum and The Modern Girl around the World Research Group, *The Modern Girl around the World*.

35. "La edad del automóvil," *EH*, September 22, 1926, 5.

36. "Innovaciones Ridiculas," *LDC*, March 17, 1926, 5.

37. "Notas morales: La moda," *Acción y Fe*, October 1922, 719.

38. The flapper—or "jazz-baby," as some called her—began appearing on the screen as early as 1920, when Selznick Pictures Corporation released *The Flapper*, starring Olive Thomas. A flurry of flapper-themed films followed, including *The Country Flapper* (Dorothy Gish Productions, 1922); *The Married Flapper* (Universal, 1922); *The Cowboy and the Flapper* (Phil Goldstone Productions, 1924); *The Painted Flapper*, Chadwick Pictures, 1924); *The Perfect Flapper* (Associated First National, 1924), which again featured Moore; *Flapper Wives* (Trimble and Murfin Productions, 1924); and *The Exalted Flapper* (Fox Film Corp., 1929). Moore's star turn in *Flaming Youth* and Clara Bow's appearance in *It* (Famous Players–Lasky, 1927), directed by Clarence Badger, were by far the most popular and controversial of the flapper's on-screen incarnations.

39. "La mujer y el progreso," *EH*, May 22, 1929, 3.

40. "Como buenos imitadores," *EH*, June 3, 1925, 5.

41. "La vanidad," *Armonia Social*, November 1921, n.p.

42. Leon Rey, "¡Mujeres honradas!," *LDC*, September 1, 1923, 4.

43. Gamboa, *Santa*.

44. Gamboa, *Santa*, 90.

45. On the prostitute in nineteenth-century Mexico, see French, "Prostitutes and Guardian Angels"; Bliss, *Compromised Positions*, chapter 2.

46. Reyes, *Filmografía*, 119, 151, 163.

47. Bliss, *Compromised Positions*, 71, 91.

48. "Deben fumar las mujeres," *RR*, December 12, 1926, 31.

49. José Elguero, "La mujer contemporánea," *RR*, January 6, 1924, 4.

50. Carlos Serrano, "El reinado de las pelonas: Una moda Americana que invade nuestro medio," *RR*, May 25, 1924, 9.

51. Serrano, "El reinado de las pelonas," 9.

52. Hershfield, *Imagining la Chica Moderna*, 127–55.

53. Obdulia [pseud.], "Las apariencias," *EH*, June 29, 1927, 5.

54. Obdulia, "Las apariencias."

55. Sanchez Filmador [Gustavo F. Aguilar], "Charlas dominicales," *EU*, July 27, 1924.

56. Doane, "The Economy of Desire," 132. See also Friedberg, *Window Shopping*.

57. For a detailed account of the cases of Alicia Olvera (1920), Pilar Moreno (1922), Luz González (1925), and Magdalena Jurado (1921), see Reyes, *Cine y sociedad*, 2:71–98. The films *Rendición*, *La puñalada*, *La banda del cinco de oro*, *La audacidad de una coqueta*, *Carmen*, and *El Secreto*, which either told the stories of particular cases or were loosely based on these cases, are considered lost. De los Reyes bases his account of them on newspaper coverage and advertising material. On the concept of honor in nineteenth- and twentieth-century Mexican legal thought and practice, see Speckman Guerra, "De méritos y reputaciones."

58. "La edad de automóvil."

59. "Esther Borgia Sforza," *EH*, November 19, 1924, 4.

60. "Fueron capturados los asesinos del cajero Ángel Oñate," *EU*, November 10, 1924.

61. Quoted in "Fueron capturados los asesinos." See also "Esther Rivera hace horrible descripción del asesinato," *EU*, November 18, 1924.

62. "Esther Borghieri [*sic*] Sforza y Moisés Rivera, estoicos en el lugar del crimen," *EU*, November 23, 1924.

63. "Esther Borgia Sforza."

64. "Mundo demonio y carne: El shimmy," *EUI*, May 26, 1921, 31.

65. John Page, "The Spread of American Customs," *Mexican American*, January 31, 1925, 5.

66. Rey, "¡Mujeres honradas!," 4.

67. José Alvarez, "El patriotismo y el cine," *EH*, February 20, 1924, 21.

68. See, for example, "Los Estados Unidos por dentro," November 20, 1921, 8, and January 1922, 8; "Efecto del cosmetico," February 1922, 8; "La muvimania," April 1922, 10, all in *El Heraldo de la Raza*.

69. "Un reprobable atentado contra las pelonas," *Excélsior* (hereafter *EX*), July 23, 1924.

70. "Un atentado que deshonra la ciudad," *EU*, July 24, 1924.

71. "Un reprobable atentado contra las pelonas."

72. Rubenstein's analysis of this incident focuses on the debate over new gender norms and the *pelona*'s connection to "the revolution and its gendered educational projects" ("The 'War on las Pelonas,'" 71). Rubenstein ultimately concludes that the pelona, or *la chica moderna*, as she came to be known, became aligned more closely with the revolutionary state through her participation in national rituals such as sporting events.

73. "Viriles y caballerosos jóvenes defienden a las pelonas," *EX*, July 14, 1924.

74. Reynaldo Cervantes, letter to the editor, *EX*, July 24, 1924.

75. "No hay nada que justifica el atentado a las pelonas," *ED*, July 24, 1924.

76. Quoted in "Caracteres trágicos esta adquiriendo el asunto de las jóvenes que llevan el cabello a la 'bob,'" *EX*, July 25, 1924, sec. 2, 1.

77. See Soto, *The Emergence of the Modern Mexican Woman*; Tuñón, *Women in Mexico*; Boylan, "The Feminine 'Apostolate in Society' versus the Secular State." On women workers in Mexico City, see Porter, *Working Women in Mexico City*. Porter notes that industrial development in the capital was dominated by industries that tended to hire women (xii).

78. Knight, "Popular Culture and the Revolutionary State," 396.

79. A. B. de Noriega, "El feminismo en Nuevo León," *Jueves de Excélsior*, January 1929, n.p.

80. "Degenerado," *LDC*, March 1, 1925, 16.

81. Manuel Gonzalez Ramírez, "Setenta y cinco centavos," *RR*, May 20, 1928, 20.

82. Ramírez, "Setenta y cinco centavos," 20, 21.

83. Ramírez, "Setenta y cinco centavos," 20, 21.

84. "A *El Universal y Excélsior*," 2.

85. "A *El Universal y Excélsior*," 2.

86. Margarita Santín Fontoura, "El feminismo de la mujer mexicana," *EH*, February 8, 1922, 33.

87. "El concurso de taquigrafia y mecanografía, convocado por 'Excélsior,' se efectuó ayer con el más lisonjero resultado," *EX*, November 22, 1922.

88. "Las señoritas," *EX*, November 29, 1922. Beyond the newspaper's mention of it, no record of this film exists. It may have been exhibited as part of a Camus & Company newsreel.

89. "El concurso del 'vestido económico,'" *EU*, April 20, 1928.

90. "El concurso del 'vestido económico.'"

91. Quoted in "El concurso del traje barato," *EU*, April 21, 1928.

92. "Del lujo como economía," *Heraldo de México*, October 7, 1923. See also "El concurso del 'vestido económico'" and "Mujeres preparadas por el hogar," *EU*, May 24, 1928.

93. "El concurso del 'vestido económico.'"

94. "El concurso del 'vestido económico.'"

95. Stamp, "'It's a Long Way to Filmland,'" 333.

96. Silvestre Bonnard [Carlos Noriega Hope], "Vanidad de vanidades," *EU*, November 18, 1919.

97. Bonnard [Noreiga Hope], "Vanidad de vanidades."

98. "Ambiciones de gloria," *EH*, May 26, 1926, 5.

99. On the role of fan magazines in solidifying the middle-class audience's investment in film culture, see Fuller, *At the Picture Show*.

100. See, for example, José Corral Rigan, "De cómo un extra se estrelló en Los Angeles, entrevista sin importancia," *EUI*, September 23, 1920, 6–7; "Las tragedia ignorada de Hollywood: 'La casa de los corazones rotos,'" *RR*, February 1, 1925; Baltazar Fernández Cue, "Caminos a la pantalla," *RR*, February 13, 1927, 32; "Ambiciones de gloria."

101. Bonnard [Noriega Hope], "Vanidad de vanidades."

102. "Gran exodo de mujeres mexicanas," *La Opinión* (hereafter *LO*), December 14, 1926.

103. Stamp, "'It's a Long Way to Filmland'"; Kenaga, "Making the 'Studio Girl.'"

104. All quotations in this paragraph are from "Gran exodo de mujeres mexicanas."

105. "Dos muchachas habian resuelto marcharse a California," *ED*, March 25, 1923. See also "Una aventura de cine realizada por dos niñas: Abandonaron la casa paterna en busca de emociones," *EX*, December 27, 1920; "Dos muchachas imprudentes," *El Heraldo de México* (Los Angeles), January 28, 1919, 8; "Tres jovenes resueltas," *El Heraldo de México* (Los Angeles), November 23, 1919, 4.

106. "Dos muchachas habian resuelto marcharse a California."

107. "Destruirá los prejuicos existente," *LO*, September 16, 1927. *Tepeyac* was well received by critics, including Carlos Noriega Hope, who read its portrayal of the Guadalupe myth as a Mexican analog to the western. Like most national produc-

tions, however, it did not last long in theaters. See Noriega Hope, *El mundo de las sombras*, 166–68.

108. For more on the opinions of the Spanish-speaking public about stars such as del Rio and Vélez, see A. López, "From Hollywood and Back"; Rodriguez-Estrada, "Dolores del Río and Lupe Vélez." The historian Vicki Ruiz writes: "A handful of Latina actresses, especially Dolores del Rio and Lupe Vélez, whetted [these] aspirations and served as public role models of the 'American dream'" (*From out of the Shadows*, 58). Victoria Sturtevant argues that Vélez's performance in the B comedies that dominated her later career can be understood as a form of "ethnic masquerade" that subverted dominant notions of Mexican immigrant identity as well as mainstream femininity. Sturtevant bases her argument on a reading of the English-language press and the characters Vélez played over the course of her career ("Spitfire," 21).

109. "La elección de la estrella mexicana," ED, June 2, 1923; "Jovenes: Aqui esta lo que estaban esperando!!," ED, March 23, 1923. Beauty contests had become a tried-and-true promotional strategy employed by both film studios and theater chains across the United States. For an early example, see "Universal's Beauty Contest," *Moving Picture World*, May 8, 1915, 887. In Mexico, other beauty contests had been held previously but had not received nearly as much press coverage. See, for example, "¿Quiere ud. ser estrella de cine?," EX, February 28, 1922, 7; "Jovenes," ED, March 15, 1923.

110. "El concurso," ED, March 23, 1923.

111. Adela Sequeyro, quoted in Vega Alfaro and Torres San Martín, *Adela Sequeyro*, 14; "Josefina," ED, March 26, 1923.

112. Indeed, one of the tag lines above the article about the tallying of the votes reads: "The politicians look surprised at how apt our country is in exercising the vote . . . when what brings people to the [voting] urns is a beautiful and patriotic ideal" ("La elección de la estrella mexicana"). Ángel Miquel focuses on this aspect of the contest, arguing that the process of voting in this contest functioned as a model of democracy, in anticipation of the upcoming presidential elections. See Miquel, "La Estrella del Sur."

113. "Honoria Suárez, la vencedora en el concurso cinematográfico prepara su viaje a la poética Los Angeles," ED, June 22, 1923.

114. Information on the film's screening and a summary of its scenes are drawn from de los Reyes, *Filmografia*, 254–55; "No han fracasado los artistas mexicanos que fueron a cinelandia buscando gloria," EX, September 7, 1924; Miquel, *Por las pantallas*, 156–57; "Amusements," *Mexican American*, August 30, 1924, 40; "Honras funebres de Honoria Suárez," LO, November 1, 1926.

115. "Honras funebres de Honoria Suárez."

116. José Vasconcelos, "Dos cartas importantes," LDC, July 1, 1924, 5.

117. Hallett, *Go West!*, especially ch. 3.

118. "Las estrellas mexicanas del cine," EUI, February 13, 1927, 22.

5. DENIGRATING PICTURES

The Courbet Brothers letter from which the second epigraph is drawn is located in AHSRE, 19-10-8 (III) 1.

1. James Mark Purcell, unpublished study, cited in Koszarski, *An Evening's Entertainment*, 33.

2. Claire Fox discusses the ways in which the Mexican Revolution became a spectacle for Americans. People behaved, she writes, "as if they were watching a play or a movie rather than a war" (*The Fence and the River*, 81).

3. "Picture Plays and People," *New York Times*, August 26, 1923; "The Screen," *New York Times*, September 3, 1923.

4. Anonymous letter to the Mexican consul general, New York, September 5, 1923, AHSRE 19-10-8 (I), III/833 (00-72)/1, 1.

5. Anonymous letter to the Mexican consul general.

6. Quoted in E. P. Kirby Hade to Minister of Foreign Relations, October 10, 1923, AHSRE, 19-10-8 (I), III/833 (00-72)/1, 1,

7. Copy of "Bill No. 6022, Ordinance No. 5614, New Series, Amending Section 1 of Ordinance No. 3893 (New Series) Entitled 'Regulating Motion Picture Exhibitors and Entertainments,'" AHSRE, 19-10-8 (I), III/833 (00-72)/1, 1.

8. J. A. Valenzuela to Ministry of Foreign Relations, November 8, 1923, AHSRE, 19-10-8 (I), III/833 (00-72)/1, 1.

9. Courbet Brothers to Manuel Téllez, November 1, 1923, AHSRE 19-10-8 (I), III/833 (00-72)/1, 1.

10. Manuel Téllez to Courbet Brothers, November 16, 1923, AHSRE, 19-10-8 (I), III/833 (00-72)/1, 1.

11. The MPPDA was created, in part, in reaction to the unsavory picture of the industry painted by star scandals such as Roscoe "Fatty" Arbuckle's trial for murder and state and local censorship campaigns (see Koszarski, *An Evening's Entertainment*, 203–8). The organization also focused its energy on keeping foreign markets open to American films (see Vasey, *The World According to Hollywood*, 29–49).

12. Vasey, *The World According to Hollywood*, 49–62.

13. Kuhn, *Cinema, Censorship, and Sexuality*, 127. Lea Jacobs (*The Wages of Sin*) argues that self-regulation by the industry (in her case studies, the self-regulation of depictions of the fallen woman) led to particular forms of narrative development.

14. Grieveson, *Policing Cinema*.

15. Vasey, *The World According to Hollywood*, 29.

16. For an analysis of the extensive history of depictions of Mexico in both early documentary and fiction films, see García Riera, *México visto por el cine extranjero*, 14–104.

17. On representations of Mexico in nineteenth-century U.S. literature, see Alarcón, *The Aztec Palimpsest*. On portrayals of Mexico in nineteenth-century American sensational literature, dime novels, and subsequently film, see Streeby, *American Sensations*. And on journalistic representations during the U.S.-Mexico War, see Johannsen, *To the Halls of the Montezumas*.

18. Musser, *Edison Motion Pictures*, 135.

19. As noted by Wanda Strauven, this concept was first introduced by Tom Gunning and André Gaudreault in 1986 in two essays, one by Gunning writing alone and the other by Gunning and Gaudreault (Strauven, "Introduction to an Attractive Concept," 11–12).

20. Pettit, *Images of the Mexican American in Fiction and Film*, 131–51; Keller, "The Image of the Chicano"; Ramírez Berg, *Latino Images in Film*, 66–86; Fregoso, *MeXicana Encounters*, 161–68.

21. Shelley Streeby makes this argument about nineteenth-century U.S. dime novels (*American Sensations*).

22. On representations of the Mexican Revolution in the U.S. press, see Britton, *Revolution and Ideology*. On Reed's sympathetic coverage of the revolution, see Wilson, "Plotting the Border," and Reed's own writings, which can be found in Ruffinelli, *Villa y la revolución mexicana*.

On visual representations of the revolution, see Fox, *The Fence and the River*, and Vanderwood and Samponaro, *Border Fury*.

23. For the most comprehensive analysis of U.S. cinematic representations of the revolution, see de Orellana's *La mirada circular*. De Orellana argues that films about the revolution reflect aspects of American society rather than Mexican reality.

24. De Orellana distills Mexican stereotypes into three major ones: first, the equation of the hostility of the border with the hostility of its inhabitants; second, the "greaser" and the "beautiful señorita"; and third, the docile and sensual *criolla* who "falls easily at the feet of the North American hero" (*La mirada circular*, 137–77). See also Ramírez Berg, *Latino Images*.

25. Noble, *Mexican National Cinema*, 30.

26. *A Trip through Barbarous Mexico* advertisement, *Moving Picture World*, March 22, 1913, 1269.

27. César Canseco, letter to Carter H. Harrison, August 2, 1913, AHSRE, III/524 (04)/8815, 16-9-160.

28. Gabriela Arredondo reports this in a footnote (*Mexican Chicago*, 176), though I did not find evidence of it in the papers in AHSRE.

29. "Películas que nos denigran," *Excélsior* (hereafter EX), February 2, 1920. This film should not be confused with a documentary short with the same title produced by the Mexican filmmaker Miguel Contereras Torres in 1923. This film was particularly well described, but there were others of its type. See "No se permitera la exportación de 'films' que nos denigren," EX, March 19, 1919.

30. "Películas que nos denigran."

31. "Películas que nos denigran." These types of requests were common and continued through the first half of the 1920s. See, for example, Sherwood MacDonald to President Alvaro Obregón, March 31, 1921, AGN, DGG, B.2.00.15. c.7, exp. 5, S. Jaffe to Plutarco Elías Calles, February 12, 1923, AGN, DGG, D.200.312, c. 20, exp. 27; C.J. Hubbell to Manuel G. Paredes, February 21, 1923, AGN, DGG, B. 2.00.15, c. 2, exp. 1; Erika Peterkirsten to Plutarco Elías Calles, AGN, POC, c. 321, exp. 814-P-95.

32. "Películas que nos denigran."

33. "No se permitirá la exportación de 'films' que nos denigren," *EX*, March 19, 1919.

34. Review of "El orgullo del palomar," *Revista de Revistas*, December 16, 1923, 47.

35. Luis L. Ruíz, report to Municipal Regulatory Commission, November 17, 1911, AHDF, AHA, DP, 807, 1316.

36. Quoted in Anduiza, *Legislación cinematográfica mexicana*, 17. The fear of cinema's capacity to serve as a "school of crime" was, of course, quite common. See, for example, Grieveson, *Policing Cinema*. In her 1933 study, *Motion Pictures: A Problem for the Nation*, Mary Astor notes that censors in Britain, India, Japan, and Scandanavia shared similar concerns, particularly in regard to young people. See also Blumer and Hauser, *Movies, Delinquency, and Crime*, part of the Payne Fund Studies of the effects of motion pictures on children in the United States. In Mexico the relationship between crime and cinema manifested itself cinematically in the national production *El automóvil gris* (1919). The film, based on a series of highly publicized robberies that occurred in Mexico City in 1915 and culminated in the criminals' being shot by a firing squad, was released as a twelve-part serial. Ramirez Berg analyzes the film as an example of Mexican cinema's turn from a strong documentary tradition to narrative, which displayed the influence of U.S., French, and Italian filmmaking (*"El autómovil gris"*).

37. See Guerrero, "La imagen de la revolución," 141–43.

38. Secretaría de Gobernación, *Reglamento de censura*, 4. The council eventually, though it is not clear when, became a subdepartment of the Secretaría de Gobernación. No materials related to the office exist in any of the archives I have consulted. My speculation, which coincides with that of other scholars, is that the papers were lost or destroyed in subsequent changes of administration or as the material was moved from one office to another.

39. Secretaría de Gobernación, *Reglamento de censura*, 4.

40. Secretaría de Gobernación, *Reglamento de censura*, 4.

41. To the surprise of the male-dominated film industry, Carranza appointed two very young women, the sisters Dolores and Adriana Ehlers, to head the Department or Council of Censorship and Department of Cinematography, respectively, another new entity that was to make films that supported or showcased government activities. The sisters, who were supporting themselves as photographers, had met Carranza in Veracruz in 1914 when they had been asked to photograph a military parade. According to an unpublished magazine profile of the sisters and an oral history of Dolores Ehlers conducted in the 1970s, Carranza was so impressed with the sisters' professionalism that he provided them with the funds to study photography in Boston at the Champlain Studios and to learn about motion pictures at the Bureau of Commercial Economics in Washington, D.C.; the Nicholas Power Company in New York; and an unidentified motion picture studio in New Jersey, probably Universal. In a 1920 newspaper article, exhibitors and distributors expressed their displeasure that censorship had been "placed in the hands of young women who neither understand films, nor are capable of understanding the topics [of the films] that could offend our country, *buenas costumbres*, or morality" ("Fueron aprehendidos varios dueños de cinematógrapho," *EX*, July 8, 1920). The Department of Cine-

matography was initially a dependency of the Secretaría de Bellas Artes (Ministry of Fine Arts). It is unclear how many, if any, films were produced on Adriana's watch (A. L. Parker, untitled manuscript, March 20, 1920, decimal file 812.4061/16; National Archives Microfilm Publication M1370, roll 148; Records of the Department of State Relating to the Internal Affairs of Mexico, 1919–29, Record Group 59, National Archives at College Park, MD [hereafter Records]).

42. "La clausura de cinematógrafos," EX, February 4, 1920.

43. This type of rhetoric is mobilized in articles covering the debate over the censorship fees. See "Los empresarios de cines piden que se las rebajen las contribuciones," EX, June 19, 1919; "Dificultades por el nuevo impuesto a los cines de la capital," EX, June 25, 1919; "Películas que nos denigran," EX, February 2, 1920.

44. "Fueron aprehendidos varios dueños de cinematógrapho."

45. Press release, 1992, AHDF, A, SP, prensa, 4015.

46. Press release, 1992, AHDF, A, SP, prensa, 4015.

47. Head of the Department of Public Diversions, "Informe Annual," November 15, 1922, AHDF, A, DP, 809, 1589. The office was to charge two centavos per meter for the first six rolls of film and one centavo for each additional meter. An average five-roll feature (with 1,000 feet or 914 meters per roll) would be subject to a revision fee of approximately thirty pesos. There is no paper trail for the censorship arm of this office in subsequent years, although I have come across tantalizing references to boxes containing material cut by the censor. Dolores Ehlers remembers the Consejo de Censura operating for one to two years. She recalls that by 1922 she and her sister were devoting themselves exclusively to the production of industrial films and newsreels under the auspices of their own studio, Casa Ehlers. Dolores Ehlers interviewed by Aurelio de los Reyes, September 7, 1974, PHO (E) 2/12, Palabra.

48. Ministry of Foreign Relations to Manuel Téllez, Mexican Embassy, Washington, D.C., February 10, 1923, AHSRE, 19-10-8 (III) 1.

49. The text of this warning is reproduced in J. Garza to Minister of Foreign Relations, March 3, 1922, AHSRE, 19-10-8 (I), D-44.

50. These complaints can be found in AHSRE, 19-10-8 (I), III/833 (00-72)/1, 1. See letters from J. Garza Zertuche to Minister of Foreign Relations, March 3, 1922; G. Ludero to Secretario, April 20, 1922; and M. Barrera to Secretario, April 21, 1922, all in AHSRE, 19-10-8 (I), D-44; and J. Garza to Secretario, May 27, 1922, in AHSRE, 19-10-8 (I), E-44-A.

51. Luis [illegible] L., special inspector, Report to Miguel Lerdo de Tejada, head of the Department of Public Entertainments, March 16, 1922, AHDF, A, DP, 809, 1632. It is unclear precisely which film is being referred to here. My most creative interpretations of the title's possible English original have not led to any films whose plots match that described in the report, but it may have been the 1912 Griffith film *Musketeers of Pig Alley* that had entered recirculation or a pirated film that had been imaginatively re-titled. Inspector Alfonso Icaza also complained about this film, writing that it was a shame "that in our own country they be allowed to denigrate us like this." Report, Icaza to Head of Public Diversions, March 16, 1922, AHDF, A, DP, sección teatros y cines, 840,192.

52. Report, Icaza to Head of Public Diversions.

53. Report, Icaza to Head of Public Diversions.

54. Actos de Cabildo, February 6, 1922, 73–74, Archivo Municipal de Guanajuato, Guanajuato, Mexico.

55. Actos de Cabildo, February 6, 1922, 73–74.

56. Álvaro Obregón to Alberto J. Pani, April 4, 1922, AGN, POC, 121-R-P-6.

57. Álvaro Obregón to Alberto J. Pani, June 5, 1922, AGN, DGG, C.2.00.5.3, c. 28, exp. 3.

58. Ministry of the Interior, letter to Ministry of Foreign Relations, quoting a communication from Mexico's "agente commercial" (commercial agent) in Toronto, Ontario, August 29, 1922, AHSRE, 19-10-8 (I).

59. Quoted in "Se pedirá no se exhiban 'films' que resulten ser denigrantes para México," EX, April 7, 1919.

60. J. B. Bristol, letter to President Álvaro Obregón, February 23, 1923, AGN, POC, c. 38, exp. 104-P-1.

61. Anonymous letter to the Mexican consul general.

62. Jack S. Connolly, letter to Charles E. Hughes, June 1, 1922, decimal file 812.4061/28; National Archives Microfilm Publication M1370, roll 148; Records.

63. U.S. Department of Commerce, Latin American Division, U.S. Trade with Latin America in 1922, 34.

64. See Seabury, The Public, 283, 288–89; Seabury, Motion Picture Problems, 413; Strauss, "Foreign Distribution," 309.

65. Vasey, The World According to Hollywood, 7.

66. Strauss, "Foreign Distribution," 307.

67. Strauss, "Foreign Distribution," 307.

68. Usabel, The High Noon, xv.

69. Claude I. Dawson, American consul general in Mexico City, to Secretary of State, October 30, 1922, 812.4061/31; National Archives Microfilm Publication M1370, roll 148; Records.

70. Enoch Pariagua, "Informes generales del Sr. Enoch Pariagua, sobre la industria cinematográfica con relación a México," August 10, 1929, AHSRE, numeración corrida, 491, 491-15/B830.

71. Quoted in FKN to Hanna, June 8, 1922, decimal file 812.4061/28; National Archives Microfilm Publication M1370, roll 148; Records.

72. Quoted in Lewis I. Clarke to Álvaro Obregón, September 26, 1922, AGN, POC c. 249, exp. 803-C-32.

73. On the reactions of European countries to "stereotypical" representations, see Vasey, The World According to Hollywood, 41–60.

74. The text of this agreement is reproduced in Reyes, Cine y sociedad, 1:187, and can also be found in FKN to Hanna.

75. Adolfo B [illegible], consul general in Berlin Ministry of Foreign Affairs, August 18, 1922, AHSRE, 19-10-8 (III) 1.

76. Ruth Vasey points to the incident with Mexico as the beginning of the MPPDA's later foreign policy. In 1923 the MPPDA's Foreign Department was headed

by Major Frederick "Ted" Heron. In 1924 Will Hays pressured the U.S. Department of Commerce for a special motion picture section within the Bureau of Foreign and Domestic Commerce, a section that was in operation by 1929 (*The World According to Hollywood*, 29–61).

77. This plot summary is drawn from the description of the film in the AFI catalog, http://www.afi/chadwyck.com (accessed May 29, 2009).

78. Some of these complaints were merely noted in passing in diplomatic correspondence. Others have been preserved in their entirety. See AHSRE, numeración corrida, 491, 19-10-8 (III) 1.

79. Quoted in Report, April 1922, AHSRE, numeración corrida, 491, 19-10-8 (III) 1.

80. My analysis of these changes is based on a comparison of the list of changes held in the AHSRE and a continuity script at the Margaret Herrick Library, Academy of Motion Picture Arts and Sciences, Los Angeles, California (hereafter Herrick). The George Eastman House in Rochester, New York, holds a print of the film as it was originally released, but since there is no extant copy of the changed version, these two documents provide the most relevant basis for a comparison.

81. Clara Berenger, "Her Husband's Trademark," Famous Players–Lasky Corp., undated, Master File 744, 6, Herrick.

82. Continuity script, "Her Husband's Trademark," Famous Players–Lasky Corp., undated, Master File 744, 23, Herrick.

83. Report, April 1922, AHSRE.

84. Report, April 1922, AHSRE.

85. Juan E. Anchondo, letter to Ministry of Foreign Relations, September 29, 1923, AHSRE, 19-10-8 (I), III/833 (00-72)/1, 1.

86. Harold Lloyd, letter to E. P. Kirby Hade, October 19, 1923, AHSRE, 36-30-36, H/833 (04) (73-59).

87. Courbet Brothers, letter to Manuel C. Téllez, October 19, 1923, AHSRE, 19-10-8 (I), III/833 (00-72)/1, 1.

88. The products of Pathé Frères, the French company, were also banned until the Mexican government realized that the two companies were unrelated.

89. As I have discussed elsewhere, Helen Delpar ("Goodbye to the Greaser") and Aurelio de los Reyes (*Cine y sociedad*, 2:173–206) each devote attention to the conflict. Delpar argues that Hollywood had an economic motive for phasing out the "greaser" and, following Vasey (*The World According to Hollywood*), that the agreement reached with Mexico served as a model for later agreements entered into by the MPPDA and other countries, such as France. De los Reyes questions some of the outrage over these films. Serna, "'As a Mexican I Feel It's My Duty.'"

90. "Una cinta de cine, con 'La paloma,' que nos denigra," *El Universal* (hereafter *EU*), December 7, 1927.

91. Baltasar Fernandez Cue, "El fracaso de la paloma," *EX*, March 11, 1928.

92. Fernandez Cue, "El fracaso de la paloma."

93. "Mexico Prohibits Girl of the Rio," *Los Angeles Times*, May 10, 1932.

94. Anonymous letter to the Mexican consul general.

95. The heroine of the film, Val Hannon, supposedly introduces soap and water

to the children on the ranch. See "En el Teatro 'Grauman' se esta exhibiendo una película que lastima el sentimiento mexicano," *La Prensa*, May 21, 1922.

96. "Note 382," Subsecretary of the Ministry of Foreign Relations to Ministry of the Interior, June 6, 1922, AHSRE, 19-10-8 (II).

97. J. Garza Zertuche, consul in San Francisco, letter to Ministry of Foreign Relations, May 17, 1922, AHSRE, E-44-A.

98. Manuel Tellez, letter to Courbet Brothers, November 16, 1923, AHSRE, 19-10-8 (I), III/833 (00-72)/1, 1.

99. J. E. Anchondo, consul in Salt Lake City, UT, note attached to report, September 9, 1923, AHSRE, 19-10-8 (I).

100. M. Esparza, Cónsul Particular in El Paso, TX, report to Cónsul General, El Paso, TX, August 23, 1923, AHSRE, 19-10-8 (IV).

101. J. E. Anchondo to Ministry of Foreign Relations, September 29, 1923, AHSRE, 19-10-(8).

102. Perhaps the best analysis of the construction of Mexican national culture after the revolution can be found in Pérez Montfort, *Estampas de nacionalismo popular mexicano* (particularly 121–48). Helen Delpar discusses this cultural nationalism and the sudden popularity and standardization of folk culture in *The Enormous Vogue of Things Mexican* (12–14). See also Benjamin, *La Revolución*. Alex Saragoza discusses the use of this visual lexicon in the development of both domestic and international tourism in "The Selling of Mexico."

103. For an overview of the presence of American artists, journalists, and intellectuals in Mexico during the revolution and in the 1920s, see Oles, *South of the Border*. Aurelio de los Reyes discusses the production of mexicanidad in *Cine y sociedad* (2:205–9), arguing that the arts became the arena in which Mexico sought to counter negative images of the country in U.S. films.

104. Subsecretary of the Interior Ministry to the Ministry of Foreign Relations (excerpting E. G. García, Luís S. Berenguer, and others, July 1922), July 20, 1922, AHSRE 19-10-8 (III); Luis Lezama, letter to Interior Ministry, September 23, 1923, AGN, DGG, D.2.03.10, c. 16, exp. 10; Dionisio Torres, Galveston, TX, letter to President Álvaro Obregón, June 4, 1924, AHSRE 19-10-8 (VI).

105. F. B., Circuito Olimpia, letter to H. Ayuntamiento de la Ciudad de Mexico, April 29, 1922, AHDF, A, DP, 811, 1632.

106. Enrique Rivera, report to chief of the Department of Public Diversions, October 16, 1922, AHDF, AHA, 815, 13.

107. Miguel T. Gonzalez, letter to Plutarco Elías Calles, Ministro de Gobernación, August 23, 1922, AGN, DGG, C.2.03.21, c. 12, exp. 2.

108. See, for example, Alfonso Sayago, letter to Plutarco Elías Calles, August 30, 1922, AGN, DGG, C.2.03.21, c. 12, exp. 2.

109. Gonzalez to Calles.

110. B. Trasviña, Tampico, Tamaulipas, telegram to Gobernación, September 26, 1922, AGN, DGG, C.2.03.21, c. 12, exp. 2.

111. "Piden la clausura de los cines que exhiben películas anti-mexicanas," *EU*, May 23, 1924.

112. Luis Lezama, letter to Gobernación, September 24, 1923, AGN, DGG, D.2.03.10, c.16, exp. 10.

113. Alfonso Villegas, General Secretary, Sindicato de Empleados Cinematografistas del D.F., letter to Álvaro Obregón, October 4, 1924, AGN, POC, 104-P-79.

114. Villegas to Obregón.

115. Vice-Consul Farrell, letter to John L. Bacon, mayor of San Diego, February 22, 1923, AHSRE, 19-10-8 (III).

116. Miguel Castillo, letter to Ministry of the Interior, December 1, 1922, AGN, DGG, C.2.03.74, c. 15, exp. 1.

117. Castillo to Minister of the Interior.

118. Torres letter to Obregón.

119. Torres letter to Obregón. I have been unable to identify the specific film to which Torres refers; it could have been any one of the numerous westerns being churned out by U.S. studios.

120. Anderson, *Imagined Communities*.

121. Torres letter to Obregón.

122. Marquez, consul in Laredo, TX, to Ministry of Foreign Relations, July 31, 1923, AHSRE, 19-10-8 (I).

123. The letter was reprinted in "Continuán en su labor de denigrarnos," *El Nacional Revolucionario*, June 3, 1930, 8. The confederation was a loose-knit organization of Mexican mutual aid, social, and political organizations in Los Angeles that had been established in 1925 at the suggestion of the Mexican consul, Rafael Avelyra (Balderrama, *In Defense of La Raza*, 8).

124. "Continuán en su labor de denigrarnos," 8.

125. For a history of the play, the silent version (1923), and the sound version (1930), see Alonzo, *Badmen, Bandits, and Folk Heroes*, 68–84. Alonzo does not mention the production of the Spanish-language version, but that topic is addressed by Jarvinen (*The Rise of Spanish-Language Filmmaking*, 63–75).

126. José Alvarez, "El patriotismo y el cine," *La Dama Católica*, February 20, 1924, 21.

127. "Continuán en su labor de denigrarnos."

128. "Continuán en su labor de denigrarnos."

129. Gunckel reads this as a moment that highlights the shifting cultural power in Mexican Los Angeles, as cinema became increasingly important at the expense of Spanish-language theater ("The War of the Accents"). See also Jarvinen, *The Rise of Spanish-Language Filmmaking*, 60–82.

130. Guaitsel, "Nuestra opinión: *El hombre malo*," *Cinelandia*, September 1930, 917.

131. It is unclear whether the Mexican government was being asked to supervise production of both the Spanish and English versions.

132. "Censura de la Película Cinematográfica *El hombre malo*," consular communication 02767, AHSRE IV-266-14, (73)/833.1/1.

133. "Mexico" (511), Motion Picture Association of America, Administrative Files, MPAA Production Code Files, Special Collections, Herrick.

134. Cónsul de México en Los Angeles, "Informe sobre producción de pelícu-

las cinematográficas," May 25, 1932, VIII.353.22.2, 1-13-8-95, Bellas Artes, Archivo Histórico de la Secretaría de Educación Pública. See also Luis Padilla Nervo, letter to Ministry of Foreign Relations, June 17, 1932, VIII.353.22.2, 1-13-8-95, Bellas Artes, Archivo Histórico de la Secretaría de Educación Pública.

135. "Informes generales del Sr. Enoch Pariagua."

136. Manuel Telléz to William A. Orr, MGM Pictures, October 21, 1929, AHSRE, 491-19 B/830 (73-0)/2 1929. *Tampico* was ultimately made by Columbia as *The Woman I Stole* (1933), with its location changed to North Africa. The need to placate Mexico may have led to the avoidance of Mexican-themed productions in favor of locating stories in countries with less critical, or at least less vocal, audiences. On this tactic, see Vasey, *The World According to Hollywood*, 59–60.

137. Rubenstein, "Raised Voices at the Cine Montecarlo."

138. "Mexico" (511).

6. AL CINE

"El Lavaplatos" epigraph reproduced in Manuel Gamio, *The Mexican Immigrant*.

1. Gunning, "An Aesthetic of Astonishment"; Bottomore, "The Panicking Audience?"

2. Venegas, *Las aventuras*, 124; see also 113–18.

3. Kanellos, "Introducción," 10.

4. See "Lista de Empresas Mexicanas en . . . ," undated typescript, folder 5, box 3, pages 2–7, Notes gathered for his book *Mexican Immigration to the United States* and related material, 1926–1929, BANC MSS Z-R 5, Bancroft Library, University of California, Berkeley (hereafter Gamio Notes).

5. Weber, *Dark Sweat*, 59.

6. Monroy, *Rebirth*, 173.

7. "Mexican Survey—Los Angeles City Schools," 11, n.d., folder 31, carton 10, Taylor Papers, Special Collections, University of Chicago.

8. Williams and Hanson, *Mexican Families in Los Angeles*, 231, 99. In this study, spending on recreation followed only that on food, clothing, housing, household operations, and transportation. For information on Mexican families in San Diego, see Panunzio, *How Mexicans Earn and Live*, 50.

9. Ruiz, *From out of the Shadows*; Monroy, *Rebirth*; Sanchez, *Becoming Mexican American*.

10. García, *Desert Immigrants*.

11. Ruiz, *From out of the Shadows*, 53–71.

12. Monroy, *Rebirth*, 176.

13. García, *Desert Immigrants*, 208, 211–12.

14. Sanchez, *Becoming Mexican American*, 173.

15. The encounters of international audiences have been the subject of increasing scholarly attention. The essays in Stokes and Maltby, *Hollywood Abroad*, constitute an excellent entry point into this research.

16. Waller, "Another Audience"; Carbine, "The 'Finest outside the Loop'"; Stewart, *Migrating to the Movies*.

17. Fregoso, *MeXicana Encounters*, 148–68.

18. Social historians of Mexican migration to the United States generally agree on a figure of 1 million to 1.5 million. Discrepancies have to do with the spottiness of migration records (in both countries) from this period. See Romo, *East Los Angeles*, 42, 61; Camarillo, *Chicanos in a Changing Society*, 200–201; Sanchez, *Becoming Mexican American*, 18; Gutierrez, *Walls and Mirrors*, 40.

19. Weber expands on the relationship between the disappearance of the independent Mexican peasantry and immigration in the late nineteenth century (*Dark Sweat*, 48–78). See also Barton, "At the Edge of the Storm."

20. The Immigration Quota Act of 1921 limited European migration to 3 percent of each national group's resident population, according to the 1910 census. The Johnson Reed Act of 1924 reduced European migration quotas even further and completely prohibited immigration from Asia. See Ngai, *Impossible Subjects*, especially chapters 1 and 2.

21. Sanchez, *Becoming Mexican American*, 10, 15; Arredondo, *Mexican Chicago*.

22. Arredondo, *Mexican Chicago*, 92–105.

23. See Aguila, "Protecting 'México de afuera'"; Kuehnert, "Pernicious Foreigners and Contested Compatriots"; Bustamante, *Cruzar la línea*; Durand, *Migración México-Estados Unidos*.

24. Quoted in Cardoso, *Mexican Emigration to the United States*, 104.

25. Durón Gonzalez, *Problemas migratorios de México*, 71. See also Fabila, *El problema de la emigración*, a pamphlet on the impact of migration on Mexico, published in 1929.

26. "¿Quien tiene la culpa? La emigración de trabajadores," *El Demócrata* (hereafter *ED*), April 4, 1923.

27. "¿Quien tiene la culpa?"

28. "Los mexicanos que van a los estados unidos regresan en la miseria," *ED*, April 15, 1923. See also, "En las calles," *ED*, May 26, 1923.

29. "Laredo Texas es la meta dolorosa," *ED*, May 26, 1923.

30. Francisco Medrano, interview by Luis Felipe Recinos, Los Angeles, April 6, 1927, box 2, folder 10, Gamio Notes.

31. Gamio was educated at Columbia University, and his early work focused on Mexico's native populations. In the late 1920s and 1930s he turned his attention to migration. See González Gamio, *Manuel Gamio*. There is no biography of Gamio in English.

32. Gamio, *Mexican Immigration*, 68.

33. Sanchez, *Becoming Mexican American*, 25. Sanchez observes that this process began during the porfiriato when rural Mexico received "new ideas and material goods" via the country's newly established railroad networks. Thus, new technologies like the railroad and the sewing machine coexisted alongside older ways of doing things like grinding corn for tortillas using a *molcajete*.

34. Gamio, *Hacia un México nuevo*, 173. Secularization was particularly important to Gamio and other liberal intellectuals who believed that fanatical Catholicism drove many of the country's civil conflicts and prevented its modernization.

35. The synopsis and quote from an unnamed source come from Reyes, *Filmografía*, 2:167.

36. The weekly popular fiction series was initiated by Noriega Hope, then editor of *El Universal Ilustrado*, to showcase young Mexican authors. The series, which published novellas and short stories on cheap paper, ran from November 1922 to sometime in 1925. In this series, Noriega Hope republished Mariano Azuela's *Los de abajo*, one of the most important novels of modern Mexican literature and the revolution, which had been originally published in serial form in the El Paso, TX, newspaper *El Paso del Norte* in 1915. See Miquel, *Disvolvencias*, 81–98. Miquel argues that *"Che" Ferrati* "copies" Noriega Hope's nonfiction account in *El mundo de las sombras* (83). My view is that Noriega Hope uses fiction to expand and develop some of the themes from this earlier work.

37. Noriega Hope, *"Che" Ferrati*, 11.

38. Noriega Hope, *"Che" Ferrati*, 9.

39. Noriega Hope, *"Che" Ferrati*, 11–12. This thematic trope—the appropriate adoption of elements of U.S. mass culture—would be repeated in the short novel *Pero Galín* (1926) by Genaro Estrada, then Mexico's undersecretary of foreign relations. In the novel, the protagonist Galín and his wife visit Hollywood, that "supposedly marvelous world of cinema," which is eventually revealed to be a place of make-believe and illusion, before returning to become generous, if paternalistic, landowners of the kind found in nationalist pastoral scenarios (9).

40. For a pithy summary of the emergence of the "Mexican Problem," see Manuel Gonzáles, *Mexicanos*, 146–47.

41. See, for example, Carson, *Settlement Folk*; Sanchez, "'Go after the Women'"; Deutsch, *No Separate Refuge*; and Ruiz, *From out of the Shadows*, 33–50.

42. The Payne Fund Studies were published in eight volumes between 1935 and 1939 and summarized in Henry Forman's *Our Movie Made Children*. See Garth Jowett and Kathryn Fuller's analyses of the studies and their legacy in *Children and Movies*. Prior to or around the same time that those extensive studies were undertaken, other studies on media and children in urban areas, rural areas, black audiences, and the Midwest were also undertaken. See, for example, C. Perry, *The Attitudes of High School Students*; A. Mitchell, *Children and Movies*. Other sociological studies, like those undertaken by Emory Bogardus and his students at the University of Southern California, included an investigation of moviegoing practices, as did Robert Lynd and Helen Lynd's study of a Midwestern town, *Middletown*.

43. Jowett and Fuller, *Children and Movies*. See also Fuller, *At the Picture Show*, 169–93; deCordova, "The Child Audience."

44. McEuen, "A Survey of the Mexicans in Los Angeles," 67.

45. Hymer, "A Study of the Social Attitudes of Adult Mexican Immigrants," 48.

46. Lanigan, "Second Generation Mexicans in Belvedere," 52.

47. Culp, "A Case Study," 62.

48. Quoted in Lanigan, "Second Generation Mexicans in Belvedere," 53.

49. Lanigan, "Second Generation Mexicans in Belvedere," 55.

50. Merkley, "A Survey of the Leisure Time Activities," 93.

51. McEuen, "A Survey of the Mexicans in Los Angeles," 70.

52. Culp, "A Case Study," 52.

53. Culp, "A Case Study," 52.

54. McCombs, *From over the Border*, 31.

55. Bogardus, *The Mexican*, 52.

56. Peek, "The Religious and Social Attitudes," 47.

57. Peek, "The Religious and Social Attitudes," 48–49.

58. Quoted in Lanigan, "Second Generation Mexicans in Belvedere," 55.

59. Lanigan, "Second Generation Mexicans in Belvedere," 56.

60. White, "The Apperceptive Mass of Foreigners," 22.

61. "Social Data on Mexican People in Fort Worth, Texas, December 6–8. 1920," typescript, Center for American History, Special Collections, University of Texas, Austin.

62. Cady, *Report of the Commission*, 21.

63. Quoted in P. Taylor, *Mexican Labor in the United States: Dimmit County*, 416–17.

64. Field note series A, set I, 79, folder 4, carton 10, BANC MSS 84/38 c, Paul Schuster Taylor papers, Bancroft Library, University of California, Berkeley (hereafter Taylor).

65. Interview with Alfredo Vasquez, Mexican consul, Kansas City, MO, 1929, field note series B, set I, 29, folder 5, carton 10, Taylor.

66. Interview with Annie C. Watson, International Institute, San Antonio, TX, 1929, field note series B, set I, 179, folder 5, carton 10, Taylor.

67. P. Taylor, *Mexican Labor in the United States: Chicago*, 232.

68. Interview with B. Valles, Presbyterian preacher, Neighborhood House, Gary, IN, 1929, field note series B, set I, 121, folder 5, carton 10, Taylor.

69. P. Taylor, *Mexican Labor in the United States: Chicago*, 232.

70. Interview with Dr. Jaime, Kansas City, MO, field note series B, set I, 35, folder 5, carton 10, Taylor.

71. Watson interview, Taylor.

72. Interview with J. Mendoza, Mexican School, Luling, TX, 1929, field note series B, set I, 201–2, folder 5, carton 10, Taylor.

73. B. Valles interview, 121.

74. Interview with Mr. Corona, Bethlehem, PA, March 7, 1929, field note series B, set I, 72, folder 5, carton 10, Taylor.

75. P. Taylor, *An American-Mexican Frontier*, 265.

76. P. Taylor, *Mexican Labor in the United States: Chicago*, 232.

77. P. Taylor, *Mexican Labor in the United States: Chicago*, 232.

78. Quoted in P. Taylor, *Mexican Labor in the United States: Chicago*, 232.

79. Quoted in P. Taylor, *Mexican Labor in the United States: Chicago*, 233.

80. P. Taylor, *Mexican Labor in the United States: Chicago*, 233.

81. Quoted in P. Taylor, *Mexican Labor in the United States: Chicago*, 233.

82. Grace Hale uses this phrase to describe the segregated South (*Making Whiteness*, 284).

83. "La bella Pola Negri pasó por esta ciudad," *El Continental* (El Paso, hereafter *EC*), April 15, 1927; "El Paso Brunets Rally around Paying Homage to Pola Negri," *El Paso Herald* (hereafter *EPH*), April 16, 1927.

84. "El Paso Brunets."

85. García notes poor record keeping and a tendency by U.S. officials to undercount Mexicans, meaning that the Mexican population in El Paso may in fact have been much larger (*Desert Immigrants*, 35).

86. García, *Desert Immigrants*, 85.

87. My description of social life in El Paso is drawn primarily from García, *Desert Immigrants*.

88. Delgadillo and Limongi, *La mirada desenterrada*, 20.

89. García, *Desert Immigrants*, 211.

90. Between 1903 and 1907, cinema entrepreneurs such as Carlos Mongrand and Federico Bouvi, whose routes have been meticulously traced by film historian Aurelio de los Reyes, stopped in Juarez, other northern Mexican towns, and smaller, primarily Mexican communities on the U.S. side of the border (*Cine y sociedad*, 1:42–45).

91. Actos de cabildo, September 11, 1904, Archivo Histórico de Ciudad Juárez, Ciudad Juárez, Chihuahua, Mexico.

92. Siegifrid F. Pallin, in business with a projectionist named Leonardo Lujan, owned the Cine Azteca. The wood structure burned to the ground approximately six months after it was built in November 1912. See Delgadillo and Limongi, *La mirada desenterrada*, 84.

93. Delgadillo and Limongi, *La mirada desenterrada*, 85. On the *zarzuela* tradition in the United States, see Sturman, *Zarzuela*. On Spanish-language performance traditions in Texas, see E. Ramirez, *Footlights across the Border*; Kanellos, *A History of Hispanic Theatre*.

94. Delgadillo and Limongi, *La mirada desenterrada*, 140.

95. Haines, *Showtime!*, 19.

96. In 1922 that block housed a variety of small businesses, including shops owned by first-generation European immigrants. By 1925 this same block had become increasingly Mexican, retaining that character throughout the 1920s. In 1928 among the thirty-three shops on the southern strip of South El Paso Street were several restaurants and barbershops, a hotel, a furniture store, and a tattoo shop, all owned by Mexicans. The remaining businesses included a Chinese-owned grocery, three stores selling dry goods, a fruit market, a jewelry store, and a tattoo parlor, all of which were owned by European immigrants. This analysis is based on my study of the *El Paso City Directory* from 1922 to 1928.

97. "Screen 'Coming Back' in Mexico," *Moving Picture World* (hereafter *MPW*), July 27, 1918, 527.

98. "Spanish Heralds," *Vitagraph Family*, April 20, 1918, 32.

99. "Down Rio Way," *Vitagraph Family*, May 18, 1918, 48.

100. Quoted in "Picture Theater Problems in Border Towns," *MPW*, January 26, 1918, 559.

101. The extent of the Calderón brothers' commercial holdings in Chihuahua is

difficult to determine in detail. In 1916 an El Paso newspaper reported that the Calderóns owned one of the biggest stores in Juárez that catered to the Mexican trade. According to the article, the store had been worth $50,000 in 1916 (the year it was incorporated), but the article does not mention the name of the store ("Calderon Brothers," *El Paso Times*, May 21, 1916). In addition to this retail business, the brothers also owned Calderón Hermanos Sucesores, "the oldest house of Mexican music in the United States" (Angel Calderón, letter to Silvestre Terrazas, May 20, 1916, Silvestre Terrazas Collection, box 10, correspondence received, Part 1, BANC MSS M-B 18, Bancroft Library, University of California, Berkeley), which sold Columbia gramophones, musical instruments, and records throughout Texas. In 1916 the Calderóns sought to build the company's capital by selling shares at $10.00 apiece, seeking investors "not from foreign sources, but sources completely Mexican" (Angel Calderón to Silvestre Terrazas).

102. Information on Salas Porras is drawn from the Camara de Comercio, Servicio y Turismo de Chihuahua website, "Juan Salas Porras," http://www/canacochihuahua .com.mx/A_presi_salasporras.html (accessed June 2, 2005; site discontinued). He later became mayor of Ciudad Chihuahua.

103. On the early history of cinema exhibition in Ciudad Chihuahua, see Montemayor, "El cine silente en la Ciudad de Chihuahua," 79–95; Montemayor, *Cien años de cine*.

104. The Calderóns were related to Alarcón by marriage.

105. International Pictures was the exclusive distributor for Vitagraph films in Mexico and Central America (Haines, *Showtime!*, 75–76). It is not clear how closely the two entities worked together initially. Although Haines has examined the articles of copartnership filed with the County of El Paso, the local press did not seem to connect the two companies in any significant way until International Pictures came under control of the Calderóns.

106. "Lo que dice el gerente de la Compañía Internacional de Diversiones de El Paso," *La República*, January 26, 1920.

107. "El Pasoan Plans to Educate Peon with Movie Show," *El Paso Morning Times*, August 17, 1919. See also "Siguen siendo los favoritos las series en Méjico," *Cine-Mundial*, January 1920, 154.

108. "La empresa Calderón y Salas Porras ensancha su camp de acción," *México en Rotograbado*, August 11, 1927, n.p.

109. "New Theater to Be Built Here," *EPH*, April 12, 1919. The owners, Lacoma and Quinn, also owned the Estrella and the Cristal. The Estrella opened in 1913 and operated, according to listings in the *El Paso City Directory*, until 1925. The Cristal opened in 1919 and operated under that name until 1922. Before the Calderóns bought the theater, it was briefly under the control of the owner of the Standard Candy Company, a Mr. Goldberg, who was also part owner of the Follies Review Company, which performed at the Texas Grand in El Paso. See "Quinn Leases Colon House to Goldberg," *EPH*, June 8, 1921.

110. "New Theater to Be Built Here."

111. "El publico mexicano espera con ansia loca contemplar *Los cuatros jinetes del apocalipsis*, la obra maestra de Rodolfo Valentino," EC, February 1, 1927.

112. "Nuestro espectáculos: De viernes a viernes," EC, February 18, 1927.

113. "Exhibieron la película," EC, August 8, 1928.

114. "Dolores Cassinelli en el Alcázar," *La República*, March 15, 1920; El Teatro Colón es obra de la revolución," EC, August 29, 1937.

115. "El publico mexicano espera."

116. "Función teatral a beneficio de la Alianza Hispano-Americana," EC, February 12, 1927. The Alliance would later use the YMCA in Smelter Town, just west of El Paso, to hold a benefit screening of films, including the then six-year-old Mexican film *El hombre sin patria*, the proceeds of which were to support building a monument in honor of aviator Emilio Carranza. "Habra funciones a beneficio de un monumento," EC, August 8, 1928.

117. Estimates of the Mexican and Chicano population are drawn from Camarillo, *Chicanos in a Changing Society*, and Sanchez, *Becoming Mexican American*.

118. Sanchez, *Becoming Mexican American*, 171–87.

119. Olsson, "Hollywood's First Spectators," 195. Japanese immigrants also had their own theaters in downtown Los Angeles (see Ogihara, "The Exhibition of Films").

120. McEuen, "A Survey of the Mexicans in Los Angeles," 67.

121. McEuen, "A Survey of the Mexicans in Los Angeles," 77–78.

122. Culp, "A Case Study," 52.

123. "Sera boicoteado un cine de Wilmington," *La Opinión* (hereafter LO), September 4, 1927.

124. Luis Aguinaga, interviewed by Luis Felipe Recinos, Los Angeles, April 6, 1927, no. 63, folder 2, box 2, Gamio Notes.

125. José Roche, interviewed by Luis Felipe Recinos, Los Angeles, April 8, 1927, no. 8, folder 14, box 2, Gamio Notes.

126. José Roche interview. Roche's unnamed wife was interviewed at the same time, and the two interviews were catalogued together.

127. María Rovitz Ramos, interviewed by Luis Felipe Recinos, Los Angeles, April 6, 1927, no. 7, folder 18, box 2, Gamio Notes.

128. See, for example, Miguel García interviewed by Felipe Recinos, April 1927, no. 6, folder 7, box 2, Gamio Notes, and Francisco Medrano interview.

129. Marez, "Subaltern Soundtracks," 57.

130. Alamillo, "Peloteros in Paradise," 196.

131. "Dolores del Río, reina," LO, October 2, 1927.

132. *Fiesta de la raza* advertisement, LO, October 5, 1927.

133. *El gaucho* advertisement, LO, December 5, 1927. On Grauman's creation of the prologue as an element of film exhibition, see Beardsley, *Hollywood's Master Showman*.

134. Borrah Minevitch was a Russian émigré. He became the leader of the first all-harmonica band and commanded extremely high performance fees on the vaudeville circuit.

135. "Gran función de gala en el Teatro Chino: Será en honor de la colonia mexicana," *LO*, January 8, 1928.

136. Quoted in "Gran función de gala en el Teatro Chino."

137. "Gran función de gala en el Teatro Chino." Chorus girls had long been associated with dubious sexual mores in Mexico. In the 1920s theaters and cabarets became associated with prostitution. See Bliss, *Compromised Positions*, 153–83. On Vélez's career and the way it was perceived by Mexican critics, see Rodríguez-Estrada, "Dolores del Río and Lupe Vélez." On her performance in the stereotyped films that marked her later career as ethnic masquerade, see Sturtevant, "Spitfire."

138. "Dos inconscientes ofensas," *LO*, January 10, 1928.

139. "Dos inconscientes ofensas."

140. All quotes in this paragraph are from "Dos inconscientes ofensas." Slavery had in fact been outlawed in Mexico in 1829 by the liberal President Guadalupe Victoria. From then on, Mexico became a destination for fugitive slaves. This presented a particularly acute problem for Texas slaveholders both before and after statehood. See R. Campbell, *An Empire for Slavery*; Taylor, "Fugitive Slaves in Mexico."

141. Luis Felipe Recinos, "Entrevista con un nino hijo de un bootlegger," Arizona, folder 6, box 1, Gamio Notes.

142. Recinos, "Entrevista con un nino."

143. Margarita Alvarez de Castillo, interviewed by Luis Felipe Recinos, Los Angeles, CA, May 15, 1927, no. 42, folder 3, box 1, Gamio Notes.

144. Juana Martínez, interviewed by Luis Felipe Recinos, El Paso, Texas, March 12, 1927, folder 2, box 2, Gamio Notes.

145. The history of Mexican labor in the film industry remains to be written. Elizabeth Nielsen briefly mentions Mexican American women who did piece work for studio costume departments in "Handmaidens of the Glamour Culture." On the place of "extra girls" in Hollywood's labor economy, see Kenaga, "Making the 'Studio Girl.'" On the gendering of extras' work as female, despite the preponderance of men working as extras, see McKenna, "The Photoplay or the Pickaxe." On the discourse on women's emancipation and work in the film industry, see Hallett, *Go West Young Woman!*, especially chapters 1 and 2.

146. Allied World War Veterans (various) to Los Angeles City Council, June 14, 1919, folder 1324, vol. 1066, box A-104, City of Los Angeles, Municipal Archive, Los Angeles.

147. On Hollywood's labor history, see Steven Ross, *Working-Class Hollywood*; Pintar, "Behind the Scenes." Ross directs readers to Perry and Perry, *A History of the Los Angeles Labor Movement*.

148. See, for example, the newspaper's coverage of the case of Silvio Romano ("Una victima de las leyes migratorias," *LO*, August 4, 1927). The article recounted how Italian silent film actor Romano had been on the verge of signing a contract with a studio when he was nabbed by the immigration service. His case, according to *La Opinión*, illustrated the unfairness of U.S. immigration policy. I have been unable to locate any information about an Italian actor by that name. It is possible that he was yet another would-be star who knew a writer at the paper.

149. "Hollywood, la nueva torre de Babel," *LO*, September 22, 1926.

150. "La 'atmosfera extranjera' en el cine," *LO*, September 17, 1926.

151. "Fuera los directores y artistas extranjeros! ¡Guerra al invasor!," *LO*, October 18, 1926.

152. "¡Fuera los directores y artistas extranjeros!"

153. "Los jingoistas del cine," *LO*, October 19, 1926.

154. "La parte que nos toca," *LO*, December 23, 1927. In November 1926 *Variety* reported "several extensive 'drives' have been made to deport such aliens with one investigation carried on through the studios in Hollywood. Strategies proposed by the Commissioner General of Immigration Henry Hull included an amnesty that would confer citizenship on those that had overstayed their visas" ("May Legalize Aliens over Here Illegally," *Variety*, November 3, 1926).

155. "La parte que nos toca."

156. "La parte que nos toca."

157. "La parte que nos toca."

158. For example, see "Un mexicano sucederá a Valentino: Tal es la opinión del gerente de Artistas Unidos," *LO*, January 29, 1927; "Otro mexicano en Hollywood," *LO*, October 29, 1927; "Se buscan seis de las mas hermosas muchachas," *El Heraldo de México*, August 23, 1919; "Mi amiga Armida Vendrell," *LO*, November 30, 1926.

159. "Los 'extras' mexicanos de los studios cinematográficos en una promisoria bonanza," *LO*, February 27, 1928.

160. "Los 'extras' mexicanos."

161. Gabriel Navarro, "La ciudad de irás y no volverás," *La Prensa*, December 1926–January 1927.

162. Lanigan, "Second Generation Mexicans in Belvedere," 51.

CONCLUSION

1. Victoriano Medina, letter to Emilio Portes Gil, April 20, 1929, AGN, EPG, 59, 3/632/205.

2. "Notas Filmicas," *El Universal*, April 29, 1929.

3. "En el teatro Colón se estan efectuando grandes mejoras," *El Continental* (El Paso), September 25, 1929.

4. On the formal aspects of Figueroa's cinematography, see Ramírez Berg, "The Cinematic Invention of Mexico."

5 Paranaguá, *Mexican Cinema*. English-language studies of this period, some of which extend their analysis into the second half of the twentieth century, include Hershfield and Maciel, *Mexico's Cinema*; de la Mora, *Cinemachismo*; Ramírez Berg, *Cinema of Solitude*; Dever, *Celluloid Nationalism*; Hershfield, *The Invention of Dolores del Río*; Tierney, *Emilio Fernández*; and Noble, *Mexican National Cinema*. The Spanish-language literature on this period is also extensive. Exemplary works include García Riera, *Historia documental del cine mexicano*; Tuñón Pablos, *Mujeres de luz y sombra*; Ayala Blanco, *La aventura del cine mexicano*; Vega Alfaro, *La industria cinematográfica*.

6. "Las películas habladas en ingles," *El Universal*, May 25, 1929.

7. "La cinematografía nacional necesita impulso colectivo," *El Nacional Revolucionario*, June 3, 1930.

8. Fein, "Hollywood and United States-Mexico Relations." Paranaguá writes that the Mexican film industry emerged with the "approval" of U.S. studios, noting that "nationalism and imitation would be woven together" ("Ten Reasons," 8).

9. Gunckel, "'A Theater Worthy of Our Race'"; D. Garcia, "There's No Place Like Home." See also Jarvinen, *The Rise of Spanish-Language Filmmaking*.

10. See, for example, A. López, "From Hollywood and Back"; A. López, "A Cinema for the Continent"; Gunckel, "'A Theater Worthy of Our Race'"; D. Garcia, "There's No Place Like Home"; Jarvinen, *The Rise of Spanish-Language Filmmaking*; Heredia, "From Golden Age Cinema."

BIBLIOGRAPHY

ARCHIVAL SOURCES

Mexico

Archivo de la Palabra, Proyecto de Cine, Mexicano Instituto Nacional de Antropologia e Historia, Mexico City

Archivo General de la Nación, Mexico City
  Álvaro Obregón–Plutarco Elías Calles
  Departamento del Trabajo
  Dirección General de Gobierno
  Galería del Periodo Revolucionario
  Propiedad Artística y Literaria

Archivo Histórico de la Secretaría de Educación Pública

Archivo Histórico de la Secretaría de Relaciones Exteriores, Mexico City

Archivo Histórico del Distrito Federal, Archivo Histórico del Ayuntamiento, Mexico City
  Diversiones Públicas
  Municipalidades
  Oficialía de Partes
  Secretaría General
  Secretaría Particular del Presidente Municipal

Archivo Municipal de Ciudad Juárez, Ciudad Juárez, Chihuahua, Mexico

Archivo Municipal de Guanajuato, Guanajuato, Mexico

Archivos Económicos de la Biblioteca Lerdo de Tejada, Mexico City

Centro de Estudios Sobre la Universidad, Universidad Nacional Autónoma de México, Mexico City, Fondo Palomar y Vizcarro

Fideicomiso Archivos Plutarco Elías Calles y Fernando Torreblanca, Mexico City
  Fondo Plutarco Elías Calles

Hemeroteca Nacional, Universidad Nacional Autónoma de México, Mexico City

United States

Bancroft Library, University of California, Berkeley
Manuel Gamio, Notes gathered for his book *Mexican Immigration to the United States* and related material
Silvestre Terrazas Collection

Center for American History, University of Texas, Austin

Charles E. Young Research Library Department of Special Collections, University of California at Los Angeles, Los Angeles, California
Albert E. Smith Collection

City of Los Angeles, Municipal Archive, Los Angeles

Cinema Corporation of America Collection, Special Collections, Florida State University Libraries

Margaret Herrick Library, Academy of Motion Picture Arts and Sciences, Beverly Hills, California

Nettie Lee Benson Latin American Collection, University of Texas at Austin, Austin, Texas

Phelps Dodge Corporation Corporate Archives, Phoenix, Arizona

U.S. National Archives and Records Administration, College Park, Maryland, Records of the Department of State Relating to the Internal Affairs of Mexico, 1919–29, Record Group 59

Warner Bros. Archives, School of Cinematic Arts, University of Southern California, Los Angeles, California

Wisconsin Center for Film and Theater Research, Wisconsin Historical Society, Madison, Wisconsin
Harry and Roy Aitken Papers
United Artists Collection

PERIODICALS

Mexico

Acción y fe (Guadalajara)
Armonia social (Nuevo León)
Boletín mensual del Departamento de Trabajo
El Continental
La Dama Católica
El Demócrata
Excélsior
Filmográfica
La Gaceta del Espectador
Heraldo Commercial

El Heraldo de la Raza
El Heraldo de México
El Heraldo Ilustrado
El Hogar
Jueves de Excélsior
Magazine Fílmico
Matehuala (Matehuala, San Luis Potosí)
The Mexican American
Mexican Life
Mexico en Rotograbado
Mujer

El Nacional
La República (Monterrey)
Revista de Revistas
La Semana

El Universal
El Universal Gráfico
El Universal Ilustrado
Zig-Zag

United States

Americas (New York)
Cinelandia (Hollywood)
Cine-Mundial (New York)
El Continental (El Paso)
El Paso Herald (El Paso)
El Paso Morning Times (El Paso)
El Paso Times (El Paso)
El Heraldo de México (Los Angeles)
Los Angeles Times

México (Chicago)
Missionary Review (New York)
Motion Picture News (New York)
Moving Picture World (New York)
New York Times
La Opinión (Los Angeles)
La Prensa (San Antonio)
Vitagraph Family (New York)

PRIMARY SOURCES

Astor, Mary. *Motion Pictures: A Problem for the Nation*. Washington: National Council of Catholic Women, 1933.

Ayuntamiento Constitucional de México. *Reglamento de Diversiones Públicas de la Ciudad de México: Año de 1922*. Mexico City: Talleres Linotipgraficos de "El Hogar," 1922.

Blumer, Herbert, and Philip Morris Hauser. *Movies, Delinquency, and Crime*. New York: Arno, 1933.

Bogardus, Emory. *The Mexican in the United States*. Los Angeles: University of Southern California Press, 1934.

Carlos Noriega Hope. Mexico City: Instituto Nacional de Bellas Artes / Secretaria de Educación Publica, 1959.

Chaplin, Charlie. *My Autobiography*. New York: Simon and Schuster, 1964.

Chase, Stuart. *Mexico: A Study of Two Americas*. New York: Macmillan, 1931.

Cleland, Robert Glass, ed. *The Mexican Year Book: The Standard Authority on Mexico, 1920–1921*. Los Angeles: Mexican Year Book, 1922.

Culp, Alice Bessie. "A Case Study of the Living Conditions of Thirty-Five Mexican Families of Los Angeles with Special Reference to Mexican Children." Master's thesis, University of Southern California, 1921.

Departamento de la Estadística Nacional. *Resumen del censo general de habitantes de 30 Nov. 1921*. Mexico: Tallers gráficos de la nación, 1928.

Departamento de Salubridad Pública. *Memoria de los trabajos realizados por el Departamento de Salubridad Pública, 1925–1928*. Mexico City: Ediciones del Departamento de Salubridad Pública, 1928.

Durón Gonzalez, Gustavo. *Problemas migratorios de México*. Mexico City: Talleres de la Cámara de Diputados, 1925.

Estrada, Genaro. *Pero Galín*. 1926. Reprint, Mexico City: Instituto Nacional de Bellas Artes Departamento de Literatura, 1967.

Flores Rivera, Salvador. *Relatos de mi barrio: Autobiografía de Salvador Flores Rivera (Chava Flores)*. Mexico City: EDAMEX, 1988.

Forman, Henry J. *Our Movie Made Children*. New York: Macmillan, 1935.

Gamboa, Federico. *Reconquista*. Mexico City: E. Gómez de la Puente, 1908.

———. *Santa*. Mexico City: Ediciones Leyenda, 2004 (orig. pub. 1903).

Gamio, Manuel. *Hacia un México nuevo: Problemas sociales*. Mexico City: n.p., 1935.

———. *Mexican Immigration to the United States*. Chicago: University of Chicago Press, 1930.

Hymer, Evangeline. "A Study of the Social Attitudes of Adult Mexican Immigrants in Los Angeles and Vicinity." Master's thesis, University of Southern California. 1921. Reprint, San Francisco: R and E Research Associates, 1971.

Icaza, Alfonso de. *Así era aquello . . . (60 anos de vida metropolitana)*. Mexico City: Ediciones Botas, 1957.

International American Conference. *Fourth International Conference of American States*. Senate Document 744. Washington: Government Printing Office, 1911.

Kinsila, Edward Bernard. *Modern Theatre Construction*. New York: Moving Picture World, 1917.

Lanigan, Mary. "Second Generation Mexicans in Belvedere." Master's thesis, University of Southern California, 1932.

Lynd, Robert S., and Helen Merrell Lynd. *Middletown, a Study in Contemporary American Culture*. New York: Harcourt Brace, 1929.

McCombs, Vernon M. *From over the Border: A Study of Mexicans in the United States*. New York: Council of Women for Home Missions and Missionary Education Movement, 1925.

McEuen, William. "A Survey of the Mexicans in Los Angeles." Master's thesis, University of Southern California, 1914.

Merkley, John Lawrence. "A Survey of the Leisure Time Activities of Junior High School Boys." Master's thesis, University of Southern California, 1933.

Mitchell, Alice Miller. *Children and Movies*. Chicago: University of Chicago Press, 1929.

Motts, Irene Elena. *La vida en la Ciudad de México en las primeras decadas del siglo XX*. Mexico City: Editorial Porrua, 1973.

Noriega Hope, Carlos. *"Che" Ferrati, Inventor*. Mexico City: Publicaciones Literarias de El universal ilustrado, 1923.

———. *El mundo de las sombras: El cine por fuera y por dentro*. Mexico City: Librería Editorial Andrés Botas e Hijo, 1919.

Novo, Salvador. "Cine." In *XX Poemas*. Mexico City: Talleres Gráficos de la Nación, 1925.

———. "Del pasado remoto." In *Poesía: XX poemas / espejo / nuevo amor / Poesías no coleccionadas*, 109–16. Mexico City: Fondo de Cultura Económica, 1961.

———. *La estatua de sal*. Mexico City: Consejo Nacional para la Cultura y las Artes, 1998.

Panunzio, Constantine. *How Mexicans Earn and Live: A Study of Incomes and Expenditures of One Hundred Mexican Families in San Diego, California*. Berkeley: University of California Press, 1933.

Paramount Pictures. *The Story of the Famous Players-Lasky Corporation, Paramount Artcraft Motion Pictures.* New York: Bartlett-Orr, 1919.

Peek, Rena B. "The Religious and Social Attitudes of the Mexican Girls of the Constituency of the All Nations Foundation in Los Angeles." Master's thesis, University of Southern California, 1929.

Perry, Clarence Arthur. *The Attitudes of High School Students toward Motion Pictures.* New York: National Board of Review of Motion Pictures, 1923.

Rodríguez, Horacio F. *Propiedad artística y literaria.* Buenos Aires, Argentina: A. M. de Tommasi, 1929.

Seabury, William Marston. *Motion Picture Problems: The Cinema and the League of Nations.* New York: Avondale, 1929.

———. *The Public and the Motion Picture Industry.* New York: Macmillan, 1926.

Secretaría de Gobernación. *Reglamento de censura.* Mexico City: n.p., 1919.

Snider, Guy Edward. *Selling in Foreign Markets.* Washington: Government Printing Office, 1919.

Strauss, William Victor. "Foreign Distribution of American Motion Pictures." *Harvard Business Review* 8 (1930): 307–15.

Taylor, Paul S. *An American-Mexican Frontier, Nueces County, Texas.* Chapel Hill: University of North Carolina Press, 1934.

———. *Mexican Labor in the United States: Chicago and the Calumet Region.* Berkeley: University of California Press, 1932.

———. *Mexican Labor in the United States: Dimmit County, Winter Garden District South Texas.* Berkeley: University of California Press, 1930.

Unión de Estudiantes Pro-Obrero y Campesino. *Estatutos.* Mexico City: Talleres Gráficos de la nación, 1930.

U.S. Department of Commerce. *Statistical Abstract of the United States, 1920.* Washington: Government Printing Office, 1921.

U.S. Department of Commerce, Latin American Division. *Promotion of Trade with Latin America Services of the Latin American Division: Department of Commerce Bureau of Foreign and Domestic Commerce.* Washington: Government Printing Office, 1922.

———. *U.S. Trade with Latin America in 1922.* Supplement to the *Trade and Economic Review for 1922.* Washington: Government Printing Office, 1923.

Venegas, Daniel. *Las aventuras de Don Chipote: O, cuando los pericos mamen.* Edited by Nicolas Kanellos. Houston, TX: Arte Publico, 1999.

Way, Eugene Irving. *Motion Pictures in Mexico, Central America, and the Greater Antilles.* Washington: U.S. Department of Commerce, 1931.

White, Alfred. "The Apperceptive Mass of Foreigners as Applied to Americanization, the Mexican Group." Master's thesis, University of California, Berkeley, 1923.

Williams, Faith L., and Alice C. Hanson. *Mexican Families in Los Angeles: Money Disbursement of Wage Earner and Clerical Workers in Five Cities in the Pacific Region.* Washington: Government Printing Office, 1939.

SECONDARY SOURCES

Abel, Richard. *The Red Rooster Scare: Making Cinema American, 1900–1910.* Berkeley: University of California Press, 1999.

Acuña, Rudy. *Occupied America: A History of Chicanos.* New York: Harper and Row, 1981.

Agostini, Claudia. "Popular Health Education and Propaganda." *American Journal of Public Health* 96, no. 1 (2006): 52–61.

Aguila, Jaime R. "Protecting 'México de afuera': Mexican Emigration Policy, 1876–1928." PhD diss., Arizona State University, 2000.

Alamillo, José M. "Peloteros in Paradise: Mexican American Baseball and Oppositional Politics in Southern California, 1930–1950." *Western Historical Quarterly* 34, no. 2 (2003): 191–211.

Alarcón, Daniel Cooper. *The Aztec Palimpsest: Mexico in the Modern Imagination.* Tucson: University of Arizona Press, 1997.

Alarcón, Francisco X. "Un Beso Is Not a Kiss." In *From the Other Side of Night.* Tucson: University of Arizona Press, 2002.

Almoina, Helena. *Notas para la historia del cine en México, 1896–1925.* Mexico City: Filmoteca de la Universidad Nacional Autónoma de México, 1980.

Alonzo, Juan J. *Badmen, Bandits, and Folk Heroes: The Ambivalence of Mexican American Identity in Literature and Film.* Tucson: University of Arizona Press, 2008.

Alston, Lee, Shannon Mattiace, and Tomas Nonnenmacher. "Coercion, Culture, and Contracts: Labor and Debt on Henequen Haciendas in Yucatán, Mexico, 1870–1915." *Journal of Economic History* 69, no. 1 (2009): 104–27.

Amador, Maria Luisa, and Jorge Ayala Blanco. *Cartelera cinematográfica 1920–1929.* Mexico City: Filmoteca de la Universidad Nacional Autónoma de México, 1980.

Anderson, Benedict. *Imagined Communities: Reflections on the Origin and Spread of Nationalism.* London: Verso, 1991.

Anderson, Danny J. "Literary Reading and the Nation: Publics in Postrevolutionary Mexico." Paper presented at the Latin American Studies Association Congress, Dallas, TX, March 27, 2003.

Anderson, Rodney. *Outcasts in Their Own Land: Mexican Industrial Workers, 1906–1911.* DeKalb: Northern Illinois University Press, 1976.

Anduiza V., Virgilio. *Legislación cinematográfica mexicana.* Mexico City: Filmoteca de la Universidad Nacional Autónoma de México, 1983.

Arredondo, Gabriela. *Mexican Chicago: Race, Identity, and Nation 1916–1939.* Urbana: University of Illinois Press, 2008.

Aurrecoecha, Juan Manuel, and Armando Bartra. *Puros cuentos: La historia de la historieta en México.* Mexico City: Consejo Nacional de Arte y Cultura, 1988.

Ayala Blanco, Jorge. *La aventura del cine mexicano: En la época de oro y después.* Mexico City: Editorial Grijalbo, 1993.

Balderrama, Francisco. *In Defense of La Raza, the Los Angeles Mexican Consulate, and the Mexican Community, 1929 to 1936.* Tucson: University of Arizona Press, 1982.

Balio, Tino. *United Artists: The Company That Changed the Film Industry.* Madison: University of Wisconsin Press, 1987.

Barrera, Mario. *Race and Class in the Southwest: A Theory of Racial Inequality.* Notre Dame, IN: University of Notre Dame Press, 1979.

Barton, Josef. "At the Edge of the Storm: Northern Mexico's Rural Peoples in a New Regime of Consumption, 1880–1940." In *Land of Necessity: Consumer Culture in the United States–Mexico Borderlands*, edited by Alexis M. McCrossen, 217–47. Durham, NC: Duke University Press, 2009.

Bartra, Armando. "The Seduction of the Innocents: The First Tumultous Moments of Mass Literacy in Postrevolutionary Mexico." In *Everyday Forms of State Formation*, edited by Gilbert M. Joseph and Daniel Nugent, 301–25. Durham, NC: Duke University Press, 1994.

Bean, Jennifer. "Technologies of Early Stardom and the Extraordinary Body." In *A Feminist Reader in Early Cinema*, edited by Jennifer Bean and Diane Negra, 404–43. Durham, NC: Duke University Press, 2002.

Beardsley, Charles. *Hollywood's Master Showman: The Legendary Sid Grauman.* New York: Cornwall, 1983.

Beezley, William H. *Judas at the Jockey Club and Other Episodes of Porfirian Mexico.* Lincoln: University of Nebraska Press, 1989.

Beltrán, Mary C. *Latina/o Stars in U.S. Eyes: The Making and Meaning of Film and TV Stardom.* Champaign: University of Illinois Press, 2009.

Benjamin, Thomas. *La revolución: Mexico's Great Revolution as Memory, Myth, and History.* Austin: University of Texas Press, 1990.

Bertellini, Giorgio. *Italy in Early American Cinema: Race, Landscape, and the Picturesque.* Bloomington: Indiana University Press, 2010.

Berumen Garcia, Frank Javier. *The Chicano/Hispanic Image in American Film.* New York: Vantage, 1995.

Bliss, Katherine E. *Compromised Positions: Prostitution, Public Health, and Gender Politics in Revolutionary Mexico.* University Park: Pennsylvania State University Press, 2001.

Blum, Ann S. "Breaking and Making Families: Adoption and Public Welfare, Mexico City, 1938–1942." In *Sex in Revolution: Gender, Politics, and Power in Modern Mexico*, edited by Jocelyn Olcott, Mary Kay Vaughan, and Gabriela Cano, 127–44. Durham, NC: Duke University Press, 2006.

Borge, Jason. *Latin American Writers and the Rise of Hollywood Cinema.* New York: Routledge, 2008.

Bottomore, Stephen. "The Panicking Audience? Early Cinema and the 'Train Effect.'" *Historical Journal of Film, Radio, and Television* 19, no. 2 (1999): 177–216.

Boylan, Kristina A. "The Feminine 'Apostolate in Society' versus the Secular State: The Unión Feminina Católica Mexicana, 1929–1940." In *Right-Wing Women: From Conservatives to Extremists around the World*, edited by Paola Bacchetta, 169–81. New York: Routledge, 2002.

Britton, John A. *Revolution and Ideology: Images of the Mexican Revolution in the United States.* Lexington: University Press of Kentucky, 1995.

Bunker, Steven. "'Consumers of Good Taste': Marketing Modernity in Northern Mexico, 1890–1910." *Mexican Studies / Estudios Mexicanos* 13, no. 2 (1997): 227–69.

Bustamante, Jorge A. *Cruzar la línea: La migración de México a los Estados Unidos.* Mexico City: Fondo de Cultura Económica, 1997.

Camarillo, Albert. *Chicanos in a Changing Society: From Mexican Pueblos to American Barrios in Santa Barbara and Southern California, 1848–1930.* Cambridge, MA: Harvard University Press, 1979.

Campbell, Craig W. *Reel America and World War I.* Jefferson, NC: McFarland, 1985.

Campbell, Randolph B. *An Empire for Slavery: The Peculiar Institution in Texas, 1821–1865.* Baton Rouge: Louisiana State University Press, 1989.

Carbine, Mary. "The 'Finest outside the Loop': Motion Picture Exhibition in Chicago's Black Metropolis, 1905–1928." *Camera Obscura* (May 1990): 8–41.

Cardoso, Lawrence A. *Mexican Emigration to the United States, 1897–1931.* Tucson: University of Arizona Press, 1980.

Carson, Mina Julia. *Settlement Folk: Social Thought and the American Settlement Movement, 1885–1930.* Chicago: University of Chicago Press, 1990.

Ceceña Cervantes, José Luis. *México en la órbita imperial.* Mexico City: Ediciones "Caballito," 1970.

Chavez, Ernesto. "'Ramon Is Not One of These': Race and Sexuality in the Construction of Silent Film Actor Ramón Novarro's Star Image." *Journal of the History of Sexuality* 20, no. 3 (2011): 520–44.

Ciuk, Perla. *Diccionario de directores del cine mexicano.* Mexico City: CONACULTA, 2000.

Cohen, Lizabeth. *A Consumer's Republic: The Politics of Mass Consumption in Postwar America.* New York: Knopf, 2003.

———. "Encountering Mass Culture at the Grassroots: The Experiences of Chicago Workers in the 1920s." *American Quarterly* 41 (March 1989): 6–33.

Contreras Delgado, Camilo. *Espacio y sociedad: Reestructuración espacial de un antiguo enclave minero.* Tijuana, Mexico: El Colegio de la Frontera Norte, 2002.

Cooper, Mark C. "Pearl White and Grace Cunard: The Serial Queen's Volatile Present." In *Flickers of Desire: Movie Stars of the 1910s,* edited by Jennifer M. Bean, 174–95. New Brunswick, NJ: Rutgers University Press, 2011.

Cruz Rodríguez, María Soledad. *Crecimiento urbano y procesos sociales en el Distrito Federal (1920–1928).* Mexico City: Universidad Autónoma Metropolitana, 1994.

D'Agostino, Annette M. *An Index to Short and Feature Film Reviews in the* Moving Picture World: *The Early Years, 1907–1915.* Westport, CT: Greenwood, 1995.

Dallal, Alberto. *El "dancing" mexicano.* Mexico City: Editorial Oasis, 1982.

Dávalos Orozco, Federico, and Esperanza Vázquez Bernal. *Filmografía general del cine mexicano, 1906–1931.* Puebla, Mexico: Universidad Autónoma de Puebla, 1985.

Davis, Diane. *Urban Leviathan: Mexico City in the Twentieth Century.* Philadelphia, PA: Temple University Press, 1994.

DeCordova, Richard. "The Child Audience, The Hays Office, and Saturday Matinees." In *Looking Past the Screen: Case Studies in American Film History and*

Method, edited by Jon Lewis and Eric Smoodin, 229–45. Durham, NC: Duke University Press, 2007.

De Grazia, Victoria. *Irresistible Empire: America's Advance through Twentieth-Century Europe*. Cambridge, MA: Belknap Press of Harvard University Press, 2005.

De Grazia, Victoria, and Ellen Furlough, eds. *The Sex of Things: Gender and Consumption in Historical Perspective*. Berkeley: University of California Press, 1996.

De la Mora, Sergio. *Cinemachismo: Masculinities and Sexuality in Mexican Film*. Austin: University of Texas Press, 2006.

De León, Arnoldo. *They Called Them Greasers: Anglo Attitudes toward Mexicans in Texas, 1821–1900*. Austin: University of Texas Press, 1983.

Delgadillo, Willivaldo, and Maribel Limongi. *La mirada desenterrada: Juárez y El Paso vistos por el cine, 1896–1916*. Ciudad Juárez, Mexico: Cuadro por Cuadro, 2000.

Delpar, Helen. *The Enormous Vogue of Things Mexican: Cultural Relations between the United States and Mexico, 1920–1925*. Tuscaloosa: University of Alabama Press, 1992.

———. "Goodbye to the Greaser: Mexico, the MPPDA, and Derogatory Films, 1922–1926." *Journal of Popular Film and Television* 12, no. 1 (1984): 34–41.

Deutsch, Sarah. *No Separate Refuge: Culture, Class, and Gender on the Anglo-Hispanic Frontier in the American Southwest, 1880–1940*. New York: Oxford University Press, 1987.

Dever, Susan. *Celluloid Nationalism and Other Melodramas: From Post-Revolutionary Mexico to fin de siglo Mexamérica*. Albany: State University of New York Press, 2003.

Díaz, María Elena. "The Satiric Penny Press for Workers in Mexico, 1900–1910: A Case Study in the Politicisation of Popular Culture." *Journal of Latin American Studies* 22, no. 3 (1990): 497–526.

Doane, Mary Ann. *The Desire to Desire: The Woman's Film of the 1940s*. Bloomington: Indiana University Press, 1987.

———. "The Economy of Desire: The Commodity Form in/of the Cinema." In *Movies and Mass Culture*, edited by John Belton, 119–34. New Brunswick, NJ: Rutgers University Press, 1996.

———. "Film and the Masquerade: Theorising the Female Spectator." *Screen* 23, nos. 3–4 (1982): 74–88.

Dueñas, Pablo. *Las divas en el teatro de revista mexicano*. Mexico City: Asociación Mexicana de Estudios Fonográficos, 1994.

Duffey, J. Patrick. "'Un dinamismo abrasador': La velocidad del cine mudo en la literatura iberoamericana de los años veinte y treinta." *Revista Iberoamericana* 68, no. 199 (2002): 417–40.

Durand, Jorge. *Migración México–Estados Unidos: Años veinte*. Mexico City: Consejo Nacional Para la Cultura y las Artes, 1991.

Durand, Jorge, and Patricia Arias. *La experiencia migrante: Iconografía de la migración México-Estados Unidos*. Talquepaque, Jalisco, Mexico: Instituto Tecnológico de Estudios Superiores de Occidente, 2000.

Eckert, Charles. "The Carole Lombard in Macy's Window." In *Stardom: Industry of Desire*, edited by Christine Gledhill, 30–56. New York: Routledge, 1991.

Enstad, Nan. *Ladies of Labor, Girls of Adventure: Working Women, Popular Culture, and Labor Politics at the Turn of the Twentieth Century*. New York: Columbia University Press, 1999.

Fabila, Alfonso. *El problema de la emigración de obreros y campesinos mexicanos: Estudio de difusión popular*. Mexico City: Talleres Gráficos de la Nación, 1929.

Feeney, Megan J. "Hollywood in Havana: Film Reception and Revolutionary Nationalism in Cuba before 1959." PhD diss., University of Minnesota, 2008.

Fein, Seth. "Film Propaganda in Cold War Mexico." In *Close Encounters of Empire: Writing the Cultural History of U.S.–Latin American Relations*, edited by Gilbert M. Joseph, Catherine C. LeGrand, and Richard D. Salvatore, 400–450. Durham, NC: Duke University Press, 1998.

———. "Hollywood and United States–Mexico Relations in the Golden Age of Mexican Cinema." PhD diss., University of Texas at Austin, 1996.

Fell, Claude. *José Vasconcelos: Los años del águila, 1920–1925. Educación, cultura y iberoamericanismo en el México postrevolucionario*. Mexico City: Universidad Nacional Autónoma de México, 1998.

Fiske, John. "The Cultural Economy of Fandom." In *The Adoring Audience: Fan Culture and Popular Media*, edited by Lisa A. Lewis, 30–49. New York: Routledge, 1992.

Folgarait, Leonard. *Mural Painting and Social Revolution in Mexico, 1920–1940: Art of the New Order*. Cambridge: Cambridge University Press, 1988.

Foster, Anne L. *Projections of Power: The United States and Europe in Colonial Southeast Asia*. Durham, NC: Duke University Press, 2010.

Fox, Claire F. *The Fence and the River: Culture and Politics at the U.S.-Mexico Border*. Minneapolis: University of Minnesota Press, 1999.

Frank, Patrick. *Posada's Broadsides: Mexican Popular Imagery, 1890–1910*. Albuquerque: University of New Mexico Press, 1998.

Fregoso, Rosa Linda. *MeXicana Encounters: The Making of Social Identities on the Borderlands*. Berkeley: University of California Press, 2003.

French, William. "Prostitutes and Guardian Angels: Women, Work, and the Family in Porfirian Mexico." *Hispanic American Historical Review* 72, no. 4 (November 1992): 529–33.

Friedberg, Anne. *Window Shopping: Cinema and the Postmodern*. Berkeley: University of California Press, 1993.

Fuller, Kathryn H. *At the Picture Show: Small-Town Audiences and the Creation of Movie Fan Culture*. Washington: Smithsonian Institution Press, 1996.

Gallo, Rubén. *Mexican Modernity: The Avant-Garde and the Technological Revolution*. Cambridge, MA: MIT Press, 2005.

Gaonka, Dilip P. *Alternative Modernities*. Durham, NC: Duke University Press, 2001.

Garber, Marjorie. *Vested Interests: Cross Dressing and Cultural Anxiety*. New York: Routledge, 1992.

Garcia, Desiree. "There's No Place Like Home: Race, Cinema, Migration, and the Hollywood Musical, 1900–1950." PhD diss., Boston University, 2008.

García, Gustavo. *El cine mudo mexicano*. Mexico City: Martín Casillas Editores; Cultura/SEP, 1982.

García, Mario T. *Desert Immigrants: The Mexicans of El Paso, 1880–1920*. New Haven, CT: Yale University Press, 1981.

García Canclini, Néstor. *Hybrid Cultures: Strategies for Entering and Leaving Modernity*. Minneapolis: University of Minnesota Press, 1995.

García Riera, Emilio. *Historia documental del cine mexicano*. 18 vols. Mexico City: Universidad de Guadalajara, Gobierno de Jalisco, and Consejo Nacional para la Cultura Instituto Mexicano de Cinematografia, 1992.

———. *México visto por el cine extranjero*. Vol. 1: *1894–1940*. Mexico City: Ediciones Era, 1987.

García Rodríguez, Irene. "Mimí Derba and Azteca Films: The Rise of Nationalism and the First Mexican Woman Filmmaker." In *Women, Ethnicity, and Nationalisms in Latin America*, edited by Natividad Gutiérrez Chong, 170–94. Aldershot, UK: Ashgate, 2007.

Garrido, Felipe. *Luz y sombra: Los inicios del cine en la prensa de la ciudad de México*. Mexico: Consejo Nacional para la Cultura y las Artes, 1997.

Garvey, Ellen Gruber. *The Adman in the Parlor: Magazines and the Gendering of Consumer Culture, 1880s to 1910s*. New York: New York University Press, 1996.

Gilroy, Paul. *The Black Atlantic: Modernity and Double Consciousness*. Cambridge, MA: Harvard University Press, 1993.

Gomery, Douglas. "U.S. Film Exhibition: The Formation of a Big Business." In *The American Film Industry*, edited by Tino Balio, 218–28. Rev. ed. Madison: University of Wisconsin Press, 1985.

Gonzáles, Manuel G. *Mexicanos: A History of Mexicans in the United States*. Bloomington: Indiana University Press, 1999.

Gonzales, Michael J. "Imagining Mexico in 1921: Visions of the Revolutionary State and Society in the Centennial Celebration in Mexico City." *Mexican Studies / Estudios Mexicanos* 25, no. 2 (2009): 247–70.

———. *The Mexican Revolution, 1910–1940*. Albuquerque: University of New Mexico Press, 2002.

González Casanova, Manuel. *"Por la pantalla": Génesis de la crítica cinematográfica en México, 1917–1919*. Mexico City: Dirección General de Actividades Cinematográficas, Universidad Nacional Autónoma de México, 2000.

González Gamio, Angeles. *Manuel Gamio: Una lucha sin fin*. Mexico City: Universidad Nacional Autónoma de México Instituto de Investigaciones Estéticas, 1987.

González Mello, Renato. "El régimen visual y el fin de la revolución." In *Hacia otra historia del arte: La fabricación del arte nacional a debate (1920–1950)*, edited by E. Acevedo. Mexico City: CONACULTA, 2003.

González y González, Luis. *San José de Gracia: A Mexican Village in Transition*. Austin: University of Texas Press, 1974.

Grieveson, Lee. *Policing Cinema: Movies and Censorship in Early-Twentieth-Century America*. Berkeley: University of California Press, 2004.

Griffiths, Alison. *Wondrous Difference: Cinema, Anthropology, and Turn-of-the-Century Visual Culture*. New York: Columbia University Press, 2001.

Gruesz, Kirsten Silva. *Ambassadors of Culture: The Transamerican Origins of Latino Writing*. Princeton, NJ: Princeton University Press, 2002.

Guerin-Gonzales, Camille. *Mexican Workers and American Dreams: Immigration, Repatriation, and California Farm Labor, 1900–1939*. New Brunswick, NJ: Rutgers University Press, 1994.

Guerrero, Maria Consuelo. "La imagen de la revolución y de la mujer en la novela y el cine de la revolución mexicana." PhD diss., University of Texas, Austin, 2005.

Gunckel, Colin. "'A Theater Worthy of Our Race': The Exhibition and Reception of Spanish Language Film in Los Angeles, 1911–1942." PhD diss., University of California, Los Angeles.

———. "The War of the Accents: Spanish Language Hollywood Films in Mexican Los Angeles." *Film History* 20, no. 3 (2008): 325–43.

Gunning, Tom. "An Aesthetic of Astonishment: Early Film and the (In)Credulous Spectator." *Art and Text* 34 (spring 1989): 31–45.

Gutierrez, David. *Walls and Mirrors: Mexican Americans, Mexican Immigrants, and the Politics of Ethnicity*. Berkeley: University of California Press, 1995.

Haines, Cynthia F. *Showtime! From Opera Houses to Picture Palaces in El Paso*. El Paso: Texas Western Press, 2006.

Hale, Grace A. *Making Whiteness: The Culture of Segregation in the South 1890–1940*. New York: Vintage, 1999.

Hall, Linda B. *Oil, Banks, and Politics: The United States and Postrevolutionary Mexico, 1917–1924*. Austin: University of Texas Press, 1995.

Hall, Stuart. "Encoding/Decoding." In *Culture, Media, Language*, edited by Stuart Hall, Dorothy Hobson, Andrew Lowe, and Paul Willis, 128–38. London: Hutchinson, 1980.

Hallett, Hilary A. *Go West Young Woman! The Rise of Early Hollywood*. Berkeley: University of California Press, 2012.

Hansen, Miriam B. *Babel and Babylon: Spectatorship in American Silent Film*. Cambridge, MA: Harvard University Press, 1994.

———. "Early Cinema: Whose Public Sphere?" In *Early Cinema: Space, Frame, Narrative*, edited by Thomas Elsaesser, 228–46. London: BFI, 1990.

———. "Fallen Women, Rising Stars, New Horizons: Shanghai Silent Film as Vernacular Modernism." *Film Quarterly* 54, no. 1 (2000): 10–22.

———. "Universal Language and Democratic Culture: Myths of Origin in Early American Cinema." In *Myth and Enlightenment in American Literature (In Honor of Hans-Joachim Lang)*, edited by Dieter Horlacher and Friedrich W. Horlacher, 321–42. Germany: Erlanger Forschungen, 1985.

Hart, John Mason. *Empire and Revolution: The Americans in Mexico since the Civil War*. Berkeley: University of California Press, 2002.

Heredia, Juanita. "From Golden Age Cinema to Transnational Border Feminism: The Community of Spectators in *Loving Pedro Infante*." *Aztlán* 33, no. 2 (2008): 37–59.

Hershfield, Joanne. *Imagining la Chica Moderna: Women, Nation, and Visual Culture in Mexico, 1917–1936*. Durham, NC: Duke University Press, 2008.

———. *The Invention of Dolores del Río*. Minneapolis: University of Minnesota Press, 2000.

Hershfield, Joanne, and David R. Maciel, eds. *Mexico's Cinema: A Century of Film and Filmmakers*. Wilmington, DE: Scholarly Resources, 1999.

Higson, Andrew. "The Concept of National Cinema." In *Film and Nationalism*, edited by Andrew Williams, 52–67. New Brunswick, NJ: Rutgers University Press, 2002.

Jacobs, Lea. *The Wages of Sin: Censorship and the Fallen Woman Film, 1928–1942*. Berkeley: University of California Press, 1995.

Jarvie, Ian. *Hollywood's Overseas Campaign: The North Atlantic Movie Trade, 1920–1950*. Cambridge: Cambridge University Press, 1992.

Jarvinen, Lisa. *The Rise of Spanish-Language Filmmaking: Out from Hollywood's Shadow, 1929–1939*. New Brunswick, NJ: Rutgers University Press, 2012.

Johannsen, Robert W. *To the Halls of the Montezumas: The Mexican War in the American Imagination*. New York: Oxford University Press, 1985.

Joseph, Gilbert M. *Revolution from Without: Yucatan, Mexico, and the United States, 1880–1924*. Cambridge: Cambridge University Press, 1982.

Joseph, Gilbert M., Catherine C. LeGrand, and Richard D. Salvatore, eds. *Close Encounters of Empire: Writing the Cultural History of U.S.–Latin American Relations*. Durham, NC: Duke University Press, 1998.

Jowett, Garth, Kathryn H. Fuller, and Ian C. Jarvie. *Children and Movies: Media Influence and the Payne Fund Controversy*. New York: Cambridge University Press, 1996.

Kanellos, Nicolas. *A History of Hispanic Theatre in the United States: Origins to 1940*. Austin: University of Texas Press, 1990.

———. "Introducción." In Daniel Venegas, *Las aventuras de Don Chipote: O, cuando los pericos mamen*, 1–10. Houston, TX: Arte Público, 1999.

———. "A Socio-Historic Study of Hispanic Newspapers in the United States." In *Recovering the U.S. Hispanic Literary Heritage*, edited by Ramón Gutierrez and Genaro Padilla, 110–17. Houston, TX: Arte Público, 1993.

Katz, Friedrich. *The Secret War in Mexico: Europe, the United States, and the Mexican Revolution*. Chicago: University of Chicago Press, 1981.

Keller, Gary D. *Hispanics and United States Film: An Overview and Handbook*. Tempe, AZ: Bilingual Review, 1994.

———. "The Image of the Chicano in Mexican, United States, and Chicano Cinema." In *Chicano Cinema: Research, Reviews, and Resources*, edited by Gary D. Keller, 13–58. Tempe, AZ: Bilingual Review, 1985.

Kenaga, Heidi. "Making the 'Studio Girl': The Hollywood Studio Club and Industry Regulation of Female Labour." *Film History* 18, no. 2 (2006): 129–39.

Kirihara, Donald. "The Accepted Idea Displaced: Stereotype and Sessue Hayakawa." In *The Birth of Whiteness: Race and the Emergence of U.S. Cinema*, edited by Daniel Bernardi, 81–99. New Brunswick, NJ: Rutgers University Press, 1996.

Knauft, Bruce M. "Critically Modern: An Introduction." In *Critically Modern: Alternatives, Alterities, Anthropologies*, edited by Bruce M. Knauft, 1–54. Bloomington: Indiana University Press, 2002.

Knight, Alan. "Popular Culture and the Revolutionary State in Mexico, 1910–1940." *Hispanic American Historical Review* 74, no. 3 (1994): 393–444.

Koszarski, Richard. *An Evening's Entertainment: The Age of the Silent Feature Picture, 1915–1928*. Berkeley: University of California Press, 1994.

Kuehnert, Lore Diana. "Pernicious Foreigners and Contested Compatriots: Mexican Newspaper Debates over Immigration, Emigration, and Repatriation, 1928–1936." PhD diss., University of California, Riverside, 2002.

Kuhn, Annette. *Cinema, Censorship, and Sexuality, 1909–1925*. New York: Routledge, 1988.

Landay, Lori. "The Flapper Film: Comedy, Dance, and Jazz Age Kinaesthetics." In *A Feminist Reader in Early Cinema*, edited by Jennifer Bean and Diane Negra, 221–48. Durham, NC: Duke University Press, 2002.

Leal, Juan Felipe, Eduardo Barraza, and Carlos Flores. *Anales del cine en México, 1895–1911*, 10 volumes. Mexico City: Ediciones Y Gráficos Eón and Voyeur, 2003.

Limón, José E. *American Encounters: Greater Mexico, the United States, and the Erotics of Culture*. Boston: Beacon, 1998.

———. "Stereotyping and Chicano Resistance." In *Chicanos and Film: Representation and Resistance*, edited by Chon A. Noriega, 3–17. Minneapolis: University of Minnesota Press, 1992.

Lomnitz, Claudio. *Deep Mexico, Silent Mexico: An Anthropology of Nationalism*. Minneapolis: University of Minnesota Press, 2001.

López, Ana M. "A Cinema for the Continent." In *The Mexican Cinema Project*, edited by Chon A. Noriega and Steven Ricci, 7–12. Los Angeles: University of California, Los Angeles, Film and Television Archive, 1994.

———. "Early Cinema and Modernity in Latin America." *Cinema Journal* 40, no. 1 (2000): 48–78.

———. "From Hollywood and Back: Dolores del Rio a (Trans)National Star." *Studies in Latin American Popular Culture* 17 (1998): 5–32.

López, Rick Anthony. *Crafting Mexico: Intellectuals, Artisans, and the State after the Revolution*. Durham, NC: Duke University Press, 2010.

———. "The India Bonita Contest of 1921 and the Ethnicization of Mexican National Culture. *Hispanic American Historical Review* 82, no. 2 (2002): 291–328.

———. "*Los más mexicano de México*: Popular Arts, Indians, and Urban Intellectuals in the Ethnicization of Postrevolutionary National Culture, 1920–1972." PhD diss., Yale University, 2001.

Macotela, Catherine. "El sindicalismo en el cine I." *Otro Cine*, no. 2 (1975): 60–61.

Marez, Curtis. "Subaltern Soundtracks: Mexican Immigrants and the Making of Hollywood Cinema." *Aztlan* 29, no. 1 (2004): 57–82.

Matute, Álvaro. *Historia de la revolución mexicana.* Vol. 5: *Período 1917–1924.* Mexico City: El Colegio de México, 1976.

———. "Salud, familia y moral social (1917–1920)." *Históricas* 31 (January–April 1991): 25–34.

Mayne, Judith. *The Woman at the Keyhole: Feminism and Women's Cinema.* Bloomington: Indiana University Press, 1990.

McAlister, Melani. *Epic Encounters: Culture, Media, and U.S. Interests in the Middle East, 1945–2000.* Berkeley: University of California Press, 2001.

McCrossen, Alexis M. "Drawing Boundaries between Markets, Nations, and Peoples, 1650–1940." In *Land of Necessity: Consumer Culture in the United States–Mexico Borderlands,* edited by Alexis M. McCrossen, 3–47. Durham, NC: Duke University Press, 2009.

McKenna, Denise. "The Photoplay or the Pickaxe: Extras, Gender, and Labour in Early Hollywood." *Film History* 23, no. 1 (2011): 5–19.

Meyer, Jean, and Leslie Bethell. "Revolution and Reconstruction in the 1920s." In *Mexico since Independence,* edited by Leslie Bethell, 201–40. Cambridge: Cambridge University Press, 1991.

Meyer, Jean, Enrique Krauze, and Cayetano Reyes. *Historia de la revolución mexicana, 1924–1928: La reconstrucción económica and estado y sociedad con calles.* Mexico City: El Colegio de México, 2002.

Meyer, Lorenzo. "La institutionalización del nuevo régimen." In *Historia General de México,* 823–46. Mexico City: COLMEX / Centro de Estudios Historicos, 2002.

Meyer, Michael C., William Sherman, and Susan Deeds. *The Course of Mexican History.* New York: Oxford University Press, 1999.

Miquel, Ángel. *Disvolvencias: Literatura, cine y radio en México (1900–1950).* Mexico City: Fondo de Cultura Económica, 2005.

———. "La Estrella del Sur." *El Acordeón,* no. 11 (April–June 1994): 5–9.

———. *Los exaltados: Antologia de escritos sobre cine en periodicos y revistas de la ciudad de México, 1898–1929.* Guadalajara, Mexico: Universidad de Guadalajara, Centro de Investigación y Enseñanza Cinematográficas, 1992.

———. *Mimí Derba.* Harlingen, TX: Archivo Fílmico Agrasánchez; Mexico: Filmoteca de la UNAM, 2000.

———. *Por las pantallas de la ciudad de México: Periodistas del cine mudo.* Guadalajara, Mexico: Universidad de Guadalajara, 1995.

——— Salvador Toscano. Guadalajara, Mexico: Universidad de Guadalajara; Puebla: Gobierno del Estado de Puebla; Xalapa, Veracruz: Universidad Veracruzana; Mexico: Universidad Nacional Autónoma de México, 1990.

Miyao, Daisuke. *Sessue Hayakawa: Silent Cinema and Transnational Stardom.* Durham, NC: Duke University Press, 2007.

Monroy, Douglas. *Rebirth: Mexican Los Angeles from the Great Migration to the Great Depression.* Berkeley: University of California Press, 1999.

Monsiváis, Carlos. "All the People Came and Did Not Fit onto the Screen: Notes on the Cinema Audience in Mexico." In *Mexican Cinema,* edited by Paulo A. Paranaguá, translated by Anna M. López, 145–51. London: BFI, 1995.

Montejano, David. *Anglos and Mexicans in the Making of Texas, 1836–1986.* Austin: University of Texas Press, 1987.

Montemayor, Alma. *Cien años de cine en Chihuahua.* Ciudad Chihuahua, Mexico: Cuadernos de Solar, 1998.

———. "El cine silente en la Ciudad de Chihuahua." In *Microhistorias del cine en México,* 79–95. Guadalajara, Mexico: Universidad de Guadalajara, 2000.

Mora, Carl J. *Mexican Cinema: Reflections of a Society, 1896–2004.* 3rd ed. Jefferson, NC: McFarland, 2005.

Mora-Torres, Juan. *The Making of the Mexican Border: The State, Capitalism, and Society in Nuevo León, 1848–1910.* Austin: University of Texas Press, 2001.

Moreno, Julio. *Yankee Don't Go Home! Mexican Nationalism, American Business Culture, and the Shaping of Modern Mexico, 1920–1950.* Chapel Hill: University of North Carolina Press, 2003.

Morgan, Tony. "Proletarians, Politicos, and Patriarchs: The Use and Abuse of Cultural Customs in the Early Industrialization of Mexico City, 1880–1910." In *Rituals of Rule, Rituals of Resistance: Public Celebrations and Popular Culture in Mexico,* edited by William H. Beezley, Cheryl English Martin, and William E. French, 151–71. Wilmington, DE: SR, 2001.

Mould, David H. *American Newsfilm 1914–1919: The Underexposed War.* New York: Garland, 1983.

Museo Nacional de Arte. *Posada y la prensa ilustrada: Signos de modernización y resistencias.* Mexico City: Instituto Nacional de Bellas Artes, 1996.

Musser, Charles. *Edison Motion Pictures, an Annotated Filmography, 1890–1900.* Washington: Smithsonian Institution Press, 1997.

Naylor, David. *American Picture Palaces.* New York: Van Nostrand Reinhold, 1981.

Negra, Diane. *Off-White Hollywood: American Culture and Ethnic Female Stardom.* New York: Routledge, 2001.

Ngai, Mae M. *Impossible Subjects: Illegal Aliens and the Making of Modern America.* Princeton, NJ: Princeton University Press, 2005.

Nielsen, Elizabeth. "Handmaidens of the Glamour Culture: Costumers in the Hollywood Studio System." In *Fabrications: Costume and the Female Body,* edited by Jane M. Gaines and Charlotte Herzog, 160–79. New York: Routledge, 1990.

Noble, Andrea. *Mexican National Cinema.* New York: Routledge, 2005.

Noriega, Chon A., ed. *Chicanos and Film: Essays on Chicano Representation and Resistance.* Minneapolis: University of Minnesota Press, 1992.

———. *Shot in America: Television, the State, and the Rise of Chicano Cinema.* Minneapolis: University of Minnesota Press, 2000.

Ogihara, Junko. "The Exhibition of Films for Japanese Americans in Los Angeles during the Silent Film Era." *Film and History* 4, no. 2 (1990): 81–87.

Oles, James. *South of the Border: Mexico in the American Imagination, 1914–1947.* With an essay by Karen Cordero Reiman. Translated by Marta Ferragut. Washington: Smithsonian Institution Press, 1993.

Olsen, Patrice Elizabeth. "Revolution in the City Streets: Changing Nomenclature, Changing Form, and the Revision of Public Memory." In *The Eagle and the Vir-*

gin: Nation and Cultural Revolution Mexico, 1920–1940, edited by Mary K. Vaughan and Stephen E. Lewis, 119–34. Durham, NC: Duke University Press, 2006.

Olsson, Jan. "Hollywood's First Spectators: Notes on Ethnic Nickelodeon Audiences in Los Angeles." Aztlán 26, no. 1 (2001): 181–95.

Orellana, Margarita de. La mirada circular: El cine norteamericano de la revolución mexicana 1911–1917. Mexico City: Artes de México, 1999.

Ortiz Gaitán, Julieta. Imágenes del deseo: Arte y publicidad en la prensa ilustrada mexicana (1894–1939). Mexico City: Universidad Nacional Autónoma de México, 2003.

Paranaguá, Paulo Antonio, ed. Mexican Cinema. Translated by Ana M. López. London: British Film Institute, 1995.

———. "Ten Reasons to Love or Hate Mexican Cinema." In Mexican Cinema, edited by Paulo Antonio Paranaguá, 1–13. London: British Film Institute, 1995.

———. Tradición y modernidad en el cine de América Latina. Madrid: Fondo de Cultura Económica de Espana, 2003

Paxman, Andrew. "William Jenkins, Business Elites, and the Evolution of the Mexican State: 1910–1960." PhD diss., University of Texas, 2009.

Peiss, Kathy. Cheap Amusements: Working Women and Leisure in Turn-of-the-Century New York City. Philadelphia, PA: Temple University Press, 1986.

Pensado, Patricia, and Leonor Correa. Mixcoac: Un barrio en la memoria. Mexico City: Instituto Mora, 1996.

Pérez Montfort, Ricardo. Estampas de nacionalismo popular mexicano: Diez ensayos sobre la cultura popular y nacionalismo. Mexico City: Centro de Investigaciones y Estudios Superiores en Antropologia y Sociologia, 2003.

Perry, Louis B., and Richard S. Perry. A History of the Los Angeles Labor Movement, 1911–1941. Berkeley: University of California Press, 1963.

Pettit, Arthur G. Images of the Mexican American in Fiction and Film. College Station: Texas A&M University Press, 1980.

Piccato, Pablo. City of Suspects: Crime in Mexico City, 1900–1931. Durham, NC: Duke University Press, 2001.

Pick, Zuzana M. Constructing the Image of the Mexican Revolution: Cinema and the Archive. Austin: University of Texas Press, 2010.

———. "Jesús H. Abitía: Cinefotógrafo de la revolución y epopeyas de la revolución mexicana." In Fotografía, cine y literatura de la revolución mexicana, 31 48. Cuernavaca, Mexico: Universidad Autonóma del Estado de Morelos; Mexico City: Ediciones Sin Nombre, Fundación Toscano, 2005.

Pintar, Laurie. "Behind the Scenes: Bronco Billy and the Realities of Work in Open Shop Hollywood." In Metropolis in the Making: Los Angeles in the 1920s, edited by Tom Sitton and William Deverall, 319–38. Berkeley: University of California Press, 2001.

Porter, Susie E. Working Women in Mexico City: Public Discourses, Material Conditions, 1879–1931. Tucson: University of Arizona Press, 2003.

Pratt, Mary Louise. Imperial Eyes: Travel Writing and Transculturation. New York: Routledge, 1992.

Rabinovitz, Lauren. *For the Love of Pleasure: Women, Movies, and Culture in Turn-of-the-Century Chicago*. New Brunswick, NJ: Rutgers University Press, 1998.

Radkau, Verena. *La fama y la vida: Una fábrica y sus obreras*. Mexico City: Centro de Investigaciones y Estudios Superiores en Antropologia Social, 1984.

Ramirez, Elizabeth C. *Footlights across the Border: A History of Spanish-Language Professional Theatre on the Texas Stage*. New York: Peter Lang, 1990.

Ramírez, Gabriel. *El cine yucateco*. Yucatán, Mexico: Fondo Editorial Ayuntamiento de Mérida, 2006.

———. *Crónica del cine mudo mexicano*. Mexico City: Cineteca Nacional, 1989.

Ramírez Berg, Charles. "*El automóvil gris* and the Advent of Mexican Classicism." In *Visible Nations: Latin American Cinema and Video*, edited by Chon A. Noriega, 3–32. Minneapolis: University of Minnesota Press, 2000.

———. *Cinema of Solitude: A Critical Study of Mexican Film, 1967–1983*. Austin: University of Texas Press, 1992.

———. "The Cinematic Invention of Mexico: The Poetics and Politics of the Fernández-Figueroa Style." In *The Mexican Cinema Project*, edited by Chon A. Noriega and Steven Ricci, 13–24. Los Angeles: University of California, Los Angeles, Film and Television Archive, 1999.

———. *Latino Images in Film: Stereotypes, Subversion, and Resistance*. Austin: University of Texas Press, 2002.

Ramírez Plancarte, Francisco. *La ciudad de México durante la revolución constitucionalista*. Mexico City: Ediciones Botas, 1941.

Reyes, Aurelio de los. *Cine y sociedad en México: 1896–1930*. Vol. 1: *Vivir de suenos*. México: Universidad Nacional Autónoma de México, Instituto de Investigaciones Estéticas, 1993.

———. *Cine y sociedad en México: 1896–1930*. Vol. 2: *Bajo el cielo de México*. México: Universidad Nacional Autónoma de México, Instituto de Investigaciones Estéticas, 1993.

———. *Filmografía del cine mudo mexicano, 1896–1920*. Mexico City: Filmoteca de la Universidad Nacional Autónoma de México, 1986.

———. *Filmografía del cine mudo mexicano, volumen II, 1920–1924*. Mexico City: Dirección General de Actividades Cinematográficas, Universidad Nacional Autónoma de México, 1994.

———. *Medio siglo de cine mexicano (1896–1947)*. Mexico City: Editorial Trillas, 1987.

———. *Los orígenes del cine en México (1896–1900)*. Lecturas Mexicanas. Mexico City: Fonda de Cultura Economica, 1984.

Reyes de la Maza, Luis. *Salón Rojo: Programas y crónicas del cine mudo en México*. Mexico City: Dirección General de Difusión Cultural, UNAM, 1968.

Ríos-Bustamante, Antonio. "Latino Participation in the Hollywood Film Industry." In *Chicanos and Film: Representation and Resistance*, edited by Chon A. Noriega, 18–28. Minneapolis: University of Minnesota Press, 1992.

Rodriguez, Clara E. *Heroes, Lovers, and Others: The Story of Latinos in Hollywood*. Washington, DC: Smithsonian, 2004.

Rodríguez O., Jaime E., ed. *The Revolutionary Process in Mexico: Essays on Political and Social Change, 1880–1940.* Los Angeles: University of California, Los Angeles, Latin American Center, 1990.

Rodríguez-Estrada, Alicia I. "Dolores del Río and Lupe Vélez: Images On and Off the Screen, 1925–1944." In *Writing the Range: Race, Class, and Culture in the Women's West,* edited by Elizabeth Jameson and Susan Armitage, 475–92. Norman: University of Oklahoma Press, 1997.

Romo, Ricardo. *East Los Angeles: History of a Barrio.* Austin: University of Texas Press, 1983.

Rony, Fatimah Tobing. *The Third Eye: Race, Cinema, and Ethnographic Spectacle.* Durham, NC: Duke University Press, 1996.

Rosenberg, Emily. *Spreading the American Dream: American Economic and Cultural Expansion, 1890–1945.* New York: Hill and Wang, 1982.

Ross, Sara. "Screening the Modern Girl: Intermediality in the Adaptation of Flaming Youth." *Modernism/Modernity* 17, no. 3 (2010): 271–90.

Ross, Steven J. *Working-Class Hollywood.* Princeton, NJ: Princeton University Press, 1999.

Rubenstein, Anne. *Bad Language, Naked Ladies, and Other Threats to the Nation: A Political History of Comic Books in Mexico.* Durham, NC: Duke University Press, 1998.

———. "Raised Voices at the Cine Montecarlo." *Journal of Family History* 23, no. 3 (1998): 312–23.

———. "The 'War on las Pelonas': Modern Women and Their Enemies, Mexico City, 1924." In *Sex in Revolution: Gender, Politics, and Power in Modern Mexico,* edited by Jocelynn Olcott, Mary K. Vaughan, and Gabriela Cano, 57–81. Durham, NC: Duke University Press, 2006.

Ruffinelli, Jorge. *Villa y la revolución mexicana / John Reed: Reed en México.* Mexico City: Editorial Nueva Imagen, 1983.

Ruiz, Vicki L. *From out of the Shadows: Mexican Women in Twentieth Century America.* New York: Oxford University Press, 1998.

Salazar Alfaro, Francisco H., and Alejandro Ochoa Vega. *Espacios distantes . . . aún vivos: Las salas cinematográficas de la ciudad de México.* Mexico City: Universidad Autónoma Metropolitana Xochimilco, 1997.

Sanchez, George J. *Becoming Mexican American: Ethnicity, Culture, and Identity in Chicano Los Angeles, 1900–1945.* New York: Oxford University Press, 1993.

———. "'Go after the Women': Americanization and the Mexican Immigrant Woman, 1915–1929." In *Unequal Sisters: A Multicultural Reader in Women's History,* edited by Vicki Ruiz and Ellen C. DuBois, 250–63. New York: Routledge, 1990.

Saragoza, Alex. "The Selling of Mexico: Tourism and the State 1929–1952." In *Fragments of a Golden Age: The Politics of Culture in Mexico since 1940,* edited by Gilbert Joseph, Anne Rubenstein, and Eric Zolov, 91–115. Durham, NC: Duke University Press, 2001.

Saunders, Thomas J. *Hollywood in Berlin: American Cinema and Weimar Germany.* Berkeley: University of California Press, 1994.

Scanlon, Jennifer, ed. *The Gender and Consumer Culture Reader*. New York: New York University Press, 2000.

Schaefer, Eric. "Of Hygiene and Hollywood: Origins of the Exploitation Film." *Velvet Light Trap* 30 (fall 1992): 34–47.

Schneider, Luis Mario. *El estridentismo: O una literatura de la estrategia*. Mexico City: Instituto Nacional de Bellas Artes, 1970.

Schwartz, Jorge. *Las vanguardias latinoamericanas: Textos programáticos y críticos*. Mexico City: Cátedra, 1991.

Serna, Laura Isabel. "'As a Mexican I Feel It's My Duty': Citizenship, Censorship, and the Campaign against Derogatory Films in Mexico, 1922–1930." *The Americas: A Quarterly Review of Inter-American Cultural History* 63, no. 2 (October 2006): 225–44.

Sevilla, Amparo. *Los templos del buen bailar, memoria histórica*. Mexico City: CONACULTA, 2003.

Sheridan, Guillermo. *Los contemporáneos ayer*. Mexico City: Fondo de Cultura Económica, 1985.

Shohat, Ella, and Robert Stam. *Unthinking Eurocentrism*. New York: Routledge, 1994.

Shukla, Sandhya, and Heidi Tinsman. "Editors' Introduction." In "Our Americas: Political and Cultural Imaginings," special issue, *Radical History Review* 89 (spring 2004): 1–10.

Siegel, Micol. *Uneven Encounters: Making Race and Nation in Brazil and the United States*. Durham, NC: Duke University Press, 2009.

Sinclair, John. "Culture and Trade: Some Theoretical and Practical Considerations." In *Mass Media and Free Trade: NAFTA and the Cultural Industries*, edited by Emile G. McAnany and Kenton T. Wilkinson, 30–59. Austin: University of Texas Press, 1996.

Singer, Ben. *Melodrama and Modernity: Early Sensational Cinema and Its Contexts*. New York: Columbia University Press, 2001.

Sluis, Ageeth. "Bataclanismo! Or, How Female Deco Bodies Transformed Postrevolutionary Mexico City." *Americas* 66, no. 4 (2010): 469–99.

Smith, Robert Freeman. *The United States and Revolutionary Nationalism in Mexico, 1916–1932*. Chicago: University of Chicago Press, 1972.

Smoodin, Eric. "The History of Film History." In *Looking Past the Screen: Case Studies in American Film History and Method*, edited by John Lewis and Eric Smoodin, 1–33. Durham, NC: Duke University Press, 2007.

Soares, André. *Beyond Paradise: The Life of Ramon Novarro*. New York: St. Martin's, 2002.

Sollors, Werner. "'A World Somewhere, Somewhere Else': Language, Nostalgic Mournfulness, and Urban Immigrant Family Romance in *Call It Sleep*." In *New Essays on Call It Sleep*, edited by Hana Wirth-Nesher, 127–88. Cambridge: Cambridge University Press, 1996.

Soto, Shirlene. *The Emergence of the Modern Mexican Woman: Her Participation in Revolution and Struggle for Equality, 1910–1940*. Denver, CO: Arden, 1990.

Speckman Guerra, Elisa. "De méritos y reputaciones: El honor en la ley y la justicia

(Distrito Federal, 1871–1931)." *Anuario mexicano de historia del derecho* 28 (2006): 331–61.

Spigel, Lynn. *Make Room for TV: Television and the Family Ideal in Postwar America.* Chicago: University of Chicago Press, 1992.

Stamp, Shelley. "An Awful Struggle between Love and Ambition: Serial Heroines, Serial Stars and Their Female Fans." In *The Silent Cinema Reader,* edited by Lee Grieveson and Peter Krämer, 210–25. New York: Routledge, 2004.

———. "'It's a Long Way to Filmland': Starlets, Screen Hopefuls, and Extras in Early Hollywood." In *American Cinema's Transitional Era: Audiences, Institutions, Practices,* edited by Charles Keil and Shelley Stamp, 332–52. Berkeley: University of California Press, 2004.

———. *Movie-Struck Girls: Women and Motion Picture Culture after the Nickel-odeon.* Princeton, NJ: Princeton University Press, 2000.

Stewart, Jacqueline. *Migrating to the Movies: Cinema and Black Urban Modernity.* Berkeley: University of California Press, 2005.

Stokes, Melvyn, and Richard Maltby, eds. *American Movie Audiences: From the Turn of the Century to the Early Sound Era.* London: BFI, 1999.

———. *Hollywood Abroad: Audiences and Cultural Exchange.* London: BFI, 2005.

Strauven, Wanda. "Introduction to an Attractive Concept." In *The Cinema of Attractions Reloaded,* edited by Wanda Strauven, 11–27. Amsterdam: Amsterdam University Press, 2006.

Streeby, Shelley. *American Sensations: Class, Empire, and the Production of Popular Culture.* Berkeley: University of California Press, 2002.

Streible, Dan. *Fight Pictures: A History of Boxing and Early Cinema.* Berkeley: University of California Press, 2008.

Studlar, Gaylyn. "The Perils of Pleasure? Fan Magazine Discourse as Women's Commodified Culture in the 1920s." *Wide Angle* 13, no. 1 (1991): 6–33.

———. *This Mad Masquerade: Stardom and Masculinity in the Jazz Age.* New York: Columbia University Press, 1996.

Sturman, Janet Lynn. *Zarzuela: Spanish Operetta, American Stage.* Urbana: University of Illinois Press, 2000.

Sturtevant, Victoria. "Spitfire: Lupe Vélez and the Ambivalent Pleasures of Ethnic Masquerade." *Velvet Light Trap* 55 (spring 2005): 19–32.

Taylor, Ronnie C. "Fugitive Slaves in Mexico." *Journal of Negro History* 57, no. 1 (1972): 1–12.

Tenenbaum, Barbara A. "Streetwise History: The Paseo de la Reforma and the Porfirian State, 1876–1910." In *Rituals of Rule, Rituals of Resistance: Public Celebrations and Popular Culture in Mexico,* edited by William H. Beezley, Cheryl English Martin, and William E. French, 127–50. Wilmington, DE: SR, 1994.

Tenorio Trillo, Mauricio. *Mexico at the World's Fairs: Crafting a Modern Nation.* Berkeley: University of California Press, 1996.

———. "1910 Mexico City: Space and Nation in the City of the Centenario." *Journal of Latin American Studies* 28, no. 1 (1996): 75–104.

Thomas, Keith. "The Meaning of Literacy in Early Modern England." In *The Written*

Word: Literacy in Transition, edited by Gerd Baumann, 97–131. New York: Oxford University Press, 1986.

Thompson, Kristin. *Exporting Entertainment: America in the World Film Market, 1907–1934*. London: British Film Institute, 1985.

Tierney, Dolores M. *Emilio Fernández*. Manchester, UK: Manchester University Press, 2007.

Torres, Rebecca Maria, and Janet D. Momsen. "Gringolandia: The Construction of a New Tourist Space in Mexico." *Annals of the Association of American Geographers* 95, no. 2 (2005): 314–35.

Torres San Martín, Patricia. *Crónicas tapatías del cine mexicano, el cine en Jalisco*. Guadalajara, Mexico: Universidad de Guadalajara, 1993.

Trumpboar, John. *Selling Hollywood to the World: U.S. and European Struggles for the Mastery of the Global Film Industry, 1920–1950*. Cambridge: Cambridge University Press, 2002.

Tsivian, Yuri. *Early Cinema in Russia and Its Cultural Reception*. New York: Routledge, 1994.

Tuñón Pablos, Julia. *Mujeres de luz y sombra en el cine mexicano: La construcción de una imagen (1939–1952)*. Mexico City: El Colegio de México, 1998.

———. *Women in Mexico: A Past Unveiled*. Austin: University of Texas Press, 1999.

Ulff-Møler, Jens. *Hollywood's "Film Wars" with France: Film-Trade Diplomacy and the Emergence of the French Film Quota Policy*. Rochester, NY: University of Rochester Press, 2001.

Ulloa, Berta. *La lucha armada, 1911–1920*. Mexico City: Patria, 1976.

Usabel, Gaizka S. *The High Noon of American Films in Latin America*. Ann Arbor, MI: UMI Research Press, 1982.

Vanderwood, Paul, and Frank N. Samponaro. *Border Fury: A Picture Postcard Record of Mexico's Revolution and U.S. War Preparedness, 1910–1917*. Albuquerque: University of New Mexico Press, 1998.

Vargas, Zaragosa. *Proletarians of the North: A History of Mexican Industrial Workers in Detroit and the Midwest, 1917–1933*. Berkeley: University of California Press, 1993.

Vasconcelos, José. *A Mexican Ulysses: An Autobiography*. Bloomington: Indiana University Press, 1963.

———. *La raza cósmica: Misión de la raza iberoamericana, Argentina y Brasil*. Mexico City: Espasa-Calpe, 1976.

Vasey, Ruth. *The World According to Hollywood*. Madison: University of Wisconsin Press, 1999.

Vaughan, Mary K. *Cultural Politics in Revolution: Teachers, Peasants, and Schools in Mexico, 1930–1940*. Tucson: University of Arizona Press, 1997.

Vaughan, Mary K., and Stephen E. Lewis, eds. *The Eagle and the Virgin: Nation and Cultural Revolution in Mexico, 1920–1940*. Durham, NC: Duke University Press, 2006.

Vega Alfaro, Eduardo de la. *La industria cinematográfica mexicana: Perfil histórico-social*. Guadalajara, Mexico: Universidad de Guadalajara, 1991.

———, ed. *Microhistorias del cine en México*. Guadalajara, Mexico: Universidad de Guadalajara, 2000.

Vega Alfaro, Eduardo de la, and Patricia Torres San Martín. *Adela Sequeyro*. Guadalajara, Mexico: Universidad de Guadalajara; Universidad Veracruzana, 1997.

Viqueira Albán, Juan Pedro. *Relajados o reprimidos? Diversiones públicas y vida social en la ciudad de Mexico durante el Siglo de las Luces*. Mexico City: Fondo de Cultura Económica, 1987.

Waller, Gregory A. "Another Audience: Black Moviegoing, 1907–1916." *Cinema Journal* 31, no. 2 (1992): 3–25.

Wang, Yiman. "The Art of Screen Passing: Anna May Wong's Yellow Yellowface Performance in the Art Deco Era." *Camera Obscura* 20, no. 3 (2005): 159–91.

Weber, Devra. *Dark Sweat, White Gold: California Farm Workers, Cotton, and the New Deal*. Berkeley: University of California Press, 1994.

Weinbaum, Alys Eve, and The Modern Girl around the World Research Group, eds. *The Modern Girl around the World: Consumption, Modernity, and Globalization*. Durham, NC: Duke University Press, 2008.

Wells, Allen. *Yucatán's Gilded Age: Haciendas, Henequen, and International Harvester, 1860–1915*. Albuquerque: University of New Mexico Press, 1985.

Wells, Allen, and Gilbert M. Joseph. "Modernizing Visions, 'Chilango' Blueprints, and Provincial Growing Pains: Mérida at the Turn-of-the-Century." *Mexican Studies / Estudios Mexicanos* 8, no. 2 (1992): 167–215.

———. *Summer of Discontent, Seasons of Upheaval: Elite Politics and Rural Insurgency in Yucatán, 1876–1915*. Stanford: Stanford University Press, 1996.

Wilson, Christopher S. "Plotting the Border: John Reed, Pancho Villa, and Insurgent Mexico." In *Cultures of United States Imperialism*, edited by Donald E. Pease and Amy Kaplan, 340–63. Durham, NC: Duke University Press, 1998.

Womack, John, Jr. "The Mexican Revolution, 1910–1920." In *Mexico since Independence*, edited by Leslie Bethell, 125–200. Cambridge: Cambridge University Press, 1991.

Yellis, Kenneth A. "Prosperity's Child: Some Thoughts on the Flapper." *American Quarterly* 21, no. 1 (spring 1969): 44–64.

Zolov, Eric. *Refried Elvis: The Rise of the Mexican Counterculture*. Berkeley: University of California Press, 1999.

FILMOGRAPHY

The films listed here are those cited in the text.

UNITED STATES

The Abysmal Brute (*El bruto*). Directed by Hobart Henley. Universal Pictures (Universal-Jewel), 1923.

The Adventures of Peg o' the Ring (*La hija del circo*). Serial, 15 episodes. Directed by Francis Ford and Jacques Jaccard. Universal Film Manufacturing Company, 1916.

After Midnight (*Despues de medianoche*). Directed by Monta Bell. Metro-Goldwyn-Mayer, Corp. [Loews's Inc.], 1927.

Ah Sing and the Greasers. Lubin Manufacturing Company, 1910.

The Avenging Arrow. Directed by William Bowman and W. S. Van Dyke. Production company unknown, presumed to be Astra Film Corporation, 1921.

The Bad Man (*El hombre malo*). Directed by Edwin Carewe. Associated First National Pictures, 1923.

The Bad Man (*El hombre malo*). Directed by Clarence G. Badger. First National Pictures / Warner Bros. Pictures, 1930.

Ben Hur. Directed by Fred Niblo. Metro-Goldwyn-Mayer, 1925.

The Black Box (*La caja negra*). Serial, 15 episodes. Directed by Otis Turner. Universal, 1915.

Body and Soul (*Alma y cuerpo*). Directed by Charles Swickard. Metro Pictures Corp., 1920.

The Broken Coin (*La moneda rota*). Serial, 44 episodes. Directed by Francis Ford. Universal Film Corporation, 1915.

A Camouflage Kiss (*Los dos besos*). Directed by Harry Millarde. Fox Film Corp., 1918.

Daredevil Jack. Serial, 15 episodes. Directed by W. S. Van Dyke. Astra Film Corporation, 1920.

Doctor Neighbor (*La ciencia y el amor*). Directed by Lloyd B. Carleton. Universal Film Manufacturing Company, 1916.

Douglas Fairbanks in Robin Hood. Directed by Allen Dwan. Douglas Fairbanks Pictures Corporation (United Artists Corp.), 1923.

The Dove (*La paloma*). Directed by Roland West. Norma Talmadge Productions (United Artists), 1927.

The End of the Road. Directed by Edward H. Griffith. Famous Players–Lasky Corp. / American Social Hygiene Association / U.S. War Department, 1919.

The Exploits of Elaine (*Los mysterios de Nueva York*, also known as *Las aventuras de Elena*). Serial, 14 episodes. Directed by Louis J. Gasnier and George B. Seitz. Wharton Films, 1914–15.

Fighting Fate. Directed by William Duncan. Vitagraph Company of America, 1921.

The Fighting Trail (*El sendero sangriente*). Serial, 15 episodes. Directed by William Duncan. Vitagraph Company of America, 1917.

Flaming Youth (*Juventud ardiente*). Directed by John Francis Dillon. Associated First National Pictures, 1923.

Fool's Paradise. Directed by Cecil B. DeMille. Famous Players–Lasky Corp., 1922.

Forbidden Valley (*Valle prohibido*). Directed by J. Stuart Blackton. J. Stuart Blackton Feature Pictures, 1920.

The Fox (*El despreciado*). Directed by Robert Thornby. Universal Film Manufacturing Company (Universal-Jewel), 1920.

The Gaucho (*El gaucho*). Directed by F. Richard Jones. Elton Corp. (United Artists), 1928.

The Girl and the Greaser. Directed by Lorimer Johnston. American Film Manufacturing Company, 1913.

The Girl in the Web (*Redes del delito*). Directed by Robert Thornby. Jesse D. Hampton Productions / Robert Brunton Productions, 1920.

A Girl Named Mary (*Se llamaba Maria*). Directed by Walter Edwards. Famous Players–Lasky Corp., 1919.

Girl of the Rio. Directed by Herbert Brenon. RKO Radio Pictures Corp., 1932.

The Golden Gift. Directed by Maxwell Kirger. Metro Pictures Corp., 1922.

The Greaser and the Weakling. Directed by Allan Dwan. American Film Manufacturing Company, 1912.

The Greaser's Gauntlet. Directed by D. W. Griffith. American Mutoscope and Biograph Co., 1908.

Guilty of Love (*Culpa de amor*). Directed by Harley Knoles. Famous Players–Lasky Corp. / Paramount-Artcraft Pictures, 1920.

Hearts of the World. Directed by D. W. Griffith. D. W. Griffith Productions, 1918.

Hell's Fury Gordon. Directed by Leon De La Mothe. Canyon Pictures Corporation, 1919.

Her Husband's Trademark. Directed by Sam Wood. Famous Players–Lasky Corp., 1922.

His Debt (*Su deuda*). Directed by William Worthington. Haworth Pictures Company, 1919.

His Majesty the American (*Su majestad*). Directed by Joseph Henabery. Douglas Fairbanks Pictures Corp. (United Artists), 1919.

El hombre malo. Directed by Roberto E. Guzmán and William C. McGann. First National Pictures / Warner Bros. Pictures, 1930.

Homeward Bound (Amor pirata). Directed by Ralph Ince. Famous Players–Lasky Corp., 1923.

Honoria Suarez en Hollywood. Produced by Paramount Pictures in collaboration with the Circuito Olimpia and *El Demócrata*. 1924.

The House of Hate (El antifaz siniestro). Serial, 20 episodes. Directed by George B. Seitz. Astra Film Corporation, 1918.

I Can Explain. Directed by George D. Baker. S-L Pictures, 1922.

The Idol Dancer (La danza del idolo). Directed by D. W. Griffith. D. W. Griffith Productions, 1920.

An Innocent Magdalene (La moderna magdalena). Directed by Allan Dwan. Fine Arts Film Company Productions, 1916.

Intolerance (La doncella de Orleans). Directed by D. W. Griffith. D. W. Griffith / Wark Producing Corp., 1916.

Iron Claw (La garra de hierro). Serial, 40 episodes. Directed by Edward José and George B. Seitz. Feature Film Corporation, 1916.

It. Directed by Clarence G. Badger. Famous Players–Lasky Corp., 1927.

Jazzmania. Directed by Robert Z. Leonard. Tiffany Productions, 1923.

Jubilo. Directed by Clarence G. Badger. Goldwyn Pictures, 1919.

The Kick-Back. Directed by Val Paul. R-C Pictures, 1922.

The King of Kings (Creo en dios). Directed by Cecil B. DeMille. DeMille Pictures Corp., 1927.

Lion and Lioness (Leon y leona). Edison Manufacturing Company, 1904.

Little Lord Fauntleroy (El pequeno Lord Fauntleroy). Directed by Alfred E. Green and Jack Pickford. The Mary Pickford Company (United Artists), 1921.

The Love Nest (Nido de amor). Directed by Wray Physioc. Commercial Traders Cinema Corp., 1922.

Loving Lies. Directed by W. S. Van Dyke. Associated Authors (United Artists), 1924.

Man and His Woman (Cuerpo y alma). Directed by J. Stuart Blackton. J. Stuart Blackton Feature Pictures, 1920.

The Man of Courage. Produced by Nathan Hirsh. Aywon Film Corp., 1922.

The Marriage Circle (El circulo matrimonial). Directed by Ernst Lubitsch. Warner Bros. Pictures, 1924.

The Master Key (La llave maestro). Serial, 31 episodes. Directed by Robert Z. Leonard. Universal, 1914.

The Mastermind (Tres almas de pena), also known as *Sinners Three*. Directed by Kenneth Webb. Associated First National Pictures, 1920.

Moran of the Lady Letty. Directed by George Melford. Famous Players–Lasky Corp., 1922.

A Night in New Arabia (Una noche en Arabia). Directed by Thomas R. Mills. Broadway Star Features Co., 1917.

No Woman Knows (Lo que todo mujer ignora). Directed by Tod Browning. Universal Film Manufacturing Company, 1921.

North of the Rio Grande. Directed by Rollin Sturgeon. Famous Players–Lasky Corp., 1922.

One Exciting Day (Un día agitado). Directed by Albert Herman. Century Film, 1923.

One Week of Love. Directed by George Achinbaud. Selznick Pictures Corporation, 1922.

Orphans of the Storm. Directed by D. W. Griffith. United Artists Corp., 1921.

Pershing's Crusaders. Directed by Herbert C. Hoagland. U.S. Committee on Public Information, Division of Films, 1918.

Pollyanna. Directed by Paul Powell. United Artists Corp., 1920.

The Promised Land (Tierras de promision). Director unknown, Corsay, 1925.

Quicksands. Directed by Jack Conway. Agfar Corp., 1923.

Ramona. Directed by Edwin Carewe. Inspiration Pictures, Inc. (United Artists Corp.), 1928.

Revenge (La revancha de Duncan). Directed by Tod Browning. Metro Pictures Corp., 1918.

Sadie Thompson. Directed by Raoul Walsh. Gloria Swanson Productions, Inc. / United Artists Corp., 1928.

Second Hand Rose (La rosa del rastro). Directed by Lloyd Ingraham. Universal Film Manufacturing Company, 1922.

The Secret Four (Los cuatro secretos). Serial, 30 episodes. Directed by Albert Russell. Universal Pictures Corporation, 1921.

Short Skirts (Faldas cortas). Directed by Harry B. Harris. Universal Film Manufacturing Company, 1921.

Shoulder Arms (Armas al hombro). Directed by Charles Chaplin. Charles Chaplin Productions (United Artists Corp.), 1918.

A Small Town Idol. Directed by Erle Kenton. Mack Sennett Productions, 1921.

Smashing Barriers (Barreras infranqueables). Serial, 15 episodes. Directed by William Duncan. Vitagraph Company of America, 1919.

Smiles (Sonrisas). Directed by Arvid E. Gillstrom. Fox Film Corporation, 1920.

The Son of the Sheik. Directed by George Fitzmaurice. Feature Productions, Inc. / United Artists Corp., 1926.

A Tailor Made Man. Directed by Joseph De Grasse. United Artists Corp., 1922.

Thunderbolt Jack (Juan Centella). Serial, 10 episodes. Directed by Francis Ford and Murdock MacQuarrie. Berwilla Film, 1920.

Tony, the Greaser. Directed by William F. Haddock. Méliès Star-Film, 1911.

A Trip through Barbarous Mexico: Madero versus Díaz. America's Feature Film Co., 1913.

The Vagabond Prince (El conde vagabundo). Directed by Charles Giblyn. New York Motion Picture Company / Kay-Bee, 1916.

The Veiled Mysteries (Los crimenes misteriosos). Serial, 15 episodes. Directed by Wester Cullison, William J. Bowman, Frances Grandon, and Antonio Moreno. Vitagraph Company of America, 1920.

Vengeance and the Woman (Por venganza y por mujer). Serial, 15 episodes. Directed by Laurence Trimble and William Duncan. Vitagraph Company of America, 1917.

Viviette. Directed by Walter Edwards. Famous Players–Lasky Corp., 1918.

The Whirlwind (El torbellino). Serial, 15 episodes. Directed by Joseph A. Golden. Allgood Picture Company, 1920.

White Shadows in the South Seas. Directed by W. S. Van Dyke and Robert Flaherty. Cosmopolitan Productions, 1928.

Who Is Number One? Serial, 15 episodes. Directed by William Bertram. Paramount Pictures, 1917.

Why Change Your Wife? (*¿Porque cambia de esposa?*). Directed by Cecil B. De Mille. Famous Players–Lasky Corp., 1920.

Why Worry? Directed by Fred Newmeyer and Sam Taylor. Hal E. Roach Studios Inc., 1923.

The Woman I Stole. Directed by Irving Cummings. Columbia Pictures Corporation, 1933.

A Woman of Paris. Directed by Charles Chaplin. Charles Chaplin Productions / United Artists Corp., 1923.

The Woman Who Walked Alone (*La mujer que anda sola*). Directed by George Melford. Famous Players–Lasky Corp., 1922.

A World Apart (*El anillo de boda*). Directed by William D. Taylor. Oliver Morosco Photoplay Co., 1917.

MEXICO

Amnesia. Directed by Ernesto Vollrath. Ediciones Camus, 1921.

Amor. Directed by Froylan H. Torres. Torres Films, 1922.

El escándalo. Directed by Alfredo B. Cuéllar, Compañía Manufacturera de Películas, S.A., 1920.

Excursión a Popocatépetl. Believed to have been produced by Excélsior, Compañía Editorial, 1921.

El hombre sin patria. Directed by Miguel Contreras Torres. Producciones Contreras Torres, 1922.

Mitad y mitad. Directed by Enrique Juan Vallejo. Dieli Films, 1921.

Tepeyac. Directed by Carlos E. González, José Manuel Ramos, and Fernando Sáyago. Films Colonial, 1917.

ITALY

Il fabbro di Lauzan (*El herrero de Lauzan*). Director unknown. Aquila Films, 1915.

Gespay, fantino e gentiluomo (*Gespay o el jockey caballero*). Directed by Emilio Ghione. Caesar Film, 1915.

Hedda Gabler. Directed by Gero Zambuto and Giovanni Pastrone. Itala Film, 1920.

Maciste. Directed by Luigi Romano Borgnetto and Vincenzo Denizot. Itala Film, 1915.

Medusa. Directed by Roberto Roberti. Aquila Films, 1915.

La moglie di Claudio (*La mujer de Claudio*). Directed by Gero Zambuto. Itala Film, 1918.

Romanticismo. Directed by Carlo Campogalliani and Arrigo Frusta. Ambrosio, 1915.

Sierpe contra sierpe (*Serpe contra serpe*). Directed by Pier Angelo Mazzolotti. Bonnard Film, 1915.

Triste impegno (*Triste deber*). Directed by Emilio Ghione. Caesar Film, 1915.

GERMANY

Anna Boleyn (*Ana Bolena*). Directed by Ernst Lubitsch. Messter Film / Union-Film / Universum Film (UFA), Germany, 1920.

INCOMPLETELY IDENTIFIED

Aprended a cuidar a vuestros hijos (Mexico, circa 1927).

Día de baño (a U.S. comedy, date and English title unknown).

Falso pudor (Mexico, circa 1927).

Las joyas de los Romanoff (The Romanoff jewels; believed to have been produced by the Vitagraph Company of America, circa 1917).

Listos para vencer (Mexico, circa 1927).

Peso de menos (United States, The Universal Film Manufacturing Company, date unknown).

La plegaria del huerfano (possibly *The Orphan*, Fox Film Corporation, 1920, or *The Orphan's Prayer*, Vitagraph Company of America, 1917).

INDEX

Hayakawa, Sessue, 77, 127
Hays, William, 166, 211
Hearst, William Randolph, 159
Heraldo de la Raza, El (magazine), 136
Heraldo de México, El (magazine), 26, 180
Heraldo Ilustrado, El (magazine), 102–3, 107, *107*
Hergesheimer, Joseph, 178
Her Husband's Trademark (Famous Players–Lasky film), 164, 167–69, *168*
Hershfield, Joanne, 90, 99, 127
Hidalgo Theater, 202, 204, *204, 205*
Hiers, Walter, 107
Higson, Andrew, 4, 5
hija del circo, La (film serial), 19–20, *20*, 25
Hippodrome Theater, 204
Hispanic American Sports Association, 207
Hogar, El (magazine), 75, 102, 127, 130–31, 134–35, 136, 140, 145
Holmes, Stuart, 167
Holt, Jack, 172
Honoria Suárez en Hollywood (Paramount short film), 150
Huerta, Victoriano, 161
Hughes, Charles E., 165
Hymer, Evangeline, 189

I Can Explain (film), 169, 172
Icaza, Alfonso de, 5, 66
immigrants. *See* migrants
Imparcial, El (magazine), 88
Imperial Cinematográfica, 32
Imperial Theater, 195
India Bonita contest, 68, *69*
Infante, Pedro, 216
"inspección de los cines, La" (González Peña), 47
International Institute, 191
International Pictures Company, 36, 198

Jazz Band León, 65
jazz bands, 65–66
Jazzmania (Tiffany film), 65
Jennings, R. P., 48, 50
Jimenez, Mauro, 56
Jowett, Garth, 188
Jueves de excélsior (Noriega), 139

Jurado, Magdalena, 9
Jury, José, 56
Juventud ardiente (Dillon film), 128–29, *129*, 131, 152

Kahlo, Frida, 133
Kanellos, Nicolas, 181
Kann, George E., 33–34
Keller, Gary D., 158
Kenaga, Heidi, 146
Knight, Alan, 138
Knoles, Harley, 69
Kuhn, Annette, 157

labor strikes, 43–44, 46
Lacoma, Silvio, 195
land rights, 3
Lanigan, Mary, 189, 190, 213
Lansing, Robert, 30
latinidad, 188
"Lavaplatos, El," 180
League for the Protection of Youth, 128
Leal y Romero, Antonio, 115–16
Lee, Jane, 68
Lee, Katherine, 68
León, Eloidia, 118
Lezama, Luis, 116–17, 174
Liga Nacional de la Defensa de la Libertad Religiosa, 40
Limón, José, 10
Linder, Max, 112
Lloyd, Harold, 154, *156*, 169–70
Lola, la chica de Hollywood, 85–86, *86*, 104–5
London, Jack, 115
Lone Star jazz orchestra, 70
López, Ana, 56, 127
Los Angeles: depiction by media, 149–50; Mexican diplomatic corps in, 177–78; migrants and cinema in, 111, 177, 201–12, 214; spectatorship in, 182, 184, 188–90
Lozano, Gabriel, 93
Lozano, Ignacio, 93
Lubitsch, Ernst, 188
Lucero, Doroteo, *121*
Luna, Soledad, 109
Lydia Pinkham company, 99–100, *100*

Negri, Pola, 123, 188, 193
Negulcio, Ignacio, 55
New Federal Theater, 202
New York Commercial Bank, 28
New York Times (newspaper), 89, 154
Nielsen, Asta, 76
Noble, Andrea, 159
noche en Arabia, Una (Mills film), 128
"Noches Argentinas" (Grauman film prologue), 206, *207*
Noriega, A. B., 139
Noriega Hope, Carlos, 26, 93, 111–13, 145–46, 187
Normand, Mabel, 112, 114–15
"Notas Editoriales" (Bauche Alcalde), 47
noticieros, 2
Novarro, Ramón, 45, 85, 109, 199, 212–13
Novo, Salvador, 9, 70, 90

Obregón, Álvaro, 35, 163, 164, 165, 166–67, 174
Obrera Simpatica contest, 90
Ochoa Vega, Alejandro, 63
Official Weekly War Review, The (Committee on Public Information newsreel), 30
Ojeda, Manuel, 111
Olsson, Jan, 202
Olvera, Norberto, 71
Oñate, Ángel, 135–36
Opinión, La (newspaper), 14, 93, 96–97, 103–5, 146–48, 154, 204, 206, 207, 209–12
Orozco, Jose Clemente, 61
Orphan, The (Fox film), 27
Ortega, Francisco G., 29
Ortiz Gaitán, Julieta, 88

Padilla, Felix, 195
Pageant of Pulchritude, The, 103
paloma, La (N. Talmadge film), 170–71
Palos, Antonia, 118
Pan-American Union, 34
Paramount Pictures, 35–36, 43, 68–69, 148, 152, 165, 215
Paranaguá, Paulo, 217
Pariagua, Enoch, 166, 178
Pathé Exchange, 30, 36, 154–55, 169, 170
Paullado, José, 76

Payne Studies, 188
Peek, Rena, 190
Peiss, Kathy, 10
pelona, 124–26, 127–38, *133*, *134*, 219, 256n33
Pennway Theater, 192
Peredo, Luis, 41
Pérez Taylor, Rafael, 19–20, 25
Pershing, John J., 31
Pershing's Crusaders (Committee on Public Information film), 30–31
Pesqueira, Alfonso, 177
Pettit, Arthur, 11, 158
Phelps Dodge Mining Corporation, 57
Phipps, Sally, *102*
Picato, Pablo, 75, 81
Pickford, Mary, 38, 99, 101, 108, 109, 114
piracy: politics and, 31–34, 167; rampant, 20–21, 31, 45, 46, 217–18
Plaza Theater, 202
Polo, Eddie, 27, 112
popular press. *See* fan magazine discourse; *specific magazines*
Porter, Emerson Browne, 176
Portes Gil, Emilio, 215
Pratt, Mary Louise, 5–6
Prensa, La (newspaper), 93, 96, 212
Prevost, Marie, 112
Pringle, Aileen, 101
Propiedad Artistica y Literaria, 34
public health campaigns, 71–73, 83
Public Health Committee. *See* Consejo Superior de Salubridad
Puig Casauranc, Manuel, 176

Queen of the Universe Beauty Contest, 103

Rabinovitz, Lauren, 10
racism: in business/politics, 42–43, 176–77; of film industry, 110, 119, 209–12; in representation of Mexicans, 6, 11, 15, 155–56, 158–60, 167–68, 262n24; in sociology, 189–90, 220; in spectatorship, 183–84, 190–92, 214, 219–20; in theaters, 10–11, 191
Ramón Novarro, 45
Ramos, José. *See* Vega, Marina